Hogan's Heroes

Hogan's Heroes:
The Definitive Episode Guide

by Brian R. Young

Foreword by Jerry London

Cover Illustrations by Larry Weber

Larry Weber's illustration of Bob Crane as Colonel Hogan.

BearManor Media
2022

Hogan's Heroes: The Definitive Episode Guide

© 2022 Brian R. Young

All rights reserved.

No portion of this publication may be reproduced, stored, and/or copied electronically (except for academic use as a source), nor transmitted in any form or by any means without the prior written permission of the publisher and/or author.

Published in the United States of America by:

BearManor Media

4700 Millenia Blvd.
Suite 175 PMB 90497
Orlando, FL 32839

bearmanormedia.com

Printed in the United States.

Typesetting and layout by BearManor Media

ISBN—978-1-62933-836-1

Table of Contents

Foreword, by Jerry London	vii
Introduction	ix
Acknowledgements	xvii
Series Staples	xxiii
Hogan's Heroes: An Assessment	1
Primer for Season One	5
Season One episodes	12
Primer for Season Two	81
Season Two episodes	83
Season Three Episodes	151
Season Four Episodes	223
Primer for Season Five	285
Season Five episodes	288
Primer for Season Six	351
Season Six episodes	354

Appendix/Special Guest Stars:	411
Bruce Bilson	412
Victoria Carroll	415
Ruta Lee	419
Jerry London	422
Marlyn Mason	425
Alan Oppenheimer	428
Larry Weber	431
Index of Episode Titles	433
General Index	439

Foreword

What fun to relive the history of Hogan's Heroes! The characters and situations developed by executive producer Ed Feldman were the best time of my young, show business life. I learned so much and was given the opportunity to be one of the regular directors on the show. And now, Brian Young has done a masterful job of recreating the history for the reader. Enjoy the book and re-watch the show. I know you will laugh and become part of the gang.

Congratulations to Uncle Buzz!

Gratefully,

Jerry London

Los Angeles, February 16, 2021.

In Beverly Hills, producer/director Jerry London helps Corporal Louis LeBeau (Robert Clary) celebrate his 93rd birthday in March, 2019. Photo courtesy of Jerry London.

Introduction

I believe that *Hogan's Heroes* is the most successfully, unorthodox series in the history of American broadcast television. This belief comes from an individual with self-acknowledged, poor athletic skills, and who has spent much of a lifetime watching too much television. This introductory statement is quite an achievement considering Colonel Robert Hogan had to compete with more than just dedicated followers of the Third Reich. It was the decade of the 1960s, offering the most varied, fantastic programming choices ever seen before, during, or since. Colonel Hogan's crew had to compete with the groovy exploits of a skintight clad Batgirl (Yvonne Craig) gleefully kicking the Penguin's goons under their jawbones on ABC Television's hit, *Batman*. It was the decade where viewers embraced shapely Barbara Eden materializing from a thick, pink cloud of smoke amid the strains of a pre-J. R. Ewing, Larry Hagman, and his wails of "Jeannie!!!" Finally, there was also William Shatner - boldly going where no man had gone before.

Yet somehow, smack in the middle of all this fantastic, television entertainment, *Hogan's Heroes* was something completely different. Here we had a thirty minute situation comedy with a laugh track, set in a World War II German Prisoner of War Camp with the "funny

Nazis" and presented as a Bing Crosby Production. When the comedy debuted Friday evening at 8:30 p.m. on September 17, 1965 on the CBS network, the program had already been hammered by an endless barrage of negative criticism. War veterans, members of the Jewish community, and select, elite journalists had already transferred this program to the Russian Front. Nearly all of this mud-slinging occurred prior to its premiere broadcast. Since completing its initial run, the program continually pops up on "the worst TV shows of all time" lists in printed tomes of questionable judgment.

Was the concept of the program in bad taste? Was the idea of presenting a TV comedy based on personal tragedy of historic proportion going too far for the sake of ratings and yuks? Were Colonel Hogan's effortlessly employed schemes of sabotage and trickery farfetched, outrageous hokum? Most likely, the answer is yes, on all accounts.

However, was the show consistently funny, buoyed by the professional cast who balanced smart line readings with hilarious, facial expressions? No matter how high the stakes, how insuperable the odds, did the good guys always come out victors and often in well-calculated, spectacular fashion? Was it *not* mere coincidence that Werner Klemperer notched two TV Emmy Award wins for his portrayal of Kommodant, Wilhelm Klink? Again, the answer is undeniably yes, on all accounts.

Moreover, and more important to the network front office, *Hogan's Heroes* averaged national viewer ratings in the top twenty, most watched, prime time programs in its first two seasons. The program rated as numbers nine and seventeen, respectively. Although it eventually slipped out of the top thirty ranked programs its numbers were strong enough to sustain its six season run. Despite the wave of backlash, millions of viewers regularly tuned in to the madcap antics and crafty maneuvers taking place at Stalag 13.

The program was the creative mindset of Bernard Fein, who audiences knew as Private Gomez on *Sergeant Bilko*, another scheming, service comedy, that starred the unforgettable king of scams, Phil Silvers, and Albert S. Ruddy, who later produced such wildly contrasting motion pictures as *The Godfather* (1972) for Paramount and *The Cannonball Run* (1981) for 20th Century-Fox. The Hogan's production team immediately realized that the only way a "concentration camp comedy" would win *any* public acceptance was to establish an unbroken series of detailed plots where the good guys, the Allied Forces, always succeeded and the bad guys, the Nazi Germans, always failed. In fact, this was a stipulation that Jewish actor Klemperer insisted before accepting the role of Colonel Klink. CBS handed over the producing reins to Edward H. Feldman, who one year earlier had cut his teeth producing thirteen episodes of yet another, wildly popular CBS service comedy, *Gomer Pyle U.S.M.C.* Over the course of six seasons and 168 episodes, producer Feldman and his writers and directors concocted tales of espionage and adventure, of farce and buffoonery. Colonel Hogan and his mainstay crew of four comrades blew up German bridges, destroyed radio towers, helped defectors defect, rescued Underground allies from the Gestapo, and wired a train for demolition in honor of Hitler's birthday. Corporal Newkirk cracked open safes and fooled the guards dressed as an elderly fraulein, while Corporal LeBeau distracted Sergeant of the Guard, Hans Schultz, with freshly baked strudel. More often than not, Hogan made many a successful contact with the many, beautiful, female agents of the Underground while blatantly carrying on an open affair with Klink's secretary! Whether it was Helga or Hilda, Hogan took his choice.

Senior Prisoner of War officer, U.S. Army Air Force, Colonel Robert Hogan, and his men were all incarcerated at Stalag 13 of the German Luftwaffe, the aerial warfare branch of the Wehrmacht during WW II. Located some fifteen kilometers from the town of Hammelburg (although this location would vary in later episodes), the camp found itself in a permanent, winter setting. Although the Allied members were prisoners of war, it was quickly established that the camp was truly being run by Hogan's Heroes, unknowingly aided and abetted by the easily conned Kommodant and the dim-witted indifference of his Sergeant of Guard. In this particular POW camp, a breakaway bunk bed led to a network of secret tunnels allowing unlimited access in and out of the camp, Colonel Klink's quarters, and even the dreaded, detention cell, known as the "cooler". A secret radio antenna elevated out of a rooftop flagpole; a periscope emerged and submerged from within a rain barrel. Every private conference held in the Kommodant's office was under surveillance thanks to the bug in Klink's office, conveniently hidden in the microphone in a portrait of Hitler delivering a speech. The story lines and the numerous devices readily available to the prisoners to execute their missions frequently reached absurdist proportions, but as Michael Fried, a longtime friend and colleague, reminded me: "It's best not to try and second guess Hogan's Heroes."

Like any television success story, this caper comedy relied on the strength of its talented cast members, who brought humor and earnest conviction to the most ridiculous of plot developments. Led by the easygoing, wise cracking charm of Bob Crane as Colonel Hogan, the team included Corporal Peter Newkirk (Richard Dawson), expert safe-cracker, vocal impersonator, and all round con man, Corporal Louis LeBeau (Robert Clary), master chef and tailor, Sergeant Andrew Carter, (Larry Hovis), expert at munitions, chemistry, and any chance to blow something up, and Staff Sergeant James Kinchloe, (Ivan Dixon), Underground radio technician and amateur boxer. The casting of Dixon was a major step in the 1960s of a black actor regularly appearing and being credited in a prime time network series. After Dixon left the program, he was replaced by another African American actor, Kenneth Washington, as Sgt. Richard Baker, who resumed the secret radio transmissions for the Heroes in its final broadcast season.

On the other side of the war effort was Werner Klemperer, unforgettable as the easily influenced camp Kommodant, who became alternately pompous, paranoid, arrogant or humble, strict yet lenient, and always terrifically funny. Many of the greatest moments of the series relied on the classic verbal exchanges between Hogan and Klink, which will receive further discussion in the commentaries of specific episodes. The other constant presence, and a large one, was John Banner's Sergeant of Guard, Hans Schultz, who due to his own incompetence - and fearful of the consequences of his ineptitude and complicity - often willfully looked the other way, preferring to hide behind his trademark lines: "I know nothing! I see nothing!" Doubtlessly, this character was inspired by the comic German actor Sig Ruman, who ran afoul of the Marx Brothers in three of their features, and who similarly played the role of Sgt. *Schulz* for director Billy Wilder's *Stalag 17* (1953), who many believe inspired *Hogan's Heroes*. (In the least it inspired the writers of the 1951 play to unsuccessfully sue Bing Crosby Productions for copyright infringement. Although the jury ruled in favor of the plaintiffs, the decision was overruled by the judge who found the two different prisoner of war stories to be of far contrasting dramatic tone and nature.)

Further bolstering the proceedings were the excellent efforts of the casting department, who consistently peppered the story lines by hiring talented guest stars. Leading the way was the Jewish, Austrian born actor, Leon Askin, who played Klink's immediate superior, Luftwaffe General Albert Burkhalter, in sixty-seven episodes. Riding his coattails was Howard Caine's diminutive, snarling Gestapo agent, Major Wolfgang Hochstetter, who frequently suspected Hogan's crew of sabotage escapades but could never quite find the proof. On those rare occasions where both Burkhalter *and* Hochstetter figured into the story line, viewers were guaranteed a doubly good show. The other regularly featured character was the angelic Helga (Cynthia Lynn) as Klink's secretary in season one, who morphed into shapely, sexy Hilda (Sigrid Valdis) for the next five seasons. Prolific character actors including Bernard Fox, Nita Talbot, Harold Gould, Gavin MacLeod, Ruta Lee, Alan Oppenheimer,

Harold J. Stone, Kathleen Freeman, Marlyn Mason, Victoria Carroll, Antoinette Bower, Henry Corden, Noam Pitlik, and John Hoyt were all regular contributors to *Hogan's Heroes*. Even Harvey Keitel got an early big break, playing a non-credited German soldier in the season one outing, "The Great Impersonation."

This book is intended to be a fan guide to all 168 episodes of *Hogan's Heroes*. It's the kind of book you can leave next to your television set or DVD player and use as a reference point after watching an episode. Each episode will be broken down into three sections: a story summary, followed by production notes, and finally, my personal evaluation of that particular episode. The episodes will be concluded by using the movie rating system made popular by Leonard Maltin and other film biographers and journalists. However, the American Eagle will serve in place of the Star. (I considered using a rating system employing German Swastikas but my better senses prevailed!) Keep in mind, this is not *Stalag 17* or *The Bridge on the River Kwai* (1957) that we're talking about. This is *Hogan's Heroes* and my critical comments will be based on the merits of each episode as it measures up to the rest of the members within the family.

The ratings indicate:

FOUR EAGLES: Excellent episode; *Hogan's Heroes* at the top of its game.
THREE EAGLES: Superior episode; may not be the best but plenty to like in this one.
TWO EAGLES: Average episode; a passable entry with a few choice moments.
ONE EAGLE: Disappointing episode; "HH" at the bottom of its game.

The use of the ½ fraction will also be utilized between eagles in the episode ratings.

Hogan's Heroes continues to capture modern audiences with its constant re-runs on Memorable Entertainment Television (ME TV), Sundance TV, and other broadcast stations around the globe. It has been documented, ironically, that the POW comedy enjoys a particularly strong following in Germany. Considering all the factors that add up to its success, ultimately, the series' strength must be credited to its star, Bob Crane. Much has been written elsewhere about Mr. Crane's personal life off camera, including his purported infidelities, and tragically, his unsolved homicide in Scottsdale, Arizona on June 29, 1978, at the far-too-young age of forty-nine. This book bears no intention to pass judgment on what many would deem as Crane's "swinging lifestyle" or the factors that led to his murder. I'll save those kinds of judgments for the fellow I face in the mirror each morning upon awakening. However, some clear similarities between Bob Crane, the womanizing celebrity, and Colonel Hogan, the womanizing character, bear out occasional distinctions. Frankly, I cannot watch a single episode to this day (and I have seen every episode several times) where, even for the slightest moment, I must reflect with sadness on the loss of his life. I always get a bittersweet taste in my mouth as the final credits play out. Every time.

You can say whatever you want about Bob Crane the person, his romances, and his sexual proclivities, but this is what I know to be truth. The man was a charming, gifted, and highly individual talent, who deftly balanced the comedy and drama of the series in a somewhat goofy yet always charismatic fashion. In the world of the theater, where certain days of the week traditionally "go dark," June 29, 1978 may be one of the darkest days in the annals of show biz.

Di – smissed!

Dedication

For Bob Crane

Acknowledgements

The great joy of writing this book has been the opportunity to interview many of the creative artists that were actually associated with *Hogan's Heroes*. The last time I had interviewed a celebrity was when I was in high school and wrote an article about Anita Garvin, comedy queen of the silent short subjects, for *The Big Reel* newspaper. Now, some years later, I am particularly grateful to Bruce Bilson, who was the first artist to respond to my letters of inquiry, and not through an office or an agency. Bruce simply called me up and said, "Sure, I'll talk with you about *Hogan's*." Bruce is the best. Special thanks go to my other "guest stars," especially Victoria Carroll Bell, and her constant enthusiasm, grace, and encouragement, and for helping me connect with "Major Buckles" himself, Alan Oppenheimer. You rock, Victoria! Thank you to Ruta Lee, a real Hollywood class act, and her keen observations about the program and the business, and to Judy Diamond, "Ruta's Gal Friday and Everyday," who kindly scheduled that interview. The participation of Marlyn Mason has been purely delightful, and I am grateful for her continued emails and off-the-wall text messages that keep me in laughter. I was so lucky to track down Jerry London, who really helped glue together the final cracks of the *Hogan's Heroes* back story, and for graciously providing a foreword to this episode guide. Although Robert Clary and Antoinette Bower politely declined interviews, I am grateful to have their spirit within these pages. Finally, a huge thank you to artist Larry Weber and his beautifully realized caricatures that should keep you smiling as you work your way through this guide.

Thanks also to Memorable Entertainment Television, which allowed me to re-discover *Hogan's Heroes* with their continued re-runs while spending most of my 2020 in quarantine. At least something beneficial occurred to me during the pandemic. Further thanks to the Internet Movie Data Base (IMDb), TV.Com, Wikipedia, CBS Television Inc., and the *Los Angeles Times* (obituary of Edward H. Feldman). The writers associated with these internet research sources are providing an outstanding service for preserving show business history. A big, local thank you goes out to Santos and Carol at Minuteman Press in Portland for their help in printing my letters of inquiry and their invaluable help in the categorizing and image filing of this book's photos, many being published for the first time.

I am exceedingly indebted to my long time circle of family and friends in Oregon for their unwavering support, humor, and encouragement: Michael Fried, for his continued friendship and astute comments made during our *Hogan's* viewings and never-ending cribbage matches, Joseph Buttler, for sharing my love of classic Hollywood and providing the photos from the day we met Bernard Fox, John Killeen, a dear pal and one of a kind talent, Marc Belmont, who has always been my reminder that life is a moving picture, and old buddy, Duane Hanson, whose recently published book, *Rideshare Confessions,* inspired me to get motivated and write.

Thanks also to my oldest brother Michael, the wise sage of the Young family, for his keen suggestions and professional advice, and the continued good cheer provided by his wife, Halah. There's a good reason, Michael, you've got that PhD! Big love to Richard and Joy Young, and their continued, enthusiastic encouragement;

my niece, Kimberly Meyers, for her gracious words of kindness and interest, and to my brother and housemate, Kevin, who has endured many a sleepless night listening to the *Hogan's Heroes* theme music and canned laughter drift up from our basement, screening room.

Finally, I am grateful to my late father, Clarence James Young Jr., for a lifetime of love, support, and constant reminder to look upon any task as a personal challenge. If I possess any love for show business, it clearly comes from my mother, Ileana Martha Kaufmann Young, who once modeled and acted in films in her native Argentina, and later sewed costumes for my grade school theatrical endeavors while "shushing" the kids in the audience during my line reads on stage. Her constant nudging for me to "keep writing" during those periods of procrastination is the key contributor to this publication. To say "I love you" would be the understatement of a lifetime.

Series Staples

In order to get a better appreciation of – and not summarily dismiss – *Hogan's Heroes* as television entertainment, the discerning viewer should be aware of several staples inherent to the program. Awareness and acceptance of these signature staples will doubtlessly encourage one's overall enjoyment of the series.

Stalag 13: Moving and Relocation, and other Services

The pilot episode established that Colonel Robert Hogan and company initially operated an Underground relocation service directly out of Stalag 13 for escaped prisoners of war. Hogan's "travel agency" provided tailor-made clothing, counterfeit German money, and forged travel papers for fugitive prisoners and their safe passage to London. This initial operation quickly expanded to include fugitive Allied soldiers (generally US Air Force and British Royal Air Force) *and* German soldiers and civilians looking to defect from the Third Reich. Further covert operations included the receiving and delivery of war information to Allied agents and acts of sabotage (which quickly became the chief focus of the Heroes).

Stalag 13: The Tunnel Network

The Heroes' secret base operated several feet below the barracks where a tunnel network existed. Access to the tunnels began from a breakaway set of bunk beds that opened to reveal a descending ladder. The main emergency tunnel provided an exit to the outside of camp from a carved-out tree stump. Other tunnels led in and out of other barracks, Colonel Klink's private quarters (a wood burning stove on wheels would conveniently roll to one side), and the solitary detention cell known as the "cooler." The other primary entrance/exit to the tunnel network was located in the guard dog kennel. A dog house actually flipped up and back for access.

Guard Dogs: Prisoners of War's Best Friends

The German civilian breeding and training the stalag guard dogs, Oscar Schnitzer, was actually a member of the Allied Underground resistance and an ally to Hogan and company. Schnitzer's dogs had been trained to barely cooperate with the German guards yet act like happy puppies with the POWs (LeBeau in particular). In a few cases, the Schnitzer character would be replaced by a similar dog training ally.

"Radio London Kinch"

The tunnel network housed a radio operations system where messages could be transmitted and received to London and to other Underground operatives. A radio antenna was installed inside the Nazi flagpole directly above Klink's office. A majority of the episode plots revolve around the orders received by radio. Sgt. James Kinchloe was Hogan's primary radio operator; in the sixth season he would be replaced by Sgt. Richard Baker, who would continue the radio operations.

The Double-talk Routine in Klink's Office

Close to two thirds of the series' programs rely on Hogan double-talking his way into Klink's confidence, generally in the Kommodant's office. Hogan, the master of concocting and enacting an elaborate yarn, would find ways to tap into Klink's pride, ego, ignorance and paranoia in order to further the plot and Hogan's personal objectives. In many cases, the "double talk" routine is the standout driving scene of the featured episode, with all the proceeding factors hinged to it.

Colonel Robert Hogan, "Idea Man"

The Heroes' capers are typically formulated by the scheming mind of Colonel Hogan. Often enough, something said by one of the prisoners creates inspiration for Hogan's crafty mind. The prisoners frequently remind the viewers that they are fighting against all odds by declaring their next assignment as "impossible" or "not having a chance" of success, which always means Hogan will quickly come up with a solution. Creating a diversion which will distract Klink, Schultz, and the other guards, is often a component of Hogan's clever ideas. In the episode "Monkey Business," Freddie the chimpanzee mimics Hogan's pacing as, together, they contemplate his next move.

"No One Has Ever Escaped from Stalag 13"

A big factor in the success rate of Hogan's clandestine operations revolves around the imperative of preserving Colonel Klink's status as the Kommodant of Stalag 13. Since Hogan has Klink wrapped around his finger, it's crucial to keep Klink and his superiors believing that his record is clean with no prisoners ever successfully escaping. This is a bragging point for Klink who blows his horn to General Burkhalter and nearly every visitor that drops in to Stalag

13. Since Schultz is also easily conned, and often flat out bribed, the Heroes also have the rotund sergeant on their silent protection plan. Their operation exists as long as they do.

A Sergeant of the Guard that Sees and Knows Nothing

Picking up the previous thread, from the pilot episode forward, Schultz is established as an easily fooled, conned, and/or bribed German soldier with doubts concerning the cause of his Fatherland. On many occasions the rotund sergeant offers up secret information in exchange for candy bars, aftershave, or an extra stake in Corporal Newkirk's crooked card games. As a result, Hogan holds that complicity over Schultz's head and blackmails him when needs arise. A running gag depicts Schultz actually witnessing aspects of the team's secret operation (such as the bunk beds opening and closing) but for fear of his life he prefers to embrace the motto of "knowing and seeing nothing."

It's Cold in Russia

In order to influence Klink and Schultz's decision making process, Hogan often spooks them by believing they may be reprimanded by Berlin and transferred to the Russian (Eastern) Front. The Nazi war offensive in Russia was a cold, brutal, miserable experience for any German combat soldier, and Klink's biggest fear was losing his cushy stalag job for a doomed transfer east. A transfer to the Russian Front is a frequent threat delivered on the series, particularly during conversations in Klink's office, with not just Hogan, but any number of visiting Nazi characters. In a rare instance, Hogan has his ally "Olga" (Ruta Lee) persuade Klink to actually request a transfer to the Russian Front in the final season anomaly, "To Russia Without Love."

Colonel Robert Hogan, "Ladies' Man"

A natural activity for actor Bob Crane to engage in, Hogan frequently becomes romantically involved with the many beautiful women associated with the series. During season one, he has an ongoing "office" romance with Helga, which continues with the arrival of Klink's next secretary, Hilda, in season two. These two women at times are in collusion with Hogan and participate in components to influence Col. Klink. Sometimes Hogan enjoys affairs with women loyal to the Third Reich, but this is to generally gather information. A staple within this staple is the "kiss me the Germans are looking" routine, which forces Hogan to make out with a female Underground agent to avoid the suspicions of prowling German soldiers. What this man is willing to do for the Allied cause is admirable – and envious.

Colonel Wilhelm Klink, "Ladies' Man"

Many of the latter capers involve Hogan instilling false confidence into Klink's mind that he is most desirable to the opposite sex. Usually the ulterior motive is to use Klink as an unwitting "carrier pigeon" by setting him up with a false, romantic rendezvous with a female agent posing as a wealthy widow or some admiring, local fraulein. Klink's uniform is often manipulated to mask some secret information that can be delivered back and forth between Hogan and his contacts. In later episodes, Klink begins to enjoy romantic interludes with genuinely attractive women that are not necessarily employed on Hogan's secret payroll.

The Call Center

The Heroes operate a switchboard down in the tunnels and have a direct line wired to Klink's office phone. This allows, most frequently, Newkirk and Carter to assume various Nazi characters to divert Klink (and even Major Hochstetter) off the course of business. Sometimes Kinchloe will assume a German identity if the other fellows are busy with some other clandestine activity.

The Bug in Klink's Office

A surveillance bug has been planted in Klink's office and hidden right in the microphone pictured in a photograph of Hitler delivering a speech. Back in the barracks, the men are able to listen in on every privileged conversation taking place with the receiving device inside a coffee pot. A wardrobe in the reception area to the office has a sliding panel which allows live eavesdropping into Klink's office (through the eyeballs of a portrait) when the men need an alternative method for their snooping. Strategically located periscopes are also hidden about the camp both inside and outside of the fencing, offering different visual perspectives, with the most frequently used being the periscope hidden in a rain barrel just outside the men's barracks.

Corporal Louis LeBeau, Master Chef

In order for Hogan to make contact with a visiting Luftwaffe General or other dignitary, Hogan will offer the services of Corporal LeBeau to prepare a gourmet dinner. During the dinner party, Hogan's other boys are often up to no good. LeBeau frequently distracts Schultz from his guard duties by bribing him with food. Hot baked apple strudel is frequently the choice delicacy of diversions.

The Mighty Hogan Art Players

Two decades before Johnny Carson would takes the reins of *The Tonight Show* and dub his acting troupe the "Mighty Carson Art Players," Hogan makes this late night talk show reference to Newkirk in regards to their sensitive handling of General Schmidt (guest star Roger C. Carmel) in the first season caper, "The Prisoners' Prisoner." Acting jobs will continually spark the team's ensuing capers, with Sergeant Carter's impersonation of Adolph Hitler ranking high as a fan favorite. The tunnel network also functions as a wardrobe department offering numerous costume choices in both German uniform and civilian apparel. The telephone switchboard system provides ample opportunity for voice acting, and in cases where the barracks have been bugged, the men will act out scenes from scripted pages as if performing their lines on old-time radio. The men will also cleverly stage performances in front of Klink and/or Schultz to help guide and influence their decision making processes.

Hogan's Heroes: An Assessment

Rating and ranking, criticizing or praising episodes of *Hogan's Heroes* is, of course, a very subjective undertaking. What might be one of my favorite outings may be tucked away in the forgotten file of other viewers. My assessments are largely plot based, and I believe the best episodes derive from well plotted details that justify the ridiculous scheming of Colonel Hogan and company. The program is what I would call a "bill of goods" show, and some episodes are much better at selling that "bill of goods" than others. Season two's "Diamonds in the Rough" and the final season's "The Gestapo Takeover" carefully lay out the bill of goods in dramatic fashion with the comedy used as a supporting device. In my humble opinion, these are the better episodes in the series because they maintain a credibility factor within the framework of an absurdist farce. When *Hogan's Heroes* presents a comedy drama half hour, the results are typically more gratifying than a purely, situation comedy driven half hour.

This is not to ignore the comedy the program offers. The regular cast was one of the funniest, most talented ensembles assembled for an American program. Sometimes, though, the characters are forced to indulge in too much comedy, laboring the story development. This is at times the case with John Banner's Sergeant Schultz, a brilliantly comic characterization that sometimes gets saddled with carrying some of the more tired elements of the comedy. Schultz works best in fits and starts; when he is forced to carry long sequences of comedy the labored element surfaces. In short, a little Schultz can go a long way. This criticism could also be applied to Larry Hovis's Carter, whose running gag is to over explain details and drag out dialogue, successfully fatiguing Hogan and the viewers. Or maybe that's the point.

Many of the most successful comedies are character driven pieces, where all the plot details hang around the actions and motivations of one such character. "Klink's Escape" is an excellent example of this approach because of the familiarity the regular viewers have gained about Klink's persona, which justifies his actions and decisions as the story progresses. His superb acting as he plays each discovery with complete seriousness is another rewarding factor. Character driven pieces also benefit Bob Crane's style of acting, especially when focused on his scheming mind and rapid fire development of "diversions" to employ his covert operations. Crane's serious, thoughtful approach, particularly when the comedy is handled by a visitor such as Colonel Crittendon, makes for agreeable, and credible viewing.

The series greatly benefits from its impressive roster of guest stars, keeping Stalag 13 a never dull home away from home. The steady contributions of Leon Askin's General Burkhalter and Howard Caine's Major Hochstetter cannot be overlooked. Many a humdrum episode is immediately uplifted by the weight of their sheer presence, punctuated by those instantly recognizable voices and countenances which significantly bolster any whale of a tale. With its World War II setting, the program also boasted the most "international" cast regularly featured in a network program before, during, or since. Nita Talbot's sparkling Russian spy, Bernard Fox's bumbling British Colonel, Felice Orlandi's French Underground ally, and all those visiting Germans and lovely frauleins dot the richly presented, international landscape of the show.

Of the Heroes, my two favorites are Richard Dawson's Peter Newkirk, and Larry Hovis's Andrew Carter, both masters at donning German costumes and characterizations. Hovis's off the rails interpretations of Hitler are legendary among the fans, and Dawson, in nearly all cases, is clearly brilliant with his expert voice work and dramatic line readings. The episodes that allow him to perform his excellent repertoire of voice impersonations are pure delights. Ivan Dixon serves as mostly a straight man for the others, and a terrific one. Unfortunately, he isn't allowed as much footage as his colleagues and often misses out on some of their more colorful escapades.

Robert Clary's Louis LeBeau, who effortlessly presents his inherent charms and musical talents, is also typically the most mean-spirited of the bunch and never hides his disdain for his German captors, even towards the well meaning, Sgt. Schultz. His frequent insults are more petulant than funny, and he often confuses his skill as a chef with arrogance.

One core attitude of the program is its, pun intended, "no prisoners held" approach to storytelling. The series maintains a very bold attitude that never makes any apology for its behavior. No matter how ridiculous the plot devices unfold, *Hogan's Heroes* essentially informs its viewers: "this is the premise, and these are its staples, now get on the boat or off." Once you accept these dictations, getting on the boat can be lots of fun. In some ways its unforgiving demeanor would be mirrored two decades later with Fox Television's *Married with Children* (1987-1997), the ground-breaking, anti-family comedy, that also embraced a no holds barred approach to its outrageous story telling. Both Colonel Hogan and Al Bundy, and their immediate family members, are two examples of the most unapologetic characters television viewers could expect to encounter.

Hogan's Heroes is a good-looking half hour, and consistently, handsomely produced with well-paced stories that keep moving in and out of camp, the woods, country fields and roads, and Bavarian hotels and restaurants. My favorite episode title is "Bad Day in Berlin" (it just sounds cool to say it); my least being "Fat Hermann, Go Home" (I've never been a fan of calling large people *fat*). I hope to make the acquaintance of my readers so we can debate and argue, laugh and recall that roller coaster ride of a television series known to its millions of fans as *Hogan's Heroes*.

Primer for Season One

Primary Cast

Colonel Robert Hogan:	Bob Crane
Kommodant Wilhelm Klink:	Werner Klemperer
Sgt. of Guard, Hans Schultz:	John Banner
Corporal Louis LeBeau:	Robert Clary
Corporal Peter Newkirk:	Richard Dawson
Sergeant James Kinchloe:	Ivan Dixon
Sergeant Andrew Carter:	Larry Hovis
Helga (recurring character):	Cynthia Lynn
General Albert Burkhalter (recurring):	Leon Askin
Olsen (recurring):	Stewart Moss
Cpl. Langenscheidt (recurring):	Jon Cedar
Oscar Schnitzer (recurring):	Walter Janovitz
Vladimir Minsk (pilot only):	Leonid Kinskey

The principal players of the first season demonstrate the fine art of digging an escape tunnel. Pictured clockwise from bottom left: Bob Crane as Col. Robert Hogan, Cynthia Lynn as Helga, Werner Klemperer as Col. Wilhelm Klink, John Banner as Sgt. Hans Schultz, Richard Dawson as Cpl. Peter Newkirk, Robert Clary as Cpl. Louis LeBeau, and Ivan Dixon as Sgt. James Kinchloe. Missing in action is Larry Hovis as Sgt. Andrew Carter. Author's collection/CBS Television Inc.

According to Albert S. Ruddy, who co-created *Hogan's Heroes* with Bernard Fein, the original concept was to set the program in a U. S. jail with Hogan acting as the Captain of the guards and the "Klink" character serving as the warden. But Ruddy claimed that no network or sponsor wanted to run a series set in a jailhouse. Some months later, Ruddy and Fein decided to transfer the action to a World War II prisoner of war camp in Germany, and a production deal was struck with Bing Crosby Productions (BCP) and the CBS Television Network. BCP was already enjoying a healthy production run with *Ben Casey*, which debuted in 1961 on ABC.

CBS hired Edward H. Feldman to produce their new POW comedy. Feldman had already enjoyed an established relationship with CBS as a producer of *Gomer Pyle, U.S.M.C.*, a spin off series from *The Andy Griffith Show*, and starred Jim Nabors as the good-natured, small town bumpkin, Gomer, whose efforts of earnest usually resulted in disappointments for short tempered Gunnery Sergeant, Vince Carter (Frank Sutton). Feldman held a background in the advertising business and at one time headed the commercial division of Desilu Productions. His debut as a television producer came with *The Box Brothers*, a CBS comedy starring Gale Gordon (Mr. Mooney on *The Lucy Show*) and Bob Sweeney, who Feldman would later recruit to direct seventeen episodes of *Hogan's*. Several actors and writers associated with *Gomer Pyle* also found recurring work thanks to Feldman and his new WWII series.

Two primary sets were used to film *Hogan's Heroes*. CBS had the Stalag 13 set constructed on the RKO Forty Acres lot in Culver City, California, which had been purchased by Desilu Productions in 1957. The wired gates, guard tower, infamous Delousing Station, and barracks buildings all stood on the "Tara" lot where *Gone with the Wind* (1939) had originally been filmed. "40 Acres" was the home to numerous television programs including the town of Mayberry on *Andy Griffith*, Fort Henderson on *Gomer Pyle*, Gotham

City on *Batman,* and was also used in three episodes of *Star Trek.* During the 1960s it was quite common to see the same actors, writers, and directors moving back and forth from one production unit to another. All interior scenes were filmed at the Desilu Studios, formed in 1950 as initially a television production facility for Desi Arnaz and Lucille Ball. Director Bruce Bilson filled me in about the history of "40 Acres" and Desilu:

I Love Lucy started at another studio, a rental studio in Hollywood. They were so successful they bought the studio on Cahuenga. It was actually right near my parents' home; I saw it being built while I was going to college. They bought that studio and that was Desilu, and then they bought RKO, which was down the street, so to speak, and then they bought the studio . . . Selznick? . . . the studio where *Gone with the Wind* was made in Culver City, and that became Desilu Culver. The "forty acres" was part of Desilu Culver, it was attached to that studio. It still had the old Atlanta station where all the corpses, all the wounded from the war were in that train station. And "Tara," the remains of where it had been burned down, were also there.*

Casting for the pilot episode and first season was managed by the team of Milt Hamerman and Lynn Stalmaster. Many of the guest actors cast in later episodes were often return artists directly welcomed back to the program by Ed Feldman. Fein's early suggestion was Walter Matthau for Hogan, but Feldman didn't believe Matthau would be effective at playing comedy. (This was prior to Matthau winning the Oscar for Billy Wilder's *The Fortune Cookie* {1966}). CBS executives offered the Hogan role to Van Johnson, who had spent much of the 1940s playing in war films, but the actor passed. Ultimately, the man who scored the lead role was not a film or television personality, but rather a radio personality – and one with a monumental following. Bob Crane was the morning drive deejay on KNX-AM Los Angeles, and spent the first half of the 1960s interviewing celebrities, playing on-air practical jokes, and playing his beloved set of drums. Odds were, in the early 1960s, if you were an actor driving across town to audition or a studio employee on your way to work, Crane was the voice on your car radio. Frequent *Hogan's* guest star Ruta Lee recalled:

I think I had met him when he was doing his radio show, and I believe it was on KMPC which was a big station that was either purchased then or later by Gene Autry. I can't remember why I would've been on his show . . . maybe publicizing something I was trying to get done. At least that's what tickles my brain. (His) charisma carried across the radio waves. When he was on radio he had a great following because he had that easygoing charm . . . a smile in his voice at all times.**

Both Werner Klemperer and John Banner were early, affirmative casting approvals by Feldman and CBS, although Banner was favored as Klink and Klemperer as Sgt. Schultz. Fortunately, smarter minds prevailed, and the role reversals were finalized. British comedian Richard "Dickie" Dawson read for the Hogan role, but when he couldn't effectively voice an American, he quickly landed the role of Corporal Newkirk. Dawson screen-tested the character with a Scouse accent, common to the people of Liverpool, England, but the network complained that it rendered him incomprehensible. He switched to a standard English cockney which easily resonated with a wider audience. After the Beatles invaded America, Dawson reportedly reminded everyone at the network of his original, vocal choice. Feldman knew Larry Hovis's work from *Gomer Pyle* and cast him for the pilot only as Lt. Carter. After Leonid Kinskey deserted, Hovis got bumped up as a regular, but bumped down in rank to "Sgt. Carter."

Cinematographer Gordon Avil, whose professional career dated back to 1929 (he filmed the all black musical *Hallelujah* {1929} for King Vidor), was already familiar to CBS executives for his work on *Sergeant Preston of the Yukon*. He was hired as the Director of Photography (DP) for *Hogan's* first five seasons until circumstances intervened. Some of Avil's singular accomplishments as DP included the Edmond O' Brien starred and co-directed *Shield for Murder*

(1954), a crime noir about a renegade cop. This one featured a skillfully staged and photographed sequence in an indoor high school swimming pool location that offered an exciting gun battle between O' Brien's crooked cop and all round crooked Claude Akins. Avil was also DP on *The Black Sleep* (1956), a "Monster Mash" re-union featuring Basil Rathbone, Lon Chaney Jr., John Carradine, Akim Tamiroff, and horror legend Bela Lugosi in his final film role (not considering his patched together, postmortem "guest" appearance in Ed Wood Jr.'s *Plan 9 From Outer Space* (1959).

Feldman and his art department (Rolland M. Brooks and Howard Hollander) staged the series in a permanent, wintery setting. This way, episodes were not constrained to follow a chronological timeline and could be broadcast in any order, although several episodes do make direct references to earlier situations. The snare drumming heard in the first part of Jerry Fielding's memorable theme music was performed by Crane.

*Telephone interview with the author, October 26, 2020.
**Telephone interview with the author, December 4, 2020.

Pilot Episode: "The Informer" 09/17/1965.

Director (D): Robert Butler
Writer (W): Richard M. Powell, Bernard Fein, Albert S. Ruddy

Guest Cast: Noam Pitlik (Wagner), Leon Askin (Col. Burkhalter), Larry Hovis (Lt. Carter), Stewart Moss (Olsen), Richard Sinatra (Sgt. Riley), Cynthia Lynn (Helga), Walter Janowitz (Schnitzer).

Storyline: Germany 1942. Camp 13, a Nazi occupied Prisoner of War camp, outside of Hammelburg. Col. Robert Hogan acquires two new men to his barracks: Lt. Carter, who has escaped from another POW camp and is awaiting a final escape to England, and captured flier, Wagner. Hogan and his men are actually fronting an operation to help escaped Allied soldiers gain safe access to England. Using the name of a fictitious Major, Hogan realizes Wagner is a liar and a spy. They confirm this after listening in on his conversation with Colonel Klink. Hogan decides to set up Wagner by blindfolding him, pretending the tunnel entrance is under the water tower, and giving him an elaborate tour of their Underground operations. The tour includes stops at a counterfeit printing press, a metal shop where they are manufacturing German lugers that are actually cigarette lighters, a steam room, and a barber shop, which includes Helga, Klink's secretary, as the manicurist! When Colonel Burkhalter arrives, Wagner's revelations fail in high fashion; Klink comments that spies are unreliable, and Burkhalter suggests Wagner cool off at the Russian Front.

Program Notes: Filmed in early 1965 in black and white, the pilot features Leonid Kinskey as Soviet POW, Vladimir Minsk, the resident tailor. When the program was picked up, Kinskey felt uncomfortable with a show about comical Nazis and declined to continue. Producer Edward Feldman, pleased with the work of guest star, Larry Hovis, offered him a regular spot even though his character, Lt. Carter, escaped Camp 13 at the pilot's conclusion. Feldman didn't see this as a problem, reportedly saying "no will care." Stewart Moss, as Olsen, Hogan's "outside man," also was offered a regular role but declined. However, Moss did return to the series for seven future assignments, three more times as the "Olsen" character. This was Noam Pitlik's first of seven, unrelated, character roles. Leon Askin debuts as "Colonel Burkhalter," in his first of sixty-seven guest appearances. The final credits roll over "lobby cards" of scenes earlier presented in the program.

Assessment: A good introduction to the overall tone and humor of the series and to establishing the three essential characters: Col. Hogan, the quick-witted, wise-cracking, brains of the operation, Colonel Klink, the vain and arrogant, but easily manipulated Kommodant, and Sergeant Schultz, the lovable buffoon, who would rather "see and know nothing" than become implicated in the schemes of Hogan and company. Helga is presented as a romantic ally to Hogan, particularly enjoying his gift of silk nylons (a scene recaptured by director Paul Schrader in *Auto Focus* {2005}), and, later, appearing in the barber shop as the boys' manicurist. The episode gets a boost from venerable actor Noam Pitlik, who performs with great enthusiasm, especially as his attempts to rat out Hogan fail at every turn under the disbelief of Askin's already suffering, Colonel Burkhalter. The strength of this pilot rests on the shoulders of the actors, who, out of the gate, perform their roles with ease and assurance, as if this operation has been running for some while and *not* being presented for the first time. Fortunately, too, some of the more fantastic details will be pared down as the series prepares to move into regular season territory.

Season 1, Episode 1: "Hold that Tiger" 09/24/1965.

D: Robert Butler W: Richard M. Powell

Guest Cast: Arlene Martel (Tiger), Henry Rico Cattani (Gen. Hofstader), Cynthia Lynn (Helga), Jon Cedar (Cpl. Langenscheidt).

Storyline: In an effort to spread Nazi propaganda, Klink brags to the prisoners about the recent successes of the Third Panzer Division's newest weapon, the Tiger Tank. Hogan quickly lays out his plan to steal a tank, disassemble it, and send its blueprints to England via his Underground contact "Tiger." Newkirk is cast as a Gestapo agent, and is sent out to sequester a Tiger Tank while LeBeau is sent to meet the other "Tiger" and arrange a temporary switch of clothing to smuggle her into camp. Hogan is put off when "Tiger" is revealed to be a female agent, and, reluctantly, he has her outfitted as a POW while Newkirk's Gestapo agent rolls into the camp along with fake papers. General Hofstader arrives, fuming for the whereabouts of his missing tank, and while the Heroes create a diversion involving the driver-less, runaway tank, the female "Tiger" is smuggled out of camp along with the blueprints.

Program Notes: Several changes took place as the show transitioned from "pilot" mode to "regular series" mode. For the 1965-66 network season, CBS made a push to color, and the *Hogan's Heroes'* pilot became an anomaly – the only episode broadcast in black and white. Other CBS series making the move to color included *Andy Griffith*, its spinoff, *Gomer Pyle U.S.M.C.*, (featuring Larry Hovis in a recurring role), *Gilligan's Island,* and for its following season, *The Wild, Wild West*. Leonid Kinskey is now removed from the opening credits, and replaced by Hovis, who is seen turning a metal crank, which bleeds in to the opening shot of the episode depicting the team's radio antenna rising from the flagpole on the rooftop of Klink's office! Several shots are now altered for the opening credit sequence and the drumming in the theme music is of a more upbeat tempo. The elaborate setup of counterfeit press, steam room, and barber shop seen in the pilot are all gone from Camp 13, now re-titled "Stalag 13." Viewers catch the opening and closing of the breakaway bunk beds for the first time in this episode. Jon Cedar makes his first credited appearance as Corporal Langenscheidt (he was briefly seen in the pilot); he would continue playing (generally) this role fifteen more times. By the sixth season he would morph into the role of Oskar Danzing for one episode. This is the first of seven appearances of Arlene Martel. Usually seen as the Underground operative "Tiger," she too would occasionally appear as other characters. *Star Trek* fans will remember her turn as Spock's Vulcan bride in the 1967 episode "Amok Time." The closing credits now picture the familiar US Air Flier hat draped over the German war helmet.

Assessment: The big spectacle of this first, regular episode broadcast is, sadly, also its weakest component. Now just how in the world did Corporal Newkirk wander over to the Third Panzer Division, steal a Tiger Tank, and then drive right into Stalag 13, and, apparently, right through one of its wired gates? The program is already requesting its viewers not to ponder such doubtful thoughts. Better here are the smaller components that say much about the series still being hatched. Col. Hogan's character is confirmed to be a "come up with a plan and worry about the details later" kind of leader. Crane has a nice scene with Martel where she explains why she volunteered for the mission, wanting to meet the man "who could've escaped but has chosen to remain in Germany helping others escape." It's a nice point about the Hogan character that is rarely addressed, and when the two finally kiss, it's a genuinely sweet moment. Curiously revealing of the actor is Hogan's line about why a prisoner wanted to escape: "He received a letter from home today. His girl sent him a candid snap shot." Also revealing is the underwhelming appearance of Henry Rico Cattani's General Hofstader, sporting probably the worst German accent of the entire series, in, thankfully, his only series sighting. Oddly missing from the second half of this loony outing is the recently demoted "Sgt." Carter. With Olsen not present and accounted for, perhaps Carter went to the other side of the fence for "outside man" duty.

Best exchange:

Cpl. Langenscheidt: (reporting to Klink that an unidentified Gestapo officer wishes to leave):
  "He has a pass, but they have no record of him entering!"

Klink: "What do I care? If he wants out, let him out. The sooner the better."

Season 1, Episode 2: "Kommodant of the Year" 10/01/1965.

D: Robert Butler W: Laurence Marks

Guest Cast: Woodrow Parfrey (Col. Schneider), William Allyn (Maj. Hauser), Victor French (Commando).

Storyline: A giant rocket is hauled into Stalag 13, accompanied by Major Hauser and tightened security. London radios the crew and informs them that they will send in a Dr. Schneider and three commandos to rendezvous with the Heroes. LeBeau sneaks out of camp and meets the four men, carefully taking their measurements so they will be outfitted later as Nazis. Schneider needs ten minutes to sneak over to the rocket so he can photograph its control panel. Hogan devises a scheme to keep Klink and his men off guard. He has Newkirk forge papers indicating that Klink has been chosen the "Kommodant of the Year" and that "Colonel Schneider" and his soldiers will arrive to present Klink with an award and scroll during a special ceremony. While Hogan encourages Klink to prattle on during his acceptance speech, Schneider sneaks off to get his photographs of the secret rocket and dodge the ambitious Major Hauser. He also sets a detonator timer which launches the rocket and eventually destroys half the Hamburg airport. This ends the "Kommodant of the Year" ceremony in most unceremonious fashion.

Program Notes: Viewers get a first look at the team's periscope which slowly ascends from a water barrel, right next to an oblivious Schultz! Stock shots of this exact activity would crop up in later episodes. Making its debut is the bug in Klink's office hidden in the microphone in the framed picture of Hitler. Although not seen, yet now promoted, General Burkhalter is referred to throughout the story.

Assessment: The program is still slowly finding itself in an okay storyline which would become a typical plot thread – a top secret war device is held at Stalag 13 where it will be safe from enemy attack, and Hogan and his crew must find a way to blueprint and/or destroy it by creating some elaborate diversion. "The Kommodant of the Year" concept sounds stronger than it is played out, despite Klink's jovial, long-winded speech and the overboard enthusiasm of the POWs (directed by Hogan's hand gestures). This particular story scenario of finding a diversion tied into Klink's ego and self love would skillfully be developed as the series progressed.

Season 1, Episode 3: "The Late Inspector General" 10/08/1965.

D: Robert Butler W: Laurence Marks

Guest Cast: John Dehner (Gen. Von Platzen), Jon Cedar (Cpl. Langenscheidt), Cynthia Lynn (Helga), Stewart Moss (Olsen/Uncredited).

Storyline: Hogan's plan to send out Olsen to destroy an ammunition train during roll call gets derailed when Klink pulls Hogan into his office and warns him of the expected visit of Inspector General Von Platzen. Ultimately impressed with Klink's efficiency record of never having a successful escape, the General states he will recommend to Berlin that Klink be promoted to senior officer of *all* Prisoner of War camps. Hogan, determined to ruin Klink's transfer, sets off a series of small pranks to discredit Klink in the eyes of Von Platzen. They go so far as to replace the motor of his car with a smoke bomb which prompts the Inspector General to believe Klink is trying to assassinate him. Von Platzen orders another staff car to take him to the train station for his departure. Luckily for Hogan, this happens to be the same ammo train he wishes to destroy so now he can derail the train and the pesky Inspector General with one stroke!

Program Notes: There is a slight change in the opening credits. Larry Hovis is no longer pumping up the radio antenna. Now he is seen mixing chemicals in his makeshift chemistry lab. Here's the first of three visits from John Dehner, who acted in nearly all the hit shows of the 1960s and 1970s, especially in the Western genre. He would return for a two-part assignment in the following season. The POW camp is now referred to as "Camp 13" again for the final time. This episode was produced right after the pilot, but held back as the fourth episode broadcast.

Assessment: Another plot device is introduced that would be revisited throughout the program's six year run, which we will call the "let's make Klink look bad so he will have to stay" campaign. It's now clear to the audience that Hogan must keep Klink as their Kommodant because no other German officer would allow the POWs to get away with their daily deeds of larceny. Unfortunately, the schemes employed here to discredit Klink (a radio plays in the barracks but no one can find it, Von Platzen's wallet gets lifted to be found by Klink, etc.) all feel undercooked. It's another plot point that would be revisited, revamped, and improved with time. Actually, blowing up Von Platzen with the train feels, oddly, rather mean-spirited. His character is certainly one of the less despicable Nazis the program will introduce. Here is a case where the writer, Laurence Marks, looked for a quick wrap up as the minutes ticked away from this half hour. What is quite remarkable, however, is how with time and development, the series would execute some tightly-woven story threads where every minute counted in the credit or discredit of Wilhelm Klink.

Season 1, Episode 4: "The Flight of the Valkyrie" 10/15/1965.

D: Gene Reynolds W: Richard M. Powell

Guest Cast: Bernard Fox (Col. Crittendon), Louise Troy (Lili), Cynthia Lynn (Helga), Jon Cedar (Cpl. Langenscheidt/Uncredited.).

Storyline: Klink, dejected by all the "funny business" taking place in his camp, decides to remove his "bad luck charm" by replacing Hogan with Colonel Rodney Crittendon, Royal Air Force (RAF), as the new senior POW officer. This upsets two of Hogan's current plans: the safe passage of a German Baroness out of Stalag 13, and the rebuild project of a small airplane the boys are working on down in the tunnels. Although Crittendon wholeheartedly agrees that a prisoner's objective is to plan an "escape, escape, escape," he does not hold the same opinions as Hogan regarding clandestine operations of sabotage. The Heroes aid Crittendon in his latest escape attempt to make him appear a threat to Klink's command and help the Baroness fly out of camp during the confusion.

Program Notes: This is the introduction of Bernard Fox to the program where he would chock up a total of eight related appearances throughout the entire run. Amassing a heavy resume of film and TV credits, Fox is permanently etched in the minds of the public for his nineteen turns as Dr. Bombay on *Bewitched*. The first of three visits from Louise Troy, who was later married to Werner Klemperer (1969-1975). The first of thirty-four directing assignments for Gene Reynolds (1923-2020). In this outing, Klink makes direct references to previous incidents: the Tiger Tank "disappearing and reappearing in the rec hall" from episode 1, and that "trains are blowing up" from episode 3.

"The Flight of the Valkyrie" introduces Bernard Fox's well meaning, but bungling, Colonel Crittendon for his first of eight, outrageous contributions. Author's collection CBS Television Inc.

Assessment: Similar to the fantastic concept of stealing the tank in the first episode, "The Flight of the Valkyrie" is a vast improvement because all the details regarding the discovery and rebuild of the crashed airplane are shown throughout the run time. Fox's debut as Crittendon is a strong one, with more humor of a slightly wry nature and less of a cartoon nature, as, sadly, the character would evolve. In later episodes, Col. Crittendon would move into full throttle Schultz territory as another lovable buffoon. Here Fox is somewhat more centered and his comments about how easy an escape should happen are contrasted with the funny business of his botched tunnel departure and attempt to cut the fence wires (a hilarious sight gag with the entire fence falling over). Newkirk and Carter make a good team here, and the final flight, complete with Wagner as a background deterrence, makes for a good show, old bean.

☆ ☆ ☆

Season 1, Episode 5: "The Prisoner's Prisoner" 10/15/1965.

D: Gene Reynolds W: R. S. Allen, Harvey Bullock

Guest Cast: Roger C. Carmel (Gen. Karl Schmidt), John Orchard (Sgt. Walters), Inge Jaklin (Fraulein).

Storyline: Sgt. Walters, incarcerated at Stalag 13, and five other British commandos have been captured while trying to blow up the headquarters of General Schmidt. Hogan decides to go back and finish the assignment by convincing Klink it would look better for his record if all the commandos were moved to his stalag. Klink sends Schultz and his men to transfer the other five men, a ruse for Hogan and Carter to hide in the transport truck headed for General Schmidt's HQ. After finishing the wire job for detonation, the duo subdues Schmidt, who is entertaining a pretty fraulein, and Hogan decides to haul him back to camp since he feels even the POWs should be entitled to have a prisoner of their own. At Stalag 13, Klink fails to believe Schmidt is actually a German general and not one of the transferred prisoners and throws him into the barracks with the rest of his POWs. London informs Hogan that Schmidt has top secret info regarding a pending Nazi offensive, so in order to persuade Schmidt to reveal such knowledge, the Heroes make believe the general has developed a deadly fever. Hogan gets the general to talk and he has Schmidt and Walters smuggled out to London.

Program Notes: The *M*A*S*H* connection takes off with John Orchard's first of three, unrelated, appearances. He would be featured as recurring character Capt. "Ugly John" Black during the first season of *M*A*S*H*, with some of these episodes to be directed by Gene Reynolds. Roger C. Carmel is a very familiar face. *Star Trek* fans will remember him as Harry Mudd; *Batman* bat-fans will remember him in a two-parter as Colonel Gumm in which he attempts to convert Batman, Robin, the Green Hornet, and Kato into life-sized postage stamps! Two decades before Johnny Carson assumes host of *The Tonight Show*, Hogan references the "mighty Hogan Art Players."

Assessment: Despite some good, psychologically based humor and other detailed moments, "The Prisoner's Prisoner" unfolds in a somewhat, incomprehensible manner, even for *Hogan's Heroes* standards. After rigging his headquarters to detonate, it's not clear why Hogan would drag the unconscious general back to camp. How this gets accomplished in the guarded transport truck they just stowed away in is a big riddle. Hogan almost plays the notion off as a lark. It's just dumb luck when Hogan learns later that London wants info out of him. The bits of business convincing Schmidt he has "barracks fever" (sliding the candles under his bunk, LeBeau wrestling with a giant pine box, etc.) are quite humorous and there is a cute bit with Hogan's first off-campus kiss - he pulls the general's date into his arms and into the darkened cellar, plants a smacker, and sends her on her bewildered way. Less memorable is the oddball Yuletide scene where the men try to convince Schmidt it is now Christmas. Guest Carmel gives a somewhat low-key performance. The two writers would have benefited his character with more dumbfounded, debate driven footage with Klink. Most underwhelming is the final scene where Schmidt makes his exit through the trick bunk beds without protest, without a syllable. Perhaps he's ready to leave this stalag in search of a more coherent script. Instead, for who knows what reason, we get Sgt. Schultz as Santa Claus. Better presents yet to come next Christmas.

Season 1, Episode 6: "German Bridge is Falling Down" 10/29/1965.

D: Gene Reynolds W: Laurence Marks

Guest Cast: Cynthia Lynn (Helga), Forrest Compton (Pilot), Hal Lynch (Co-pilot), Jon Cedar (Cpl. Langenscheidt/Uncredited), Roy Goldman (POW/Unc.).

Storyline: During a night roll call requested by Hogan, all the men light up cigarettes creating an illuminated arrow in order to signal an overhead American bomber looking to air strike Adolph Hitler Bridge. When the air strike misses its target, Hogan instructs Carter to whip up an explosive using the ammonia and bleach stored in the camp kitchen. Carter's chemistry tests set off several, minor explosions, but the men cover by posting civilian construction signs indicating that periodic blasting will take place. With no success, Hogan devises a new plan. They will steal ammo and gunpowder out of the storage unit, build a timer explosive, and sneak it into the sidecar of the mail courier. To access the ammo building, the men graffiti the outside walls with anti-Nazi slanders. Klink forces Hogan's men to repaint the building and they deliberately stall the detail to buy time for Newkirk to pick the lock and for the men to sneak in individually and remove the gunpowder from numerous cartridges. The boys slip the newly devised time bomb into the courier's sidecar, and after his run to Dusseldorf, the courier's timed route must take him right over the target bridge.

Program Notes: The *M*A*S*H* connection tightens up as writer Marks (sixty-seven *Hogan's* scripts) and director Reynolds (thirty-four) enjoy their first collaboration. They would be two of the guiding forces behind the "Henry Blake" era of *M*A*S*H*. The two, different, opening credits of Larry Hovis as Carter conducting his chemistry experiments used for the series are culled from this episode. Upon seeing the arrow signal in the opening scene, the pilot smiles and quips: "Hogan's Heroes."

Assessment: Pacing is one of the series' best friends and it is used to great advantage in this clever story line that minimizes the more ridiculous aspects of the program, although it's hard not to roll your eyes when LeBeau posts the civilian construction sign in English! The episode gets off to a flying start with the terrific sight gag of the giant arrow signal formed from all the men lighting up cigarettes and standing on their marks. Another wild sight gag is the appearance of Carter, who pops out of a tunnel from within a large locker on the floor of the barracks! The show keeps moving at a nice clip and the graffiti painted on the exterior of the storage unit ("Hess is a Mess," etc.) provides some good chuckles. Well-timed, too, is the planting of the time bomb in the sidecar, set to go off in twenty minutes, and some rapid improvising on Hogan's part, making Klink believe the courier accepted a bribe so Klink will notify the guard station to keep the courier to his timed route. Speaking about that poor courier . . . talk about an innocent pawn in one of Hogan's schemes. The guy shows up to deliver mail and ends up part of a human booby trap to blow up a bridge. Talk about war being hell.

Season 1, Episode 7: "Movies Are Your Best Escape" 11/05/1965.

D: Howard Morris W: Laurence Marks

Guest Cast: Cynthia Lynn (Helga), Henry Corden (Gen. Von Kaplow), John Crawford (Lt. Ritchie), William Christopher (Lt. Donner).

Storyline: Two British airmen, Ritchie and Donner, arrive to the barracks via the escape tunnel. Their transfer to London is stalled by the unannounced arrival of General Von Kaplow, who is en route to Berlin with important documents sealed in an attaché case handcuffed to his wrist. Hogan, of course, wants to know the contents of those documents, so he sets up a friendly, high cuisine dinner courtesy of Chef LeBeau in honor of an American holiday, the "repeal of prohibition." During dinner, Newkirk is able to sneak under the table and remove the documents. Hogan encourages Klink to play the violin for Von Kaplow and Helga in order to stall for time while LeBeau photographs the document pages in the kitchen and Newkirk returns them to the attaché case. Hogan discovers they are top secret war plans and plots to get them delivered to London despite the heavy German security surrounding the stalag. He decides to throw the Germans off guard by concocting a scheme that implies the Third Reich is losing the war. First, he holds a Russian language class to convince Schultz that the camp will soon be liberated by the Russians. He also spreads rumors that Berlin and Hamburg are "in shambles." Then he has Newkirk fake a live broadcast of Hitler announcing that "negotiation talks are underway." Next, Hogan casts the two airmen as Nazi photographers who have been assigned to shoot movie film of Stalag 13 for "archival purposes." Their movie camera is a dummy prop, however, containing the negatives of Von Kaplow's war plans. When Von Kaplow returns and stifles the rumors with news of German victories on all fronts, an outraged Klink throws the two filmmakers out and they make their escape to London with the secret negatives.

Program Notes: A couple of firsts are introduced including Klink's debut as a violinist and LeBeau's first employment as master chef to entertain German VIPs and help disguise Hogan's true motives. Howard Morris, long remembered as a regular member of Sid Caesar's comedy troupe in the 1950s, launches his first of fourteen directorial assignments. This is the first of five guest shots for prolific actor Henry Corden, perhaps most fondly remembered as the voice of Fred Flintstone, after the passing of Alan Reed in 1977. William Christopher begins the first of his four visits who, during the 1960s, would bounce back and forth between the *Hogan's* set and its neighbor, the *Gomer Pyle U.S.M.C.* set. Along with several of his *Hogan's* colleagues, he would make the move to the 4077th playing Father Mulcahy for all eleven seasons of "M*A*S*H."

Assessment: This is the best episode to this point, with a fast moving plot, lots of funny ideas, and a big boost from guest star Corden. The high point of this episode – that crams in so many plot details you may feel dizzy by the end of the half hour – has to be the riotous Hitler speech delivered with great gusto from Corporal Newkirk who finishes by telling the Fatherland to "keep schmiling." "Keep smiling? He wants us to keep smiling?" counters Klink in incredulous, hilarious fashion. Brightly funny, also, are the scenes of the fake cameramen shooting archive footage. Klink, convinced the Russian forces will liberate the camp at any moment, encourages the men in their project and even takes over as director (suggesting we "try moving the camera over there," etc.) The shining star, however, may be Corden's Von Kaplow, complete with eye patch over right eye. Unlike the later superiors that would pay visits and generally berate and belittle poor Klink, this General is delighted to be wined and dined, endures Klink's violin concerto, and ogles Helga. When he returns on his way back from Berlin, providing a plot point to confirm to Klink that the Third Reich is *not* losing the war, it's simply because he's hoping to score another gourmet dinner *and* score with Helga. Now that's a hip general!

Season 1, Episode 8: "Go Light on the Heavy Water" 11/12/1965.

D: Howard Morris W: Arthur Julian

Guest Cast: Cynthia Lynn (Helga), John Stephenson (Capt. Mueller), Lawrence Montaigne (Sgt. Steinfeld), Eddie Firestone (Scotty).

Storyline: Pinned down by enemy fire, a Nazi transport truck headed for Berlin is diverted to the safety of Stalag 13. Capt. Mueller, highly secretive of the cargo he possesses, informs Klink that he is delivering water from Norway to Berlin. Hogan's men learn that the truck carries a large barrel of "heavy water," to be used for nuclear testing. London warns Hogan that the heavy water must be destroyed at all costs. Hogan convinces Klink that the precious water comes from a Norwegian spa renowned for restoring youth to those that drink it. Suspicious, Klink sneaks into the transport truck to sample its contents. The next day, both Helga and Hogan confirm that Klink appears more youthful, that he appears to have grown more hair, and that there is a more youthful stride to his step. Obsessed, Klink plots to steal the barrel and have it switched and talks Schultz into being his accomplice in crime. Capt. Mueller spoils the fun when he finally reveals the true contents and purpose of the "heavy water." Hogan's initial plot foiled, the Heroes stage a fire in Klink's office, and during the confusion switch out the "heavy water" with a barrel of plain water for Berlin.

Program Notes: Robert Clary does not appear in this episode and his name is not featured in the end credits. Eddie Firestone fills out the shoes of the fourth hero as "Scotty". Many fans regard director Howard Morris' funniest work as an actor in the films of Mel Brooks, particularly as Dr. Lillolman in *High Anxiety* (1977) and as Nero's flamboyant court speaker in *History of the World Part I* (1981).

Assessment: A fitfully amusing outing based on how well you buy into Hogan's con that the water barrel contains the fountain of youth. (I didn't.) Hogan is now clearly established as a womanizer, and he gets three scenes to make time with Helga to prove the point. Helga has now become a willing co-conspirator; she openly lies to Klink about his new, youthful appearance. Most interesting is that Klink is willing to commit larceny against the Fatherland by plotting to lift the water. Less interesting is the wrap up with the fake fire in a ruse we will encounter in many future tales, and the ensuing slapstick at Klink's expense. It's only a short matter of time before you know he will meet up with a blast of fire hose water. Uncanny how those mischievous POWs are always there to run amok during an unexpected crisis while Klink's men are left to run around in circles.

Season 1, Episode 9: "Top Hat, White Tie, and Bomb Sights" 11/19/1965.

D: Gene Reynolds W: Laurence Marks

Guest Cast: Leon Askin (Gen. Burkhalter), Edward Knight (Maj. Klopfer), Monroe Arnold (Willie), Sigrid Valdis (Gretchen), Thordis Brandt (Elsa/Uncredited).

Storyline: Hogan's assignment from London is to make contact with agent "Willie" at the Hausner Hof restaurant in nearby Hammelburg. Klink is having his men automate and electrify the gates so the normal escape route is blocked. While Hogan thinks of an alternative plan to meet Willie, he discovers that Klink has had his living quarters bugged. The gang delivers scripted lines for Klink's benefit, indicating that Hogan has now developed a pro-Germany attitude. He even drops clues that as an Army airman he was involved in the development of the "Norden." General Burkhalter is anxious to have Hogan reveal his knowledge of the Norden, so he has Klink set up a small dinner party at the Hausner Hof complete with wine and a couple of pretty women. While Hogan makes time with Gretchen, Klink's date, on the dance floor, Klink fumes while Burkhalter is amused. Hogan finds Willie and slips him a message. Back in Klink's office, Hogan draws out a map of the Norden for the General, the Kommodant, and Major Klopfer, who realizes that the "Norden" is actually an American vacuum cleaner!

Program Notes: Leon Askin returns to Stalag 13, now promoted to "General Burkhalter." Sigrid Valdis appears as "Gretchen." Moviegoers had recently enjoyed an eyeful of Valdis in the Rat Pack comedy, *Marriage on the Rocks* (1965) as a bikini-clad candidate interviewing as Dean Martin's personal secretary – and stealing the scene from Dino! Valdis would return the following season to assume the role of Helga's replacement, Hilda. Oddly enough, Cynthia Lynn does not appear in this episode but her future substitute does.

Assessment: A smartly written, funny episode that lends formal introduction to General Burkhalter in less than dignified manner. When the general arrives, Klink is anxious to show off his newly automated front gates. Of course, Kinchloe has rewired them to randomly open and close creating some silly slapstick with Klink stumbling into Burkhalter and knocking both men to the ground three times. As childish as this sounds on paper, it plays better on film and the physical antics conjure the spirit of a Laurel and Hardy routine. At the Hausner Hof, Sigrid Valdis melts the screen with her smoldering personality, and actor Monroe Arnold, who bears a strong resemblance to comedian Louis Nye, contributes a brief, but very funny bit as a nervous spy, prompting Hogan to quip: "It's a pleasure to work with spies with nerves of steel."

Classic Exchange:

Klink: "You may not know this about me, General, but when I turn on the charm, I have been known to be irresistible."

Burkhalter: "Really? I have no trouble resisting you!"

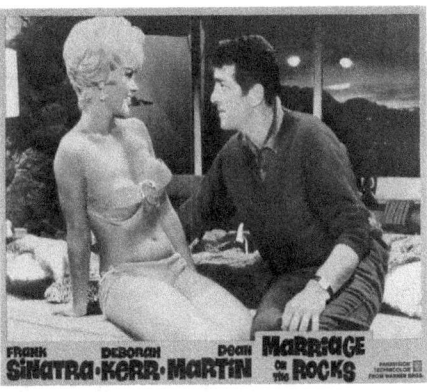

Original lobby card for *Marriage on the Rocks,* the final "Rat Pack" comedy, more than bolstered by the steamy presence of Sigrid Valdis who performs the impossible – stealing a scene from the great womanizer, Dean Martin. Author's collection/National Screen Service Corp./Warner Brothers Pictures.

Season 1, Episode 10: "Happiness is a Warm Sergeant" 11/26/1965.

D: Gene Reynolds W: Laurence Marks

Guest Cast: Cynthia Lynn (Helga), Norman Alden (Sgt. Krebs), Bruce Yarnell (Capt. Winslow), Jon Cedar (Guard), Norbert Schiller (Max).

Storyline: Kinchloe needs replacement parts for the team's radio transmitter so this means sending someone into town to meet their Underground contact at the local pub. Newkirk fakes a toothache and Schultz is ordered to take him to the local dentist, but the crafty Brit persuades his escort to visit the pub for one beer. While waiting for the barkeep, Max, to fetch the radio parts, Newkirk inebriates Schultz by dumping shots of whiskey into his beer stein. Seven hours later, the men return to Stalag 13 with Newkirk rolling a drunken Schultz up to the gate in a wheelbarrow! Furious, Klink orders an immediate transfer for Schultz and his replacement, the no-nonsense Sgt. Krebs, reports for duty. Clearly a threat to their operation, the gang goes to work to discredit Krebs. First, Carter buddies up to him by handing over a makeshift radio the other POWs designed. Klink is delighted with the discovery until the gag radio squirts water in his face. Then Kinchloe pretends to communicate to Hogan through the ground near the barracks. When Krebs ushers Klink over to the spot, the Kommodant disappears six feet under. Finally, the Heroes stage an escape and while Newkirk stalls Krebs in the barracks with his card tricks, Hogan, Carter, and LeBeau allow themselves to be captured by Schultz, winning back the confidence of Klink and insuring the exit of Krebs.

Program Notes: Norman Alden's professional acting resume is a mile long, with over one hundred appearances in the cult soap opera *Mary Hartman, Mary Hartman* alone. He would return for the final *Hogan's Heroes* broadcast, "Rockets or Romance."

Assessment: An amiable little adventure, affording some nice, sympathetic moments for John Banner's Schultz, who through no fault of his own becomes intoxicated by the scheming business of the prisoners. The episode revs up a notch with Norman Alden's energetic Sgt. Krebs and the trickery to get him displaced. Hogan comments that it took "us six months to get Schultz to look the other way," and one suspects that with some time and psychology, the Heroes would eventually bring Krebs around to their way of thinking. He seems to be willing enough as he buddies up to Carter with ease and quickly falls for the sleight of hand deceptions of Newkirk. The rigged escape attempt is quite charming, with Hogan and company encouraging Schultz to raise the alarm and foil their group effort. Schultz, however, has been stuck walking guard duty outside the wire day and night, and has completely lost interest in saving himself, so, of course, it's up to the Heroes to restore order by giving themselves up.

Season 1, Episode 11: "The Scientist" 12/03/1965.

D: Howard Morris W: Laurence Marks

Guest Cast: Parley Baer (Prof. Altman), Maurice Marsac (Emil Du Bois), Forrest Compton (1st Officer), Buck Young (2nd Officer), Jayne Massey (Marie DuBois/Uncredited), Bard Stevens (Capt. Krug/Unc.).

Storyline: At nightfall, Prof. Du Bois is ushered in to an empty storage building by armed guards. Allowing Schultz to join their blackjack game, Hogan discovers that their new guest is a French scientist cooperating on experiments with the Nazis. Hogan talks Klink into letting LeBeau join Du Bois as his assistant. LeBeau learns that the only reason Du Bois has feigned cooperation is because the Nazis are holding his daughter hostage at a local hotel. Posing as an ill-tempered German General from Hitler's staff, Hogan, accompanied by Newkirk, force the German officers at the hotel to forfeit the scientist's daughter, Marie, over to them. They ride off in a motorcycle with Marie seated in "General Von Himmelburger's" lap in the sidecar! The Heroes next reunite father and daughter and plan to have them flown out of Germany. When Klink learns of the Du Bois escape, he panics, and accepts Hogan's plan to have LeBeau impersonate the scientist for the impending arrival of Nazi Professor Altman, who will be checking up on his progress. LeBeau pulls off the ruse and after the departure of Altman the Heroes erase the existence of Du Bois with a well timed explosion.

Program Notes: Parley Baer is best remembered as Mayor Roy Stoner on "The Andy Griffith Show." This was his first of four appearances. Forrest Compton, in his second of six guest shots, played the role of Colonel Edward Gray in forty-one episodes of *Gomer Pyle U.S.M.C.* In this episode, Klink's private sleeping quarters are attached to Helga's reception area, though this location would later change.

Assessment: A pretty dull affair, "The Scientist" has some plot implausibilities that even Colonel Hogan can't talk his way out of. Klink's acceptance of the Du Bois escape is unusually weak as he doesn't question *how* it occurred or even attempt to send out a search party. This weakness is matched by his all-too-quick willingness to allow LeBeau to step in to the doc's shoes. This also taints all of Klink's future boasts that "no one ever escapes from Stalag 13." Apparently this boast only pertains to prisoners of war and not kidnapped scientists. The sequence with LeBeau as the impostor is devoid of laughs. Newkirk plies the two Germans with brandy while "Du Bois" prattles on and on and no one chuckles. Worse yet is the tacked - on conclusion with the contrived explosion meant to close the Du Bois chapter. However, wouldn't the Nazis search the wreckage for any remains of the body? Ah, but there I go, trying to second guess *Hogan's Heroes* again. Barely successful is the rescue of Marie Du Bois with "Von Himmelburger" and his aide riding into the courtyard of a well appointed set and entering the equally handsome hotel interior. Crane, spouting close to the worst German accent ever, performs a ballet of destruction as he throws a temper tantrum contrasting the fatigued takes of Dawson. The whole spectacle is more bizarre than funny. The sight of the pair riding off with Marie in the General's lap is . . . well, let's just say the less said about this one the better . . . .

Season 1, Episode 12: "Hogan's Hofbrau" 12/10/1965.

D: Gene Reynolds W: Laurence Marks

Guest Cast: Cynthia Lynn (Helga), Frank Marth (Capt. Milheiser), Paula Stewart (Hilda), Willard Sage (Lt. Schmidt), Roger Heldfond (Soldier).

Storyline: A German Panzer division is sighted near camp and Hogan and London want to know what their plans are. Hogan dons a Luftwaffe Major's uniform and plans to scope out Hilda's Hofbrau where all the German soldiers have been patronizing hoping to pick up on any idle conversation. Meanwhile, Capt. Milheiser and his aide, Lt. Schmidt, pay Klink a visit in order to solicit a contribution for the "beautify Bertesgarten" campaign. The enforcers coerce Klink into pledging 5000 marks. At the Hofbrau, Hogan, disguised as "Major Hoople," buddies up to Milheiser and Schmidt, claiming to be on temporary assignment at Stalag 13. Hogan sets up Newkirk and Carter as waiters and LeBeau as the chef so they can also troll for information. Schultz strolls in and nearly has a coronary when he spots all his POWs present and not accounted for, but chooses to wait outside where he can see and know nothing. The next day, Klink, still getting the shakedown from Milheiser and Schmidt, agrees to meet them at the Hofbrau that evening with his "donation." While trying to pacify the two men at the pub, Klink nearly has his own coronary when he recognizes the Heroes out of camp. But "Major Hoople" smoothes it all out for his Kommodant by paying off the extortionists with 5000 marks in hot money.

Program Notes: This is the first of five Nazi characterizations for Frank Marth, who, as a personal favorite of Jackie Gleason's, supported "the Great One" in over fifty television programs in the 1950s and 1960s. This is also the first episode where Klink clearly identifies his POWs as AWOL, and yet somehow accepts that Hogan and his men have the freedom to come and go from Stalag 13, although the epilogue allows Hogan an explanation for this behavior.

Assessment: Laurence Marks delivers his finest script yet by removing the explosive spectacles of the series and paring it down to a simple plot – Hogan and his men going undercover at the Hofbrau and snooping for enemy information. Stockpiled around this basic premise are numerous laugh out loud moments including Schultz's reactions to seeing the boys at work, and Klink being harassed by the questionably philanthropic blackmailers. This includes a terrific camera shot from the back of Milheiser and Schmidt's heads as they stare down Klink in his office. Frank Marth exudes subtle sleaze as Milheiser and the audience gets a taste of crime noir, Nazi Germany style. The comedy with the gang at the Hofbrau favors a Marx Brothers picture with LeBeau, Newkirk, and Carter inexplicably joining the restaurant staff, and running afoul of Schultz and Klink. The boys might not be serving up *Duck Soup* (1933) but maybe come a little closer to offering a taste of *Room Service* (1938). Priceless too, in an episode with many choice bits to choose from, are Schultz's clumsy attempts to stall Klink in his office from departing for the Hofbrau including this:

Classic Exchange:

Schultz: "Herr Kommodant. I have a problem."

Klink: (dryly) "That is the understatement of the year."

Season 1, Episode 13: "Oil for the Lamps of Hogan" 12/17/1965.

D: Howard Morris W: Laurence Marks

Guest Cast: Cynthia Lynn (Helga), Leon Askin (Gen. Burkhalter), William Mims (Fritz Bowman), Jon Cedar (Cpl. Langenscheidt/Uncredited).

Storyline: General Burkhalter arrives along with German industrialist, Fritz Bowman, and his plans to build a new, synthetic fuel plant at Stalag 13, a site safe from Allied attack. Burkhalter informs Klink that all the POWs will be reassigned to other stalags "temporarily" while a new Stalag 13 is constructed. Fearing the end of their escape operation, Hogan conspires to turn Burkhalter off on the idea. First, he slowly convinces Klink that once dispersed they will not be coming back (Hogan has "seen it happen before") and that Klink will be pressed back into aviation duty. Then a phony escape attempt is staged and Newkirk, Carter, and LeBeau are hauled into Klink's office with fresh oil smeared on their faces. Carter blabs they had to stop tunneling and come up for air because they were drowning in "all the oil down there." In privacy, Hogan spins a yarn that a former prisoner was also a geologist who confirmed that a river of oil flows under the camp. Klink and Hogan agree to be partners after the war, buy the deserted stalag, and start their oil empire. Burkhalter is pulled into the oil scheme but they can't convince Bowman to build elsewhere so Hogan stages a dummy air attack complete with threatening leaflets dumped in the compound effectively breaching the security of the industrialist's plans and allowing Hogan and company to stay put.

Assessment: Laurence Marks continues his writing stride, and aided by Howard Morris' snappy direction, another smart comedy emerges. The farfetched idea of black gold flowing under the stalag is capably realized thanks to some longer than usual Hogan/

Klink banter, and a brief, but very funny and well timed Burkhalter/Hogan exchange that Hogan twists to his advantage. Crane and Klemperer wonderfully perform together as Hogan sells Klink on the evidence of oil and what that means for them. Watching the manic glee and excitement Klemperer exudes is to watch a masterful comic actor at work. Jon Cedar gets a longer than usual scene where the boys stage a fight in Klink's office so LeBeau can crawl into Klink's safe for eavesdropping purposes! Schultz actually shows some muscle by breaking the scene up and encouraging the young corporal to "get tough so they will respect you!" The final wrap up is more than satisfactory with the fake air raid (complete with wired explosives to lend authenticity and the hailstorm of blackmail leaflets) and Hogan pacifying Klink's fears about Burkhalter's interest in the oil disappearing once the *Allies* have won the war.

Season 1, Episode 14: "Reservations are Required" 12/24/1965.

D: Gene Reynolds W: Laurence Marks

Guest Cast: Cynthia Lynn (Helga), Robert Hogan (Braden), Dennis Robertson (Mills), Mike Murphy (Comminsky).

Storyline: Out on an unspecified night mission, LeBeau encounters Braden and Mills, who have just tunneled their way out of Stalag 9 and are looking to take advantage of Hogan's escape and relocation service. Unfortunately, the men are only two of twenty escapees and Hogan reluctantly holes them up at Stalag 13 while his boys go to work on crafting fake German IDs and civilian attire for all. Impatient, Braden and Mills attempt to escape on their own by sneaking into the water truck which could spoil plans for the others and the entire operation, so Hogan breaks this plan up by tipping off Schultz. The gang digs a special escape tunnel out of Barracks Three and Hogan instructs Newkirk, LeBeau, and Carter to escape and then surrender. While Klink storms Barracks Three with all his men, the twenty escapees utilize the emergency tunnel to make their genuine escape. Klink orders Hogan's men to fill up the tunnel from Barracks Three, proud that he foiled their plans and that his no escape record is still clean.

Program Notes: Rumor has it that actor Robert Hogan was a friend of co-creator Bernard Fein, who used the actor's name for the title character of this show. *M*A*S*H* fans will remember Hogan from the fourth season "Smilin' Jack" episode, where his plans to become "chopper pilot of the year" are shot down by Hawkeye and B. J.

Assessment: A bit of mid-season humdrums settle in as this program seems to already be recycling previous themes with the exception being the size of the lot needed to be moved (twenty escapees instead of the usual two or three). The idea of staging a fake escape as a distraction for the true, intended scheme taking place shows up again. There are a couple of nice bits, however, such as Hogan searching Barracks Three for the location of the new tunnel, enhanced by an unusual, high angle shot overlooking the set. Effective also is Klink stamping his foot twice to fit into his boot which unknowingly signals the men underground to move out. Still, this outing feels a bit weighed down by an already, business-as-usual fatigue.

Season 1, Episode 15: "Anchors Aweigh Men of Stalag 13" 12/31/1965.

D: Howard Morris W: David Chandler, Jack H. Robinson

Guest Cast: Cynthia Lynn (Helga), Leon Askin (Gen. Burkhalter), Jon Cedar (Cpl. Langenscheidt/Uncredited), Fredd Wayne (Kristman), Michael St. Clair (Capt. Michaels).

Storyline: Schultz catches Hogan and LeBeau outside of camp in broad daylight, but they are more concerned with their rendezvous with British Capt. Michaels, who has just escaped from Stalag 5. He pulls up in a stolen German truck carrying a newly-developed gunsight that can spot aircraft by computer. The boys sequester Michaels and the stolen gunsight back to camp leaving Schultz with the task of ditching the truck in the woods. Hogan plots to transport Michaels and the entire gunsight back to London by convincing Klink of the need for a new officers' club, and he has one constructed as a sail boat to capture a "yacht club" theme. Klink plans to throw a big party to launch the opening of his new club and invites General Burkhalter to attend. When London changes the timetable of Michaels' scheduled transport it conflicts with Klink's party night so Hogan has Carter convince Klink that Burkhalter recently got furious with another Kommodant's frivolous spending on a similar officers' club. Klink orders a squadron to remove the boat immediately, and his soldiers have it towed sixty miles to the North Sea along with Michaels and the gunsight as stowaways.

Program Notes: Producer Edward H. Feldman brought on the writing team of David Chandler and Jack H. Robinson for this and two ensuing scripts. Leon Askin is mistakenly billed as "Col. Burkhalter" in the closing credits.

Assessment: It took two scriptwriters to unleash the worst story of the first season that starts with a ridiculous chapter and never improves. Schultz actually busts Hogan and LeBeau in the opener, but, naturally, chooses to do nothing about it. Hogan even dismisses his presence to Michaels stating "he's sort of one of us." The idea of Michaels escaping in a German truck, complete with the gunsight aboard, is absurd; worse yet, even though Schultz is left to ditch the stolen vehicle the three men somehow haul the gunsight back to camp through, apparently, the escape tunnel! The idea of building a nautically-themed, officers' club in an attempt to *sail* Michaels back to England is, to put it mildly, farfetched. Clumsier yet is that Klink allows LeBeau to supervise the construction of the club and order his men about. The whole script is a complete mess; a case of two new writers not really having a handle on the basic plot developments of a particular program. Even in its most inane circumstances, *Hogan's Heroes* typically clings to some form of logic, sometimes more successfully in some cases than others. Here there is no logic to be found. Instead we are left with a show where the POWs do whatever the hell they want and Klink parades around in a skipper costume, similar to the type of behavior we might expect from Ralph Furley on a late season outing of *Three's Company,* but not necessarily from the Kommodant of the "toughest prisoner of war camp in Germany."

Memorable Exchange:

Klink: (in Skipper uniform)"I am a man of many sides. You didn't know that behind that stern soldier there is a world traveler, a dreamer, a lover!"

Helga: "You *are* a dreamer."

Season 1, Episode 16: "Happy Birthday, Adolf" 01/07/1966.

D: Robert Butler W: Laurence Marks

Guest Cast: Cynthia Lynn (Helga), Howard Caine (Maj. Keitel).

Storyline: In honor of Hitler's upcoming birthday, the Allied forces are planning an airstrike at a general sector a short distance from Stalag 13. After nightfall, LeBeau goes out on an undercover mission, dressed as a little old lady, and reports back to Hogan that a nearby squadron has several large artillery guns ready to defend any air attacks. Donning the identity of "Captain Hoganburg," Hogan and LeBeau, as "Corporal Doberman," meet with Major Keitel, the commanding officer of the battalion, and hand over forged papers stating his men are to relieve command on the eve of Hitler's birthday celebration. Keitel checks the validity of these orders, but Kinchloe and Newkirk have tapped into his phone line and validate them. Newkirk further instructs Keitel to beautify the installation's recreation building for a birthday bash. Off the phone, Keitel frets he is undermanned for such a frivolous duty, but Hoganburg suggests he borrow the POWs from the nearby Stalag 13, and ironically force *them* to perform the labor of party setup crew. The night of the party, Hoganburg returns stating his men are to stand guard while Keitel and his men celebrate Hitler's birthday. Keitel demurs, until Helga and a sexy girlfriend arrive, which changes the Major's mind. Keitel now out of the way, the Heroes go to work on the big guns creating quite the birthday surprise once the Allied air strike begins.

Program Notes: A milestone of sorts is achieved as brilliant actor Howard Caine begins a long and fruitful association with *Hogan's Heroes*. He would play one more unrelated character early in the second season before settling in to his infamous Gestapo officer, Major Hochstetter, for thirty-seven nods. This is the fifth and final directing assignment from Robert Butler, who launched the series by directing the pilot, "The Informer." He finished out the 1960s with several directing assignments for *Batman* and the two-part space classic "The Menagerie" on *Star Trek*. In 1982 he co-created and remained a guiding light for the *Remington Steele* series, which made Pierce Brosnan a household name.

Howard Caine (left) begins his rightfully celebrated tenure with the series as Major Keitel before returning as another Major distraction. Author's collection/CBS Television Inc.

Assessment: Less spectacle and more character driven, "Happy Birthday Adolf" moves at a good tempo and is well worth the time to watch Caine in an early role. Bob Crane, perhaps realizing his German accent floundered in "The Scientist," appears to abandon any attempts at dialect during his lengthy dialogue scene with Major Keitel. Probably a wise move, since the scene plays better for it allowing Crane to do what he often does best, light dramatic work with a self serving subtext. Caine is excellent delivering a reserved performance and banters well with Bob Crane's "Hoganburg." Caine's subtle reactions to Hoganburg's constant barking at Corporal Doberman (most likely a nod to *The Phil Silvers Show* and Maurice Gosfield as Private Duane Doberman) show the actor is far more capable than just rants and raves. The ridiculous finish, with gag banners reading "Happy Birthday Adolph," is an implausible stretch, but allows Caine to execute his first, on screen, temper tantrum. Nice too is the final tag scene where Klemperer and Caine square off for the first time; a rare moment where Klink is able to pull rank and "Di-Smiss" the Major's accusations of POW sabotage. These are all just a glimpse of funnier altercations around the corner. Finally, let's not dismiss Helga's contribution, as any program that features her shapely legs as a strategic diversion is reason enough to enlist for duty at any military installation.

Season 1, Episode 17: "The Gold Rush" 01/14/1966.

D: Howard Morris W: Laurence Marks

Guest Cast: Cynthia Lynn (Helga), Rick Traeger (Major Krieger/Gestapo), Tom Hatten (Capt. Martin), Pitt Herbert (German #1).

Storyline: Schultz and a squad of guards return to Stalag 13 four hours later than expected along with a new prisoner, Captain Martin. In Klink's office, Schultz explains the delay was caused by a German transport truck that has seized hundreds of gold bars from the French National Bank and is moving the fortune to Berlin. As Martin clears out his pockets onto Klink's desk, Hogan slips in a false note describing a planned Allied attack. Hogan convinces Klink that the Allies will attack while the Nazis are preoccupied with the gold movement and that Stalag 13 would be the safest hideout for the gold until the threat blows over. Klink relays this information to Major Krieger, who is handling the gold transport, and he diverts the truck off course to Stalag 13. The men arrange an elaborate mission to steal the gold bricks and have them replaced with gold painted, mason bricks. The transport moves on with the phony fortune and Klink proudly addresses the POWs from the newly installed *brick steps* leading to his office.

Program Notes: In one scene, John Banner engages in some improvised, German dialogue with two of Krieger's transport guards. Although at the end of this episode the painted red *gold* bricks have been permanently installed in front of the Kommodant's office, subsequent episodes revert back to wooden steps again.

Assessment: Not a remake of Charles Chaplin's 1925 masterpiece, this "Gold Rush" breezes along thanks to several well plotted moments and a general spirit of teamwork. Outside of the core regulars, the entire barracks pitch in by helping move the metal lockers of gold from the truck to the bunk beds and down into the tunnel and then vice versa after performing an elaborate paint job (the gold now becomes red bricks and plain bricks are painted gold). There are several strategic particulars that help sell this bill of goods: the fake war plans in Klink's office, the drugging of the coffee pot and making the guards believe they both fell asleep, and the sabotage of Klink's wooden steps so the boys can go to work with bricks and mortar. Newkirk and LeBeau play a wonderful scene with Schultz as they schmooze him about gold and drug his coffee pot while Banner strikes poses every time the searchlight passes them by. Variations of this funny gag would crop up in later episodes. Perhaps the sweetest moment, in an episode with a high likability factor, is when the team saws away at the wood supports to the steps while all whistling the theme instrumental in unison, a nice example of a team truly "whistling while they work."

Season 1, Episode 18: "Hello Zolle" 01/21/1966.

D: Gene Reynolds W: David Chandler, Jack H. Robinson

Guest Cast: Gavin MacLeod (Major Zolle), Gilbert Greene (General Hans Stofle), Britt Nillson (Ingeborg), Ramon Bieri (Steiner), Horst Ebersberg (Gunther).

Storyline: A longtime friend and school chum of Klink's, General Hans Stofle, drops in to Stalag 13, along with his beautiful, young mistress. Greene is commanding officer of the Afrika Corps and will be leading a major offensive against the Allies. London directs Hogan and his men to detain the general for at least twenty four hours so they can get the jump on the German war plans. An unexpected visitor, Gestapo agent Major Zolle and his team, also show up to both Stofle and Klink's surprise. Zolle is curious about Stalag 13's perfect record of no escapes and begins snooping about the grounds using the latest technology to search for escape tunnels and other security breaches. Hogan plants the idea to Klink, and later Stofle, that his young fraulein is actually a sweetheart of Himmler's. The two Germans now believe that is the reason for Zolle's unsanctioned arrival. Hogan agrees to smuggle Stofle out of camp dressed as a POW in a staff car, but instead tips off Schultz who captures the "defector." Zolle, delighted to have finally discovered a security breach, has his men haul away Stofle whose absence guarantees a victory for the Allies.

Program Notes: Stalag 13 welcomes Gavin MacLeod for the first of four visits. One of the most recognizable faces in the history of broadcast television, MacLeod has the distinction of being a regular on three hit network programs: *McHale's Navy*, as Happy (seventy-three appearances), *The Mary Tyler Moore Show*, as Murray Slaughter (168), and most famously, as Merrill Stubing, the stern but lovable Captain of the Pacific Princess on the long sailing *Love Boat* (a whopping 250 cruises). Immediately after this role, Gilbert

Greene moved over to *McHale's Navy* to play a German, submarine Captain.

Assessment: Certainly an improvement over the last Chandler/Robinson teleplay, "Hello Zolle" spins an amicable but decidedly muddled story line. The contrivance of having the General's unnamed lady friend (listed as "Ingeborg" in the credits only) pawned off as Himmler's girlfriend seems too simple a ploy to throw off the commander of the Afrika Corps. Her character is sorely underutilized and her lack of dialogue hinders the ruse. This plot is juxtaposed with Zolle's efforts to prowl the camp for clues which turns into nothing more than a Warner Brothers cartoon. Still, the gags are amusing and MacLeod, sporting a Hitler mustache of his own, spectacles, and a permanent smirk, performs with great enthusiasm, offering just a slight, accented voice. There's a zippy, sleazy, little charm he brings to the role and his confidence in recruiting Schultz as his accomplice is rather refreshing. John Banner has a delicious moment when prior to digging up the ground, he stops and strikes a minimalist pose with shovel in hand, before resuming the dig. If there was ever sharp humor found in brevity this is a terrific example. Schultz ironically becomes the hero of the piece when he enacts the capture of the "defector" allowing Zolle and crew to make an arrest and leave. Why Klink chooses not to defend his old friend during the arrest is unclear. Foggier yet is how the Heroes are able to sabotage the tracking devices of the Gestapo and lead Zolle and his men to various booby traps such as the leaky water main, etc. Then again, a script that uses Warner Brothers cartoons as its inspiration may not be concerned with such trifling logistics. Best moment: LeBeau performs a wonderful pantomime to silently explain to Hogan how the drugged champagne was consumed by Ingeborg and not Stofle.

Season 1, Episode 19: "It Takes a Thief... Sometimes" 01/28/1966.

D: Howard Morris W: Richard M. Powell

Guest Cast: Cynthia Lynn (Helga), Michael Constantine (Capt. Heinrich), Claudine Longet (Michelle), Edgar Winston (Adolph), Chris Anders (Wolfgang).

Storyline: During a rigged poker game in the barracks, Schultz leaks out secret information regarding recent sabotage activity in the vicinity. Hogan, not able to account for these deeds, ventures off campus to meet with the Underground group responsible. He and LeBeau encounter the small gang of saboteurs, led by Heinrich, in a small barn and agree to an alliance just as an air raid takes place. Hogan romances the young French woman of their group, Michelle, and they ponder the uncertainties of the war and their lives after it. The next day, Hogan and his men learn that Heinrich is actually a Gestapo Captain working undercover with his group to trap the real saboteurs active outside of Stalag 13. In their next meeting, Hogan informs Heinrich they need to bomb Stalag 13 while freeing the prisoners and that rounding up the dynamite will be Heinrich's responsibility. Dumbfounded, Heinrich agrees to the plan and confides to Klink that he will carry out the plan by using fake dynamite. The POWs are ordered to load Heinrich's truck but do so with real dynamite, a maneuver observed by Schultz who "sees nothing" lest he be ratted out for gambling with the prisoners. That night, Hogan changes the plan. Now they are going to destroy the last strategic target in the area, a railroad tunnel. Heinrich secretly radios Klink with the plan change but his call is intercepted by Kinchloe, impersonating Klink, who agrees to send a squad of men to surround the tunnel. Michelle tries to protect Hogan by revealing Heinrich's true identity and he holds all at gunpoint, boasting that the tunnel is actually wired with fake dynamite. To prove his point he hits the detonator, promptly blowing the tunnel to bits. Escaping in the fake sabotage team's civilian truck, he makes a beeline for Stalag 13 and is met with a barrage of gunfire from Klink's men, believing their stalag is under attack.

Program Notes: This is the only series guest role for Michael Constantine, who will always be remembered for his Emmy award-winning role of Principal Seymour Kaufman on the urban comedy-drama, *Room 222* (1969).

Assessment: The most densely plotted story of the first season, "It Takes a Thief . . . Sometimes" benefits from some gritty developments, Constantine's excellent performance as the impostor/villain, and Crane's assured swagger as a romantic, leading man. Powell's script is an effective change of pace focusing more on the intricacies of the sabotage business and less on boffo humor. We open with a strong start as the POWs squeeze Schultz for info during their rigged poker game. When his Jacks full of Aces full house loses to Hogan's four Kings, *Schultz loses it* and wildly stuffs some of the cards in his mouth in complete disbelief and frustration. Hilarious. Crane is excellent when romancing Michelle and there is a sweet yearning to their hopes of a post-war reunion. French actress Claudine Longet sadly underwhelms; her line reads sound like a stock portrayal of a baby-voiced, French teenager by an *American* high school student. Far more successful is Michael Constantine's double agent role. He brings plenty of menace balanced with light comedy in his confrontations with both Hogan and Klink. When this Nazi rat makes his escape, he meets up with one of the grittier demises seen to date – a hail of gunfire from Klink's men defending their beloved stalag. It's up to Hogan to suggest that Heinrich was actually killed "fleeing from saboteurs," an idea warmly embraced by Klink and successfully capping a very successful episode.

Season One episodes • 53

Sgt. Schultz in the act of "seeing and knowing nothing" as the boys perform the old shell game with crates of dynamite. The actor on the far right, Roy Goldman, regularly appeared as a mostly silent, background character before moving on to a similar role on M*A*S*H. Author's collection/CBS Television Inc.

Season 1, Episode 20: "The Great Impersonation" 02/041966.

D: Gene Reynolds W: Laurence Marks

Guest Cast: Bert Freed (Major Bernsdorf), James Frawley (Gestapo Capt.) Harvey Keitel (Gestapo Officer/Uncredited).

Storyline: After successfully detonating an explosion and derailing a German train, Hogan's Heroes find themselves lost in the woods. While Kinchloe scales a tree to get a bearing on their location, a German squad apprehends Newkirk, Carter, and LeBeau. Kinchloe reports the bad news to Hogan who persuades Schultz to not report the three missing men at roll call. The trio are carted to Stalag 4, but thanks to their phony dog tags the Gestapo make little progress in their interrogations. Hogan and Kinchloe go to work on Schultz making him believe the boys will blab to the Gestapo about the sergeant's indifference to their schemes and rampant willingness to accept bribes in exchange for food. Schultz unwillingly agrees to impersonate Colonel Klink, and accompanied by Hogan and a fake phone call from "General Kinchmeier," coerce the Kommodant of Stalag 4 to release the three prisoners to "Klink."

Program Notes: Bert Freed spent most of his career playing cops and robbers and can be spotted in several crime noirs of the early 1950s. A decade before cementing his work relationship with director Martin Scorsese, Harvey Keitel launches his pro acting career in this episode (although the young Keitel unmistakably resembles his acting colleague, Robert DeNiro).

Assessment: Truly a character driven piece, this outing affords John Banner a nice opportunity to showcase his acting skill by being much more than just a lovable buffoon. There's a nice sequence where Schultz auditions as "Klink" in front of Hogan and Kinchloe. When he first steps out of Hogan's quarters dressed as the Kommodant, the shy and sheepish sergeant channels the spirit of Oliver

Hardy with his timid grace and gentility. With three of the boys tied up at Stalag 4, Kinchloe finally gets pushed forward into the limelight and performs equally well. Director Reynolds frames a lovely bit at the program's conclusion. As the Gestapo agent confers with Klink describing a "three hundred pound man dressed as an officer" that removed his prisoners, Schultz dimly stands unnoticed in the background looking like a human bowling pin filling out the frame.

Season 1, Episode 21: "The Pizza Parlor" 02/11/1966.

D: Gene Reynolds W: Arthur Julian

Guest Cast: Hans Conried (Major Bonacelli), Joey Tata (Tony Garlotti), Ernest Sarracino (Mr. Garlotti), Harry Lauter (Submarine Capt.), Elsa Ingram (ATS Sgt.), Jack Good (Capt. Henderson), "John" Cedar (Corporal Langenscheidt), Bard Stevens (German driver).

Storyline: En route to Stalag 13, Italian POW camp commander, Major Bonacelli, holds his driver at gunpoint daydreaming about making his escape to Switzerland. An air raid breaks up this scene and the driver flees, but Cpl. Langenscheidt arrives to escort Bonacelli to Stalag 13, where he is expected. Klink has been assigned to give the Italian Major some pointers because of his "no escape" record, but the Italian is clearly disillusioned with Italy's alliance with Germany and his homesickness for Italian cuisine. Hogan wants to corral Bonacelli to his extended team of Underground operatives by keeping him as a POW commander and tries to bribe him by securing a recipe for pizza which LeBeau serves up. When the injured driver returns to Stalag 13 and spots Bonacelli, he rats him out to Klink, who has him arrested. To make him look like a true friend of the German cause, Hogan stages a ten prisoner escape and allows Bonacelli to escort the POWs back to Stalag 13 winning Klink's approval.

Program Notes: Was there a TV show in the 1950s and 1960s that Hans Conried *didn't* appear in? Doubtful, as the master character actor chocked up over two hundred roles in film and television dating back to the late 1930s. Many fans will always remember his two turns as misguided aviator "Wrong Way" Feldman on *Gilligan's Island*. Perhaps even more fondly, he will always be remembered for providing the narration and extra voices in the animated Dr. Seuss classic, *Horton Hears a Who!* (1970). Langenscheidt is mistakenly billed as "John" Cedar in the closing credits. Major Bonacelli would return, but not Hans Conried, in the fourth season show aptly titled, "The Return of Major Bonacelli."

Assessment: Good natured and charming, this episode may not be hilarious, but it's one a- sweet, a pizza pie. Up to this point, Hans Conried was probably the biggest name guest star visiting the series and writer Julian and director Reynolds wisely give him ample elbow room in the opening sequence where he attempts to bribe his driver to take him to Switzerland! Skillful, and unusual, is the sequence where Hogan needs to get the recipe for pizza from Tony Garlotti's father in Newark, so a chain message travels from Kinchloe to the sub commander to Allied Headquarters to Garlotti's restaurant and back (hence the larger than usual supporting cast). The smiles continue up to the closing sequence as Bonacelli marches the boys back home as they all whistle their theme tune in unison. Home, oddly, doesn't seem like such a bad place.

Season 1, Episode 22: "The 43rd, A Moving Story" 02/25/1966.

D: Howard Morris W: James Allardice, Tom Adair

Guest Cast: Cynthia Lynn (Helga), Sandy Kenyon (Major Hans Kuehn), Hal Lynch (Lynch), Leon Askin (Gen. Burkhalter).

Storyline: The Allies are looking to bomb a chemical factory, but the Germans are ready to receive with a major, anti-aircraft battery so Hogan plots to get the Germans to move the battery to another location. Klink has now received a new Executive Officer, Major Kuehn, who prods Klink by suggesting his tenure is only "temporary." He begins making affirmative decisions without Klink's consent and reminds him that his uncle is a Field Marshall with Hitler's core staff. Hogan suggests to Klink and Helga that the Allies are looking to bomb Hammelburg, but Kuehn sees this as a trap. Later, Hogan addresses all his men outdoors knowing Kuehn is eavesdropping and informs them that their usual Red Cross care packages might get "blown up" this time around. This is enough for Kuehn to secretly contact General Burkhalter and insist the Nazis move their anti-aircraft battery to Hammelburg. Burkhalter arrives and confirms to Kuehn that the strategic moving of the battery was a huge success – *for the Allies*. Klink acknowledges that he will be able to function fine without a second in command.

Program Notes: This is the only writing contribution of the team of James Allardice and Tom Adair, and the first of five guest roles for Sandy Kenyon, who notched several parts on *The Dick Van Dyke Show* and made three trips to *The Twilight Zone*. The team moves down to the underground tunnel for their "coffee pot" surveillance of Klink's office instead of in Hogan's living quarters. Kuehn states that Stalag 13 has had 293 escape attempts; Klink counters that two do not count since they were actually his own soldiers! Hogan concurs with this fact.

Assessment: The only James Allardice/Tom Adair offering is something less than special. Hogan needs to figure out a way to get the Germans to move their anti-aircraft battery and does so by staging a fake address to his men. It's a pretty cut and dry ruse and not nearly as well calibrated as so many of the other schemes that have a more psychological bent. Director Morris manages to conjure up some inspired bits of business, the best being the gang dodging a visit from Schultz, relaxing after he exits, then scurrying back to their previous spots when the sergeant unexpectedly returns. The group timing here is perfectly executed. There's also a fun, extended bit involving the team's water barrel periscope repeatedly avoiding the snooping Kuehn. Sandy Kenyon brings appropriate Nazi arrogance to this role while Burkhalter is merely tossed in at the show's conclusion as, once again, the bearer of bad news. This would be a trend in later episodes, unfortunately, where the talented Leon Askin would be shoehorned into a marginal scene or two for plot sake only. A big talent like Leon Askin certainly deserves a bigger amount of screen time.

Memorable Exchange:

Helga: "Have you done something naughty?"

Hogan: "No, but I might as well." (Moves in for the kiss).

Season 1, Episode 23: "How to Cook a German Goose with Radar" 03/04/1965.

D: Gene Reynolds W: Phil Sharp

Guest Cast: Cynthia Lynn (Helga), J. Pat O' Malley (General "Cpl." Tillman).

Storyline: A new POW is transferred in, Tillman, who appears to be the world's oldest corporal in the US Army. Grouchy and uncooperative, Hogan wants him transferred out and has the men stage a fire outside Klink's office, blaming it on Tillman. Tillman claims he is actually a general and on a secret mission to help the Allies bomb a new rocket plant by placing radar devices in a trail leading up to the strike point. Stalag 13 is the last strategic point for planting the last radar unit. London confirms his identity so Hogan uses Helga as a diversion in order to scale the guard tower and plant the device. When Hogan realizes the placement of the device is off by six inches (which could throw the bombers' target off by two thousand yards) the boys scramble to rectify the error and insure an explosive result for the Allied air strike.

Program Notes: This is the first of sixteen scripts to be penned by Phil Sharp, a writer with a huge comedy background who created teleplays for Joan Davis, Sid Caesar, and Phil Silvers. J. Pat O' Malley's career spanned five decades including voicing three characters in the Disney classic, *101 Dalmatians* (1961). He would return in the third season for "D Day at Stalag 13." Contemporary jazz music is used during one scene.

Season one publicity shot of Bob Crane and Cynthia Lynn, whose physical charms are exploited by Col. Hogan, creating a tantalizing diversion in "How To Cook a German Goose with Radar." Author's collection/CBS Television Inc.

Assessment: A pretty straightforward, mild caper punctuated by some decidedly offbeat flourishes, this outing gets off to a charming start during the opening sequence when Schultz escorts Hogan, who incorporates a playful skip to his stride, over to see the Kommodant. Helga, who typically is a willing accomplice in Hogan's schemes, now becomes an unwitting pawn when Hogan charms her into posing as a model for LeBeau's filmless camera – and in a swimsuit no less! This is plenty to divert the lookout guard's attention while Hogan scales the tower with the radar unit. Admirers of pin-up girls will find so much to marvel at; members of the ME TOO generation will roll their eyes. Still, this is the 1940s and the pin-up girl was a woman routinely admired by men and often women, too. Surprisingly, it's Robert Clary snapping the pics and not Bob Crane. The payoff to this outing is one of the craziest gags in the entire canon. Hogan uses a car jack to elevate *the entire guard tower* the extra six needed inches while the men all tilt to one side to convince the lookout guard that everything is still on the level! This is a truly wild sight gag that brings this episode to a satisfying finish.

Season 1, Episode 24: "Psychic Kommodant" 03/11/1966.

D: Gene Reynolds W: Phil Sharp

Guest Cast: Cynthia Lynn (Helga), Joseph Mell (Kintzler), Leon Askin (Gen. Burkhalter).

Storyline: Newkirk is playing the "old shell game" in the barracks and this pulls in the curiosity of Schultz. Klink barges in but before he can render the game kaput Hogan pulls him into the game and Newkirk rigs it so Klink wins every time. Hogan leads Klink to believe that he possesses the powers of ESP and that Otto Von Tillerman's book confirms the German brain is renowned for such extraordinary gifts of the mind. Burkhalter phones Klink to brief him about a pending top secret mission that will involve Stalag 13. Before Hogan can hear more the wiring in their bugging device shorts out. When the General arrives with Kintzler, Hogan sneaks a walkie-talkie into Klink's office so the Heroes can resume their covert eavesdropping. Kintzler has perfected the "noiseless" aircraft, a huge advantage to the German cause, and the final demonstrations will take place at Stalag 13 for an audience of Nazi big wigs. The boys sneak out at night, remove the engine for photographing and blue printing purposes, and then sneak the altered engine back into the airplane. The big demonstration party miserably fails when the engine is revealed to be anything *but* noiseless.

Assessment: Phil Sharp's second script is a disappointing affair and the proceedings are a synonym for the opening scene - a tired, old shell game. It's never really established what Hogan has in mind when he cons Klink into believing he now has powers of ESP. There's no development to the concept nor is it integral to the story line or its conclusion despite earning the episode's title. Less than credible is the lifting and returning of the airplane's engine, with Klink's men proving no hindrance to the task whatsoever. There's some humor to be found during the demonstration of the "noiseless" aircraft, but the unconvincing preceding matters at hand encourage the viewing audience would best join the Nazi party in their staff car – who drive away without uttering one word of acknowledgment.

Season 1, Episode 25: "The Prince from the Phone Company" 03/18/1966.

D: Gene Reynolds W: Richard M. Powell

Guest Cast: Cynthia Lynn (Helga), Isabelle Cooley (Princess Yawanda), Lee Bergere (Count Von Sichel), Stewart Moss (Captain), Ivan Dixon (Prince Makabana).

Storyline: The men have their hands full with a large group of escapees who are lacking one item to trigger their departure - money. The Germans have recalled their currency rendering Hogan's counterfeit marks useless. A sudden dogfight results in a German plane going down and a surprise visitor, Prince Makabana of Africa. He is in negotiations with the Germans to set up a submarine port in his country. As he bears an uncanny resemblance to Kinchloe, Hogan performs a switch and the new Prince now recognizes Hogan as an old classmate and friend. They enjoy the comforts of Klink's private quarters when they learn that the Prince's German contact, Count Von Sichel, and the Prince's wife will meet them shortly. Although recognizing the fake, Princess Yawanda, estranged from her actual husband, agrees not to blow Kinchloe's cover. Still posing as the Prince, and using Hogan as his negotiator, Kinchloe cuts a deal with Von Sichel for several hundred thousand marks and the German subs head for their new African port. Hogan has already informed London of the deal and the German subs are met by an Allied attack rendering Von Sichel obsolete. He agrees to defect and escape with Yawanda (and the other escapees who now have spending money) and she vows to meet Kinchloe in Toledo, of all places, after the war.

Program Notes: The final credits list "Ivan Dixon also appearing as Prince Makabana." John Banner would similarly enlist for double duty in the following season's "Heil Klink." The prime time soap opera was kind to Lee Bergere, who amassed numerous appearances on both *Dynasty* and *Falcon Crest*. He would return in the final season as the betrothed to "Kommodant Gertrude." Stewart Moss, who passed on a regular role with the series, couldn't pass apparently on a recurring paycheck.

Assessment: Ivan Dixon finally takes center stage in a script crafted around Kinchloe and his lookalike, the arrogant Prince Makabana. Dixon offers a slight variation in his Makabana role presenting the Prince as a droll and humorless dignitary. He plays his scenes with Isabelle Cooley with complete confidence and sincerity and there is a nice romantic chemistry between the two. The episode generally avoids the more extraordinary elements of the series although how the boys are able to whip up an identical African costume in record time is anybody's second guess. Unfortunately, the episode also avoids big laughs for the most part, although the expression on Schultz's face when he spots the bunk beds slowly closing downwards is worth the price of admission, or worthy of the admission of "seeing nothing!"

Season 1, Episode 26: "The Safe Cracker Suite" 03/25/1966.

D: Howard Morris W: Laurence Marks

Guest Cast: Walter Burke (Alf the Artist), Antony Eustrel (Maj. Kronman), Booth Colman (Capt. Guenther/Gestapo).

Storyline: Major Kronman, an old friend of Klink's, turns up unexpectedly for a visit, but before his intentions are clear, Captain Guenther and his Gestapo team storm in and arrest the Major for treason. Before he is hauled away, he slips a key on a metal chain to Hogan in secrecy. Hogan realizes the key will open a safe deposit box within the safe of a local hotel and plots to discover its contents. Newkirk refers the safe cracking job to "Alf the Artist," the best in the business, and London agrees to parachute him in and the boys smuggle him into the barracks. Hogan, realizing he will need Klink's involvement, shows the key to him and spooks him into believing his goose will be cooked if the Gestapo suspect a collusion between Klink and Kronman. Klink agrees to an alliance with Hogan and he hosts a party at the hotel for the local dignitaries while Kinchloe moves Alf to the safe and the others provide a distraction as singing waiters. The contents of the box reveal that Kronman was plotting an assassination attempt on Hitler and Klink's name is implicated. Klink burns the evidence as Hogan negotiates for an increase in amenities for his men.

Program Notes: Walter Burke jump-started his career by appearing in several classic film noirs including Jules Dassin's *The Naked City* (1950), *Dark City* (1950), and Joseph Losey's thoughtful remake of *M* (1951).

Assessment: A tightly conceived script by Laurence Marks is further elevated by the uneasy alliance of Hogan and Klink, which provides many laughs. For the first time, the senior POW officer and his enemy Kommodant are now truly in cahoots and this is set up by the best scripted, to date, dialogue scene between the men in Klink's office, which has now truly evolved into a staple of the series. Hogan agrees to call the shots and even informs Klink that he will have "to look the other way" for their scheme to retrieve Kronman's secret papers to work. There's also a fun contrast between the two men at the hotel party as Klink nervously babbles and continually downs glasses of champagne while Hogan remains seriously alert. Fun too are the singing waiters (Carter, LeBeau, and Newkirk) who provide Alf extra time to hide from the snooping Capt. Guenther. Klink has now decided to adopt the mantra of his Sergeant-in-Arm, and when he spots Alf inexplicably in the prisoners' barracks while Hogan dangles the incriminating safety deposit box key in plain view, Klink admits: "For the first time since I've taken command here, I want to know nothing, nothing!"

Season 1, Episode 27: "I Look Better in Basic Black" 04/01/1966.

D: Howard Morris W: Arthur Julian

Guest Cast: Jean Hale (Kathy Pruitt), Edward Knight (Capt. Heinrich), Jackie Joseph (Charlene Hemsley), Jayne Massey (Ginger Flintrin).

Storyline: The men from Barracks Three are emptied out and moved into Hogan's barracks to make room for three captured American women, who will be taken to Berlin. Hogan has his men tunnel their way into Barracks Three and they learn that the women are entertainers who had the misfortune of witnessing a stockpile of German rockets at a military base. To insure their silence, the Germans plan to have them incarcerated in Berlin, so Hogan looks to smuggle them out to safety in London. A collapse in their new tunnel forces Hogan to consider an alternative escape method. He decides to have Newkirk, LeBeau, and himself dress as the women and have the girls don the clothes of the POWs. That night, the "women" are hustled into a transport truck, but shortly after leaving camp the female Hogan feigns illness, a ruse which allows the boys to overpower Capt. Heinrich and his guards. Kinchloe, meanwhile, has radioed London which effectively puts an end to the Germans' rocket business.

Program Notes: Jackie Joseph played Audrey in Roger Corman's infamous quickie *Little Shop of Horrors* (1960) and later voiced "Melody" for the animated *Josie and the Pussy*cats. This was the second of ten appearances for Edward Knight.

Assessment: This is about as silly as the series gets with a slim to none plot in which everyone ends up acting and dressing – well, silly. Having three women showing up in a camp surrounded by lonely men turns everyone into sappy suitors, including Schultz and Klink, who saunter into Barracks Three with bottles of wine and delusions of grandeur. The girls perform with cheery enthusiasm and certainly provide a smorgasbord of eye candy. Jean Hale, in particular, displays little to no modesty from her tight, yellow sweater. There are chuckles to be had at the three men in drag in a comic device that probably dates back to the Mack Sennett silent era, and been exploited by nearly every comic since. The sight of Crane in a push-up bra and that yellow sweater lays claim to *the* most bizarre sighting of the series, and the expected double takes of Schultz as the "ladies" board the bus add to the chuckles. But in the end, what we get is a goofy excursion, one where three men in drag are able to clobber their Nazi captors with handbags, and where the POW colonel is able to race back to the stalag for a farewell kiss with Kathy, who appears to mouth the words, "Oh, Bob," during the fade out.

Werner Klemperer attempts to maintain his serious demeanor despite being surrounded by a suddenly modest Bob Crane, sleepy-eyed Robert Clary, and dazzled Richard Dawson during the exuberantly goofy filming of "I Look Better in Basic Black." Author's collection/CBS Television Inc.

Season 1, Episode 28: "The Assassin" 04/08/1966.

D: Edward H. Feldman W: Richard M. Powell

Guest Cast: Cynthia Lynn (Helga), Bernard Fox (Col. Crittendon), Larry D. Mann (Dr. Vanetti), and Leon Askin (as Gen. Burkhalter).

Storyline: The team listens in on a private conversation with Burkhalter and visiting Dr. Vanetti in Klink's office regarding the secret lab work Vanetti must conduct in complete silence at Stalag 13. Hogan recognizes the Vanetti name as a researcher of atomic energy and as a catastrophic danger to the Allied cause. He coldly informs his men that Vanetti must be eliminated. Uncomfortable with the role of assassin, Hogan learns of a Sgt. Garraeux, a known assassin imprisoned at Stalag 16. Hogan sends Carter and LeBeau to meet Garraeux in the woods and have him smuggled into camp, but Col. Crittendon has tagged along and clumsily alerts the Stalag 13 guards, who shoot and detain Garraeux while the British colonel makes his way to the escape tunnel. Hogan, infuriated with the capture of Garraeux, reluctantly accepts the services of Crittendon, who demands to carry out the assassination of Vanetti. They try by crossbow but Hogan changes his mind when he learns that Vanetti no longer wants to cooperate with the Nazis. Hogan convinces Klink that the assassination attempt is meant for him and he agrees to sneak out of camp in disguise and go into temporary hiding. Hogan also convinces Crittendon to ride along with the disguised "Vanetti" and that he can eliminate their target with two gun shots. With the two colonels busy, Hogan smuggles the real Vanetti out to safety and then stages a lab explosion destroying the atomic scientist's existence much to the bewilderment of General Burkhalter.

Program Notes: Executive Producer Feldman now takes the reins for his first directorial effort. He would direct a total of twenty eight episodes. Bernard Fox returns for his second of eight appearances, all as the bumbling, unpredictable Colonel Crittendon. Hogan makes a reference to playwright Joseph Kesselring's famed black comedy, *Arsenic and Old Lace*. Bob Crane would star as Mortimer Brewster in a made-for-TV movie adaptation of *Arsenic* that aired on network television in 1969.

Assessment: Feldman's first directorial assignment is a big shift in tone that hinges around Hogan's cold-blooded determination to have Vanetti eliminated. Within that framework is a Powell teleplay cluttered with an overabundance of ideas and plot details, which are tough to dislike, but possibly tougher to defend. The unexpected presence of Crittendon is a lark, of course, and he now praises Hogan for his Underground operations (completely about-face from his previous attitudes about POWs engaging in sabotage, which Hogan points out). The creative team clearly realized that if they were going to continue writing in the Crittendon character, then he would have to willingly conspire to the rules of the game. Hogan spends most of this episode in serious mode, honoring the cold nature of the business at hand. It's a good change of pace and allows Crane to continue to demonstrate his skill as a dramatic actor. Some of the extraneous details distract, including the subplot involving Klink's fear of assassins and Carter's ridiculous lab explosions that have supposedly been ordered by Crittendon in order to discover an explosive method of assassination, and which continue to fuel Klink's fears. Schultz is haphazardly tossed into these plot points and he must admit to "knowing nothing" about a hundred times in this episode. Less can be more, but that's not the case with this script. Despite these dopier elements, the program is well directed and includes a funny encounter with Klink recognizing Crittendon from his earlier appearance, and Crittendon's less than heroic retreat. Fortunately for our cowardly Brit, Hogan thoughtfully had the guards' rifles loaded with blank ammo, yet another reminder that logic is not always the hallmark of this series. For the finale, the program dusts off the resolution of "The Scientist" where once again the existence of this latest scientist is obliterated, another sign that the creative well is running a bit dry.

Best Observation:

Burkhalter: (studying the crater left from the explosion) "How can he be so brainy and dumkopf enough to blow himself up?"

Season 1, Episode 29: "Cupid Comes to Stalag 13" 04/15/1966.

D: Howard Morris W: Phil Sharp

Guest Cast: Kathleen Freeman (Mrs. Linkmeyer), George Tyne (Ferguson) Inger Stratton (Lottie), and Leon Askin (as Gen. Burkhalter).

Storyline: The POWs harbor Ferguson, an escaped prisoner with stolen maps valuable to the Allied cause, but Hogan delays his departure due to Klink's unusual "prowling" of the camp grounds late at night. Burkhalter arrives and suggests to Klink that being single may be holding back his chance for promotion and states on his next visit he will be accompanied by his sister and her daughter. Klink assumes the General is suggesting a match with his niece, and he is delighted to find her a young, attractive beauty. He writes her a charming note while Hogan arranges a romantic dinner for two, but the note moves to Burkhalter's sister, Gertrude, the actual, intended, matrimonial match. Hogan bails Klink out by telling Gertrude that Klink has requested a transfer to the Russian Front, and this is enough for her to dismiss any wedding plans. Now content, Klink is finally able to catch up on his sleep, an opportunity for Hogan to finally smuggle Ferguson and his hot maps out of camp.

Program Notes: Kathleen Freeman debuts in her first of four appearances as Burkhalter's sister, Gertrude Linkmeyer. A real favorite of the "total filmmaker" Jerry Lewis, she has key supporting roles in several of the comedy giant's films including: *The Errand Boy* (1961), *The Nutty Professor* (1963), *The Patsy* (1964), and *Which Way to the Front?* (1970), a comedy many believe to be loosely inspired by *Hogan's Heroes*. A new periscope is introduced that affords the POWs a different perspective of the surrounding, interior camp grounds.

Assessment: As season one approaches the finish line, the creative team decides to spin a family comedy involving the Burkhalters, a theme the show would revisit from time to time. Gone are the usual escape attempts and deeds of espionage and sabotage; instead we get a mild marital comedy with no big laughs or moments of suspense. Still, director Morris gets a bright energy from the players and the half hour moves with a bouncy rhythm, especially during the domestic scene featuring show biz veterans Askin and Freeman, who truly resemble brother and sister. Most unusual, and of great interest, is the unexpected delay to Hogan's typically executed relocation business thanks to Klink's sleepless nights and unprecedented "prowling" of the camp at night. It's quite ironic that the Heroes have pulled off wild capers and transported escaped POWs, defecting Germans, and pretty entertainers all season long, but Klink's unanticipated behavior now screeches the entire operation to an awkward stop. It's oddly funny. Klink is now turning to Hogan in a somewhat regular fashion for advice, a sign that a real relationship is forming between the two men, despite being on opposite sides of the war. It is this relationship, perhaps, that becomes the cornerstone of the series and makes it transcend the usual gripes that the comedy was solely based on a clever POW constantly pulling the wool over the eyes of his dimwitted captor.

Funniest Line:

Klink: (Deadpan) "Hogan, I'm going to have you shot and no court martial will convict me."

Season 1, Episode 30: "The Flame Grows Higher" 04/22/1966.

D: Howard Morris W: David Chandler & Jack H. Robinson, and Laurence Marks (teleplay), David Chandler & Jack H. Robinson (story).

Guest Cast: Cynthia Lynn (Helga), Susanne Cramer (Eva), Hannie Landman (Margit), Charles Radilac (Willie), Irene Tedrow (Jennie), Todd Martin (Gestapo Officer), Jerry Ayres (Capt. Warren/Uncredited).

Storyline: Hogan is astonished to see Capt. Warren apprehended and brought to Stalag 13, especially after the team negotiated his escape earlier. Hogan suspects there is a rat somewhere within their escape network and decides to follow the trail which begins at the Kaiserhof restaurant, operated by Eva and Margit. The boys stage a fake forest fire up on a hill above the camp, and Klink dispatches Hogan and his men to put it out. The Heroes ditch Schultz and visit the Kaiserhof. While Newkirk and LeBeau flirt with Margit, Hogan learns from Eva that after this checkpoint, the escapees next move to a farmhouse down the road for their next set of instructions. The boys move to the farmhouse and despite Hogan being overpowered by the couple who live there, he believes they are innocent. The girls from the Kaiserhof phone in with a change of plan, stating the three "escapees" are to depart along the south road, and Hogan's suspicions about the two women are confirmed. Newkirk notifies the local Gestapo in a thick German voice that three escaped prisoners will be convening at the Kaiserhof. The men return there to flirt and stall which makes Eva decidedly nervous, and brings the arrival of the flustered Schultz and the Gestapo team. Schultz is made to look a hero by capturing three escaped POWs and the girls are hauled away as double agents.

Program Notes: The final writing contribution from the team of David Chandler and Jack H. Robinson. Hannie Landman is listed as born in 1949 which made her the tender age of sixteen when she appeared in this episode. She also was featured in *Billy the Kid vs. Dracula* (1965), a cult classic (of sorts) directed by the King of Z's, William "One Shot" Beaudine.

Assessment: The final Chandler/Robinson offering (aided by Laurence Marks) yields their best work with a fast paced adventure of war time intrigue. The ruse of starting a forest fire with smoke bombs atop the hill is a simple and clever scheme to send the boys out on the detective trail. The bookends of this piece plant Schultz firmly into buffoon soil as he opens the program wildly searching for his keys, which the prisoners have moved to the backside of his belt, and ends the program uproariously laughing like a crazed hyena. The POWs continue to harass him once they become fire fighters, leaving him deserted in a smoke bomb cloud and even stealing his truck as he attempts to radio Klink on a walkie-talkie unit. His temper tantrum here is quite amusing. Yet, somehow, he becomes the hero of the piece when the Gestapo believe he alone is responsible for rounding up the trio of escaped prisoners. Once again, there's some zippy, contemporary music used to underscore the trio's entrance into the Kaiserhof although the antics of the sex starved LeBeau and Newkirk are becoming more annoying than funny. Newkirk, or rather Richard Dawson, seems genuinely perturbed that he must stand guard at the door and miss out on trying to score with the frauleins. The oft reported uneasy off camera relationship of Bob Crane and Dawson seems to boil under the surface here. Quite effective is the scene where the couple subdue Hogan with a wooden chair attack and the subsequent rescue by LeBeau and Newkirk, which restores order to the aforementioned, tenuous friendship.

Season 1, Episode 31: "Request Permission to Escape" 04/28/1966.

P/D: Edward H. Feldman W: Laurence Marks

Guest Cast: Cynthia Lynn (Helga), Martin Blaine (Gestapo Officer), Mary Mitchell (Mady), John Crawford (Officer #1), William Christopher (Private).

Storyline: One of the team's Underground contacts has slipped a cigarette lighter containing microfilm into Klink's staff car, so the boys immediately set to giving the vehicle a car wash. The lighter is discovered under the hood of the car and it contains phony war plans that the Underground wants to deliberately slip into the hands of the enemy. Mail call brings a "Dear John" letter to Carter from his fiancé, Mary Jane, who has accepted the love of another. Carter submits the title request, hoping he can return home and repair his relationship. Reluctantly, Hogan honors the request and looks for a volunteer to escape into Hammelburg and immediately get captured, allowing the Gestapo to find the lighter and the tainted microfilm. When the others refuse the mission finding it too risky, Carter volunteers knowing the result will be thirty days in the cooler, after which Hogan guarantees his escape to freedom. In town, Carter has a devilish time getting arrested. Despondent, he is befriended by Mady, a consoling waitress who restores his confidence with a kiss to the cheek. The Gestapo, believing Carter is one of their own, offer to give Carter a ride to Stalag 13 and en route finally believe his story of being an escaped POW. The Gestapo return Carter to the custody of Klink and depart with the incriminating microfilm. After serving his time in the cooler, Carter prepares to leave through the emergency tunnel, but assures Hogan he will return shortly after paying a visit to Mady, his *new* object of affection.

Program Notes: This marks the second of seven guest roles for big and burly character actor John Crawford, who amassed over two hundred guest roles in a five decade career. Mary Mitchell, the sympathetic bar maid, Mady, would return the following season in "Everyone Has a Brother-In-Law." The concept of trying to get arrested and repeatedly failing was a routine worked to perfection by Bud Abbott and Lou Costello in their film *The Noose Hangs High* (1948/Eagle Lion) and later in an episode of their television series, "The Dentist Office" (1952).

Assessment: The first season concludes with a sentimental, pleasant finish, though not quite on par with the best the series has to offer. The episode opens with some unremarkable slapstick involving Schultz, a water hose, and Klink, the unfortunate recipient. Somewhere in Werner Klemperer's contract must have been a clause stating that once every ten episodes he would get doused with water! The Kommodant and his rotund sidekick step into the background as Larry Hovis gets his turn to move forward. Hovis brings his usual warmth to his character and this permeates his extended sequence in the local hofbrau, which includes an amusing encounter with Bill Christopher as a private on leave and some jovial irony from John Crawford. There's a gentle sweetness that director Feldman achieves during the Carter/Mady scene although it triggers the rather abrupt decision of Carter forgetting about Mary Jane and his urgency to return home all together. It's enough for the sweet and simple story to succeed, but not exactly the spectacular finish one might expect from a season closer.

Primer for Season Two

Primary Cast

Colonel Robert Hogan:	Bob Crane
Kommodant Wilhelm Klink:	Werner Klemperer
Sgt. of Guard, Hans Schultz:	John Banner
Corporal Louis LeBeau:	Robert Clary
Corporal Peter Newkirk:	Richard Dawson
Sergeant James Kinchloe:	Ivan Dixon
Sergeant Andrew Carter:	Larry Hovis
Hilda (recurring character):	Sigrid Valdis
General Albert Burkhalter, Luftwaffe (recurring):	Leon Askin
Colonel Rodney Crittendon, RAF: (recurring)	Bernard Fox
Cpl. Langenscheidt (recurring):	Jon Cedar
Oscar Schnitzer (recurring):	Walter Janovitz
"Tiger" (recurring):	Arlene Martel
Major Wolfgang Hochstetter, Gestapo: (recurring)	Howard Caine

Hogan's Heroes in production at the Stalag 13 compound set at Forty Acres, Culver City, CA, and now featuring Sigrid Valdis as "Hilda," next to Crane. To her left is Bruce Bilson, director of twenty five adventures. Photo courtesy of Bruce Bilson/CBS Television Inc.

The fundamental change taking place between the first two broadcast seasons was the replacement of Cynthia Lynn as "Helga," with Sigrid Valdis as "Hilda," who would continue the recurring role of Klink's new secretary through the sixth and final season. No story explanation was made for the change in Klink's staff. Valdis made a strong impression with both viewers and Bob Crane when she appeared as "Gretchen" in season one's "Top Hat, White Tie, and Bomb Sights." Reportedly Crane pushed for Valdis to become a permanent cast member which meant that Lynn was pushed out (although she did return in two later, non-credited, guest appearances.) Bernard Fox and Arlene Martel, who made their debuts in season one, began to chock up return visits. Nita Talbot would debut as Marya, "the White Russian," in the two-part adventure "A Tiger Hunt in Paris," before becoming a recurring fixture in the following season. Howard Caine, who earlier portrayed two different Nazi officers, one Luftwaffe and the other Gestapo, debuted as Major Hochstetter in "Heil Klink," a role he would dominate until the tail end of the series. Likewise, Leon Askin began to visit Stalag 13 with more frequency, bringing along his masterful characterization of General Albert Burkhalter.

Season 2, Episode 1: "Hogan Gives a Birthday Party" 09/16/1966.

D: Gene Reynolds W: Richard M. Powell

Guest Cast: Sigrid Valdis (Hilda), James Gregory (Gen. Biedenbender), Peter Marko (Lt. Karras), L.E. Young (Lt. Hardy).

Storyline: The Heroes have safely housed two bomber pilots, Lieutenants Karras and Hardy, shot down while flying to Stuttheim to destroy a refinery. Hogan inspires Klink to set up a research facility including a replica of a Heikel bomber for test purposes. Kinchloe takes secret snapshots of the plane in order to brief London. Berlin sends General Biedenbender to supervise the flight tests and startles Hogan with his knowledge of several personal details. It seems Biedenbender was responsible for Hogan being shot down on his final air mission and becoming a prisoner of war. He prides himself on how he has been able to get inside Hogan's head, master his sense of scheming, and has continued to keep watch on Hogan. Hogan's team, along with Karras and Hardy, hijack the German bomber and overpower the general, who has insisted to fly out a night early sensing a trick on Hogan's part. The men successfully bomb the refinery, parachute to safety, and their prisoner Biedenbender finds himself on a one way flight to London.

Program Notes: Sigrid Valdis debuts as Hilda, Klink's new secretary, with no explanation to the absence of Helga. If you listen carefully, you will hear Klink mistakenly call her "Helga" in an early scene that director Reynolds missed. Unmistakable by looks and voice, James Gregory spent most of his successful career alternating as police officers and military officials. Two performances well worth seeking out include his crafty insurance investigator in the 1956 film noir *Nightfall*, and his standout turn as the political puppet, Senator Iselin, in John Frankenheimer's superb cold war thriller, *The Manchurian Candidate* (1962).

Assessment: To launch their second season, the Heroes take to the air in an inspired adventure highlighted by the presence of a formidable opponent from Hogan's past. Much of the strength of the teleplay lies in the psychological banter between Crane and guest star Gregory, who work exceedingly well together. With his deep, somewhat gravely voice, Gregory wisely applies only the slightest of German accents. He dominates the proceedings whether prodding Hogan, partying in Klink's office, (his genuine laughter at one of Crane's one-liners is a lovely revelation), or ogling Hilda, who exudes a much more blatant sexuality than her predecessor. The messiest element involves Klink's abrupt decision to establish the aircraft research post with Berlin's complete cooperation, and this quickly segues to a scene where Klink conducts a tour for Hogan as if playing the cooperative Bond villain who happily reveals all details of his secret organization. Pretty absurd too is Carter's immediate unveiling of an arsenal of bombs ready to drop on the refinery. Having Schultz dragged in to the proceedings and forced to fearfully parachute with the others is just that – a forced comic element. Yet overall, the program succeeds thanks to the strength of the Hogan and Biedenbender confrontation and a jaunty air mission that tips its pilot's cap to *Dr. Strangelove* (1964) with an overzealous Carter anxious to drop his explosive children into the lap of the refinery.

Season 2, Episode 2: "The Schultz Brigade" 09/23/1966.

D: Gene Reynolds W: Richard M. Powell

Guest Cast: Sigrid Valdis (Hilda), Leon Askin (Gen. Burkhalter), Parley Baer (Col. Burmeister), Lou Krugman (Col. Bussie).

Storyline: Schultz meekly posts an announcement mandated by the Minister of Propaganda regarding the voluntary enlistment to the Luftwaffe by POWs. To rattle him, Hogan states he will start an enlistment service of his own with defecting German officers who will train German prisoners to fly for the Allies, and he dubs the program "The Schultz Brigade." Klink is hosting fellow stalag commanders Burmeister and Bussie, who have plotted to discredit General Burkhalter, knowing one will be promoted to his position and guarantee a life of luxury for the other two. Before they can secure Klink's cooperation, Burkhalter arrives unforeseen and has all three men placed under arrest to await their court martial. Hogan visits Klink and agrees to act as a witness on his behalf, but during the court martial proceedings, Hogan's testimony inexplicably incriminates Klink and exonerates the other two men! After Hogan threatens to rat out Burmeister and Bussie, who agree to defect, Newkirk and Carter don their uniforms and clown masks and take Burkhalter hostage. Hogan, Klink, and Schultz attempt to storm the quarters and a wild gun battle ensues, with the two fake Kommodants fleeing. Burkhalter sees Klink as a hero, all is forgiven, and back in the barracks, Hogan insists that the two defecting Germans will launch a new training program called "The Schultz Brigade."

Program Notes: Lou Krugman made several appearances on *I Love Lucy* (and later, *The Lucy Show*), *The Untouchables*, and *Gunsmoke*, and would return for the season four opener, "Clearance Sale at the Black Market."

Assessment: The team of Reynolds and Powell deliver a fast moving comedy script with credible plot development, and less humor based on absurd coincidence and random slapstick. This is Leon Askin's finest contribution to date; his character is well incorporated into and throughout the story line, and he gets to shine with many choice lines of dialogue married with his signature squealing vocal tones. Hilda continues her sultry compliance with German high brass; she appears ready and willing to please. She is also now established as a willing participant as she knowingly admits the two masked gunmen into Burkhalter's quarters. Hilda is clearly in on this caper. Klink proves to be a surprisingly efficient defense attorney during his court martial. All he needs is a more cooperative witness than Hogan. For the second airing in a row we appear to receive a Stanley Kubrick reference. This time it's the stickup man in a clown mask resembling Sterling Hayden in *The Killing* (1956). Least successful, however, are the "two muffled gun shots" and Hogan declaring that the two fugitives have shot themselves. Doubtlessly, Burkhalter would have demanded to investigate the dead bodies for confirmation. Still everything else goes so well in this outing that to forgive is divine. Lastly, remember, Carter and Newkirk have the *real bullets*.

Classic Ultimatum:

Burkhalter: "I will see to it that you get a fair trial immediately, after which you will be shot."

Season 2, Episode 3: "Diamonds in the Rough" 09/30/1966.

D: Gene Reynolds W: Laurence Marks

Guest Cast: Paul Lambert (Hegel), Ulla Stromstedt (Myra), Martin Blaine (secret Policeman).

Storyline: Myra, a German local, visits the camp selling tin cups of milk to the men and slyly slips a note to Hogan in Carter's cup requesting a scheduled meeting for later that evening. Hogan feels uneasy as these kinds of instructions usually come straight from London, but he ventures out anyway. In a clearing, Hogan meets Myra, who holds him at gunpoint and reveals she is an agent of the Gestapo. The others arrive and are forced to ditch their weapons. They are taken to a Gestapo hideout operated by Major Hegel, who explains in detailed words complete knowledge of their Underground operations at Stalag 13. In order to spare their lives (and supposedly allow the continuance of their covert operations), Hegel demands that London provide one million dollars worth of diamonds, and gives Hogan one week to cough up the bribe. Hogan goes to Klink for help and suggests Klink order a road detail with the POWs as laborers as an excuse to meet with Hegel. Klink, dressed as a private, creeps to the back of Hegel's staff car and eavesdrops on his conversation with Hogan, which not only confirms the blackmail but also includes disparaging comments about Klink's command. London parachutes down a parcel revealing the finest counterfeit diamonds a war can buy. The Heroes deliver the hot ice and Hegel casually mentions the unfortunate disappearance of Myra. Klink and his men surround the barn and announce their intent to storm the building in two minutes. Hogan pleads with Hegel to take the diamonds and lam it, but Hegel, satisfied with the payoff, will now conspire *with* Klink and order the prisoners shot. He storms out waving his gun and is promptly shot to death by Klink's trigger happy squadron. Later, in Klink's office, a German arbitrator listens to Hogan's testimony and concludes that Hegel "was a casualty of war and died a war hero."

Program Notes: This marked the first of four visits from Paul Lambert, who was an actual US Army Air Corps Lieutenant in WWII. Sigrid Valdis does not appear in this episode. This is the first episode that demonstrates the escape tunnel leading out of an old tree stump. This would be the most commonly used exit for the remainder of the series.

One of the few comedic sequences in the expertly plotted "Diamonds in the Rough" necessitates the role reversal of Schultz and Klink, so he and Hogan can spy on a common enemy. Author's collection/CBS Television Inc.

Assessment: The future *M*A*S*H* team of writer Marks and director Reynolds contributes their finest half hour to date in a story that combines an exciting blackmail tale with a nifty resolution in which Klink comes to the rescue of Hogan and his men. Paul Lambert is a smooth as silk Nazi villain (his casual mention of Myra now dead is particularly nasty) and his long monologue in the Gestapo hideout might as well be a complete series primer for any virgin viewers tuning in. For the first time, Hogan goes directly to Klink for help beyond his typical control. It is precisely this concept, that at times the two men must put aside their inherent differences and willingly help each other, that makes *Hogan's Heroes* a bit more special (and credible) than is oft regarded. Similar to the finish of last season's "It Takes a Thief . . . Sometimes," the Nazi villain meets a hail of Klink's bullets, except this time Klink has his men knowingly shoot to kill. Klink also pleasantly steps up to bat in the final scene, detracting the arbitrator's initial plan of sending Hogan to Berlin for further questioning, and insisting that as "his" prisoner, Hogan will remain at Stalag 13, further insuring the continuance of the series and their relationship.

Season 2, Episode 4: "Operation Briefcase" 10/07/1966.

D: Gene Reynolds W: Laurence Marks

Guest Cast: Oscar Beregi (Gen. Stauffen), Willard Sage (Maj. Gunther), Barry Ford (Hercules), Eddie Firestone (Sgt. Wilson), Peter Hellmann (Guard), Chris Anders (Sentry), Roy Goldman (POW/Uncredited).

Storyline: London instructs the team to meet and transport back to the barracks "Hercules," who will be parachuting down into the woods late that evening. Badly wounded when his plane was shot down, "Hercules" barely survives the trip through the escape tunnel and into the camp. He explains he is carrying a briefcase with a built-in timing mechanism and powerful explosive, before dying. General Stauffen will be paying a visit to Stalag 13 to give Klink an award, but his real purpose is to swap out his identical briefcase with the deadly one and then proceed to a staff meeting with Hitler where he will attempt an explosive assassination. Hogan and his men are able to make the switch during a party in Klink's quarters and the next day Stauffen rushes through Klink's award ceremony in order to proceed with the assassination. Schultz inadvertently triggers the briefcase timer just before Stauffen rides off in his staff car. With thirty minutes to spare, Hogan stages a rapid prisoner escape and encourages Klink to set up road blocks within a twenty mile radius. This halts the General's car and Hogan arrives in time to deactivate the briefcase timer. Stauffen continues his mission and later in Klink's office a telegram arrives informing all of a failed, assassination attempt on the Fuhrer.

Program Notes: Hungarian born actor Oscar Beregi skillfully played European heavies and war criminals of strong intellect in an accomplished career that included some terrific visits to *The Twilight Zone*. He played the mastermind of the gold heist in "The Rip Van Winkle Caper" and, unforgettably, the former Kommodant who pays a pompous, post-war visit to his old concentration camp in the chilling ghost story, "Deaths-Head Revisited" (both 1961).

Rehearsal time on the Forty Acres, Stalag 13 set as John Banner examines the deadly device that Sgt. Schultz will innocently trigger in "Operation Briefcase." Author's collection/CBS Television Inc.

Assessment: The second season continues its strong stride with a nifty, war time assassination plot that also becomes a race against time thriller. A fairly serious tone carries the proceedings along with the assured performance of guest star Oscar Beregi, the go to Nazi actor of 1960s television. Unfortunately, some of the plot points stumble. If Hogan is already in cahoots with Stauffen, would it really be necessary to stage such an elaborate diversion to make the briefcase switch? Further mind boggling is Klink's immediate acceptance to set up *road blocks* to deter the escaped prisoners, a tactic never before employed despite the nearly three hundred previous escape attempts. Also, unbelievably silly is Carter's distraction of a sentry by getting the guard to help him look for his escaped mouse, Felix! Many of the ploys used by our Heroes to create diversions are of a clever nature, yet this just isn't one of them. Still, the pacing and race against time sequence is skillfully handled and there is a mild ad lib fest that occurs between Schultz, Gunther, and Stauffen, who definitely reacts to Schultz's go to admission that "he knows nothing!"

Season 2, Episode 5: "The Battle of Stalag 13" 10/14/1966.

D: Robert Sweeney W: Richard M. Powell

Guest Cast: Sigrid Valdis (Hilda), Jacques Aubuchon (Gen. Von Kattenhorn), Janine Gray (Greta), Howard Caine (Col. Feldkamp/Gestapo), Walter Alzmann (Schneider).

Storyline: Greta, a beautiful Underground member and part of the network the prisoners use, is smuggled into camp through the dog house tunnel in front of Schultz's bewildered eyes. She informs Hogan that his reckless behavior of sabotage has brought intense heat on Hammelburg and that the Gestapo plan to arrest and interrogate every local in sight. Von Kattenhorn arrives and informs Klink that plans are underway to renovate Stalag 13 into a retirement home for German officers and that most of his POWs will be relocated. Col. Feldkamp of the Gestapo storms in and demands that he assume operations of the camp for his Hammelburg interrogations. Hogan decides to pit the two men against one another. First, he has the General's staff car stolen by Newkirk and Carter dressed as Gestapo, which puts the blame on Feldkamp. Then, dressed as Wehrmacht officers, Hogan's team raids Feldkamp's temporary office, holds the Germans at gun point, and triggers a release of several civilians held for interrogation, including Greta. The Heroes escape in Feldkamp's staff car, effectively putting the blame on Von Kattenhorn. A standoff occurs between the two Nazi officers later at Stalag 13 but Hogan restores order by stating both their cars are safely parked over by the recreation building. Both the men claim their vehicles and a short distance from camp two separate explosions are heard. Hogan pacifies Klink by explaining that the two men tried to double cross each other and that any further investigation would only damage Klink's rep with Berlin.

Program Notes: Director "Bob" Sweeney was already a familiar face on the CBS lot, having directed eighty episodes of *The Andy*

Griffith Show. Later, he would assume the role of supervising producer of *Hawaii Five – O* and direct several episodes of the anthology-based series *Fantasy Island* and *The Love Boat*. Howard Caine returns for his second assignment; his next one, later in this season, would be of a more permanent nature. The team's aerial antenna rising up from the flagpole atop Klink's office is now getting regular use.

Assessment: Hogan gets tough talk from a fetching fraulein in the program's opener, complaining that his "going boy scout and blowing up bridges" has caused enormous heat on the locals, and this is just one of many small delights found in "The Battle of Stalag 13." The Heroes now blatantly go about their business disregarding the presence of Schultz by routinely sneaking outsiders in through the dog house and opening the breakaway bunk beds, all right before his disbelieving eyes. The big jolt to the funny bone stems from the return of Howard Caine, now in fully growling Gestapo mode. His first scene in Klink's office with Von Kattenhorn reveals a big man in a small frame, and he employs a real shot-out-of-a-cannon approach to his acting style. He makes many of the preceding Gestapo characters we've encountered seem dull in comparison and it is no surprise that producer Feldman offered him a regular recurring role, one destined to become a true fan favorite. He even gets to introduce his signature line, "Who is this MAN?" for the first of his many heated encounters with Hogan. Caine also appears to slip in an ad lib within the middle of a line of dialogue to Klink, when he casually inquires: "Why are you smiling?" There's a bit of a silliness pervading this episode but the overall bright energy carries it along through the explosive finish courtesy of one of Carter's "finer efforts" (his words). In the end, Hogan merrily strolls off satisfied knowing two big pests have been removed and order has been restored, and although Caine's Colonel Feldkamp has been blown to bits, a resurrection of sorts looms in the horizon.

Season 2, Episode 6: "The Rise and Fall of Sgt. Schultz" 10/21/1966.

D: Gene Reynolds W: Laurence Marks

Guest Cast: Whit Bissell (Gen. Kammler), Laurie Main (Col. Franz), Edward Knight (Gestapo officer).

Storyline: Becker, an Underground operative, has been captured by the Gestapo and before they work him over, London wants Hogan and company to spring him. Carter and Newkirk, dressed as Gestapo, attempt to get a release with orders from "Col. Hoganmeier," but the agent holding Becker will not cooperate. Becker will be moved to a local hotel for security reasons, they learn. A new area commander, General Kammler, arrives for inspection and immediately recognizes Schultz as a WWI comrade who once saved his life! Suddenly, the sergeant's popularity stock rises and even Klink attempts to clumsily befriend him. Hogan has LeBeau stage a scene where the little French man picks a fight with Newkirk, screams for his freedom, and promptly runs smack into the belly of Schultz. Hogan oversells his praise of Schultz to Klink and suggests that he should be awarded a medal at an honorary party with Schultz's dear old friend, General Kammler, in attendance. Of course, the party takes place at the local hotel where Becker is being held and, of course, Hogan's men will provide the wait staff duties. At the party, Kammler awards the intoxicated Schultz the Iron Cross and moments later the gang start a fake fire. During the confusion, Newkirk and LeBeau sneak Becker out which ends Kammler's military career and erases any respect Schultz had earned from Klink.

Program Notes: Going through the resume of Whit Bissell (1909-1996) is akin to reading a textbook on the history of the motion picture. His career regularly juggled between the "A" pictures: *The Caine Mutiny* (1954), *The Defiant Ones* (1958), etc. and, most definitely, the "B"s: *I Was a Teenage Werewolf* (1957), *I Was a Teenage Frankenstein* (1958), etc.

Assessment: The second season, creative steam begins to evaporate as a slight adventure gets bogged down in implausibility and routine monkey business. The idea of a general singling out Schultz as an old war buddy is a good one, but we never get to hear or see the two war buddies reminisce or acknowledge about those good old days. Instead, we hear and see "no-thing" about their former history. What we do get are some stock scenes, such as Klink now coddling the sergeant as his suddenly caring buddy. There is some sharp humor with Newkirk and Carter's visit to the local Gestapo headquarters, on the orders of "Col. Hoganmeier," and LeBeau's wildly frenzied ham acting during his escape attempt. There's also some curiosity to guest Laurie Main's few line reads which are pretty off the charts. But it all seems to stutter during the concluding sequence at the hotel where Schultz gets drunk, Klink screams for "water" and gets hit in the face with two buckets full, and Newkirk and LeBeau overpower the hotel guards with some poorly staged fight combat moves. The old ploy of starting a fire to create chaos is wearing thin; thinner yet is the contrivance of holding the award ceremony party in the exact, same hotel where Becker happens to be housed. If only all wars were this convenient.

Season 2, Episode 7: "Hogan's Springs" 10/28/1966.

D: Gene Reynolds W: Laurence Marks

Guest Cast: Sigrid Valdis (Hilda), Leon Askin (Gen. Burkhalter), Sidney Klute ("Sparrow"), David Frank (Driver), Walter Janowitz (Schnitzer).

Storyline: Four Underground operatives are being transported in a German truck and the Heroes trigger their release. They smuggle them into barracks through the tunnel under the dog house. Meanwhile, Kinchloe reports that a water pipe has broken causing a mud slide into their primary escape tunnel, so now the boys go to work bailing buckets of mud while Kinch patches the break. The pressure reverts upward and now water is streaming above ground. Hogan pretends it is pure mineral water, which Klink doubts, but he tells Schultz to draw up two bottles so they can send it into town for a lab analysis. The boys switch the bottles with water specially prepared in Carter's lab and the report comes back stating the water has a high content of sulfate and rock salt. Hogan suggests that his men build a bath house and invite General Burkhalter and other staff generals to the grand opening. While the general, Klink, and the others are hosted by Newkirk and LeBeau in the bath tubs, Hogan and the others steal their uniforms and suit up Sparrow and his men. Now dressed as Germans, Carter drives them off base, deposits them safely in the woods, and high tails it back to camp with the uniforms. Burkhalter and company realize their clothing is missing but Hogan returns, wheeling their uniforms up on a wardrobe cart, and explaining they just had their uniforms cleaned and pressed.

Assessment: A decidedly daffy, ridiculous story is more than compensated for by its consistent charm and humor. If there was ever an all round pleasant half hour, this has to be it. The plot points of *Hogan's Heroes* often push the limits of the viewers' credibility with some episodes selling the bill of goods far better than others.

This story works because Marks' script includes the detail of Carter's water samples being analyzed by the local scientist, which sells the caper to Klink in convincing fashion. The episode begins with a lovely sequence where the Heroes halt the German transport utilizing Carter as a private on patrol and the others providing the muscle. Perhaps learning from their previous outing, the stage combat here is much better realized. The use of Jerry Fielding's music is bright and cheery as the allies all pile into the "next truck that comes along." There are plenty of sweet moments to savor: the water switch with Schultz in which Newkirk and Kinchloe suddenly change places, a terrific dialogue scene in Klink's office where Hogan sells the idea of building the bath house, and the sight of Burkhalter and Klink smoking cigars and drinking cognac in the bathtubs. Leon Askin's laugh out loud reaction to a LeBeau punchline is a priceless moment. Fielding's music continues to punctuate many a moment, my favorite being the departure of "Sparrow" and his Underground men dressed as the Luftwaffe. Questions arise, such as why Klink doesn't order his men to dig up the ground around the spring leak to investigate. More ironic is that Klink and the others have a marvelous time enjoying the mineral baths, never realizing that it's just plain water.

Classic Admission:

Hogan: (to Sparrow) "We're a small organization, but with a very large payroll."

Season 2, Episode 8: "A Klink, A Bomb, and a Short Fuse" 11/04/1966.

P/D: Edward H. Feldman W: Phil Sharp

Guest Cast: Sigrid Valdis (Hilda), Leon Askin (Gen. Burkhalter).

Storyline: London wants photos taken of the newest Nazi code book, so Newkirk lifts it and Carter takes the snaps while Klink hounds the men for its return. Burkhalter arrives and informs Klink that Allied radio transmissions are coming from his camp, and he has brought a detecting device to prove his point. The device indicates that the radio transmissions are coming from Hogan's barracks, but all they discover is a percolating coffee pot in a foot locker. Carter realizes that he never loaded film into the camera so the boys trick Klink into removing the code book from his office safe (to prove it is actually there!) and manage another round of snapshots. Now they need to transmit the information to London, but Burkhalter's detecting device will prevent this. Hogan gets an idea during an Allied air strike near the stalag. He has Carter create a fake bomb which the men will plant in the compound hoping to distract the Germans. Hogan adopts a cavalier attitude as he attempts to defuse the "live bomb" in front of Klink and Schultz, until Kinchloe arrives with bad news. During the air raid, Carter and his fake bomb got trapped in the emergency tunnel, so Hogan is operating on an actual bomb! Stifling his fear, Hogan finally deactivates the bomb by *not* heeding the advice of Klink.

Program Notes: Gene Reynolds must have remembered this scenario because the idea of a live, ticking bomb in a military compound and its subsequent deactivation turns up in the first season *M*A*S*H* episode, "The Army Navy Game," (1973).

Assessment: Despite a few, clever set pieces, the story this time feels a bit cluttered with plot details that are rougher than smooth. Effective is the radio detecting device introduced in Klink's office which we then follow over to the barracks. Less effective is the con game with Klink posing for photographs with his POWs while LeBeau has the code book pose for its own set of pictures. The idea of planting a fake bomb as a diversion feels pretty far out of left field, even for this show, but it does lead to the best sequence of the program, where Hogan makes the split second decision of cutting the wire *not* suggested by Klink, knowing that whatever choice Klink would make would certainly be the wrong one!

Season 2, Episode 9: "Tanks for the Memory" 11/11/1966.

D: Gene Reynolds W: Laurence Marks

Guest Cast: Leon Askin (Gen. Burkhalter), Vincent Van Lynn (German Major), Robert Gibbons (Civilian Technician), Margareta Sullivan (Girl).

Storyline: While out on a daylight mission, Newkirk spends his time enjoying a picnic and the favors of a local girl. They observe a small German tank approach on the road below followed by a vehicle with two men. It seems the Nazis are experimenting with a miniature, remote controlled tank, but decide to move the unit to the local stalag where it will require further testing. Hogan wants to photograph the interior control panel of the tank to transmit to London, and he learns that Klink will house the unit in Building 12. Now the men need to dig an additional six feet from their emergency tunnel so they will be able to access Building 12. In order to hide the dirt from the extra tunneling, Kinchloe writes a fake letter to Klink announcing a "Camp Beautification" contest and the men volunteer by providing their gardening skills. Completing the tunnel extension, the gang takes photos while Kinchloe removes the control panel just as Burkhalter and his high brass are escorted to Building 12. With no time to reinstate the control panel, the men retreat with it and Hogan forces LeBeau to crawl inside the tiny tank. Once the tank is maneuvered behind the barracks, LeBeau is pulled out and replaced by one of Carter's explosives. With no driver or control panel, the mini-tank runs amok and causes an explosion with the general's staff car. Hogan suggests they head back "to the old drawing board" knowing his men will transport the control panel and photos to London to analyze.

Assessment: The stand out sequence of this episode is the tiny tank demonstration accompanied by Hogan continually belting out the maneuver instructions for LeBeau's ears and to which Schultz, standing next to Hogan, finally responds, "I heard you!" The Camp Beautification contest isn't exactly the scheme of the century and can best be written off as just another little diversion, an excuse to sweep some dirt under the carpet. At some point, Richard Dawson must have registered a complaint to producer Feldman that he wasn't engaging in enough lip lock with the local frauleins like his ranking officer continued to enjoy. As a result, this episode opens with the absurd scene of Newkirk cavorting with a local beauty in broad daylight, a scene that no one really requested other than, probably, Corporal Newkirk.

Left to right, Schultz, Hogan, Gen. Burkhalter (Leon Askin), Klink, and guest stars Vincent Van Lynn (far right) and Robert Gibbons (seated) prepare to demonstrate the newest example of German artillery in "Tanks for the Memory." Author's collection/CBS Television Inc.

Season 2, Episodes 10 & 11: "A Tiger Hunt in Paris"

Part 1: 11/18/1966. Part 2: 11/25/1966.
D: Robert Sweeney W: Richard Powell

Guest Cast: John Dehner (Col. Backscheider), Nita Talbot (Marya), Arlene Martel (Tiger), George Neise (Capt. Mueller), Dave Morick (Cpl. Sontag), and Henry Corden (as Antonovich/Himmler).

Storyline: Klink announces to the POWs that he will be taking a one week leave to Paris, and it is decided that Schultz will accompany him, leaving Capt. Gruber in temporary command. Hogan gets word that their Underground contact, Tiger, has been apprehended and taken to Gestapo headquarters in Paris. Hogan, along with a wad of counterfeit French money, recruits LeBeau, and the two men bribe Schultz into letting them hide in the luggage rack atop Klink's staff car. In Paris, Hogan and LeBeau steal the staff car while Klink has gone to check in with the hotel. Schultz is left to explain that the vehicle and luggage was suddenly commandeered by the Gestapo. Hogan holds court in a hotel suite, expecting a visit from the Gestapo, and they comply. Hogan forms an alliance with Colonel Backscheider, explaining how he escaped from Stalag 13 (as Sgt. Frank Durkin) and how he has amassed a small fortune through the black market in Paris. Backscheider's men find the stash of counterfeit cash which perks the colonel's interest. Hogan claims that Backscheider's prisoner, Tiger, used to work for him and that he could probably get her to talk alone. Backscheider complies since he has Tiger's cell bugged, but Hogan finds the bug and disconnects it. Hogan looks for any information he can use against Backscheider, and Tiger suggests he connect with a Russian fortune teller who frequents the White Russian cafe and has been romancing the Gestapo colonel. (It seems that all the high ranking, German officers are obsessed with astrology and fortune telling since their Fuhrer also has this passion.) Hogan stalls Backscheider by telling him that Tiger's contact in Paris was none other than Wilhelm Klink, so the Gestapo have him arrested. The Russian woman, Marya, strikes a deal with Hogan. She will help Hogan spring Tiger if he can steal information regarding secret fighter bases being developed near Hammelburg. Knowing his hotel phone has been bugged by Backscheider, "Durkin" pretends he will be expecting a visit from his dear friend Heinrich Himmler. While Backscheider awaits Himmler's arrival at the airport, Hogan and an actor posing as Himmler spring Tiger from Gestapo headquarters along with the plans to the secret fighter bases. Klink is finally released and ready to end the worst week of his life as he boards his relocated staff car, with the two stowaways again hiding out in the luggage rack.

Program Notes: The first two-part adventure of the series enlisted the Forty Acres back lot to pose as Paris. John Dehner returns for his second of three appearances, and Nita Talbot debuts as the Russian double agent, Marya. She would return as Marya on six more memorable occasions. Likewise, Arlene Martel chocks up her second of seven appearances, five as the Underground operative "Tiger." Early in his film career, Henry Corden worked as a contract player at Universal-International, and lent support to two of the biggest comics in the business, in the films: *Abbott and Costello in the Foreign Legion* (1950) and *Abbott and Costello Meet Dr. Jekyll and Mr. Hyde* (1953).

A jaunty Bob Crane looks rightfully delighted to find himself between beautiful co-stars Nita Talbot and Arlene Martell during shooting of the first two-part adventure of the series, "A Tiger Hunt in Paris." Author's collection/CBS Television Inc.

Assessment: Big on spectacle, low on brains, "A Tiger Hunt in Paris" moves Hogan off campus for a spirited, though not entirely successful escapade. The road trip begins with the most unconvincing scene of Hogan and LeBeau threatening Schultz to let them stowaway in Klink's luggage rack. It's the sergeant's word against theirs, but for the series to function Schultz has no faith in his own word. In Paris, Klink is reduced to stooge status as the boys steal his staff car and luggage. Then viewers are afforded the sensational sight of Hogan now relaxing in a Paris suite, sipping champagne, and awaiting the arrival of the Gestapo. John Dehner's Col. Backscheider is a curious performance, and the actor speaks in such low tones it is often difficult to comprehend his dialogue. Apparently, he is the equal of Klink because he is duped rather easily, especially when his men confirm the existence of a "Sgt. Durkin" that had escaped from Stalag 13. Here we must assume a forged personnel file has found its way into Klink's file cabinet. Backscheider gets suckered instantly by the fake francs and a bribe, the keys to Klink's staff car! Arlene Martel as Tiger isn't given much to do other than look scared and sexy, and be ready on cue to kiss Crane. Meanwhile, back at camp, the new Stalag 13 being run by the efficient Capt. Gruber and his triple dose of bed checks, fails to discover the absence of the senior POW officer for an entire week!

The two part-er gains advantage with the introduction of Nita Talbot's Marya, "the nutty Russian," as Hogan would repeatedly reference her. She is a real firecracker and makes the most of every minute on screen, whether talking turkey with Hogan, interrogating him in the back of Klink's staff car (which would develop as a running gag of sorts in later outings), or ensnaring Backscheider with her astrological mumbo jumbo. Best of all, is the terrific return of Henry Corden (last seen as the groovy General Von Kaplow in "Movies are Your Best Escape"), who cleverly steals the show as Russian ham actor, Antonovich, and his alter ego, Heinrich Himmler. (When LeBeau recognizes him as the doorman of the cafe where they convene, Corden quips in an ego driven, actor's manner: "Not one of my better parts"). Corden is terrifically funny when he questions Capt. Mueller, then breaks downstage with Hogan who cues his next line, and then returns to Mueller without breaking stride. This is very funny stuff, especially for anyone who has ever walked the boards on stage. Klink, who has been hung out to dry for most of the hour, is allowed the very humorous, comical thread of continuing to see and hear Hogan. After spotting Hogan and LeBeau in a cafe, Klink calls Capt. Gruber back at Stalag 13, but gets the vocal master, Newkirk, at work. Kinchloe is able to patch the call into Hogan's hotel room, thus proving he is still at Stalag 13. Hogan even snidely asks how the staff car is running which leads Klink to the observation: "He knew. Somehow he knew!" The final bit is also strong, with Klink grousing about the terrible week he's spent in Paris, heightened by his continued seeing and hearing of the "insufferable" Col. Hogan! A clever, muddy voiceover of Hogan protesting the "insufferable" insult is heard and this spooks Klink back into the vehicle, ending this vacation of lost and mixed bags.

Season 2, Episode 12: "Will the Real Adolf Please Stand Up?" 12/02/1966.

D: Gene Reynolds W: Laurence Marks

Guest Cast: Leon Askin (Gen. Burkhalter), Bonnie Jones (Christina), William Christopher (Foster), Forrest Compton (Maj. Krantz), and Larry Hovis as (Adolph).

Storyline: Major Krantz has a document detailing the German forces defending the English Channel sea ports, and Hogan and the Underground want to photograph it. Christina, an Underground ally, stages a car breakdown on the road Krantz is traveling, and he has his driver attend to the repair while he escorts Christina to the local pub. Newkirk, Carter, and LeBeau have already subdued the waiters and assumed their professions. Hogan enters, costumed as Major Hoganlauffer, and joins Krantz and Christina. Newkirk slips Krantz's overcoat into the storeroom and Kinchloe photographs the secret document. The next day, Klink informs Hogan that he knows all about the previous night, but then goes on to say that two escapes have simultaneously occurred at two other stalags, and that he will be doubling the guard. LeBeau attempts to sneak out so he can deliver the film negatives to their contact "Karl," but the civilian is apprehended. Hogan thinks of another way to get the very important film to their Underground allies while Carter clowns around doing his Hitler impersonations. At first, Hogan is angry with him, but then he realizes the answer. Snagging a car from the motor pool, the Heroes stage the arrival of "Hitler" and three Luftwaffe officers. The ruse works fooling Klink, scaring off General Burkhalter, and allowing an escape route for Carter to safely leave the camp and deliver the vital film negatives.

Program Notes: Forrest Compton returns for the third of his six assignments along with the third of four, unrelated, appearances for Bill "Father Mulcahy" Christopher. Bonnie Jones would follow

Christopher over to the *M*A*S*H* set, playing Lt. Barbara Bannerman during its first season before retiring from professional acting. Klink's opening dialogue with Hogan in his office was reworked by director Paul Schrader in his film *Auto Focus* (2005) which featured Kurt Fuller as Werner Klemperer and Greg Kinnear as Bob Crane.

Assessment: This episode opens with a well-directed, well-paced sequence where the Heroes infiltrate the local cafe and assume the roles of the staff: Newkirk as waiter, LeBeau as bartender, Carter as a customer, and Kinchloe as a photographer in hiding. There is just enough footage of the two real waiters bound and gagged to lend credibility to the entire operation. Knowing the top secret map is hidden in the coat lining of Major Krantz's overcoat, Hogan joins the group as "Capt. Hoganlauffer" so an overcoat switch can be made. This leads in to a priceless dialogue scene where Klink spooks Hogan with his knowledge of all the details from the previous evening. As expected, Klink is referring to completely different circumstances creating a false scare for Hogan. Superior too, is the next office scene in which the senior POW is confident he can get Klink to move his security forces by revealing an intended escape plan by his men. In a rare instance, Klink turns the tables on Hogan by not only doubting the entire story but ordering reinforcements, and taking a brief moment to mimic Schultz's stock lines of knowing and seeing nothing! Hogan thinks he has "lost his touch." The final sequence centers on Larry Hovis's hilarious interpretation of Adolph Hitler. Physically he is a dead ringer for the Fuhrer and vocally he is quite impressive, especially while slipping in some terrific non sequitur comments such as, "love the barbed wire." This sequence also includes a laugh out loud cameo visit from General Burkhalter, who suddenly pulls up in his staff car, overhears "Hitler" ranting and raving about his dumb generals who are losing the war, and immediately retreats as his driver exits the uncomfortable scene in reverse! More than anything, this episode is a wonderful example of what could have been another broad, impossible premise more than justified through the commitment of the writing, direction, and top performances of its game and talented cast.

Season 2, Episode 13: "Don't Forget to Write" 12/09/1966.

D: Gene Reynolds W: Laurence Marks

Guest Cast: Leon Askin (Gen. Burkhalter), Sandy Kenyon (Col. Bessler), Dick Wilson (Capt. Fritz Gruber), George Tyne (Luftwaffe Doctor), Roy Goldman (POW/Uncredited).

Storyline: Luftwaffe officer Colonel Bessler pays Klink a social visit but his real motive is to recruit officers to the Russian Front. After listening to Klink brag about his days as a flyer with the 410th Bomber Crew, Bessler springs his trap and informs Klink that pending his physical, he will be transferred to the Russian Front. Hogan plots to foil the transfer and his men go to work on Klink attempting to get him out of shape and fail the physical. The Luftwaffe Doctor arrives and even though Klink is in miserable physical shape, the doc approves his transfer anyway. General Burkhalter arrives and announces Klink's successor, Captain Gruber, in front of the entire company. Gruber, a strict disciplinarian, threatens the operation so Hogan orders LeBeau, Carter, and Newkirk to flee out the emergency tunnel and hole up at their "primary escape hide outs": a barn near the Hammelburg Road, a cave, and a haystack. While Gruber frantically searches for the three escapees, Hogan fills in Klink on their hideout locations so he can get back into the good graces of Burkhalter. Klink rounds up the three men, Gruber is ousted, and Klink is reinstated as the Kommodant of Stalag 13.

Program Notes: This is the first of eight guest performances for character actor Dick Wilson, who nearly any TV addict will remember as the Charmin tissue pitchman, Mr. "Don't squeeze the Charmin" Whipple, the biggest fusspot on television since Joe Besser whined his way through *The Abbott and Costello Show*. Roy Goldman gets to enjoy a rare line of dialogue in this episode: "Atta boy Fritz Baby!" which earned him a trip to the cooler for thirty days.

Assessment: A residential comedy that focuses more on the inherent characters and less on covert capers and espionage, "Don't Forget to Write" has its fair share of pleasures although much of the proceedings seem to tread on familiar ground. The episode kicks off with a cute, bizarre occurrence, with the men trying to get Herman the Chicken to lay one more egg so LeBeau can finish making a souffle! Unfortunately, this triggers Schultz to dopily cackle like a chicken himself to encourage the fowl maneuver. Sandy Kenyon breezes in and out of his guest role as the sly Colonel Bessler. Laboring the war effort, next is the sluggish sequence of the men trying to ruin Klink's health status for the physical: they starve him, Klink tries to force Schultz to give up half his lunch, they make him sleep outside all night, they try to keep him awake, and they execute other "tired" gags. Easily the funniest moments occur when Klink gleefully studies Gruber and his guards' frantic efforts through binoculars, along with the subsequent dialogue between Klink and Hogan. Here the sight of Klink cackling at the misfortunes of his former platoon yields some nice laughs without the egg laying.

Classic Medical Summation:

Luftwaffe Doctor: "You have passed the one important test for a combat assignment to the Russian Front."

Klink: "I have?"

Luftwaffe Doctor: "You're breathing."

Season 2, Episode 14: "Klink's Rocket." 12/16/1966.

D: Robert Sweeney W: Art Baer, Ben Joelson

Guest Cast: Sigrid Valdis (Hilda), Harold Gould (Gen. Von Lintzer), John Orchard (Billett).

Storyline: Klink brags to the men at formation about the recent successes of the Luftwaffe, their superiority in the air, and the Blitzkrieg they have brought down on London. Hogan looks to turn the tide and builds his plotting around an abandoned warehouse in London, which he plays up as an Allied factory for the development of rocket guns. He further beefs up this claim by staging a paratrooper stuck in a tree outside camp and employing a metal, lampshade part clipped from Klink's office and later claimed by Carter. Klink tries to interrogate Carter as to the location of the rocket gun factory and he is joined by an old colleague, General Von Lintzer. They finally discover the name of the factory location, Leadingham, and Von Lintzer declares he will lead the air attack. The Germans are received by Allied anti-aircraft artillery resulting in the loss of sixty two Nazi bombers – including Von Lintzer's.

Program Notes: Art Baer and Ben Joelson begin the first of four writing assignments. The team also drafted many scripts for *Andy Griffith*, *Gomer Pyle U.S.M.C.*, and much later, *The Love Boat*. This marks the first of four guest shots for long time show biz fixture, Harold Gould. Take your pick as to your favorite Gould performance, however, his con man role of "Kid Twist" in the best picture of 1973, *The Sting*, is easily a contender." "Ugly John" Orchard makes a return visit, counting down the days until his transfer to the 4077th Mobile Army Surgical Hospital.

Assessment: Two new writers contribute to a teleplay that feels more clunky than clever, and only sporadically funny. Harold Gould, probably sensing how *big* the other Nazi characterizations have been, downplays his role of Von Lintzer leaving the viewer with little impression. It's easy to see why Feldman continually hired Leon Askin (and later Howard Caine) as his regular go to Nazis since both of those actors looked and sounded German and performed with incredible zeal. The only real enthusiasm Gould musters is fawning over Sigrid Valdis, not that the man is to blame. The bill of goods being sold here is the metal knob removed from Klink's lampshade and being pawned off as part of a rocket gun. Perhaps that plot detail might work better in a *Buck Rogers in the 25th Century* episode with Gil Gerard. Here it's a big stretch, but that's the irony. Even Von Lintzer is duped by the deceptive prop. Schultz is given some routine dopiness; here he somehow ends up with a helmet full of grapes crushed to his large skull. Probably even Oliver Hardy endured days like this while working at 20th Century-Fox. By far, the funniest business involves Carter being overstuffed with food by Klink and Schultz (an interesting interrogation strategy) while the POWs eavesdrop, convinced their colleague is actually being tortured, but most of the air time surrounding this tasty bit feels underfed.

Season 2, Episode 15: "Information Please." 12/23/1966.

P/D: Edward Feldman W: Laurence Marks

Guest Cast: Leon Askin (Gen. Burkhalter), Sam Melville (Lt. Crandall/Schmidt), Don Knight (RAF Capt.), John Stephenson (Maj. Kohler).

Storyline: Klink is summoned to General Burkhalter's office in Berlin. The Germans have an intelligence agent planted in London, who has informed the general of a leak of information coming from Stalag 13. Burkhalter sets a trap by having fake information regarding a rocket factory near Hammelburg leaked to Hogan courtesy of Schultz. Hogan relays the info to London and they destroy the factory with an air attack. Later, during surveillance of a conversation between Klink and Burkhalter, Hogan discovers the factory was abandoned and now Burkhalter's suspicions are confirmed. He replaces Klink with his own aide, Major Kohler, and also has a German spy, Schmidt, brought to the camp as a recently arrested prisoner. "Lt. Crandall" seems to check out okay, but Hogan has his suspicions. In the middle of the night, the men stage a small fire creating much panic. Kinchloe shouts in Crandall's ears in German to escape through the window, and the spy takes the bait. The men take Crandall into their confidence, suggesting that Major Kohler is actually their ally and radio contact to London. Then Hogan has Kinchloe contact London stating that Kohler is the mole who has been leaking out the Nazi war secrets, and because of the German spy within London high command, the information gets back to Burkhalter. The general has Kohler arrested, and Schmidt confirms what the POWs had told him earlier. Returning to the barracks, Hogan and his men force Crandall/Schmidt at gunpoint to take a permanent vacation to England.

Program Notes: John Stephenson, last season delivering "heavy water" to Stalag 13, returns in his second of eight appearances. A gifted voice actor, Stephenson has lent his voice to over three hundred animated cartoons, perhaps most recognizably as "Mr. Slate," the quick-tempered boss of Fred Flintstone. The episode title references the radio quiz show of the same name, which NBC aired from 1938 to 1951.

Assessment: Once again Laurence Marks drafts an agreeable, home-based situation in which Klink finds himself on the short end of the general's stick and Hogan must intervene in order to save the Kommodant and his clandestine operations. Probably the best bit involves Kinchloe's command of German during the fake fire, which helps ferret out the informer, as the series revisits the plot of the pilot. The resolution seems a little too soft with the implication to London, and the snooping German spy on that end, that Kohler is the actual traitor. Further complicating this logic is that Burkhalter's deliberate misleading of the information that leads to the Allied air raid on the empty rocket factory takes place *before* Kohler assumes command of Stalag 13. Yet Burkhalter still falls for the frame-up of Kohler as the traitor without considering this timeline.

Season 2, Episode 16: "Art for Hogan's Sake." 12/30/1966.

D: Gene Reynolds W: Laurence Marks

Guest Cast: Leon Askin (Gen. Burkhalter), Ina Victor (Suzette), John Crawford (1st Gestapo Agent), Norbert Schiller (Verlaine), and Jon Cedar (as Cpl. Langenscheidt).

Storyline: General Burkhalter, having avoided an enemy attack on the road to Stalag 13, entrusts Klink with an original painting stolen from the Louvre in Paris, "The Fifer," by Edouard Manet. The general plans to present it to Field Marshall Goering as a birthday present. Spying on the proceedings, LeBeau enters the office through the window after the Germans depart and sneaks the painting back to the barracks. Hogan schemes to get it back to Paris with the help of Verlaine, a painter friend of LeBeau's who can create a convincing duplicate. Klink, on the warpath for the art thief, is presented with a bowl of ashes, the supposed remains of "The Fifer." Klink threatens LeBeau with a firing squad, but Hogan points out it will be his neck also for allowing the theft to happen. Klink agrees to let Hogan and LeBeau, accompanied by Sgt. Schultz and Cpl. Langenscheidt, seek out the services of Verlaine in Paris and recover an imitation. En route, Hogan has Schultz wear a Luftwaffe General's uniform so they won't be bothered by sentry posts! In Paris, they rendezvous with Verlaine and his daughter, Suzette, and head to the painter's studio where Verlaine creates a duplicate while Schultz bluffs the Gestapo. Back at Stalag 13, Burkhalter senses the painting now appears slightly different. He recruits LeBeau, who claims he has seen the painting many times in the Louvre, to offer his opinion. After studying the painting, LeBeau concludes it is an excellent reproduction and that some time ago he learned that the original had been seized by Goering. Burkhalter accepts the analysis, relieved that LeBeau has saved him from the embarrassment of giving Goering a replica while the Field Marshall already owns the original.

Assessment: Hogan, LeBeau, and Schultz all make their return to Paris in an episode that may very well be Robert Clary's finest contribution. Schultz is allowed to dominate the proceedings even though Hogan's motivation for having the sergeant don a general's uniform is paper thin at best. Still, General Schultz gets to recycle the old Buster Keaton bit of nonstop salutes that dates back, appropriately, to *The General* (1926). Banner's badgering of the Gestapo agents ("the bully boys are here") provides some of the bigger laughs of the half hour. Jon Cedar gets to enjoy his greatest amount of screen time to date, drinking wine with his sergeant of the guard, and peeking behind the curtain of the true machinations of Col. Hogan. After this trip, Langenscheidt would best take his superior's cue to know and see nothing. The presence of Leon Askin nicely bookends this piece, but the true star is Clary's LeBeau. Whether shedding tears when he first holds the portrait of "The Fifer" (beautiful touch from director Reynolds), bantering in French with his Parisian colleagues, or playing the art appraiser who shakes off the use of a magnifying glass, Clary's warmth adds great measures of credibility to a well crafted excursion.

Season 2, Episode 17: "The General Swap" 01/06/1967.

D: Gene Reynolds W: R. S. Allen Harvey Bullock

Guest Cast: Leon Askin (Gen. Burkhalter), John Myhers (Field Marshall Von Heinke), Frank Gerstle (Gen. Barton).

Storyline: General Barton is brought to Stalag 13 along with his downed bomber plane. Klink has invited Field Marshall Von Heinke to camp and plans to create a publicity stunt around Barton's imprisonment. London sends orders to have Barton sprung so Hogan tries to make Klink believe that Barton is not really a general, but this fails when Barton shows open contempt for Hogan. Instead, Hogan and his men ambush the staff car of Von Heinke and kidnap him, pretending to be British Commandos. Then they manage to steal the dormant bomber out from under Schultz's nose and convince Von Heinke that he is being flown to England. Burkhalter and other Luftwaffe officers arrive and make plans to rescue Von Heinke. The Heroes stage a radio transmission requesting a prisoner exchange between Barton and Von Heinke. Although Klink doubts the validity of the British radio message, Burkhalter and the others accept the terms of the prisoner trade, especially after hearing Newkirk's impersonation of Churchill!

Program Notes: Frank Gerstle kicked off his professional career playing the doctor who infamously informed Edmond O' Brien, "You've been murdered," in the noir classic *D.O.A.* (1949). He amazingly chocked up 200 film and TV credits before passing at the age of fifty- four.

Assessment: Slightly somber, this Allen/Bullock concoction is a pretty straightforward caper with few moments of suspense or big comedy. The most inventive device (and the most ridiculous) is the towing away of the general's bomber and its use as a theatrical setting for the kidnapped Von Heinke's flight to England. Klink stirs up some distractions for Hogan as the *only* German officer who suspects trickery during the radio address. In fact he almost walks into the theatrically appointed British Headquarters (actually Hogan's living quarters), before being summoned back to his office. This is one time that Klink appears ahead of the game of his superiors, yet he just can't prove it.

Season 2, Episode 18: "The Great Brinksmeyer Robbery" 01/13/1967.

D: Robert Sweeney W: Phil Sharp

Guest Cast: Joyce Jameson (Mady Pfeiffer), Theodore Marcuse (Ludwig Strasser), Arthur Hanson (Bank Manager).

Storyline: An accidental tunnel explosion renders the team's radio service inoperable, so the men sneak outside Klink's office to overhear a BBC broadcast with coded information for the Heroes. That night, a parachute delivers 100,000 German marks, to be used in a bartering deal with Ludwig Strasser, who possesses a map of Nazi rocket launching sites that the Allies desire. At nightfall, Klink and Schultz are spotted headed towards the barracks, so Newkirk hides the stash of cash in their wood burning stove. As an act of discipline, Klink sets fire to Schultz's three day pass and deposits it in the stove. After Klink and Schultz finally leave, the POWs survey the destroyed marks. Hogan is determined to somehow buy the map from Strasser. He plots to rob the local bank and he and Newkirk pay a visit in disguises. The men study the map plans of the bank and realize that the vault is in a room adjacent to the apartment occupied by Mady Pfeiffer, who lives alone. Hogan shows up to Mady's door with flowers, champagne, and a yarn about his yearning affection. Hogan gets Mady drunk and plays the radio loudly while Newkirk and LeBeau sneak into her bedroom and remove the wall. Mady passes out as the men finish the heist and remove 100,000 in marks plus an extra 1000 that Hogan leaves behind for Mady. Hogan is able to make the deal with Strasser, and later Schultz informs the POWs that the local bank had been robbed yet the robber later attempted to deposit the same stolen 100,000 marks with the same bank!

Program Notes: Generally typecast in "dumb blonde" roles, Joyce Jameson was used to good advantage by producer/director

Roger Corman in his Poe adaptations: *Tales of Terror* (1962, the "Black Cat" segment) and *The Comedy of Terrors* (1963) as the daughter of horror icon, Boris Karloff. Theo Marcuse would return for two more of Colonel Hogan's adventures before tragically losing his life in an auto crash in 1969.

Assessment: Despite some okay touches, Phil Sharp's script is as preposterous as they come and there isn't much "greatness" to this bank robbery. Klink again demonstrates his unknowing power to derail Hogan's plans through mere coincidence. This time it's burning up the German marks in the stove with Schultz's three day pass. There's also the stock, but amusing, scene where Schultz spots Hogan and Newkirk at the local hofbrau, but without a pass himself, there is nothing he can do about it except bolt. The best moments of this episode are thanks to the charming presence of Joyce Jameson, who makes the most of an underwritten role. If one were to tune in late to this episode, one might think they were watching Jameson and Bob Crane on an episode of *Love, American Style*, which might be a better viewing choice than this ridiculous-beyond-belief bank debit.

Season 2, Episode 19: "Praise the Fuhrer and Pass the Ammunition" 01/20/1967.

D: Robert Sweeney W: Jack Elinson

Guest Cast: Sigrid Valdis (Hilda), Frank Marth (S.S. Col. Deutsch), David Frank (S.S. Guard).

Storyline: SS Colonel Deutsch arrives and has Klink inform the entire company that war games will be conducted in the surrounding area and that all parties must stay clear. With a sneering contempt for the prisoners, Deutsch takes a grenade from the belt of one of his own soldiers and tosses it in front of the assembly. Everyone hits the deck except Hogan who knew it was a fake all along. Hogan plots to take revenge and plans to mix real ammo with the fake ammo that will be used for Deutsch's war games. In order to access the ammo storage, Hogan stages a birthday party for Klink in one of the barracks. The POWs set up a stage and entertain Klink and Deutsch (who has only attended because he is escorting Hilda) and the rest of the prisoners. Hogan sneaks a big slice of birthday cake over to Schultz to keep him occupied while Hogan's men steal ammo from the building. Then they quickly venture out to taint the dummy ammo with live ammunition. Deutsch threatens to leave the birthday show early, but Newkirk is able to detain him while performing a magic trick at Klink's expense. Hogan returns just in time for Klink's birthday cake and a rendition of "Jolly Good Fellow." Later, Klink thanks Hogan for the marvelous time he had at his party, but receives a phone call with some bad news. Somehow live ammo was used during the war games causing an unforeseen casualty list for Deutsch.

Program Notes: This was the only writing contribution from Jack Elinson who wrote dozens of TV scripts for Danny Thomas, Doris Day, and Gomer Pyle. Later, he would achieve much success as the executive producer of *One Day at a Time* (75 episodes,

1976-1979) and *The Facts of Life* (78 episodes, 1980-1986). Frank Marth, who played the blackmailing Capt. Milheiser in last season's "Hogan's Hofbrau" returns for his second of five sojourns. Although billed in the closing credits, Larry Hovis does not appear.

A tense moment in Klink's office finds an uncertain Newkirk, bewildered Schultz, and a confident Hogan ready to square off with his Kommodant. Author's collection/ CBS Television Inc.

Assessment: Hogan wants revenge on a nasty SS Colonel, and one-shot writer Elinson drafts a script that proves to be a real irregularity to the series. The lead-in sequence is terrific with Deutsch causing a panic with the dummy grenade and his standoff with Hogan. It feels like you could be watching a scene straight out of a WWII feature film and not a sitcom. The birthday party affords many genuinely light-hearted moments including Robert Clary's spirited song and dance to "Alouette" and Richard Dawson's excellent repertoire of voice impressions of Humphrey Bogart, Sydney Greenstreet, and, especially, Peter Lorre. It's easy to see why after the war ended, Dawson would be added (along with Larry Hovis) to the ensemble of *Rowan and Martin's Laugh In*. Klink, in particular, is delightful during the performance segment. Seated upfront with an ear to ear grin, he is every bit the small child marvelously enjoying his birthday party. The dialogue between Hogan and Hilda is starting to heat up. This time there is a seductive exchange regarding her perfume choices causing Klink to intercede and remind Hogan that they are "none of his concern." There's also a nice plot point with Newkirk in possession of a small arsenal of bullets and his discredit of Sgt. Richter, which encourages Klink to switch Schultz to guard duty of the arsenal storage. Frank Marth continues his hot streak of memorable Nazi characterizations. He plays the perfect contrast to Klink's happy birthday boy and only shows enjoyment when Newkirk's magic trick backfires, leaving two raw eggs in Klink's cap!

Season 2, Episode 20: "Hogan and the Lady Doctor" 01/27/1967.

D: Gene Reynolds W: Laurence Marks

Guest Cast: Ruta Lee (Dr. Suzette Lechay), Leon Askin (Gen. Burkhalter), Curt Lowens (Gestapo Capt.), Bard Stevens (Lab Duty Officer), Karl Bruck (Dr. Krull).

Storyline: London orders the team to blow up a research facility developing synthetic fuel, and they send a female scientist to lead the operation. Newkirk and Carter return from a scouting mission of the lab and report that it is heavily guarded and surrounded by land mines and other booby traps, prompting Hogan to scrub the mission. However, Dr. Lechay continues to push for the success of the operation, even if she has to go out alone. She explains she was forced by the Nazis to help develop the synthetic fuel before going into hiding, and is now determined to see the end of their research. They agree to get her recaptured after which she is certain the enemy will take her back to the research lab to continue her work. While on a work detail, the men hide Lechay in a barn and then let her be discovered by Schultz, who initially wants to let her flee until Klink rides up in his sidecar. Burkhalter interrogates her and realizes her validity to the research project and has her ordered to be taken back. En route, the vehicle transporting Lechay is overturned by the Heroes. They force the driver at gunpoint to access the front gates of the facility and Carter is able to plant several timed explosives within the interior. They flee the facility just as the guards they had subdued return and open fire, only to hit the deck once the entire laboratory blows sky high!

Program Notes: This is the first of three, non related guest appearances for Ruta Lee, who made her professional debut in 1952 and has continued to enjoy guest roles well into the millenium. Lee previously co-starred with Werner Klemperer in *Operation Eich-*

mann (1961), an Allied Artists release that depicted the Israeli manhunt for escaped Nazi, Adolf Eichmann. The film also featured John Banner in the cast, along with frequent *Hogan's Heroes* guest stars Oscar Beregi Jr., Theodore Marcuse, and Norbert Schiller. Regarding this film and working with Klemperer, Ruta Lee recalled:

> Of course, I've always done accents and I got to do several of them as you know on *Hogan's Heroes*. This was the first time that I had worked with Werner on a movie ... it was the first movie to get residuals on television so it was the first time that anything that had been done on the big screen played on television and got paid. Not that I made but twenty-nine cents on it! And we became very good friends on the shoot ... it was fun for me because again I was playing a German accent. It was a low budget movie but not bad for what it was.

Two dinner guests who certainly do not want their photograph taken! Prior to joining up with Colonel Klink at Stalag 13, Ruta Lee (left) played spouse to Nazi war criminal on-the-run, Werner Klemperer, in Operation Eichmann. Photo courtesy of Ruta Lee/Allied Artists photo.

Assessment: "Lady, you're pushing me around, and we're not even married!" sulks Hogan, as the Colonel finds himself at odds with the stubbornly determined "lady doctor." As the title character,

Ruta Lee is terrific in the role and brings great earnestness to the French doctor who was forced to comply with Nazi Germany. This episode is molded around the caper model and much of the action centers around the team's efforts to plan, chart out, and eventually penetrate the lab facility. There is one terrifically funny sequence, however, involving Schultz, the work detail, and the capture of the lady doctor in the barn. First, we get an amusing dialogue exchange between Hogan and Schultz about his favorite meals of the day. Especially funny is the sergeant's reaction to the notion of breakfast. "I'm ca-razzy about it!!" Schultz emphatically responds. After he clumsily makes the capture of Lechay, Schultz encourages her to lam it so he doesn't have to deal with the required paperwork and extra effort the capture will entail! Only the unexpected arrival of Klink breaks up this plan. The mission to the lab facility (complete with an opportunity for Ms. Lee to flash her fabulous dancer legs) and its eventual demise is well directed, and some moments of suspense are rendered with the guards breaking their bindings and returning for gunplay involving Newkirk. Yet after all the whining and complaining from all the Heroes about how impossible this mission will be achieved, the gang sure makes it all look pretty darn easy during its execution.

Season 2, Episode 21: "The Swing Shift" 02/03/1967.

D: Edward H. Feldman W: Art Baer, Ben Joelson

Guest Cast: Hal Smith (Hans Spear), Leon Askin (Gen. Burkhalter), David Wiley (Maj. Pintz), David Frank (Kraus), Otto Waldis (Doctor), Buck Young (Factory Insp./Uncredited).

Storyline: Hans Spear, a civilian, arrives as a special guest of General Burkhalter. Spear has had much success converting manufacturing factories into war plants for the German war effort. In Hammelburg, they plan to convert an auto factory into a cannon manufacturing plant and they need extra guards from Stalag 13. Hogan notifies London but they cannot send out an air strike for six weeks so Hogan plots to destroy the plant himself. They apprehend four laborers and assume their identities on the swing shift. Inside the factory they begin to plant explosives in some of the cannons while running afoul of Schultz. A wrinkle in the plan forms when "Mueller," the foreman, and the identity assumed by Newkirk, is accepted into the German army and led away. Newkirk passes a physical with a German doctor and later must hide his face from Klink, who is recruiting new soldiers. Hogan shows the plant inspector tainted cannons and insists that productivity has sharply declined with the absence of Mueller, their former foreman. Hogan is able to get "Mueller" sprung from active duty and returned to the cannon plant and the Heroes carry out the destruction of the factory.

Program Notes: Hal Smith is best remembered as Otis Campbell in several episodes of *The Andy Griffith Show*, and lent his voice to hundreds of animated cartoons. Slapstick fans may remember him as King Theseus in *The Three Stooges Meet Hercules* (1962) with Joe DeRita as the 3rd Stooge. This is the second of four scripts from the writing team of Baer and Joelson.

Assessment: The series presents a most unusual, and quite entertaining, diversion that separates the Heroes from Klink and the usual camp settings by placing them in the cannon factory. Even more unusual is the solo adventure that Newkirk undertakes once his "Mueller" identity is accepted into the German army. This leads to some amusing incidents including a brief, but hilarious, physical exam with the Nazi doctor, and the dodging of Klink who shows up looking for recruits. Dawson is consistently tops in his solo sequences. Further amusing is the presence of Schultz who checks each laborer into the factory by examining their ID badge. After our four Heroes slip through, Schultz stops the next man and gives him an extra long, visual look over before giving him a pass. Perhaps not a top entry, this episode still diverts as an anomaly to the series, a case where two newer writers are experimenting and succeeding with different material.

Season 2, Episode 22: "Heil Klink" 02/10/1967.

P/D: Edward H. Feldman W: Richard M. Powell

Guest Cast: Sigrid Valdis (Hilda), Arlene Martel (Tiger), Howard Caine (Major Hochstetter), and John Banner (as Wolfgang Brauner).

Storyline: Wolfgang Brauner, the "money man" for the Nazi empire, is holed up in an apartment with Tiger after making an uneasy alliance to defect. Hogan appears through a tunnel, upset that Brauner bolted early in his staff car and now has the Gestapo on his tail. Hogan convinces Brauner to drive directly to Stalag 13, and that he will be directed into Klink's private quarters. Hogan reveals to Klink that the Fuhrer's life is in immediate danger, and to prove the point, a phone call from Newkirk, acting as a general, and Carter, as Adolph Hitler, confirms this gossip. Klink is instructed to privately admit a staff car with one man into Stalag 13. Brauner arrives and is able to access Klink's quarters while masking his identity. Major Hochstetter arrives demanding the whereabouts of Wolfgang Brauner, but Klink stalls him long enough to visit "Hitler." The Heroes move Brauner down into their tunnel network and set up Carter in Klink's quarters. Through the door, "Hitler" informs Klink that he is the only man to be trusted in the Third Reich and that he will appoint Klink as his successor! Meanwhile, the Heroes go to work on Brauner, and after shaving his facial hair they notice a fascinating resemblance to a certain Sergeant of the Guard. Tiger arrives to protest Hogan's plan as Schultz enters, notices the man in the barber chair, and the presence of a woman, but chooses to see nothing. Hochstetter insists he confront the man in Klink's quarters, and, upon entry, they find Schultz (actually Brauner) seated alone. Klink orders "Schultz" to assemble the guard and find the escaped man. Later, the real Schultz returns adding to the confusion. Hogan explains that Brauner, a master of disguise, fooled them earlier as Schultz, and made his escape with Tiger as his driver.

Program Notes: The end credits list "John Banner also appearing as Wolfgang Brauner." Prior to her recurring roles on *Hogan's Heroes,* Arlene Martel was generally listed as "Arline Sax." Having previously portrayed a Captain, then a Colonel, Howard Caine returns for good as legendary Gestapo enforcer Major Wolfgang Hochstetter, in a role he would triumphantly realize thirty-seven times.

Assessment: John Banner in a dual role, a surprise visit from Hitler, and the introduction of Howard Caine's Major Hochstetter, contribute to the biggest, laugh out loud caper of the season. It is especially delightful to see Banner portray the straight role of Brauner. He maintains some of his usual comic twitches, but also portrays the defector in a realistically nervous manner. Effective too is the switch when Brauner becomes Schultz, and who blankly accepts orders from Klink. This leads to the classic sight gag of the real Schultz witnessing the departure of the fake one, a gag straight out of a silent Laurel and Hardy type comedy. (This joke would've been even stronger if they had eliminated the entrance of Schultz earlier when he saw his double in the barber chair, which weakens his surprised reaction later.) The dialogue between Carter's Hitler and Klink through a closed door is also hysterical and sets up Klemperer to perform a subtle, half faint into Hogan's arms – another example of Klemperer's brilliant, physical timing. His following dialogue, fired at Hochstetter and making choice reference to the delousing station, is also prime material. Howard Caine's debut as the rip roaring Major Hochstetter performs with so much zeal that it appears the character has already been established with the program for years. Naysayers of the series should be directed to view this episode, easily one of the funniest in the entire canon. Heil writer Powell! Heil producer/director Feldman!

Season 2, Episode 23: "Everyone Has a Brother-in-Law" 02/17/1967.

P/D: Edward H. Feldman W: Laurence Marks

Guest Cast: Leon Askin (Gen. Burkhalter), Cliff Norton (Capt. Kurtz), Mary Mitchell (Eva).

Storyline: Hogan's men are wiring a section of railroad tracks for detonation when Eva, an ally, arrives and informs the saboteurs that the train from Dusseldorf carrying munitions has been delayed for several days. The men leave the wiring intact and attach the detonator to a nearby emergency phone booth and return to camp. General Burkhalter arrives with his brother-in-law, Captain Kurtz, and installs him as Klink's new adjutant. Kurtz makes life difficult for the POWs with much stricter regulations than before, including a doubling of the guard that prevents any of the men from accessing their normal escape routes. Kurtz confers with Hogan in privacy revealing his plans to desert the German army. To test his loyalty, Hogan wants Newkirk to be allowed to escape, and Kurtz says he will allow him access to the wire that night. Newkirk walks into a trap, avoids machine gun fire, and Klink sends him to the cooler for thirty days. Hogan is furious, but Kurtz insists that Klink was tipped off and hung around to supervise. Kurtz pleads his sincerity, and Hogan agrees to set up a meeting with the Underground outside of camp and to let them decide. Kurtz informs Klink about the Underground meeting involving Hogan, and Klink allows him the use of his motorcycle and sidecar. That night, Hogan drives Kurtz off camp, directly to the emergency phone booth, where they will await a phone call from the Underground contact, to coincide with the arrival of the train from Dusseldorf. Kurtz pulls a gun on Hogan and insists he will make the call as the train approaches. He does with most explosive results. Later, back in the barracks, Hogan informs Burkhalter and Klink that both Kurtz and the train were destroyed by the explosion. Upon their departure, the prisoners usher in their new hostage, Capt. Kurtz, ready to transfer to England as a prisoner himself.

Program Notes: Mary Mitchell, who played Mady, Carter's romantic interest in the finale of season one, returns for a brief and final visit to the program. Oddly enough, in both episodes, she never shared a scene with Bob Crane. Cliff Norton makes his sole appearance. He frequently supported several of the biggest comedy stars in television history, including on many occasions, Sid Caesar, Lucille Ball, Jack Benny, and Joey Bishop.

Assessment: A strong Laurence Marks script, with the main story concerning the detonation of the munitions train framed as book ends, almost overcomes a few plot deficiencies. Klink functions more as a strict Kommodant here and less the buffoon as typically portrayed in other outings. As a result, the signature scene of Hogan double-talking his way in Klink's office is removed. Schultz too is, more or less, in control of the POWs, as he bribes Newkirk for a dozen cigarettes in exchange for Newkirk holding a jitterbug dance contest – a social affair squashed by the new adjutant. Cliff Norton is a strong guest star; he effectively portrays both sides of the coin with Hogan and is a rare example of a second-in-command showing complete respect for the Kommodant. Another serious tone is the escape attempt of Newkirk, which not only is effectively shut down, but also results in a thirty day trip to the cooler, a punishment that is left unresolved at the program's conclusion. Everything percolates nicely until the less than smooth resolution. Why would Kurtz pull his gun on Hogan instead of wait it out for Hogan to complete his contact with the Underground? The answer is a case of contrivance with the writer selecting a Nazi to pull the trigger with disastrous consequences to his own cause. The final questioning from Burkhalter also goes far too smoothly with Hogan being let off the hook with nary a wrist slap. Unclear also is how Hogan is able to smuggle his new captor back into camp since the extra guards are blocking the usual escape routes. The viewer is left to conjecture that Hogan brazenly rode back to camp with his German captive in tow in the sidecar!

Season 2, Episode 24: "Killer Klink" 02/24/1967.

D: Robert Sweeney W: Harvey Bullock R.S. Allen

Guest Cast: Parley Baer (Dr. Pohlmann), Barbara Morrison (Gretchen Schultz), Walter Janovitz (Oscar Schnitzer).

Storyline: Kinchloe informs Hogan that one of their female Underground contacts in Heidelberg requires new radio parts for transmission. Hogan learns that Schultz is headed to his hometown of Heidelberg on his three day pass and asks the sergeant if he will deliver a potted plant to an old sweetheart of his (with the radio parts hidden inside.) The plan seems to gain steam until Schultz meets his wife, Gretchen, at the stalag gates, and she becomes jealous when she reads the love note attached to the potted plant. In anger, Schultz tears up his own pass. Hogan tries to get Klink to draft a replacement pass, but Klink, furious that Schultz would destroy the first pass, orders the sergeant to nonstop marching duty. Hogan schemes to get Klink to change his mind by convincing the Kommodant that Schultz needs a physical. Hogan gets Schnitzer, the dog trainer and friend of the Allies, to substitute his eighty-year-old father for Schultz and his physical. Alarmed, the doctor meets with Klink explaining that Schultz is a forty-year-old man in an eighty-year-old body, and that his health is in critical condition. After reinstating his pass, Schultz takes leave to Heidelberg and delivers the potted plant to the team's Underground contact.

Program Notes: Parley Baer returns for his third of four visits. A rare and singular instance where viewers get to meet the wife of Hans Schultz.

Assessment: The third Bullock/Allen contribution is one of the weakest stories produced. It's hard to get overly excited about a story hinging on whether or not Schultz can get a three day pass. There are a few pleasant diversions including the domestic squabble of Schultz and his wife Gretchen, and the misunderstood dialogue shared between Schultz and Klink regarding his upcoming "leave." Unfortunately, nearly all the proceedings get derailed by the fantastic idea of the doctor believing the eighty-year-old Schnitzer is actually the forty-year-old Schultz – truly a tough pill to swallow. The title, too, suggests a completely different episode when it is merely pulled from a random line of dialogue. Here's a case where two writers doesn't necessarily guarantee double the viewing pleasure.

Season 2, Episode 25: "Reverend Kommodant Klink" 03/03/1967.

D: Gene Reynolds W: Richard M. Powell and Ben Joelson & Art Baer (teleplay) Ben Joelson & Art Baer (story).

Guest Cast: Sigrid Valdis (Hilda), Howard Caine (Major Hochstetter), Felice Orlandi (Lt. Boucher), Susan Albert (Suzanne Martine).

Storyline: A French bomber is shot down near Stalag 13 and its pilot, Lt. Boucher, is hauled into camp. Major Hochstetter tries to get the location of Boucher's air base, but he only offers his name, rank, and serial number. Hochstetter infers that the lieutenant's French fiancee, Suzanne, has been unfaithful with German soldiers hoping to crack Boucher. The Heroes plot to find Suzanne and sneak her into Stalag 13 where they will stage a play about a wedding ceremony in which Klink will perform the ceremony. Hochstetter agrees to the performance hoping his cooperation will soften up Boucher. LeBeau, dressed as a Gestapo soldier, is sent to Paris and finds the actress, Suzanne, exiting the theatre, and she agrees to accompany LeBeau back to camp. At the performance, Hilda is costumed to be the bride but she is secretly switched out with Suzanne just before the "ceremony" begins. After the exchange of the wedding vows, Boucher lifts the veil of his bride and discovers that it is actually Suzanne. He holds and kisses her away from the audience. The next day, Hochstetter resumes his strategy of amicable interrogation, but Boucher, now convinced his new wife is completely faithful, only offers his name, rank, and serial number.

Program Notes: This launches the first of four invites for Italian born actor Felice Orlandi, who played a French man in all his outings. He would return as the recurring character Maurice Dubois for his next three guest turns. Hogan makes direct references to three earlier episodes: rebuilding and flying a plane out of camp ("Flight of the Valkyrie"), stealing the Tiger Tank ("Hold That Tiger"), and the kidnapping of James Gregory and bombing of his own refinery ("Hogan Gives a Birthday Party").

Assessment: As pleasant as the series can get, this episode also requires the viewer to suspend a lot of disbelief. The idea of allowing the POWs to stage the wedding ceremony is completely preposterous; even more so is that LeBeau is able to travel to Paris, round up Suzanne, and sneak her into camp in a twenty-four hour period. Major Hochstetter takes an entirely different approach as he attempts to sweet talk the information he seeks out of Boucher, in keeping with the overall genial tone of the show. There's some joy to behold in the sight of beautiful Hilda in and out of her wedding dress, and she has a nice exchange with Hochstetter during the wrap up in Klink's office. However, the overall absurdity of the plot development relegates this episode to mediocre status despite the efforts of three writers.

Season 2, Episode 26: "The Most Escape Proof Camp I've Ever Escaped From" 03/10/1967.

P/D: Edward H. Feldman W: Bill Davenport

Guest Cast: Leon Askin (Gen. Burkhalter), Edward Knight (Col. Stieffer), Mickey Manners (Sgt. Malcolm Flood), Karl Bruck (OSS Agent Huebler), Bard Stevens (Sgt. Schmidt).

Storyline: A sabotage plot to derail a German train is sidetracked by London. Hogan receives orders, however, that an Underground contact must be smuggled into camp in order to radio London with German subs plans. Burkhalter arrives with Colonel Stieffer and informs Klink that Sgt. Flood will be brought to his stalag. Apparently Flood is a master of the escape and has proven so at nine other stalags. Flood arrives and is incarcerated yet found later shaving in Hogan's quarters. Hogan orders Flood to remain confined to the barracks because he must retrieve the Underground contact without any interference from Stieffer's squadron. Hogan assigns Carter to keep watch on Flood, but Carter is later found trapped inside Hogan's footlocker! Hogan reports to Klink that Flood has escaped but claims he knows where to recover the escape artist. Klink allows Schultz to drive Hogan to the spot where Flood is hiding, but Hogan returns with the Underground agent instead claiming he mistook him for Flood. Since the man is a civilian with proper I.D., Klink tosses both men out of his office. Flood returns with Schultz, stating he had a change of heart about escaping after all. Stieffer and his men seize Flood and assert that he will be handed over to the Gestapo. As the men show concern for the final plight of Sgt. Flood, the escape master pops his head out from one of the bunks.

Program Notes: This is the first of thirteen scripts penned by William Davenport, who authored sixty-two scripts of *The Adventures of Ozzie and Harriet* (1953-1955) and later contributed teleplays to *All in the Family,* and its spin-off, *Maude.* Actors Knight,

Bruck, and Stevens all made regular stopovers at Stalag 13. Mickey Manners worked in several Jerry Lewis films, most notably the 3rd Reich inspired *Which Way to the Front?* (1971). Richard Dawson does not appear in the first half of this program.

Assessment: Bill Davenport's first script for the program is a clumsy, muddled affair and not nearly as spectacular as the unbelievable escapes effortlessly performed by Sgt. Flood. The subplot involving the pickup and smuggle in of the Underground man is also a clunky plot thread hindered by its lack of presentation. Hogan talks Klink into letting Schultz drive them to the hideout location of Flood, supposedly, and within seconds, Hogan and the Underground man are now seated in the rear of the truck and riding back to the stalag. There is no introduction of this new character, and why Schultz has agreed to transport this man back to camp is unclear. Schultz has already met the real Flood, so why would he agree to this suspicious arrangement involving a complete stranger? The remarkable escapes of Flood are just that because we are never allowed a glimpse into the escape artist's methods. They just happen time and again no matter how impossible the odds. There's not much to like with his character either. Mickey Manners is lacking in just that; he comes across as an arrogant, self-serving twit. By the end of this confounding odyssey you just might find yourself actually rooting for Col. Stieffer to put this misfit into the proverbial cell and make sure to throw away that key! Anytime you find yourself reluctantly rooting for the Nazis instead of the POWs, you just know something's rotten in Germany.

Season 2, Episode 27 "The Tower" 03/17/1967.

D: Gene Reynolds W: Laurence Marks

Guest Cast: Leon Askin (Gen. Burkhalter), Willard Sage (Capt. Berger), Elisa Ingram (Lili), Roy Goldman (POW/Unc.).

Storyline: The Germans have installed a radio tower near Stalag 13 which will increase communication efficiency with their bombers, and General Burkhalter assigns Klink's command to secure it from sabotage. Hogan knows his men need to destroy the tower, but doing so would guarantee a trip to the Russian Front for their Kommodant. Hogan plots to destroy the tower anyway and to protect Klink by blackmailing Burkhalter. First, he has Lili, a lovely Underground contact, write Klink a romantic letter of admiration. Then he suggests that Klink invite Lili to Stalag 13 for dinner and show her off in front of Burkhalter. The trio enjoys champagne on the sofa, and Lili blatantly flirts with the married Burkhalter while Kinchloe snaps photographs from an outside window. While Klink and the general are sidetracked, the men head out of camp and successfully pull Schultz and his guards away from watching the tower. Then they wire the tower with explosives and destroy it. Burkhalter is furious with Klink and imprisons him until a mysterious envelope arrives with photo enlargements of Burkhalter and Lili looking quite friendly. Attached is a note from Lili saying she has fallen in love with Klink, wants him exonerated, and includes a threat to send the negatives to Burkhalter's wife. At first Burkhalter says he can handle his wife, but he changes his mind when Hogan reminds him that Hitler hates infidelity among his soldiers. Hogan is ordered to meet the woman and he returns with the negatives which finally restores Klink to his former command.

Program Notes: This is the third of five, unrelated, guest appearances for Willard Sage, who guest starred on numerous TV westerns in the 1960s including *Gunsmoke*, *Death Valley Days*, and *Branded*.

This is one of three guest appearances on the show during the brief career of Elisa Ingram. Outside of the brief sequence cracking the safe in Klink's office, Richard Dawson does not appear during the rest of the episode.

The blackmailing of General Burkhalter (Leon Askin) is a key component to Hogan's success in saving Klink from active duty in Russia in "The Tower." Illustration courtesy of artist Larry Weber.

Assessment: Another "let's save Klink from going to the Russian Front" episode is bolstered by a terrific Leon Askin visit and the fetching presence of Elisa Ingram. The best sections of this outing revolve around the blackmail party and the hilarious photos of Burkhalter that develop from this situation. The destruction of the tower is a pretty nifty bit of sabotage, although the luring away of Schultz and the guards with Kinchloe on the megaphone is a bit of a stretch. Of the many episodes that cultivate this theme of saving the Kommodant from a transfer to misery, this one is about par for the course, although other occasions would employ more intricate, clever plot points in getting the job done.

Season 2, Episode 28 "Colonel Klink's Secret Weapon" 03/24/1967.

D: Gene Reynolds W: Phil Sharp

Guest Cast: Milton Selzer (Sgt. Franks), Stewart Moss (Lt. Bigelow), John Stephenson (Inspector General), Sidney Clute (Max).

Storyline: The men observe through their periscope a fleet of German tanks rumbling through their area which is disrupting the stability of their tunnel network. Lt. Bigelow is noting the German offensive before he prepares to secretly leave Stalag 13 and report to London. Hogan and his men are summoned to roll call just as the tunnel roof begins to collapse. Klink is fuming mad because the Inspector General recently gave his stalag the second lowest grade possible. Klink is determined to make up his poor scoring with the help of a new "secret weapon" - Sergeant Reinhold Franks, a no nonsense, by the book soldier, who makes Schultz look like a gigantic cream puff. Franks goes to work on the men by making them march double time, decreasing their sleep quota, and springing constant bed checks. At first Klink is delighted with the progress until Franks begins to ride him about his inefficiency in reporting to Berlin. Franks threatens Klink because he has a cousin who works for Goering. Meanwhile, Hogan learns from Max, the dog trainer, that Lt. Bigelow never surfaced from the tunnel, which means he's still trapped underground. The men go to work removing the dirt in the collapsed tunnel to free Bigelow and also hide the dirt from the snooping Franks. The Inspector General arrives for his re-evaluation report and the Heroes make Franks look like a failure by trashing the compound and also making alterations to his uniform including inscribing Churchill's "Victory Sign" on the sergeant's undershirt. Bigelow arrives posing as a Gestapo agent and hauls the disgraced sergeant away to both Hogan and Klink's relief.

Program Notes: Among his two hundred plus credits, Milton Selzer played the recurring role of "Parker" throughout season one of *Get Smart* (1965-1966). He would return to the Forty Acres set in the fourth season episode, "Guess Who Came to Dinner?" During the final compound scene, Richard Dawson uncharacteristically smokes a cigarette during formation.

Assessment: A bit of a revisit to the themes explored in last season's "Happiness is a Warm Sergeant," this reboot succeeds on the strength of guest star Milton Selzer, who brings much zip to his portrayal of Sgt. Franks. Selzer, in particular, works nicely with Larry Hovis. Unusually successful is the plight of Lt. Bigelow, who has spent half the episode trapped in the Heroes' tunnel network, temporarily forgotten by Hogan and the viewers. Less successful is the rapid fire conclusion with too many loose ends quickly tied up with unchallenged ease. In one scene, the men have hauled up dozens of bags of soil into the barracks when a surprise roll call is announced. The men try to momentarily stall Sgt. Franks, but once he enters the barracks everything is surprisingly back in order. Apparently within two minutes, Lt. Bigelow, working alone, has hauled every bag of soil back down into the tunnel! The finale also suffers from a rapid fire, illogical solution with the compound suddenly transformed into a garbage dump and the sergeant's uniform falling to pieces. (That's what you get, I suppose, for actually trusting Corporal LeBeau to have your uniform pressed!) Compounding the illogical mindset is the sudden arrival of Bigelow in Max the Dog Trainer's truck posing as a Gestapo agent. Apparently, his car broke down and he had to sequester the Dog Trainer's vehicle, or something like that . . .

Season 2, Episode 29 "The Top Secret Top Coat" 03/31/1967.

D: Howard Morris W: William Davenport

Guest Cast: Sigrid Valdis (Hilda), Leon Askin (Gen. Burkhalter), Inger Wegge (Maid), David Wiley (Herr Gruber).

Storyline: Mail call brings a pair of socks from Col. Hogan's Aunt Alice, but it's actually a coded message that the men play on a hand-spun sewing machine radio receiver! Hogan's mission is to attend a party hosted by Baron Von Aukberg, who will hand off secret plans for Operation Dragonfly. Hogan is able to snag Klink's party invitation from Hilda just as Klink and Burchhalter enter. In privacy, Klink and the general discuss the Von Aukberg party while Hogan and company listen in on their surveillance unit. Burkhalter informs Klink that Von Aukberg has been selling off Nazi plans for big money and that they will both attend the party in order to catch the Baron and his contact. Hogan smells a rat and has Kinchloe radio London to warn the Baron to cancel the party, but they are unable to do so. At the party, Klink receives a fake phone call from Stalag 13 that a prison break and riot have erupted sending Klink out in a hurry. Back at camp, Hogan learns that the Baron had his maid hide the Operation Dragonfly documents in Klink's topcoat. Burkhalter returns to Stalag 13 upset that Klink left in a rush and reports that the Baron was not in attendance and that the Gestapo will arrive in the morning to question Klink. Hogan makes several attempts to get Klink to remove his overcoat that fail. He has Carter pose as "Schmidt," a Gestapo agent who questions Klink in a cooperative manner and exits, deliberately taking Klink's overcoat with him. Hogan and Klink realize the error and find fake Operation Dragonfly documents in Carter's overcoat. Hogan suggests that the Baron returned posing as Schmidt. Klink shows the documents to Burkhalter and the real Gestapo agent when they arrive, and the men burn the papers satisfied that they have put an end to Operation Dragonfly (although the real papers left with Carter and Klink's topcoat).

Assessment: Although an improvement over his first contribution, Bill Davenport's second script suffers from a stockpiling of details that makes for an anything *but* smooth story progression. First, we have Hogan ordered to attend the party in disguise as Klink, so he retrieves the party invitation from Hilda. Then Hogan decides he is not going so he has to clumsily deliver the invitation back to Klink. Once Klink arrives at the party, the men back at camp have to get Klink to leave with the documents, so they fake the phone call concerning a POW riot. (Of course, at this point Hogan doesn't even know that the maid has hidden the documents in Klink's topcoat, furthering the strain of logic and motivation for the fraudulent phone call.) The script is further weakened with all the references about the Baron, who is never incorporated into the story as a living, breathing character. Why the Gestapo is now suspicious of Klink is also another mysterious detail, despite the fact that Burkhalter makes a return trip to Stalag 13 attempting to explain this plot development. The best sequence revolves around Carter's visit as Schmidt, the Gestapo Agent, and director Morris does a lovely job of framing the interrogation scene between Klemperer and Hovis in extreme close ups and to great effect. There's also some nice business from Burkhalter, as usual, particularly in his first scene in which he takes a moment to primp himself in front of the mirror while chatting with the Kommodant. These are sidebars, however, salvaged from a good director, working with a script that is mostly cluttered and clunky.

Season 2, Episode 30 "The Reluctant Target" 04/07/1967.

D: Bob Sweeney W: Phil Sharp

Guest Cast: John Hoyt (Field Marshall Von Galter), Theodore Marcuse (Pierre), Larry D. Mann (S.S. General Brenner).

Storyline: Underground contact Pierre confers with Hogan down in the tunnels concerning upcoming Nazi troop movements. The men create a diversion with LeBeau releasing the guard dogs so Pierre can safely exit, but the guards apprehend him, and Klink questions him in the compound. The men hide his papers while Schultz searches all present, and Hogan casually tosses Pierre's pistol atop the snow covered roof over Klink's office. Later, while Hogan contemplates how to spring Pierre, Carter and LeBeau attempt to retrieve the pistol from the rooftop. It drops to the ground and discharges, sending a bullet into Klink's office. Hogan uses this accident as a ploy. First, Carter sets off some explosives in the compound near Klink, and later Hogan poisons a coffee cup which causes a potted plant to wilt and die. Hogan convinces Klink that there is a mysterious assassin out to kill Klink, and that if he could set up a decoy Kommodant it would give them a chance to catch the assassin. Klink loves the plan and orders Hogan to switch identities with him. Hogan enjoys strutting around camp impersonating Klink and has the guards release Pierre. General Brenner arrives and informs the new Klink, whom he has never met, that a top secret conference will take place in Klink's office. Brenner indicates that no chances can be taken and that extreme security is cautioned. Hogan has LeBeau rig a walkie-talkie set in the outer office so Hogan can successfully relay the conference details to his men and on to the Underground. Later, when all is restored to normal, Klink is furious that Pierre was released, but Hogan points out that the assassination attempts started when he was first arrested, and they should be thankful that the man has departed.

Program Notes: John Hoyt kicks off his seven episode commitment to the series. A long time fixture on movie and television screens, film noir fans will remember his role as the ill-fated, Norwegian skipper in the poverty row cult classic *The Big Combo* (1955). One of his standout TV turns has to be the cranky, stranded bus passenger in *The Twilight Zone's* "Will the Real Martian Please Stand Up?" (1959), a role that afforded Hoyt the dexterity of using three arms! Theo Marcuse just enjoyed an appearance earlier in the season with "The Great Brinksmeyer Robbery." Bat fans will probably remember him lending crooked support to Frank Gorshin's The Riddler in the two part caper: "Death in Slow Motion/The Riddler's False Notion" (1966). This episode is often aired in syndication without a "laugh track" giving it an unusual dynamic. The principal photography, especially during the opening compound scene, is also unusually lit, framed, and contains some jarring camera movement. Ivan Dixon does not appear.

Assessment: After having had Schultz impersonate Klink in "The Great Impersonation," it seems a natural that the writers would get around to having the senior POW switch with the Kommodant. It's a pretty wacky lark and a fairly amusing one at that. Crane is pretty funny as he struts about doing his best Werner Klemperer imitation complete with the signature monocle firmly in place. Outside of Schultz, who is briefed about the change, none of the other soldiers seem to be even aware that a change has taken place. The retrieval of the pistol from the rooftop is a clumsy detail. The boys would have been better off just leaving the firearm alone – out of sight, frame, and mind. Furthermore, the gun falling to the snow-packed ground and then discharging also seems pretty unconvincing (and again, completely ignored by the stalag soldiers). There's a nice exchange between Crane and guest star John Hoyt and some good timing with Hogan in the outer office dodging the suspicious General Brenner while relaying the conference dialogue via the walkie-talkie. Likewise, there's a well timed moment with Hogan having to enter the inner office because he needs to see the name of the city being pointed to on the map. It's a good thing the general courteously kept his finger in the same spot for just the right amount of time needed for Hogan to snoop in and out.

Colonel Hogan temporarily assumes the identity and command of Colonel Klink, a role reversal concept the series would frequently employ, in the second season finale: "The Reluctant Target." Author's collection/CBS Television Inc.

Season 3, Episode 1: "The Crittendon Plan" 09/09/1967.

D: Gene Reynolds W: Richard M. Powell

Guest Cast: Bernard Fox (Col. Crittendon), Laurie Main (Maj. Shawcross), Naomi Stevens (Nadya), Cliff Osmond (Marko), Angela Dorian (Carla).

Storyline: Hogan receives detailed orders to blow up a tunnel and a German truck containing rocket fuel. He is to meet with a small Underground unit and spring the release of a British commando from Stalag 16. London describes the mission as "the Crittendon Plan," and Hogan reluctantly agrees knowing he will once again have to join forces with the bumbling Col. Crittendon. Carter escapes from camp and Klink allows Hogan, guarded by Schultz, to bring him back. Driving the German truck, Hogan first picks up several supplies, including German uniforms and explosives, all over Schultz's objections. They find Carter along one of the roads then proceed to Stalag 16 dressed as Germans and successfully release Crittendon. Next they head to a beer hall where they meet their oddball trio of Underground contacts: Marko, a suspicious man, Nadya, an agreeable woman, and Carla, an exotic, young beauty. While Hogan, Marko, and Nadya scope out the tunnel, Carla learns from Crittendon that his plan involved the planting of geraniums and not the destruction of tunnels! Apparently, London got their info confused with another Crittendon imprisoned at Stalag 2. Nevertheless, Hogan and his rag tag crew are able to halt the convoy while Crittendon attaches a time bomb to the gas tank of the fuel truck. Mission accomplished, Hogan, Carter, and Schultz finally return home to appease Klink.

Program Notes: Angela Dorian, also known by her true name, Victoria Vetri, had a small role in Roman Polanski's *Rosemary's Baby* (1968), in which Mia Farrow claims she looks like actress Victoria Vetri! Dorian posed for *Playboy* magazine (Miss September, 1967) and was later heralded as the 1968 Playmate of the Year. She also appeared in the cult classic, *Invasion of the Bee Girls* (1973). The opening credits now feature a new shot of Richard Dawson cracking open the safe in Klink's office, although he does not appear in this episode.

Assessment: A spirited, fast-moving adventure, "The Crittendon Plan" is also, sadly, burdened with excessive plot points that confuse more than clarify. The idea of two different POW officers with the last name "Crittendon" *and* both simultaneously possessing an allied, sabotage plan seems far too coincidental. Further confusing is the start of Hogan's road trip where Schultz is questioning why they made so many stops to acquire so many supplies when their orders are simply to find Carter. Apparently, Hogan just drove up to his friendly Underground Walmart for all the supplies he required. The character of Marko is most puzzling. He is part of the Underground team yet he challenges Hogan at gunpoint, is deserted by the others, later gets picked up by the German convoy, threatens to rat them out, and finally flees only to be shot by the German driver. Yet at the end of the caper, there he is, seemingly recovered and seemingly everyone's friend again! The absence of Schultz during most of this action is also a puzzler. Too often the writers burden the plots with too many extraneous details instead of providing just the right details to sell the bill of goods. Still, the story moves at a good clip and Bernard Fox is able to provide his usual amusing diversions, while shapely, sexy Angela Dorian proves to be the most fetching diversion of all – a human road block of sorts, capable to halt a German convoy dead in its tracks.

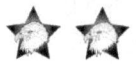

Season 3, Episode 2: "Some of their Planes are Missing" 09/16/1967.

D: Gene Reynolds W: Laurence Marks

Guest Cast: Leon Askin (Gen. Burkhalter), Stewart Moss (Olsen), John Doucette (Col. Leman), Walter Janowitz (Oscar Schnitzer/Uncredited), Bard Stevens (Sgt./Unc.), Rick Traeger (Conrad/Unc.).

Storyline: Late at night, six German soldiers arrive and are greeted by Klink. Hogan's men, hiding in several lookout points, identify the Nazis as Luftwaffe. Burkhalter and Col. Leman inform Klink and the six soldiers that they are part of Operation Albatross, which involves the Germans infiltrating the Allied cause by piloting six RAF planes and attacking their own British squadrons. The men see the six RAF fliers over camp and Klink reports to Burkhalter his suspicions. Hogan learns from Conrad, an Underground contact, that the Germans have a secret airstrip five kilometers outside of Hammelburg and Hogan plots to destroy it. To remove suspicion from himself, Hogan gets himself invited to a party hosted by Klink for Burkhalter, Leman, and their six fliers. Hogan pretends to get drunk and passes out in the bedroom. Then Olsen slips in takes his place on the bed wearing Hogan's clothes and lying face down. Hogan slips out and joins his team and they dress in German uniforms and head to the airstrip to meet Conrad and his team of saboteurs. They bully their way past the sentry post and rig several explosives to destroy the planes while Conrad leads an attack on the barracks. Hogan and his men flee as the airstrip is destroyed and race back to camp. Burkhalter is informed of the destruction and suspects Hogan, but they find the POW Colonel still passed out in bed.

Program Notes: Olsen, Hogan's original "outside man" from the pilot, returns to take the place of the inexplicably missing Newkirk. John Doucette's lengthy career started as a go-to thug in several film noirs including *Ride the Pink Horse* (1947) and *Criss Cross* (1949) and he continued playing outlaws in countless TV Westerns in the 1960s. He also played the regular role of Lt. Weston in seventy-eight episodes of *Lock Up* (1959-1961).

Assessment: An original, intriguing premise is carried out in a straightforward, effective manner. Laurence Marks' script avoids the recent overkill of multiple, confusing elements and keeps the story moving at a strong pace with just the necessary details intact. There's also a nice bit involving the sneaking in of one of the guard dogs into the tunnel in order to retrieve a message from Schnitzer attached to the dog collar. The use of the body double is a good gimmick and would be revisited in season six's "Hogan's Double Life." As is the case in many a *Hogan's Heroes* caper, questions arise. If Operation Albatross is of such secret importance, would the Nazis be so brazen as to have Hogan cavort at their private party with the six fliers present? We must assume since Hogan and his men spotted the overhead fliers earlier, apparently, they want to keep Hogan under their thumb. There's also the mind stumbling fact that Carter, who recently has shown expertise with his German dialects as Hitler and various Gestapo agents, now suddenly botches his European voice skills in less than comic fashion. Sometimes with *Hogan's Heroes* you just can't have it all.

Season 3, Episode 3: "D-Day at Stalag 13" 09/23/1967.

D: Gene Reynolds W: Richard M. Powell

Guest Cast: Sigrid Valdis (Hilda), Harold Gould (Gen. Von Scheider), Gail Kobe (Lilli), John Hoyt (Gen. Bruner), Ivan Triesault (Gen. Von Katz), J. Pat O' Malley (British General).

Storyline: This story begins in London where Hogan is summoned to report to a British General regarding the upcoming D-Day Invasion on the beaches of Normandy. Since the British high command respect Hogan for his successful reputation of executing "bizarre" schemes to undermine the Germans, the General wants Hogan and his men to stall the progress of the Chief of Staff and his aides who will be convening at Stalag 13. This will allow the Allies to have the upper hand when they storm Normandy. Chief of Staff Von Scheider and his wife Lilli arrive and Klink houses them in his guest quarters. Lilli, previously an Underground contact, then married Von Scheider for unknown reasons, so London has ceased communications with her for three years. Hogan enters through the tunnel under the stove and solicits her help with the following exchange:

Hogan: "I'm working on a plan to immobilize the General Staff. I'm making them think that Hitler is replacing Von Scheider with the most incompetent colonel in the Wehrmacht just to bring the army to heel."

Lilli: "How bizarre."

Hogan: "I'm noted for that."

Klink receives a phone call with Newkirk posing as a General in Hitler's staff followed by a recording of Hitler himself (actually Kinchloe) decrying the failures of his generals and his search for a new Chief of Staff. Lilli notifies her husband while he is in conference about Hitler's newest plan, and the other generals falsely concur they too have heard the same gossip. Then Carter arrives as a

Gestapo agent to further the idea that Hitler will select Klink as Von Scheider's successor. The other generals are wary in their support of Von Scheider. Finally, Kinchloe (again as Hitler) calls Klink to give him the job and then informs Von Scheider that he will be Klink's successor as the Kommodant of Stalag 13! Von Scheider meekly accepts as Lilli walks out of the office. The Allies invade Normandy while "Chief of Staff" Klink and his crew of generals flounder with indecision, and Von Scheider sadly attempts to locate his missing wife. Lilli, now down in the tunnel, prepares to be smuggled out to England stating she leaves nothing behind.

Program Notes: The guest cast is populated with return performers including John Hoyt, Harold Gould, and J. Pat O' Malley. After a successful career as a TV actress, including three trips to *The Twilight Zone*, Gail Kobe enjoyed an even more successful career as a producer of several daytime soap operas including *The Edge of Night* (246 episodes), *The Bold and the Beautiful* (297), and *Days of our Lives* (197).

Assessment: This episode commences with an unusually strong opener set in London where the British High Command have flown Hogan in for a one hour conference regarding D-Day. Fascinating is that Hogan has now built a reputation for his elaborate and bizarre schemes to confound the Germans, while remaining a prisoner of war. There's plenty of fun to be had with the boys planting the idea that Hitler actually wants to promote "his most incompetent colonel" as his next Chief of Staff. Carter, who most recently lost his skill with German dialect, bounces back with his funny guise as the Gestapo Agent. The real strength of this episode comes from the bittersweet, dramatic turns conveyed by Gail Kobe and Harold Gould, ably achieved by director Reynolds. In his second visit, Gould is far more effective this time around and gains much audience sympathy, particularly when he has to meekly accept his "demotion" and his new reassignment from Kinchloe's Hitler. Even more touching is when he leaves his dimwitted generals behind and in a bewildered state begins a futile search for his missing wife. Gould's dramatic acting here is terrifically sincere. Equally effective are the emotions of his estranged wife, a woman who was once used by the Underground and then discarded after her marriage into the Third Reich. Whether or not she married Von Scheider for love remains a mystery, and she pulls down the curtain with much melancholic tenderness as she departs Hogan and his Heroes by "leaving nothing behind."

Season 3, Episode 4: "Sergeant Schultz Meets Mata Hari" 09/30/1967.

D: Gene Reynolds W: Laurence Marks

Guest Cast: Howard Caine (Maj. Hochstetter), Joyce Jameson (Eva Mueller), Sidney Clute (Kurt).

Storyline: Major Hochstetter grills Klink about the mysterious acts of sabotage continually occurring near Stalag 13 and warns Hogan that he will be combing every inch of the entire camp to confirm his suspicions. Hogan makes a quick departure informing the duo that he "has things to hide." Hochstetter and Klink have their men search the barracks, and when they discover a radio it turns into a practical joke. After listening to Klink's lenient disciplinary measures, Hochstetter storms out. At Gestapo HQ, Hochstetter confers with one of his female spies, Eva Mueller. He wants her to cozy up to Sgt. Schultz and milk him for information. Later, at the Hofbrau, Eva invites Schultz to her table and takes great interest in the rotund sergeant. Back at camp, Schultz is dancing on air over his new love interest which peaks Hogan's curiosity, so he has Carter sneak into town and patronize the Hofbrau. Meanwhile, Hogan is briefed by his ally Kurt about a new German factory that they plan to blow up. Carter reports to Hogan that after her date with Schultz, he witnessed Eva enter the Gestapo HQ in Hammelburg. Hogan schemes to end the romance and has Kurt enter the Hofbrau the next evening disguised as a Gestapo Agent. Kurt has Eva arrested and orders Schultz to return to Stalag 13 while Hogan's men eliminate the factory. Down in the tunnel, the POWs inform Eva that she will be enjoying a new life as a POW herself in England. Above ground, Hochstetter is dumbfounded by the mysterious arrest and disappearance of one of his prized spies.

Program Notes: Joyce Jameson returns after Hogan used her apartment to break the bank in last season's "The Great Brinksmeyer Robberty." The exterior shot of Gestapo Headquarters is actually stock footage pulled from "A Tiger Hunt in Paris." Hochstetter is outfitted in a civilian suit during this episode and not his usual Gestapo uniform. Colonel Hogan's remark, "I've got things to hide," was reworked by director Paul Schrader into *Auto Focus* (2002).

Assessment: After getting the short end of the stick in her last appearance, Joyce Jameson's second and final appearance affords her the juicy role of a Nazi femme fatale, and she plays it to the hilt. Her subtle expressions and eye rolls in response to Schultz's sweet natured, yet clumsy attempts, as a Casanova provide some lovely moments of laughter. Banner too brings effortless, boyish charm to his romantic emotions, even to the extent of dancing around the barracks while casually noticing the opening to the Heroes' tunnel entrance from within the bunk beds and warning the crew that someone might fall in! There's some priceless dialogue, too, from Klink during the barracks search when he issues the stern warning to Hogan that he will actually cancel the men's ping pong tournament, much to the slow boiling dismay of Major Hochstetter. In his third appearance as the feisty Gestapo man, Howard Caine has quickly established himself as a regular force with even more inspired antics yet to unfold.

Season 3, Episode 5: "Funny Thing Happened on the Way to London" 10/07/1967.

D: Gene Reynolds W: Laurence Marks

Guest Cast: Lloyd Bochner (Capt. Roberts/Lt. Baumann), Howard Caine (Maj. Hochstetter), Sigrid Valdis (Hilda), Peter Hellmann (Gestapo Man).

Storyline: Major Hochstetter delivers a new prisoner to Stalag 13, RAF Captain Roberts, who is ushered into Klink's private quarters. Hogan knows him and when he requests to see Roberts, Klink and Hochstetter oddly and politely comply. After disabling a hidden microphone, Hogan learns in secrecy that Roberts was imprisoned at Stalag 9 for two months where he was photographed and voice-recorded. Knowing Roberts is a personal assistant to Churchill, Hogan smells a rat. Listening in on their surveillance unit, the men discover that the Gestapo have created a double for Roberts via plastic surgery. Their plan is to get Hogan to trigger the double's escape and then he will be safely transported to England where he will assassinate the Prime Minister. Hochstetter provides a handgun holster that will be affixed to the inside forearm of the double and that will discharge upon a handshake with Churchill. The Germans will then make the real Capt. Roberts the patsy for the assassination. Hogan has his men release the real Roberts from the cooler and instead place a lifelike dummy in the cell cot. Then Roberts is smuggled out, and he meets the German drivers that will take him to an airfield thinking he is their Nazi impostor. Meanwhile, Hogan is helping the fake Roberts cut the wire for an escape, but Schultz is tipped off and captures him. The next morning, Hochstetter and Klink realize that the real Roberts has been safely flown to England and their diabolical double remains. The fake Roberts offers Hogan a handshake for being a "worthy opponent," but Hogan jerks his arm upward sending a bullet through the cap of the mortified Klink!

Program Notes: One of the most familiar faces in the annals of television, Lloyd Bochner would certainly be remembered by fans of *Dynasty* (1981-1989) for playing Cecil Colby. *Twilight Zone* trippers will instantly recall his doomed, intergalactic tourist in "To Serve Man" (1962). Nearly thirty years later, Bochner parodied that role in *The Naked Gun 2 ½: The Smell of Fear* (1990), frantically clutching a large tome and emoting: "It's a cookbook! It's a *cookbook!*"

Assessment: The old "I see double" routine is a chestnut that's been used on everything from *I Dream of Jeannie* to *Gilligan's Island*, and it functions quite smoothly at Stalag 13. Bochner is an excellent choice for portraying the duplicity and brings the appropriate amount of evil arrogance to the Mr. Hyde side of his split personality. One of the joys of this particular outing is actually seeing Klink and Hochstetter function as deviously plotting conspirators. Klink is slightly more nefarious than usual and Hochstetter is less condescending with his German ally. The scene where the duo enjoy their schnapps and accommodate Hogan's request to visit the prisoner is a rare instance of the two men in smooth collaboration. Of course, their best laid plans of mice and men are squandered again by "Hogan's Heroes," the perennial good guys of the piece.

Season 3, Episode 6: "Casanova Klink" 10/14/1967.

P/D: Edward H. Feldman W: Bill Davenport

Guest Cast: Leon Askin (Gen. Burkhalter), Kathleen Freeman (Gertrude Linkmeyer), Woodrow Parfrey (Hugo Hindmann), Carl Carlsson (Bruno/Bartender/Uncredited), Roy Goldman (POW/Unc.)

Storyline: While Schultz attempts to get the POWs to observe lights out during their poker game, the Allied Underground are dropping bombs nearby and the men make speculations as to their targets – all to the bewilderment of Schultz. Meanwhile, Klink is hosting Burkhalter and Hindmann, a Gestapo agent who has gone undercover in the Underground. Hindmann has top secret plans of a proposed Underground target, and he wants the info locked up in Klink's safe. He also informs the men that he will have the combination lock changed as a precaution. Hogan's precaution is to have the surveillance bugs removed from Klink's office. Hilda is on leave and Klink has been badgering Burkhalter for a replacement, so the next morning he delivers his sister, Gertrude. Hogan needs to insure that both Klink and Gertrude stay away from the office at nightfall, so he insists to Klink that Gertrude has actually gone undercover for the Gestapo. Hogan suggests Klink has dinner with her to keep the woman at bay. Klink complies and the boys sneak in to the office so Newkirk can have a crack at the safe. After some difficulty, Hindmann's papers are photographed revealing that an oil refinery is the target, and Hindmann has directed the squadron guarding an ammo dump to be moved to the refinery instead. Hogan, with the help of Newkirk, tips off the Underground that Hindmann is actually a Nazi plant, and they need to switch targets. The next night the boys are again playing poker and Schultz is again trying to enforce the lights out rule when an explosion is heard. Again Schultz is mystified when the POWs inform him that the Germans just lost their ammo dump.

Program Notes: This is the second of four visits from Kathleen Freeman as Burkhalter's sister, Gertrude. Freeman found herself playing the gun moll mama of Fred Ward in *The Naked Gun 33 1/3: The Final Insult* (1994) at the latter stage of her long, comic career.

Gifted comic actress Kathleen Freeman returns for her second trip to Stalag 13 as Gen. Burkhalter's lovelorn sister, Gertrude Linkmeyer. Author's collection/CBS Television Inc.

Assessment: Underdeveloped seems to be the major symptom undermining the effectiveness of another Bill Davenport contribution. The presence of Gertrude, her romantic designs on Klink, and Klink's abject fear of the notion only get slight development. Sadly, Kathleen Freeman isn't on screen enough to further the plot line, and she shares even less time with Klemperer for any of it to gel. It's really just a subplot in order to get the two out of the office and to get Newkirk's fingers on the safe dial. The other subplot involving Hugo Hindmann also suffers from lack of action; we never see him pretending to be a collaborator with the Underground. We only get a final glimpse of this interaction when Hogan calls them up and speaks to each Underground member individually while Newkirk tries to identify which voice is the rat, which is another thin thread of logic. Still, the overall proceedings are brightened by the old hands at the game, which includes some snappy exchanges between Askin and Freeman and Crane and Klemperer. Yet these are just some of the few, brighter threads found in a somewhat trite tapestry.

Season 3, Episode 7: "How To Win Friends and Influence Nazis" 10/21/1967.

D: Bob Sweeney W: Phil Sharp

Guest Cast: Leon Askin (Gen. Burkhalter), Karl Swenson (Karl Svenson), Edward Knight (Herr Grosser), Doris Singleton (Magda Tischler).

Storyline: Dr. Karl Svenson is ushered into camp by General Burkhalter. The Swedish scientist is developing a metal that is lighter yet stronger than any before, a great benefit to the German war effort. Burkhalter wants Klink to keep the scientist happy so he will quickly finish his development plan. Klink acts chummy with Hogan in front of Svenson, and Hogan uses this to his advantage. He influences Klink to let him and his men accompany Svenson and Klink into Hammelburg and an overnight stay at a hotel. Back at camp, Kinchloe telephones Klink's hotel room and pretends to be Burkhalter. He orders the Kommodant back to camp. The men aid Schultz, their watchdog, into falling asleep, and Hogan changes into a civilian suit. He visits Svenson with a rigged, explosive fountain pen to eliminate the doctor. When Svenson explains his political neutrality, Hogan decides to take him into the lounge instead, where Svenson becomes enamored with the lounge singer, Magda Tischler. Hogan wants to stall the doctor's progress, so he approaches the singer pretending to be a Hollywood talent scout. He is able to connect the singer with the scientist. Later, Burkhalter and Herr Grosser of the Gestapo bristle that the doctor has halted his research because he is spending all his time with his new love. Svenson returns to Stalag 13 with Magda who is now set to become the doctor's fourth wife! Furious at the development, Grosser has them held for treason at Stalag 13 and leaves to make his report to Berlin. Hogan manages to slip Carter's deadly fountain pen into the departing staff car. After a terrific explosion, Hogan's men smuggle

Svenson and Magda out through the escape tunnel while Hogan explains away their departure to the attentive Klink and Burkhalter.

Program Notes: Doris Singleton first caught the eye of the American public in the recurring role of Caroline Appleby on *I Love Lucy*, figuring prominently into the plot of the classic "Lucy and Harpo Marx" episode (1955). Their professional friendship would continue with several episodes of *The Lucy Show* and *Here's Lucy*.

Assessment: Phil Sharp's script is tough to dislike, but the weight of its implausibilities threaten to tumble the house of cards. First, we get the ridiculous notion of Klink allowing Hogan and three of his men to all enjoy a hotel vacation at the expense of the Third Reich. Then we get Schultz promptly falling asleep after a few staged yawns. When will Klink learn to assign someone *other than Schultz* to guard his POWs? Suddenly, and inexplicably, we find Newkirk posing as a cocktail server in the lounge, an absurd and superfluous element added to the story. Finally, we get Hogan blatantly slipping the lethal pen into Grosser's staff car in front of everyone imaginable and the requisite cover up dialogue that Klink and Burkhalter are too eager to accept. It's unfortunate because the basic story is serviceable and we get a nice change of pace setting in the hotel lounge and even a song number from the delightful Doris Singleton. Here, yet again, is a caper that tends to confound the viewer by consuming too many extreme notions and leaving a sour aftertaste, an aftertaste clearly shared by Richard Dawson who cannot hide his disdain as Bob Crane obligatorily kisses the bride for the flimsy finish!

Season 3, Episode 8: "Nights in Shining Armor" 10/28/1967.

D: Gene Reynolds W: Laurence Marks

Guest Cast: Leon Askin (Gen. Burkhalter), Felice Orlandi (Maurice Dubois), Sigrid Valdis (Hilda), Chris Anders (Capt. Franz).

Storyline: An emergency call from London requests Hogan to retrieve a parachute drop late at night. The drop yields a crate loaded with bulletproof vests intended for the French resistance. Too heavy to move, the men have the contents buried and transport one vest back to camp. The next day, Maurice Dubois surrenders at the front gate and is brought to Klink, who secures him in the cooler. Hogan learns that Dubois is trying to recover the vests which the French were forced to drop because of swarming German patrols. As Kinchloe fixes the plumbing in the barracks, Hogan gets inspired. He has Kinch tamper with the pipes under Klink's quarters which sends a spray of water into the Kommodant's face the next morning. Furious, Klink finds he is without a plumber until Hogan informs him that the French prisoner Dubois has plumbing skills. Klink demands Dubois repair the pipes, and Hogan has Kinch crawl under the building with Dubois to begin the job. Kinch fills in Dubois on what to say and the Frenchman tells Klink that the pressure valve needs a major repair. They set him up in the workshop building, an opportunity to sneak over the bulletproof vest. Dubois pretends it is his invention and, impressed, Klink invites Burkhalter to observe a demonstration. The general wants Dubois to show the vest to Hitler. The Germans load a truck with all the vests, and Capt. Franz is directed to take Dubois and the cargo to Berlin. En route, Carter stops the truck posing as a sentry guard, and the others force Franz to yield his travel orders and his uniform. Dubois departs now posing as Franz with the valuable vests. Klink wonders how Franz, the Frenchman, and the valuable cargo vanished.

Program Notes: Felice Orlandi as Maurice Dubois continues his association with the series with two more third season appearances to follow in rapid succession. In the 1975 Charles Bronson film, *Hard Times,* Orlandi played the role of Lebeau!

Assessment: The water works flow with relative ease in a well appointed story that finally moves Kinchloe into the foreground, but clogs up as it progresses. The plumbing ploy is a clever one and results in two requisite slapstick moments, naturally at the expense of Colonel Klink. Serviceable is the action revolving around the bulletproof vests, although how they get transported from the woods and into the workshop is foggy at best ("We moved them in last night," Hogan explains away in a few seconds). Meanwhile, the Nazis kindly accept that Dubois is able to manufacture dozens of these vests in a couple of days. Inevitably, confused elements develop including a solo officer left in charge of delivering a captured inventor and their precious cargo to Hitler, the pistol that Dubois wields out of thin air, a Frenchman now posing as a German Luftwaffe officer, and the implementation of Carter as a sentry guard. Whether or not the boys hijacked a guard's sentry station or constructed it like a theatrical set piece are left to the viewers' discretion.

Memorable Consensus:

Klink: "That's exactly what I was thinking, Herr General."

Burkhalter: "I knew you would be the moment I mentioned it."

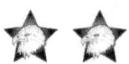

Season 3, Episode 9: "Hot Money" 11/04/1967.

D: Bob Sweeney W: Laurence Marks

Guest Cast: Sandy Kenyon (SS Major Bock), Jon Cedar (Herman Stoffel).

Storyline: Late at night, the men observe through the rain barrel periscope, a German staff car and truck pull into the compound. The next day, Newkirk runs a craps game, and Schultz starts betting big using American fifty dollar bills and then British five pound notes. On close examination, Kinchloe discovers they are fakes, and the men realize that Stalag 13 will now be hosting a counterfeit money operation under the supervision of Major Bock. Newkirk is instructed to forge Klink's signature on a bulletin board notice which is brought to the attention of Klink and Bock. After Hogan is dismissed, Newkirk confides that he wants to get in on the counterfeit racket with the Germans. Klink tosses him out and Bock cautions Klink that they cannot report the incident to Berlin because he is entirely responsible for the success of the operation with his own life on the line. Their conversation is recorded on the Heroes' sewing machine device. Hogan plots to dismantle the works by targeting Bock's key operative, Herman Stoffel, who disapproves of the counterfeit project. Kinchloe reedits the transcript while a note is slipped to Stoffel stating that "a friend" urges him to visit Barracks Three for his safety. Stoffel takes the bait, and Hogan plays the new version of the recording which now has Bock stating that Stoffel's life will be expendable once the project is completed. Agreeing to Hogan's plan, Stoffel starts a fire in the printing room and tosses a few smoke bombs into the mix. The POWs rush in as firefighters and haphazardly destroy the money plates and everything in sight, effectively putting the Nazis out of the hot money business.

Program Notes: Jon Cedar abandons the role of Corporal Langenscheidt for this particular episode. Sandy Kenyon returns for his third of five guest appearances.

Assessment: An intriguing premise receives an adequate presentation before slowly falling apart in the final minutes. The strongest gimmick of the half hour is the doctoring of the recorded conversation between Klink and Bock, a clever ruse that would be resurrected at the tail end of the series in "Klink for the Defense." Jon Cedar is promoted to a larger supporting role and offers a sympathetic take as the German money man clearly working against his own moral code. The scene where he takes the bait and meekly enters the men's barracks, along with the chilly, aloof reception by LeBeau, is quietly effective. Once again, the boys absurdly man the water buckets and fire axes for another fiery conclusion. The caprice of having the prisoners act as firefighters and blatantly destroy the currency plates while none of the German soldiers do a damn thing about it is grossly the most counterfeit element in this tale of counterfeit cash. More ironic, or moronic, is Klink's acceptance of the net result and his gratefulness to the prisoners for their skill in handling the fire!

Season 3, Episode 10: "One in Every Crowd" 11/11/1967.

D: Bob Sweeney W: Laurence Marks

Guest Cast: Paul Picerni (Jack Williams), John Stephenson (Felix), Barbara Babcock (Maria Schmidt), John Crawford (Capt. Hermann).

Storyline: Newkirk catches Williams cheating at poker in the barracks and a fist fight breaks out until Hogan busts it up. When Williams protests, Hogan snaps that he knows Williams has been stealing Red Cross packages and "selling them to the Krauts for money." Capt. Hermann arrives needing a new fuel pump for his truck which is transporting a new field gun. London orders Hogan to destroy the field gun. Williams attempts an escape at nightfall but is caught by Schultz and a guard. In private conference with Klink, Williams bargains to sell out Hogan's operation in exchange for money and safe relocation. The men overhear the dialogue, and while Klink considers the deal he moves Williams to the cooler. Carter overhears Williams provide some info to Klink regarding the recent destruction of a German bridge. Hogan's plan is to somehow destroy the field gun and pin it on Williams. Underground operative "Felix" poses as "Major Weber" and presents fake orders from Berlin regarding the Williams deal. A fake phone call sends Klink on a wild goose chase to meet General Burkhalter in Berlin leaving "Major Weber" in charge. Weber releases Williams and has him dictate everything he knows concerning the clandestine operations of Hogan, while Weber's secretary Maria takes down all the information for Williams' signature. Unknowingly, Williams also signs off some additional doctored info. Weber turns over all the signed papers to Hogan then instructs Schultz that he must leave for Berlin, and he leaves the phony signed papers for Klink's return. Klink discovers the Underground plans to blow up an arms factory in Hammelburg, and he races his entire squadron to the site to prevent the disaster. With the camp near empty, Carter rigs an explosive to destroy the field gun while the boys force Williams over to the Underground, who will see that he is tried as a traitor. Later, Hogan turns over Williams' jacket to Klink and Capt. Hermann effectively framing him as the escaped, yet tragic, saboteur.

Program Notes: The former Mayor of Tarzana, CA, Paul Picerni, flew twenty-five combat missions in WWII and was the bombardier that helped destroy the real bridge inspiring *The Bridge on the River Kwai*. In his long acting career, Picerni lent support to Robert Stack as Lee Hobson in ninety-three episodes of *The Untouchables*, (1959-1963).

Assessment: With most of the sillier hi-jinks removed, Laurence Marks offers a smart script that recaptures the tension of *Stalag 17*, aided and abetted by the excellent grit provided by guest star Paul Picerni. Things simmer with a skillful, tough opener in which Newkirk busts Williams for dealing Kings off the bottom of the deck, and this leads to a well choreographed right cross and ensuing barracks brawl. The story unfolds in a logical, credible progression that includes the smart inclusion of John Stephenson as a fake Nazi and Barbara Babcock as his attractive assistant. Three guest performers are allowed to move the plotting forward in Klink's office, an unusual yet successful approach. (This method would be revisited in the final season outing, "The Gestapo Takeover.") As is often the case, the familiar wrap up with Hogan explaining away the field gun destruction is weak and undermines the preceding logic of the piece. Why would a man ready to bargain with the Nazis suddenly turn to sabotage? Are we to assume that Williams himself blew up in the explosion, but his jacket survived intact? How in the world did Williams get his hands on those explosives to trigger his cooler escape? Best not to dwell on the little details, I suppose, when so much of this episode moves in the right direction.

Season 3, Episode 11: "Is General Hammerschlag Burning?" 11/18/1967.

P/D: Edward H. Feldman W: Richard M. Powell

Guest Cast: Barbara McNair (Kumasa/Carol Dukes), Paul Lambert (Gen. Hammerschlag), Felice Orlandi (Maurice Dubois), Dave Morick (Aide).

Storyline: Maurice Dubois is welcomed back to the barracks hoping to secure the defense plans for Paris that are in the possession of General Hammerschlag. Hitler has ordered the total destruction of Paris if the Nazis are no longer able to defend it, and the Hammerschlag plans are vital to the French Resistance. The general has been enjoying the charms of Kumasa, a night club singer in Paris. She also moonlights as a mystic, claiming she can communicate with the spirit of Otto Von Bismarck, first chancellor of the German Empire. Dubois thinks the key to the plan is to go through her, and he suggests that Kinchloe go on the mission since he actually went to the same Detroit high school with Kumasa! To hitch a ride to Paris, Hogan sends Klink a fake letter congratulating him as "The German Soldier of the Month," which includes lodging at the hotel and lounge where Kumasa sings. Hogan and Kinchloe tag along, dressed respectively as a busboy and doorman, jobs set up by Dubois. In Paris, Kinchloe is reunited with his former schoolmate who resents the idea of being used in order to secure the defense plans from Hammerschlag. She decides to stay neutral for the moment. Hammerschlag arrives and Kinchloe introduces Hogan as a mute French busboy, who when under a trance can regain his speech and communicate with the spirit of Bismark. The oddball duo, with the help of Kumasa, are able to rig a séance for the general, a ruse to switch out his war plans and have them photographed and returned, all while the busboy carries on a spirited conversation with Bismark.

Program Notes: In order to bribe Schultz to let them go to France, Hogan references the last time they went to Paris: "A Tiger Hunt in Paris" (parts one and two). In her first encounter with Kinchloe, Kumasa calls him "*Ivan* Kinchloe," and not "James."

Assessment: Producer/Director Feldman steers a lively, high spirited adventure that draws on concepts from Hogan's previous trip to Paris, including the Nazi officer infatuated with a female mystic. Ivan Dixon gets a welcome return to center stage and shows his cool smoothness in his scenes with Barbara McNair, who brings plenty of snap and sincerity to her role of "Kumasa," a woman who has hooked up with a Nazi general to afford a better deal in life. The novelty of having Hogan play a mute is an ironic twist for the regularly loose-lipped, fast-talking colonel and this leads to the funniest sequence of the night when he rediscovers his lost speech during the séance. While Dubois bicycles off with the war plans in a cylinder to have them photographed and returned, Hogan must stall the proceedings and does so by becoming a loudmouthed, brash American who not only openly talks with Otto Von Bismark but continually derides Hitler and his specific war campaigns! He rants on and on like a boorish party guest that won't shut up, and Crane plays it to the hilt in one of his funniest scenes from the entire series. Once again, Klink endures another miserable trip to Paris. As the busboy, Hogan unceremoniously dumps a bucket of mop water at Klink's legs then giddily comments on the gag to Kinchloe as if Crane the actor is commentating on the script for its comic worth. Klemperer enjoys an inspired exchange with guest Paul Lambert that includes some priceless dialogue regarding Klink's selection as "German Soldier of the Month." "Ridiculous, isn't it?" Klink admits. How the gang produces a gimmick cylinder perfectly matching the one they had never laid eyes on before doesn't stall the funny train during this raucous round trip to Paris.

Best war campaign analysis:

Hogan: (under a trance) "Stalingrad! A classic case of bungling! Classic!"

Season 3, Episode 12: "A Russian is Coming" 11/25/1967.

D: Bob Sweeney W: Phil Sharp

Guest Cast: Leon Askin (Gen. Burkhalter), Bob Hastings (Igor Piotkin), Felice Orlandi (Maurice Dubois), Bard Stevens (German officer).

Storyline: Maurice Dubois and his Underground friends deliver a tied-up package to Hogan, a Russian pilot whose plane had engine trouble and was forced to land. They have him bound since the confused Russian put up an awful struggle. Hogan wants the pilot transferred to London, but the Russian will only accept going back home to his country. Burkhalter informs Klink of the missing pilot and orders him to take charge of the search parties. Hogan visits Klink as the Kommodant is plotting a mapped strategy to recover the pilot. Klink receives a call from Lt. Huber, an aide to Field Marshall Von Gruneke, who rudely pushes Klink for his progress in the search. Klink is furious that a lieutenant dares to berate his efforts, but Hogan claims he is the nephew of Von Gruneke. Hogan has Kinchloe run a telephone line from Klink's phone into the barracks, and Hogan calls Klink pretending to be Lt. Huber. He further insults Klink and threatens to take over the operation. Then Kinchloe phones, pretending to be Von Gruneke, and states his nephew is a thief, a deserter, and a disgrace. The men disguise Igor, the Russian, as a German officer and bring him to Klink as "Lt. Huber." Klink exacts his revenge by stating that Huber will be immediately transferred to the Russian Front. The fake Huber is hustled out, Klink is delighted that justice is served, and Hogan is satisfied that the Russian will return home.

Program Notes: This concludes the fourth and final appearance of Felice Orlandi as the recurring character, Maurice Dubois. Bob Hastings will always be remembered as Lt. Elroy Carpenter on *McHale's Navy* (1962-1966). In later years, he regularly voiced the character of Commissioner Gordon for numerous animated *Batman* series. The episode title is a reference to the 1966 Norman Jewison release *The Russians Are Coming, The Russians Are Coming* which featured Alan Arkin as the primary Russian.

Assessment: Bob Hastings gives this most playful episode a spark with his feisty Russian characterization. It's refreshing to see a chapter in the playbook that's not based on death or destruction but on simply performing a good gesture, in this case, getting the Russian pilot back home. Most of this script centers on an elaborate practical joke where Hogan assumes the telephone identity of Lt. Huber, enough to infuriate the Kommodant and to get a motivation for the Russian to suit up as a German. As usual, Klemperer balances his performance with the appropriate amount of disdain (being bullied by a lieutenant) and glee (exacting revenge). There's also a well-paced routine with Schultz going one over on a bed count of ten, then returning for a second count and getting a total of *nine*. The slow burn that Banner gives Crane as he exits the first time is a slice of subtle delight.

Season 3, Episode 13: "An Evening of Generals" 12/02/1967.

D: Bob Sweeney W: Laurence Marks

Guest Cast: Leon Askin (Gen. Burkhalter), John Hoyt (Gen. Bruner), Maurice Marsac (Sgt. Jacques Mornay), Ben Wright (Gen. Felix Mercer).

Storyline: Burkhalter informs Klink that a war conference with several branch generals attending is scheduled. Klink is to host an opening night banquet at a hotel in Hammelburg while Burkhalter is detained in Berlin. Kinchloe informs Hogan that London wants all of the generals eliminated because their meeting involves the distribution of war plans for a major offensive. Hogan recruits Sgt. Mornay of the Free French to pose as the caterer for the banquet and sets him up with forged papers which satisfy Klink. Carter devises several timer bombs disguised as German centerpiece decorations which Mornay will move into place when preparing the room prior to the banquet dinner. Hogan learns that Felix Mercer will also be in attendance, and that he is actually an Allied spy, so London aborts the mission. Unfortunately, the timer bombs have already been set so the men must find a way to remove the deadly centerpieces. At the banquet, Lebeau and the others serve as assistants to the caterer, Mornay, while Hogan must pull Mercer away from the party. He has Mornay and LeBeau start a loud argument in French which disrupts the meeting. General Bruner sends Mercer into the kitchen knowing his command of French. Hogan quickly fills in Mercer about the fake centerpieces, and he immediately discovers the time bombs upon his return which evacuates the room. Mercer leaves behind his copy of the war plans deliberately, and LeBeau is able to remove them before the big explosion occurs.

Program Notes: British born actor Ben Wright begins his five episode association with the series. He was a guest star fixture on countless classic television programs including: *The Twilight Zone* (three appearances), *Gunsmoke* (eleven), *Have Gun – Will Travel* (six), and *The Outer Limits* (four). Maurice Marsac was last seen as "The Scientist" in season one. *Kolchak: The Night Stalker* fans may recognize Marsac from his guest shot in the exemplary "The Spanish Moss Murders."

The presence of Gen. Burkhalter at the onset of any episode usually dictates the general plot to follow. Case in point, Askin and Klemperer in "An Evening of Generals." Author's collection/CBS Television Inc.

Assessment: A race against time bomb is at the suspenseful center of this well crafted tale that plays more like a WWII drama and less like a situation comedy. Plenty of strong details keep the story moving, especially Carter's expertly disguised time bombs as Nazi centerpiece decorations, and a tense moment when Klink unwittingly handles one in the men's barracks. Hogan's rapid fire, innate sense of problem solving is on display, particularly late in the game when he orchestrates the kitchen fight in French, and instructs Mercer on how to clear a room with a bomb ready to blow. Well handled, also, is the extra attention lent to the caper's development as Mornay and the others study the map to the hotel during their plotting phase. Show biz veterans Ben Wright, Maurice Marsac, and John Hoyt all lend authenticity to the proceedings. The only gripe one can really harbor with this episode is that it could be accused of being not funny enough, but in a series where frequent silliness abounds, the straight and narrow approach can also bring sitcom relief.

Season 3, Episode 14: "Everybody Loves a Snowman" 12/09/1967.

D: Bob Sweeney W: Arthur Julian

Guest Cast: Sigrid Valdis (Hilda), Howard Caine (Major Hochstetter), Noam Pitlik (Capt. Morgan), Robert Pickering (Lt. Rosen).

Storyline: Carter and Newkirk barely smuggle in a crew of five into the barracks under a blanket of snowfall. Major Hochstetter arrives and informs Klink that a bomber crew attacked Gestapo headquarters, and he believes they could be hiding out in Stalag 13 until they can safely move out. He begins a search of every building, but Hogan throws him off the trail by building a fake tunnel under a sink and allowing the Major to discover it. Meanwhile, Capt. Morgan and his men challenge Hogan about wanting to leave camp immediately. Hogan, building on a suggestion from Carter, insists they must first build a snowman, which will mask a new tunnel. The men begin to build the snowman while also creating a tunnel underneath which will connect to an existing tunnel. Schultz stops in the barracks and notices that Newkirk and Carter are sweating profusely from their tunnel digging. The men all pretend it is uncomfortably hot in the barracks and pull off their shirts and open the windows. Schultz reports the strange behavior to Klink and Hochstetter, who investigate the barracks and find the POWs all huddled and shivering. Later, the bomber crew is slowly moved out via the snowman tunnel, but Schultz spots the maneuver and again reports it. The men successfully move the snowman several feet over and when Hochstetter investigates, he finds himself trapped within its snowy interior.

Program Notes: Last seen as "The Informer," the title character of the pilot episode, Noam Pitlik returns for his second of seven guest appearances. The usual opening shot of the guards patrolling at the front gate, just after the conclusion of the credit sequence, is now replaced with a new shot of the same guards surrounded by snowfall.

Assessment: Likability is the key factor to the success of this Yuletide season episode, despite containing one of the most absurd of escape solutions. Major Hochstetter receives his first extended guest appearance and Howard Caine makes the most of every featured minute. The best bit involves the discovery of the fake tunnel under a very theatrical roll-away sink, and a nice, tightly framed close up of Klink and Hochstetter inspecting the dirt under Carter's fingernails. There's also some nice dramatic tension with a crotchety Noam Pitlik attempting mutiny with his crew, and Kinchloe and the regulars defending their colonel's instructions. Sigrid Valdis benefits from some extra footage outside of her usual opening the door and announcing Hogan's visit. Although wildly illogical, the snowman escape tunnel receives a strong bill of goods, supported by some extended footage of the men's tunneling efforts and the subsequent doubts of Schultz as to why the men are perspiring their way through a winter's day. Better yet, is the moment where Schultz breaks up an argument concerning the face decorating of the snowman between the childlike Carter and LeBeau, Hogan likening Schultz to King Solomon (!), and the sergeant's unexpected return and memorable exclamation: "There's some monkey business going on in the snowman!" Hochstetter stands in for Klink for the slapstick finale where the Major and the Snowman merge into one.

Season 3, Episode 15: "The Hostage" 12/16/1967.

P/D: Edward H. Feldman W: Richard M. Powell

Guest Cast: Nita Talbot (Marya), Theodore Marcuse (Gen. Friedrich Von Heiner).

Storyline: Klink is summoned to counsel with General Von Heiner and his lady friend, Marya, the "White Russian." Von Heiner is displeased that Klink is sitting in the middle of Underground sabotage activity and has done nothing to curb it. Von Heiner is having a rocket fuel depot built just outside the camp and wants to use it as a trap to lure saboteurs. The following day in Klink's office, Von Heiner confronts Hogan by showing him a map with the fuel depot location and baits Hogan for his response. Von Heiner discovers a listening device and the Germans attempt to trace the source, but Kinchloe severs the wire. That night, Hogan and LeBeau sneak out of camp and visit Marya at her hotel to press her for information. Their efforts are aborted with the unexpected arrival of Von Heiner and they hastily depart. Hogan decides to proceed with the destruction of the fuel depot, and the men tunnel up underneath the site and place a large explosive in position. Hogan orders the tunnel back filled with dirt so that no one will be able to stop the timer explosion if Hogan is apprehended and his men must evacuate. Von Heiner orders Hogan taken to the fuel depot and imprisoned under guard as a hostage. Hogan pretends to crack and reveals to Von Heiner a fake game plan involving an Underground attack from the woods. Marya suggests that Hogan, a wealth of information, be returned to Stalag 13, while Von Heiner and his battalion ambush the impending offensive. Hogan, Marya, and Schultz all return to camp and hit the dirt right at 2000 hours as the depot explodes before the amazed eyes of Klink.

Program Notes: Nita Talbot returns as the "White Russian," as Kinchloe dubs her in reference to Hogan and LeBeau's earlier assignment in Paris. Talbot received a Prime Time Emmy Award nomination for her role in this episode in 1968 ("Best Supporting Actress in a Comedy Series"). The award went, posthumously, to actress Marion Lorne, who played Aunt Clara on *Bewitched*. Theo Marcuse closes out his three installment commitment with the series.

Assessment: The team of writer Powell and big boss Feldman create a terrific package that combines some of the best comical and suspenseful elements associated with the series, along with another race against time bomb. Marya, last residing in Paris, blasts her way back into the program and is now hanging around the bedroom of a new Nazi general. Boy, does this gal get around! Her final moments with Hogan, lying on the ground of the compound after the big noise, showcase the wonderful energy of this inspired actress. There's some cute shenanigans involving LeBeau flirting with Marya from underneath the flexible doghouse, and a fun bit where Klink, Schultz, and Von Heiner attempt to follow the wire leading from a bug discovered in the Kommodant's office. Hogan keeps pace with a largely serious dramatic tone, genuinely worried about the safety of his team in case the unpredictable Russian has sold out the operation. The big boost comes from Theo Marcuse, who completes his orders with his best characterization yet, the deliberately oily and scheming Von Heiner, a real counterpart, of sorts, to Hogan's own scheming mind. Marcuse assumes the Erich Von Stroheim approach to the role leaving an indelible Nazi impression. The ransacking of the men's barracks has a strong WWII movie-feel to it. Further impressive are the latter moments with Hogan and his engaging in a little philosophy with Schultz in order to remove their tails from impending danger. Least impressive is the beyond silly wrap up where Hogan convinces Klink, but not the viewers, that Schultz possesses powers of ESP, a plot worked to death in forthcoming, less inspired adventures.

Season 3, Episode 16: "Carter Turns Traitor" 12/23/1967.

D: Howard Morris W: Richard Powell

Guest Cast: Antoinette Bower (Leni Richter), John Myhers (Gen. Wittkamper).

Storyline: Hogan has his POWs stage a deadly sneak attack on Carter before the disbelieving eyes of Schultz. The men are taken to Klink and during questioning it slips out that before he was captured, Carter was actually a Major working on chemical warfare projects. Carter has considered switching sides which has incurred the hostility of the other prisoners. Klink dismisses the others and keeps Carter close to his side, planning to recruit a local general specializing in chemical warfare projects to interrogate Carter. The whole plan is Hogan's ruse so they can learn the location of the Nazis' new chemical plant. Gen. Wittkamper and his fetching escort, Leni Richter, arrive and attempt to smooth talk Carter in Klink's quarters. Once Carter is alone, the men appear through the tunnel underneath the wood stove and Hogan removes a cocktail glass that Leni poured for Carter. The libation burns a hole through LeBeau's cap. The men disappear and as Leni returns, she is amazed that Carter is still alive. Hogan, now fearing for Carter's life, produces a "note" Carter wrote claiming he made his story up. Wittkamper doesn't buy it and orders Carter transported to the chemical plant permanently. Hogan and his Heroes disguise themselves as a hooded Gestapo execution team and halt the general's staff car outside of camp. The masked Hogan claims that one of the general's party is a traitor to the Third Reich. Leni comes forward admitting that she is a member of the resistance, and that she has purposely been delaying the general's chemical progress. Schultz is ordered to take Carter back to camp while Hogan makes new travel plans for Leni and Wittkamper.

Program Notes: This is the debut for German born Antoinette Bower, who played the role of "Fox Devlin" on *Neon Rider*. Bower frequently guest starred on such programs as *The Fugitive*, *Mannix*, and *Mission: Impossible*, during her very prolific career. John Myhers was last seen as the kidnapped and confused Field Marshall Von Heinke from season two's "The General Swap."

Assessment: The boyish, happy-go-lucky charm of Larry Hovis captures the spotlight in an outing that kicks off with the zany sequence of the men pretending to stalk Carter as each of our Heroes stroll by Schultz with their weapon of choice in tow. It's almost a literal send up of the board game, *Clue*. The men's unique tunnel entrance into Klink's quarters, the roll away wood stove, gets some nice attention as well. The crew share a warm sequence late in the game when they suit up as Gestapo hoods down in the tunnel, and all band together to go rescue their boy, Carter. There's also a bit of grim intensity during Carter's rescue as the men pose as the hooded execution team, prompting a hilarious confession of treason out of Schultz. It also prompts guest starlet Antoinette Bower to deliver an impassioned monologue explaining her duplicity while other guest star, John Myhers, appears to duplicate the disparity and confusion of his last visit to Stalag 13.

Season 3, Episode 17: "Two Nazis for the Price of One" 12/30/1967.

D: Bruce Bilson W: Phil Sharp

Guest Cast: Howard Caine (Major Hochstetter), Alan Oppenheimer (Herman Freitag), Jon Cedar (Col. Mannheim), Barbro Hedstrom (Ilse Praeger).

Storyline: Hogan is summoned to the office of Klink by Major Hochstetter, who attempts to get the senior POW to divulge information about the Manhattan Project. Hogan offers nothing but wisecracks, despite the Major knowing about Hogan's command of the 504th Airborne prior to his capture. Hogan smells a rat at Allied HQ in London, and has Kinchloe contact Allied command with a message regarding an attempt to detonate Hitler's private train, which prompts the spy to stir to action and reveal his identity. The London spy was working for Gestapo Gruppenfuhrer, Herman Freitag, and this man now knows all about Hogan's operation. Later, Klink tells Hogan that they both have been requested to join Freitag for dinner. Freitag quickly dismisses Klink and his snooping aide, Mannheim, while Freitag and his sexy lady friend, Ilse Praeger, attempt to extort info out of Hogan. Freitag attempts to barter with Hogan in exchange for a trip to Switzerland and $50,000 in a Swiss account. He presses Hogan for any facts about the Manhattan Project. To stall, Hogan says he needs to cut a deal for his four operatives back at camp. The men make a deal, and Freitag abruptly cancels the dinner plans. The following day, Freitag appears at Stalag 13 and orders Hochstetter to contact Berlin stating that he will soon possess top secret information regarding the Manhattan Project. Freitag waits in Klink's office for Hogan to arrive but receives some unexpected, unfriendly fire from Mannheim, his disgruntled aide. Klink's outer office turns into target practice until Hochstetter arrests Mannheim, and Hogan is satisfied knowing that the secrets surrounding his operations have departed along with the recently departed Freitag.

Program Notes: What television series has veteran actor Alan Oppenheimer not guest starred on? It's hard to single out his work considering he's still working as a professional voice actor as of 2021. Many of us will remember him as Dr. Rudy Wells on *The Six Million Dollar Man*. *Happy Days* fans will certainly single out his turn as Ralph's daddy, Mickey Malph, in the 1976 installment: "A.K.A. the Fonz." This signifies the debut of director Bruce Bilson, who would helm twenty-five episodes. Bilson was working as a regular director on *Get Smart* when he made the call to Edward Feldman to enlist at Stalag 13. He continued to direct episodes for both series for the next year. Bilson explained how he first became involved with the series: *

I didn't get a phone call, I made a phone call. I was working on Get Smart, things were going well, and I knew Hogan's Heroes looked like a really good show. So I called my friend Ed Feldman and I said: "I'd love to direct your show." Ed said: "OK, Bruce, I tell you what. You send me a print of an episode of Get Smart that you're really proud of and then send me the original script." And that's what I did. And nobody else ever did that, not in my experience. The way he hired me. Nobody did that! They might say, "Show me your work," but not "Show me the script." Never.

Guest star, Alan Oppenheimer, (about his initial hiring process): **

I remember when I read for them the first time it was certainly among the first shows that I did when I came out here in the summer of 1966 . . . I read for them and they said, "Thank you very much," and I left, and one of the guys came running out to the elevator and said, "Will you come back here please?" I came back and they said, "You're not right for this part, but we have a part coming up that we'd like you to do." And, I said, "Sure." So maybe it was two or three weeks later, I played my first Nazi.

Guest stars Jon Cedar (left) and Alan Oppenheimer make a decidedly unusual duo in the aptly titled, "Two Nazis For the Price of One," an episode that marked the debuts of both actor Oppenheimer and director Bruce Bilson's successful associations with the series. For Cedar, it was a nice departure from his signature role of Corporal Langenscheidt. Photo courtesy of Alan Oppenheimer/CBS Television Inc.

Assessment: Bruce Bilson supervises a completely original addition to the series and brings a lot of punch to his premiere directing assignment. The program kicks off with a brightly humorous Q & A segment in Klink's office, in which Hogan and Hochstetter appear to be comic strip characters taken directly out of *Mad* magazine and one of Al Jaffee's "Mad's Snappy Answers to Stupid Questions." A clever, novelty prop crops up when the men need to install a larger antenna to the rooftop of Klink's office, and do so in the shape of a swastika. The casting is quite strong in this one, with memorable turns from Alan Oppenheimer as a conniving Kraut, Barbro Hedstrom as a femme fatale fraulein, and Jon Cedar, in his most offbeat role yet, as an unhinged underling. The shoot 'em up finale in Klink's outer office is wildly funny with Schultz deliberately losing his rifle, and Colonel Hogan, the perennial prankster, tricking Klink into walking into direct gunfire just for the hell of it.

*Telephone interview with the author, October 26, 2020.
**Telephone interview with the author, November 27, 2020.

Season 3, Episode 18: "Is There a Doctor in the House" 01/06/1968.

P/D: Edward H. Feldman W: Arthur Julian

Guest Cast: Sigrid Valdis (Hilda/Uncredited), Leon Askin (Gen. Burkhalter), Anthony Eustrel (Dr. Kronk), Brenda Benet (Janine Robinet), Roy Goldman (POW/Uncredited), and Howard Caine as (Major Hochstetter).

Storyline: Hogan welcomes through the emergency tunnel the beautiful, young French woman, Janine Robinet, who the men will help transport to London. Her beauty quickly becomes the object of affection for both LeBeau and Newkirk. Hogan's plan is to have Janine smuggled out of camp in the trunk of Klink's car when the Kommodant leaves for a staff meeting in Mendelburg. The next day, Schultz informs Hogan that there will be no roll call because Klink has taken ill. Hogan expresses concern that the Kommodant will miss his staff meeting and goes to visit the Kommodant. Burkhalter arrives and suspects Hogan of reading Klink "bedtime stories." He explains that Major Hochstetter will arrive soon in search of a missing girl from the French Underground and plans to send Klink to a rest camp for his recovery. Kinchloe radios London and has them parachute a medical supply box with penicillin. They go to Klink's quarters and persuade him to apply a mustard plaster to his chest with Bearnaise sauce substituting for mustard! While the men apply the plaster, Kinchloe injects Klink with the penicillin. The next day, Klink recovers and pleasantly dispenses with the house call of Dr. Kronk. Hochstetter storms in, searching for the French girl, and shows a found scarf with her scent that his guard dogs will use to track her down. Hogan manages to distract Hochstetter and smear the scarf with Bearnaise sauce. He convinces Klink to receive a second plaster treatment followed by a bicycle ride around the camp. While the guard dogs chase Klink's scent,

Janine is huddled over to the trunk of Klink's staff car and leaves Hogan a kiss goodbye.

Program Notes: This is the first of three guest star appearances for Brenda Benet, who amassed a terrific performing resume before tragically taking her own life in 1982. Although Sigrid Valdis appears as Hilda, she does not receive closing credit. Both Leon Askin and Howard Caine appear in this episode for the first time, but they do not share a scene together.

Assessment: The good guys continue their track record of helping innocent allies to safety by welcoming their loveliest visitor to date. Apparently the men still have plenty of bottles of wine leftover from their recent after hours bug sweep of Klink's office (from "Casanova Klink") as both LeBeau and Newkirk are quick to serenade Janine with offers of romance and grapes. Much of the ensuing hi-jinks revolve around the boys' attempts to cure Klink so he will keep his staff meeting date, which make for some amusing yet mostly ridiculous situations. A prime example is when Klink reacts to his sudden injection of penicillin, and Hogan's casual dismissal of the pain as a sharp spring in the bed mattress. More ridiculous is convincing the Kommodant that he is ill *again,* an excuse to get the dog sniffing detail to chase down the bicycle-riding Klink and his freshly plastered chest of Bearnaise! Per usual, Leon Askin and Howard Caine, working separately, improve the overall affair with their patented characterizations. Burkhalter's "bedtime stories" quip is the funniest line read of the night. There's also a brief but spirited visit from return guest, Anthony Eustrel, as the bewildered but not bemused Nazi doctor. Finally, there is the heavenly sight of Brenda Benet, dressed as the prettiest prisoner in Germany, carefully huddled over to the trunk of the staff car, where she receives, not surprisingly, one of Bob Crane's longer-than-usual, farewell kisses.

Season 3, Episode 19: "Hogan Go Home" 01/13/1968.

P/D: Edward H. Feldman W: Bill Davenport

Guest Cast: Bernard Fox (Col. Crittendon), Dave Morick (SS Guard).

Storyline: Hogan confers with his men about two sabotage maneuvers he plans to execute simultaneously, the destruction of the Berlin Express (carrying munitions) and the Kessling oil refinery. Kinchloe receives a startling message from London – Colonel Hogan is ordered back home where he will receive a hero's welcome. Hogan is elated when he hears the news, much to the disappointment of his loyal comrades. Klink happily summons Hogan announcing that Colonel Crittendon is being transferred to Stalag 13 and will take over Hogan's quarters as the new, senior ranking, POW. Crittendon knows about Hogan's secret transfer out of Germany, and has volunteered to take over the vacancy as he is familiar with the operation. After sharing his secret orders with Hogan, then burning them and starting a fire in a laundry basket, Crittendon discusses how Hogan will leave the camp. They agree if he can get transferred, Hogan will have an opportunity to escape with the help of the Underground. Hogan has a pitch to sell Klink but gets the cooler instead after Crittendon intercedes. Klink approves Hogan's transfer to Stalag 15 and Crittendon gives his swagger stick, concealing a sword, to Hogan as a parting gift. Klink announces that Hogan will be transported to his new camp via the doomed Berlin Express as the transport truck with Hogan rolls out. The men, with Crittendon's supervision, attempt to stall the vehicle en route by chopping down a tree to block the road. When this fails, the men catch up with the vehicle which has suffered a flat tire. At gunpoint, the Heroes rescue their beloved Colonel without the help of Crittendon, who later gets a transfer of his own after Klink's men apprehend the British officer attempting to escape his way back into Stalag 13!

Program Notes: Syndicated broadcasts of this episode sometimes present a version without the canned laugh track allowing viewers to sporadically and faintly hear the off camera chuckles of crew members, particularly during the scene when Hogan leaves his cooler cell to casually join the conversation with Klink and Schultz. This is the fourth of eight appearances of Bernard Fox's bumbling Colonel Crittendon.

Assessment: Easily the best Bill Davenport script to date, this episode is uplifted by the excellent, guiding hand of producer/director Feldman. There's plenty to enjoy in this half hour where the humor stems more from the likable characterizations and less from outlandish situations. A delightful mix of emotions surrounds the impending departure of our beloved Colonel Hogan, and this makes for the riotous return of Crittendon who within minutes of his arrival nearly sets the barracks on fire in the best "Inspector Clouseau" like tradition. Laugh provoking, too, is the cynical glee of Klink who finally enjoys the upper hand on Hogan and Klink's seizing of plum moments to "chop, chop, chop" him down. Hogan's mild panic attack as he is driven away from camp, realizing he will be a commuter on the doomed Berlin Express, is a rare example where humor is created at the frightened expense of the normally, unflappable Colonel. Finally, we receive a perfectly staged, outstanding sight gag as Crittendon plans to topple a tree trunk into the road to halt the transport truck, only to swing the final whack and watch the tree fall in the opposite direction! Hogan can only register comic disbelief as he rambles by in the truck with a ticket to board a trainload of trouble.

Professional actor, musician, second banana, and longtime friend, Joseph Buttler catches up with Bernard Fox in Los Angeles at the Hollywood Collectors Show in January, 2013. Note the sizable amount of Hogan's Heroes memorabilia that "Colonel Crittendon" was signing for his many visiting fans that day. Photo courtesy of Joseph Buttler.

Season 3, Episode 20: "Sticky Wicket Newkirk" 01/20/1968.

D: John Rich W: Richard M. Powell

Guest Cast: Ulla Stromstedt (Gretel), Howard Caine (Major Hochstetter), Jay Sheffield (Sgt.), Rita Hayworth (Pin up model), Stewart Moss (Capt. Anderson/Uncredited), and Larry Hovis as ("Gen. Von Seidelberg").

Storyline: In Hammelburg, Newkirk enjoys an evening with the lovely fraulein, Gretel, who despite seeing through Newkirk's phony German accent, appears to be friendly with the allied cause and doubtful of the stupidity of war. They discuss the recent escape of eighteen allied bombers from Stalag 6. Soldiers bust in, arrest Newkirk, and drag him out. Klink happily informs the returned Newkirk that he will be transferred to Stalag 6. Hogan hands Newkirk a firearm and orders him to flee the transport party and make his way back to England. Major Hochstetter arrives and berates Klink for transferring Newkirk; he wanted to find out why the man was in Hammelburg in civilian clothes. He claims that he has now captured eight of the missing eighteen bombers, and the one that talked said he was headed to Stalag 13. Schultz bursts in and announces that Newkirk, having produced a huge gun, has escaped from the transport team. Hochstetter wonders why Klink is allowing his prisoners to carry guns. Newkirk returns from the escape tunnel accompanied by Gretel. Knowing that Gretel has now seen their entire operation, Hogan, nonetheless, pulls down a secret chart and explains how they will move the ten airmen out of camp. Gretel reveals she's a Gestapo spy and accompanies Schultz to make a full report to Klink. Hogan orders Newkirk down below to set off an explosion that will close off the tunnel underneath the bunk beds, to flee camp, and later to return and surrender. Gretel, Klink, Hochstetter, and guards attempt to find a tunnel underneath the beds. The head of security for all POW camps, "General Von Seidelberg," drops in and appears bemused by the efforts of Hochstetter to find an escape tunnel. When Gretel shows the secret location of the chart, the Major pulls down a pin-up poster of Rita Hayworth! Von Seidelberg attempts to defend Gretel by mentioning all the secret dirt she has smeared about Hochstetter, promptly sparking her arrest. Von Seidelberg informs Klink that too many transfers create unrest among the prisoners and Klink decides to have Newkirk reinstated at Stalag 13.

Program Notes: Last seen in "Diamonds in the Rough," this was the final guest shot for beautiful Ulla Stromstedt, who went into retirement after completing this episode and sadly passed away at the age of forty-six in Cannes. The first of two directing assignments for John Rich, who would then move next door to the *Gomer Pyle* sound stages for an extended tour of duty. In the following decade, Rich would be the guiding hand behind eighty-one episodes of the landmark series *All in the Family*, during its (arguably) best era, 1971-1974.

Larry Hovis's wry masquerade as General Von Seidelberg, "Chief of Security for all Prisoner of War Camps," is the highlight of "Sticky Wicket Newkirk," an episode boasting many, despite one sticky wicket of a detail. Author's collection/CBS Television Inc.

Assessment: Newkirk falls for the temptations of the most fetching of femme fatales, the head of security for POW camps pays a surprise visit, and Major Hochstetter's funniest appearance to date, all highlight the debut of director John Rich in this tip top outing. It all stitches together with perfect precision . . . until one detail threatens to unravel the spool. Ulla Stromstedt again establishes herself as the perfect Mata Hari, and she is quite delightful in her opening scene in which Richard Dawson enjoys his opportunity to play romantic hero. This segues to the brief, but hilarious, moment where Klink gleefully announces the transfer of Newkirk, buoyed by the actor's joyful line read: "In other words, Hogan, I'm breaking up that old gang of yours!" Howard Caine's pit bull presence is on full display, and he commands his most extensive footage yet. Whether demanding that Klink stop providing handguns to the prisoners, or when snarling a variation of his trademark line, "Why is this man here?", the actor is wildly, consistently hilarious. Larry Hovis, too, continues to successfully explore variations on his imaginary, Nazi characterizations. As a terrific contrast to his bombastically, outrageous impersonations of Hitler, Hovis crafts the Von Seidelberg character with elements of drollness, sarcasm, and self serving humor. His slight, evil giggle evokes the classic caricature of the Nazi in love with his own meanness. Whether casually acknowledging his relationship with Klink or commenting on Hochstetter's proclivity with "gardening and girly pictures," the Hovis/Von Seidelberg role is a fabulous scene stealer. The one element that threatens to sink the ship is Gretel's discovery of the bunk beds and its secret passage. Hogan is able to explain part of the problem away by having an explosion close off the tunnel, although Hochstetter and the others are most forgiving and forgetting after experiencing the shock waves of the explosion. What isn't explained is how the men are *perfectly able* to replace the floor boards where the beds normally open and close. The device to open the beds along with the ladder heading down into the tunnel have mysteriously vanished.

The ensuing action with the soldiers chopping up the wooden floor feels entirely implausible. (A brief shot of LeBeau and Kinchloe smoothing out the soil and moving new floorboards into position would have greatly helped the subterfuge.) It's unfortunate, because here is an episode worthy of four eagles, but as is often the case, *Hogan's Heroes* takes no apologies for its maneuvers and often confounds the viewer by taking a Nazi Germanic stance – accept the illogical as logical.

Classic Observation:

Hochstetter: "Colonel Hogan, that you were able to operate for so long is a tribute to the stupidity of your beloved Kommodant. Or is it complicity, Klink?"

Klink: "No, indeed Major! Stupidity!"

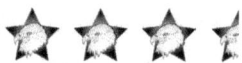

Season 3, Episode 21: "War Takes A Holiday" 01/27/1968.

D: Bruce Bilson W: Art Baer, Ben Joelson

Guest Cast: Howard Caine (Major Hochstetter), Sigrid Valdis (Hilda), Frank Marth (Inspector Gen. Busse), William Christopher (Thomas), Peter Marko (Albins), Chris Anders (Hermann).

Storyline: Major Hochstetter arrives bringing several top members of the Allied Underground into camp as his prisoners. They will be kept under maximum security until an armed transport will turn them over to Berlin HQ. At first, Hogan tries to have his men sneak the prisoners out inside old mattresses that are being replaced, but Hochstetter's early return busts up the plan. Furious that his scheme failed, Hogan tries to come up with a new idea and gets an inspiration from one of Newkirk's random observations. He decides that they will end the war prematurely to force the Gestapo to release the Underground team. First, he has Kinchloe and Thomas sneak into Hammelburg and hijack the local radio station. Kinch then broadcasts a special bulletin: "the war is over!" Klink and Hilda hear the announcement on the office radio, and, delighted, Klink notifies Hochstetter. Next, Hogan has Newkirk intercept a phone call from Hochstetter to his good friend, Col. Bomberg, in Berlin. Newkirk plays the roles of an aide, Bomberg, and several women enjoying a wild celebration! Now Hochstetter is convinced. Finally, LeBeau plants a dummy newspaper on Schultz with the same fake news on the front page. The camp turns into a party zone with Germans and prisoners alike celebrating. Hogan convinces Hochstetter to release his prisoners and allow them to borrow his staff car so they can drive back to town. A new staff car pulls in with Inspector General Busse, who sets all straight and reprimands Klink and Hochstetter for their stupidity.

Program Notes: William Christopher, as "Thomas," fills in for Larry Hovis, who does not appear in this episode. This is the third of five visits from Frank Marth. This premise is somewhat reworked in the first season *M*A*S*H* episode, "Ceasefire."

Director Bruce Bilson: (about the "Stalag 13" set): *

When I was starting to work on Hogan's, I went out to look at the location, I hadn't been there. It was after rehearsal or something, after some work. I drove out, it was like across town to Culver City, I drive into this joint and come up and park my cute little Jaguar Sedan, and the sun is just going down. And I'm standing there in front of this prison camp gate and it was fucking spooky. Because when I was going to high school and all that part of my youth was World War II and concentration camps and six million Jews – of which I'm glad I wasn't one – and so standing there at dusk with that tower and the gate . . . it was really something.

Assessment: For those who grew up with *Hogan's Heroes*, this is easily one of the most fondly remembered episodes. The dual writing team of Baer and Joelson and the direction of Bilson serve up a winner that contains a terrifically funny and precisely laid out bill of goods. The elements that pull off this prank of globally epic proportions are all in place, from the fake radio announcement, to the phone call with "Col. Bomberg," to the dummy newspaper. Hilda is a key conspirator as she gets the ball rolling by allowing Klink to wine her and then switching on the radio on cue. It's a pity she's not around later to enjoy the armistice party. Richard Dawson concocts a hilarious showcase at the switchboard as he impersonates several different male (and female) characters and employs all the audio tricks of an old time radio show, complete with doors opening and closing, ladies' high heels striking wood, and noisemakers blaring. It's probably the funniest sequence the gifted Englishman would deliver during his entire run. Schultz has a sweetly charming scene when he explains to the men in Klink's office that he was the owner of the Shotzy Toy Company, until the toy factory was taken over by the Third Reich for the war effort. In just a few lines of dialogue, Banner conveys the simple sweetness of the man and his yearning to resume his toy work for the sake of the children. Lovely, just lovely. Hogan perfectly plays the doubting Thomas of the group and some of his remarks appear to be a commentary on the actual details of deception he conjured, particularly his line about the "hokey phone call." Most intriguing of all is how the news affects the demeanor of Major Hochstetter. He must say out loud that "the war is over" a couple of dozen times (as if trying to convince himself it's true), and each time he registers some degree of quiet confusion, almost sadness, like a man lost now that he will no longer be working as a Nazi enforcer. The man is changed by the news, to the point where he frees his prisoners and actually allows them to drive off in his staff car! This is possibly one of the best of the many Howard Caine performances, and that is a truly remarkable statement regarding an actor who is typically always at the top of his game. It's up to return guest, Frank Marth, to bring everyone back to Third Reich earth, with his simple, yet painstakingly funny response to Hochstetter: "The what is *what?*"

*Telephone interview with the author, October 26, 2020.

Season 3, Episode 22: "Duel of Honor" 02/03/1968.

P/D: Edward H. Feldman W: Richard M. Powell

Guest Cast: Antoinette Bower (Erika Weidler), Howard Caine (Major Hochstetter), and Larry Hovis as (Gen. "Tiger" Weidler).

Storyline: Erika Weidler, a friend of the Underground, is brought in through the emergency tunnel. She has knowledge of a list of men plotting to kill Hitler and they need to get this list to London. After rejecting a few ideas, Hogan is inspired by Newkirk's comment of having Klink himself deliver the list. The men produce a mock newspaper with a picture and article commending Klink's record. Hogan sneaks in a perfumed letter from Erika, who claims she has fallen in love with Klink after reading his news profile. Hogan influences Klink to have the woman brought to his quarters, and he is delighted by her elegance and beauty. Romance blossoms until Erika admits that she is married, and Hogan pipes in that her husband is General "Tiger" Weidler, infamous for killing sixty-three men in saber duels. The next day, Carter as "Weidler," storms the office and threatens Klink. After challenging Klink to a duel at dawn, Weidler departs and Erika instates a plan. She has tickets and papers for the couple to meet a private plane late that night chartered for Argentina. She provides Klink with a list of coded names of "friends" in Argentina, actually the list of Hitler's conspirators. Klink meekly agrees to Erika's plan, unsure of how he ever got into this mess that is forcing him to abandon his military career. He drives to a remote air field and signals the pilot when he is suddenly joined by Major Hochstetter, who seizes Klink's papers and arrests him for treason. Hogan and his men appear, disguised as a hooded unit from Abwher. Claiming that they are on a secret mission for the Fuhrer and that Klink is their "dupe," they deliver the intelligence list to the waiting pilot who departs. The Abwher unit scares off Hochstetter and tells Klink to continue acting as a "dupe."

Program Notes: Klink finally finds romance, although deceivingly, and enjoys his first on camera kiss with the beautiful Ms. Bower. The Abwher was the German military intelligence service for the Wehrmacht from 1920 to 1945. Their objective was initially the defense against foreign espionage, and they often found their operations at odds with the Gestapo.

Antoinette Bower guest stars as a mysterious woman who tempts Klink to desert his post and join her in Argentina in the nutty entry, "Duel of Honor." Photo courtesy of Antoinette Bower.

Assessment: A sympathetic "dupe" of a Kommodant, the sparkling energy of Antoinette Bower, and a surprise visit from Major Hochstetter, prop up the proceedings of a somewhat pedestrian story line, despite the lure of freedom in Argentina. The ploy of using Klink as an unwitting carrier pigeon would be manipulated to better degree in other capers. It just seems too unlikely that Klink would so quickly abandon his entire position in Germany for a woman he is uncertain about, without consulting his own German allies, and in fear of a crazy general that he has not only never heard of but not investigated. After crafting a deft, Nazi characterization in "Sticky Wicket Newkirk," Larry Hovis resorts to an easier, far broader approach as the saber wielding "Tiger" Weidler. It's okay for cheap laughs, but a let down from his more clever turns as Hitler and the aforementioned Chief of POW security. It's also unclear what would happen if Klink actually boarded the plane supposedly headed for Argentina. This episode also suffers from situation comedy fatigue, particularly noticeable in the office scene with Klink, Hogan, and Carter's nutty general. The best turns come from Bower's passionate presence, the droll humor seized in the brief Howard Caine cameo, and the spookiness of the Abwher unit, and Klemperer himself, a master at eliciting audience sympathy. Not surprisingly, the funniest moment comes from Klink's reaction when Hogan, Erika, and Schultz all offer their admiration of the Kommodant's bravery, prompting the dumbfounded Klink to exclaim: "Are you all out of your mind?"

Season 3, Episode 23: "Axis Annie" 02/10/1968.

D: John Rich W: Laurence Marks

Guest Cast: Louise Troy (Anna Gebhart), Chet Stratton (Blue Fox), Karl Bruck (Vandermeer), Bard Stevens (Gestapo Guard), L.E. Young (Diner), and Howard Caine as (Major Hochstetter).

Storyline: Hogan and his team make a twilight rendezvous with "Blue Fox," an Underground contact being pursued by the Gestapo. Hogan receives important war documents that must be delivered to "Vandermeer," who will be staying at the Hammelburg Hotel. Blue Fox immediately drives off and the men observe a Gestapo automobile in pursuit. Klink announces to his entire company the presence of "Axis Annie," representing Goebbels and the Ministry of Propaganda, who wants to recruit prisoners to discuss the fairness of their treatment under the articles of the Geneva Convention for a radio broadcast. Hogan plots to deliver the info to Vandermeer by feigning cooperation with Klink and Annie. Hogan, Newkirk, and LeBeau all agree to participate in her radio address, in exchange for increased privileges and for a hosted dinner at the Hammelburg Hotel. Klink and Major Hochstetter bristle at the idea, but Annie sees this as a publicity coup and she drops Goebbels' name to get her way. While at dinner, Carter and Kinchloe sabotage the Germans' radio detection truck and destroy Building 9, where wax recordings of the earlier radio address have been stored. In the restaurant, Chef LeBeau enchants everyone by preparing a flaming cherries jubilee which quickly turns into an out of control fire. Hogan slips to the hotel desk and notifies Vandermeer that some important mail is waiting for him. Hogan then observes Vandermeer retrieve his mail from the desk clerk, momentarily drop the envelope, and have it returned by an obliging Colonel Klink.

Program Notes: "Axis Annie" is based on the name "Axis Sally," a generic cover for female broadcasters who attempted to demoralize Allied soldiers over the radio air waves under the supervision of Joseph Goebbels' Ministry of Propaganda. This is the second appearance of Louise Troy, who would become Mrs. Werner Klemperer the following year. Troy appeared with Burt Lancaster in the highly acclaimed cult film *"The Swimmer,"* released the same year as this broadcast.

Assessment: Inspired by war history fact, this Laurence Marks script is certainly an intriguing addition to the *Hogan's Heroes* legacy. The story combines the expected elements of outlandish diversion, such as the restaurant dinner going up in flames, along with an espionage adventure, Carter and Kinchloe's destructive raid on the radio truck and Building 9. Several components contribute to the general success of the tale, including Carters's deadly magnesium pencil bombs, Klink's joyful demeanor as the dinner party host, Hochstetter's grousing over the same, and the influence of publicity purveyor, Axis Annie. Shamelessly reworked again, the out of control fire is the ruse to distract the dinner guests, complete with the POWs tossing smoke bombs into the mix (are the "jolly jokers" ever searched prior to these unlikely social affairs?). Salvaging this stock situation is the role of Newkirk as an obnoxious drunk starting a fight with a patron's fraulein, a most amusing diversion delivered by Dawson, and the ever obliging Wilhelm Klink, who politely retrieves the momentarily displaced war plans for the departing Vandermeer.

Season 3, Episode 24: "What Time Does the Balloon Go Up?" 02/17/1968.

D: Marc Daniels W: Arthur Julian

Guest Cast: Peter Brooks (Christopher Downes), Lincoln Demyan (Sgt. McMahon), and Howard Caine as (Major Hochstetter).

Storyline: British spy Christopher Downes has just fled Berlin with a fist full of top secret documents, and he joins Hogan. The camp area crawling with Gestapo soldiers, Hogan must keep Downes hidden until an escape route becomes available. Hochstetter, wielding the signed permission of General Burkhalter, surrounds Stalag 13 and issues "shoot to kill" orders for anyone attempting to exit. Hogan becomes inspired after watching Schultz release a helium balloon that was intended for his nephew, Wolfie. Much to the bewilderment of his company, Hogan mandates orders involving basket weaving, kite flying, and the building of a tent out of old parachutes. Despite the protests of Hochstetter, the men continue with the oddball activities as a larger ruse to trigger the escape plan for Downes. Kinchloe flies a kite into some electrical wires creating a colorful diversion, while Newkirk fills the tent with hot air which is now attached to a giant basket. Despite some random interference from Schultz, the hot air balloon, with Downes and a parachute as hidden passengers, successfully departs camp meeting the satisfaction of the senior ranking POW.

Program Notes: This is the first of nineteen directing assignments for Marc Daniels, probably the most prolific director employed by the series. Daniels guided the first half of production on *I Love Lucy*, directing thirty-nine episodes. He also called the shots on numerous episodes of *Star Trek*, *Marcus Welby, M.D.*, and eighty-six episodes of *Alice*. On the opposite end of the rainbow, Daniels also directed all eight episodes of *Co-Ed Fever* and six episodes of *Life with Lucy*, effectively bookending his substantial career in TV direction.

Assessment: High likability again combines with high implausibility for a mostly enjoyable half hour. The best sequence stems from the concern of the gang over the mental stability of their intrepid Colonel Hogan, who has just laid out their marching orders: basket weaving, kite flying, and tent pitching! The idea of inviting Klink to be the judge of the men's basket weaving contest is questionable; fortunately, that old pro Werner Klemperer wisely treats the basket judging sequence with complete seriousness, another terrific example of the actor improving the material by playing it straight. More giggles are provoked by Hochstetter's appalled response to the highly unusual and oddly accepted prisoner activities of leisure. The least satisfying sequence stems from the harassment of Sgt. Schultz, who sweetly returns to camp with gifts for his little nephew's birthday, only to have Newkirk spitefully burst one balloon prompting the release of the other into the stratosphere. It's like asking the audience to laugh at the schoolyard bullies ganging up on their chubby classmate. It may have been an endeavor we all once participated in, but one that none of us can recall as one of our finer moments. Justifiably enough, the episode ends on a high note with the hot air balloon launched to the smiling satisfaction of Colonel Hogan and to most of his non-discriminating fans.

Season 3, Episode 25: "LeBeau and the Little Old Lady" 02/24/1968.

D: Bruce Bilson W: Arthur Julian

Guest Cast: Celeste Yarnall (Wilhelmina), Sigrid Valdis (Hilda), Howard Caine (Major Hochstetter), Sivi Aberg (Juliana).

Storyline: LeBeau complains about again making contact with the Underground agent, "Wilhelmina," whom he insists is a crotchety, hard of hearing, little old lady. Later, at her apartment in Hammelburg, Wilhelmina is revealed as an attractive, young woman, whom LeBeau has fallen for. Back at camp, Kinchloe gets the word that the Gestapo have arrested "Wooden Shoes," a regular contact of Wilhelmina, so LeBeau defies orders and sneaks out of camp to protect Wilhelmina. Hogan reports to Schultz that LeBeau has gone missing, but the sergeant prefers to ignore the news and falsely reports that the prisoners are all present. Hogan persists and cuts a deal with Klink to go into town with Newkirk and Carter in order to retrieve LeBeau. Klink and Schultz accompany the retrieval party. Outside Wilhelmina's apartment, the POWs enter to find LeBeau while Klink creates interference with the newly arrived Major Hochstetter out in the street. The men sneak their contact out dressed as an old lady and she misdirects the Gestapo into the building. Later, Klink and company drop the "old lady" off near a flower shop and Klink marvels at the sentimentality of LeBeau who graciously kisses her goodbye. Finally, when all the men decline to meet their newest Underground agent in town, Hogan himself accepts the task, with pleasantly gratifying results.

Program Notes: Celeste Yarnall would return in the following season's "Will the Blue Baron Strike Again?" Making the rounds of most of the hit series of the 1960s, TV trivia devotees will certainly remember Yarnall as Yeoman Randall from the 1967 *Star Trek* voyage, "The Apple." This was the only appearance of stunning Sivi

Aberg, who memorably raised temperatures as the bikini clad girlfriend of Cesar Romero's Joker in the Bat-camp-classic "Surf's Up! Joker's Under!" (1967). Director Bruce Bilson shared his memories about executive producer Ed Feldman, and the production process on *Hogan's Heroes*: *

He ran the show and he was the best. In every way. We had a rehearsal day. We would rehearse on a stage and sort of semi-stage the stuff that would be on location, and if we had an idea for a joke we would try it. And then when we were ready, we called him and said "Come on down," and he came to the set, and we ran the show for him. We were free to try and add things, and he gave us some notes. And that was it. I never had a rehearsal day on a filmed show that you then did a run thru for the boss, except on *Hogan's Heroes*.

Assessment: With Newkirk having recently enjoyed his off campus romance in "Sticky Wicket Newkirk," it seems somewhat logical that his frequent rival in romance, Louis LeBeau, would earn his place with love on the run. Fortunately, he is paired with the charming Celeste Yarnall, and there is a sincere sweetness between her and our lovelorn Frenchman, Robert Clary. The funniest scene involves the unflappable Sgt. Schultz and his refusal to rock the boat by continuing to ignore Hogan's report of the AWOL LeBeau and sticking with what he knows best - nothing. Klink adds to the ignorant humor by responding to Hogan's persistence of the missing LeBeau by innocently responding: "Missing from where?" Crane wisely plays this scene in the straight man mode of a Bud Abbott, allowing his confused captors to carry the laughs. We're also treated to some more Blake Edwards/Inspector Clouseau type gags of Schultz driving off and stranding the humiliated Kommodant. Equally fun is the final round up, complete with LeBeau's first on camera kiss and a nifty, high angle observation out the apartment window of the spectacle of Klink and Hochstetter conducting their customarily conflicted business down below. On screen for about three minutes, Howard Caine again explodes with his trademark contempt and zeal, even incurring a warning from Hogan that his shouting may "bring down the neighborhood property values!" The final sequence creates its own charm and we get a true gang comedy finish, with both the prisoners and their German wardens happily driving off together! In the epilogue, with sensational Sivi Aberg in essentially a cameo role, Hogan happily reminds viewers that "it's good to be the king."

Season 3, Episode 26: "How to Escape From a Prison Camp Without Really Trying" 03/02/1968.

P/D: Edward H. Feldman W: Bill Davenport

Guest Cast: Leon Askin (Gen. Burkhalter), Sigrid Valdis (Hilda), Willard Sage (Col. Krueger), Edward Knight (Col. Nikolas), Lyn Peters (Audrey St. Laurence), Chet Stratton (Bruno), Tom Hatten (Sgt.), Jay Sheffield (Cpl.).

Storyline: Hogan, posing as "Horst," a war correspondent, wines and romances a pretty fraulein in order to get information, only to find out she is actually with British Intelligence and already wise to his true identity. Later, the men stall Schultz waiting for Hogan to return for roll call. Klink announces he will be taking a two week leave and that Col. Krueger will act as his replacement. The Heroes listen in on their surveillance unit as Krueger and his colleague, Col. Nikolas of the Gestapo, plot a takeover of Stalag 13. Hogan attempts to persuade Klink to abandon his planned trip, but Klink dismisses the idea as one of Hogan's schemes. Meanwhile, Hogan receives the unlikely orders from London to stall the Germans' 6th Division for forty-eight hours. Hogan orders the fifteen men in Barracks One to move down into the tunnel creating a mass escape of an embarrassment for Krueger. Then he adds his own men down into the mix. Nikolas insists that they request help from the 6th Division to recover the thirty missing prisoners. At a ski lodge, Klink is having a marvelous time until Gen. Burkhalter steps in and orders him back to Stalag 13. Hogan tells Burkhalter that the men will probably turn themselves back in for fear of Klink's punishment. Burkhalter scoffs at the idea just as Schultz bolts into the office to announce the puzzling return of all thirty missing men.

Program Notes: The first of two visits from the born in Buenos Aires beauty Lyn Peters, who would return for the final season installment, "It's Dynamite." Willard Sage played the alien Thann in the *Star Trek* episode "The Empath" (1968). Klink references an earlier episode to Bruno when he states his nickname as "Killer Klink," which Burkhalter enthusiastically repeats moments later.

Assessment: Thirty prisoners missing at Stalag 13 and the Wehrmacht still doesn't suspect something unusual is happening over at Klink's place? Working within this sketchy premise is a mixed bag of elements resulting in a diverting yet hardly remarkable half hour. The opening scene with Crane and guest star Lyn Peters is a charmer, but this unfortunately segues into the longer, less amusing sequence of the men stalling Schultz by making him repeat the meaning of the word "Achtung!" along with other wordplay that fails to amuse at any level. Guest villains Willard Sage and Edward Knight fail to register much humor or tension, perhaps a reaction to a mediocre Bill Davenport script. The best moments, fortunately, arise courtesy of our old hands at the game, which includes the twist of having Hogan try to double talk Klink out of his trip for his own good, and Klink not falling for the perceived deception. There's also the classic bit of business of the proud Klink bad mouthing his "tub of lard" superior, General Burkhalter, while the rotund general carefully takes in every word behind Klink's back. Guest star Chet Stratton brings a boost of naturally pleasant cheer as "Bruno" during the ski lodge sequence. Outside of these memorable moments, the rest of this outing takes on a business as usual air.

Season 3, Episode 27: "The Collector General" 03/09/1968.

D: Bruce Bilson W: Laurence Marks

Guest Cast: Gavin MacLeod (Gen. Metzger), Sigrid Valdis (Hilda), Heidy Hunt (Lisa), John Stephenson (Karl), Dave Morick (Guard/Uncredited).

Storyline: An Underground operative, Lisa, meets with Hogan and the others in their tunnel network. She informs Hogan about an abandoned mine that the Germans have installed a large steel door locking the entrance. While Hogan wonders about its usefulness, Gen. Metzger meets with Klink to inform him that Hitler has started a new program of stashing arms and ammunition in several hiding places around Germany, including the mystery mine. Listening in, Hogan doubts the validity of Metzger's story, and has Kinchloe radio London for any background on the general. The men trick Klink into believing there is a leak in the roof over his office, and the boys set to repair work. In an elaborate ruse, LeBeau feigns injury from a rooftop fall, but actually manages to sneak into Metzger's supply truck. He reports to Hogan that the entire truck is full of art and other stolen treasures that Metzger has lifted from France. His plan is to move the haul into the mine shaft for safe keeping. London aids Hogan by staging a fake air raid and dropping dummy commandos by parachute into the woods. Klink's entire company are diverted to the woods for combat while Karl, Lisa's husband, impersonates a Luftwaffe officer and orders Schultz to abandon his post at the mine shaft. The Heroes move in and detonate the steel door and move all the treasures into an Underground supply truck. Later, Metzger is furious with Klink about the raid at the mine. Hogan suggests he call Berlin to make an official report regarding his "missing ammunition," which the general hastily declines.

Program Notes: Gavin MacLeod returns to Stalag 13 in his second of four, unrelated, German characterizations. In between his work assignments for Mr. Feldman, the prolific MacLeod kept busy with appearances on *Combat!* and *Death Valley Days*, and was invited to Blake Edwards' raucous *The Party* (1968) as the movie producer, C. S. Divot. Director Bruce Bilson shared further comments about his association with producer, Ed Feldman: * "He did not come and look over our shoulder, that's not how he worked. If he hired you - he gave it to you. He was the best. I have to keep telling you . . . about a very unusual, terrific, talented, friend of mine. Idol. All of the above."

Assessment: Picking up a cue from the second season Paris sojourn, "Art for Hogan's Sake," this episode continues the theme of greedy Nazis ransacking Europe for valuable art as an insurance policy for post-war retirement. Most of the outing clicks like clockwork, although the men's diversion of having LeBeau fall from the roof, body doubled by Newkirk back in the barracks, and then the return of LeBeau *back on the roof* creates much confusion – not just for Schultz but for the audience. At times the writers go the *long* way around the block for the sake of a simple plot development. This is such the case. Return guest star Gavin MacLeod brings much cynical sleaze to his avaricious general. His best scene is the close-out with Hogan when he attempts to schmooze the American colonel by extracting the location of his precious "ammunition." With his deceptive smirk and piercing eyes, MacLeod makes his few line reads truly sparkle with a playful demeanor masking a sinister, ulterior motive.

*Telephone interview with the author, September 14, 2020.

Season 3, Episode 28: "The Ultimate Weapon" 03/16/1968.

D: Marc Daniels W: Richard M. Powell

Guest Cast: Leon Askin (Gen. Burkhalter), Sigrid Valdis (Hilda), Marian Moses (Col. Karla Hoffmann).

Storyline: Klink proudly displays several imprisoned Allied fliers that were shot down while trying to bomb a ball bearing plant in Zuglitz. Hogan wants to aid the Allied cause with a victory in Zuglitz so he visits Klink and manages to deactivate his radio while the Kommodant is busy studying his war map. Klink is anxious to hear the six o' clock broadcast of Radio Berlin so Hogan volunteers the services of Kinchloe to repair the radio. Hogan has Newkirk lift the pocket watch of Schultz and set the time back twenty minutes. The men return the fixed radio, but Klink fumes that he missed the radio broadcast. But Hogan, Schultz, and even Hilda all state the correct time is just minutes before six. Hogan claims that Schultz predicted the Russians would make an advance on Kiev and when they listen to the broadcast, actually a recording of the earlier one, it proves that Schultz is correct. Over the next several days, Hogan continues to manipulate the predictions of the seer Schultz in the same manner. This draws the interest of General Burkhalter and Colonel Hoffman, a female officer sent from Berlin, and they treat Schultz luxuriously while they continue to hone his battle predictions. Hoffmann confides to Hogan her doubts in the future success of Hitler and an uneasy romance begins. Schultz suggests that Berlin will be the next Allied target which changes the German defense plan. The Allies successfully wipe out the undefended ball bearing plant in Zuglitz. The magic ESP powers of Sgt. Schultz have come to an end, Burkhalter is now in hot water with Berlin, and Colonel Hoffmann disappears, although Hogan is optimistic about a post-war reunion.

Assessment: The ESP themed hoax that didn't particularly work back in season one hasn't improved with age. John Banner is a gifted talent and a very funny fellow, but building an entire episode around his Sgt. Schultz isn't necessarily a best in show strategy. In short, a little Schultz can go a long way. The biggest flaw with Richard Powell's script is the time element concept of turning back the clock which might work once, but for an entire week? No one, including Klink, Burkhalter, and even Colonel Hoffmann, ever catch on to the time discrepancy factor. Why is it that Hilda too chimes in with the false time of day? One must assume that Hogan schmoozed her with a smooch and a pair of stockings in some unseen scene. Far too convenient is the SS Colonel all too quickly coming to Hogan's side and into his arms. In the end, the Germans are left with all too familiar sauerkraut on their faces, suckered by their easily manipulated sergeant of arm, and the audience suffers from a slight case of indigestion.

Season 3, Episode 29: "Monkey Business" 03/23/1968.

D: Bob Sweeney W: Arthur Julian

Guest Cast: Leon Askin (Gen. Burkhalter), Sigrid Valdis (Hilda), Jack Good (Submarine Officer), Elisa Ingram (Radio Operator), Laurie Main (Col. Wembley), and "Freddie" the chimpanzee.

Storyline: During an Allied air attack on a ball bearing plant, the Hammelburg Zoo sustains damage causing most of their animals to escape. Carter, out on a mission to deliver a radio transmitter part to the Underground, returns with a new friend, a chimpanzee that Newkirk names "Freddie." Because of the activity during the air raid, Carter was unable to deliver the part so Hogan must think of a new solution. Freddie becomes the favorite member of the prisoners, particularly Newkirk, and Schultz agrees to keep his presence a secret. Hogan realizes that they must get Freddie returned to the zoo, with the radio part hidden in his new, tailor made uniform, and the Underground can make contact with the chimp at a later time. Klink, who has been ordered to round up the escaped animals, sees the men working in the garden outside his office, including Freddie who is now wearing a miniature wardrobe like LeBeau's. Klink thinks he's losing his mind, but later meets Freddie (who salutes) and orders his return to the zoo. Schultz, fond of the little simian, suggests they keep Freddie hidden, but Hogan insists that direct orders must be carried out. Freddie makes it back to the zoo, and British Intelligence marvels at Hogan's clever use of a chimp as a secret courier.

Assessment: For a television series that often relies on charm, it just may serve up its most charming story to date. Some of the minor subplots lamely limp along including Hogan's attempt to convince Klink that LeBeau is actually a big game hunter, an out of left field trick to create opportunity for LeBeau to deliver the radio transmitter to the zoo. This leads to some subsequent nonsense

An impromptu jazz trio featuring Sigrid Valdis, Bob Crane, and guest star, "Freddie" the Chimpanzee, during production of "Monkey Business." Crane was never far from his beloved drum set, often heard in the background as the crew set up the next shooting scene. Author's collection/CBS Television Inc.

involving LeBeau practicing target range with Schultz's rifle, and General Burkhalter dodging a stray bullet as he rounds a corner. These silly distractions aside, the real star of the show, undoubtedly, is Freddie the chimpanzee, who conjures up a series of adorable moments: setting the coffee pot on the stove, working in the garden with the rest of the gang (prompting a hilarious reaction from Klink), and in the best moment of the half hour, pacing back and forth with Hogan as the chimp apes the crafty colonel's attempts to decide the team's next move. Sweetly sentimental, also, is Newkirk's fondness for the little guy. Richard Dawson appears to genuinely enjoy working with his little guest star. Commendable also is Schultz's good-natured attempt to bend the rules so Freddie can become a permanent resident of Stalag 13.

Season 3, Episode 30: "Drums Along the Dusseldorf" 03/30/1968.

D: Bob Sweeney W: Arthur Julian

Guest Cast: Sigrid Valdis (Hilda), David Frank (German Sgt.).

Storyline: On a night mission, the Heroes are wiring the Hammelburg Bridge to explode the following day when a German one-and-a-half-ton truck carrying an experimental fuel will cross. Later, Klink informs Hogan that twelve new prisoners will be added to the barracks, and that they will be transported over the same bridge, which has been rigged to explode by the weight of the truck. Hogan tries to convince Klink that the men should be transferred to a different stalag, but Klink doesn't buy the double talk. Mail call indicates that Carter is of the Sioux Indian tribe which intrigues Schultz to no end. Hogan sends Newkirk out of camp dressed like an old German lady, and he manages to detain the truck with the American prisoners long enough for another truck to pass, which destroys the bridge. Kinchloe informs Hogan that the destroyed truck was not the one they were after, and London has reported the actual fuel truck has been rerouted to pass right by Stalag 13. Hogan presses Carter into service, who has been practicing with his bow and arrow, to send a flaming arrow in the direction of the fuel truck. During night roll call, Carter manages to strike the fuel truck with the flaming arrow which creates a fiery spectacle while Klink ignorantly addresses his entire company.

Assessment: The finale to season three just floats along on flimsy material at best. The program gets bogged down in silliness with Schultz quickly becoming a child playing cowboys and Indians as he limply simulates his imitation of an Indian war dance. The stereotyped silliness continues all the way to the top as Klink caps the moronic momentum by trying on a feather headdress and posing in front of the mirror, only to get surprised, of course, by Hogan's entrance. These aren't exactly career defining moments for either actor. Even the usually reliable "Dawson in drag" routine feels time worn featuring the duped, dummkopf sergeant caving in at the mention of the old lady's granddaughter – who Newkirk claims is a "fan dancer!" Barely salvaging the half hour are two choice moments: the great sight gag of Carter firing the flaming arrow only to have it travel one foot and strike the interior window frame, and the well-staged shot of Klink bragging to his entire company about German ingenuity as the fireball of a fuel truck streaks by in the background.

Season 4, Episode 1: "Clearance Sale at the Black Market" 09/28/1968.

P/D: Edward H. Feldman W: Laurence Marks

Guest Cast: Sigrid Valdis (Hilda), Gavin MacLeod (Maj. Kiegel), Doris Singleton (Maria), Lou Krugman (Hermann), Bard Stevens (Karl).

Storyline: Schultz has taken a fancy to Maria, the bar maid at the Haufbrau, and accidentally walks in on a private meeting between her boss, Hermann, and Major Kiegel, of the Gestapo. After his departure, Kiegel states that the sergeant will be disappearing very soon to the Eastern Front. Back at camp, the men retrieve a secret message that Maria planted on Schultz regarding German troop movements. Later, Kiegel visits Klink and hand picks Schultz from the active personnel list for an immediate transfer to Russia, although Klink is dumbfounded with the selection. Klink informs Schultz of his transfer orders and the sad sergeant seeks the solace of Hogan and his men. Schultz mentions to Hogan his innocent intrusion on Hermann and Kiegel, so Kinchloe runs background checks. London reports that Kiegel and Hermann are running a black market operation out of the back of the Haufbrau. Hogan figures Schultz witnessed a payoff between the two men, and Kiegel decided to get rid of Schultz. The men infiltrate the Haufbrau, and Hogan approaches Kiegel with a wrist full of watches. He states he is a friend of Schultz and demands his protection or he will blab to Berlin all about Kiegel's crooked, black market activity. Kiegel and Hermann decide to clear out and load up a truck in the back alley full of their stolen merchandise while Kinchloe snaps several incriminating photos. Later, Klink tears up the transfer papers and informs Schultz that the Gestapo HQ arrested Kiegel after several mysterious photos were mailed to Berlin.

Program Notes: Both Lou Krugman and Doris Singleton close out their two appearance association with the series in this episode.

Assessment: A fairly routine tale of black market crime and blackmail gets a big boost from some nifty, character driven moments and Gavin MacLeod's best guest appearance to date. Schultz is the innocent party and he appears to be surrounded by antagonists on all sides. Maria pretends to flirt with him, but is only using him as an unwitting courier of Underground messages. Kiegel dismisses Schultz as "a slob," and immediately plots his wintry funeral at the Russian Front. Klink, instead of making waves with the Gestapo, is more than ready to sell him out. Then there's Colonel Hogan, who spends much of the episode tossing off unusually cruel jabs about the man's weight, and acknowledges Schultz as our "three hundred pound carrier pigeon." Ruder yet is how quickly the men abandon the sergeant each time they retrieve one of Maria's messages from the tight-fitted belt on his uniform. This allows John Banner to play some lovely scenes of sympathy, particularly with Klink, when he meekly asks his superior officer if he has "done something wrong." All of this set up makes the conclusion that much stronger as Hogan confronts Kiegel with his simple defense of Schultz: "I like him." MacLeod is excellent as the shifty Gestapo crook who quickly hits the panic button when he realizes that Hogan is a wise adversary and ready to close down his shop. Clad in a black topcoat and matching wide-brimmed hat, hurriedly loading ill gotten gain in the back alleys of bars, and shooting out incriminating light bulbs with his pistol, MacLeod embraces the cloak and dagger/film noirish elements of the evening, and the story is that much better because of it.

Season 4, Episode 2: "Klink vs. the Gonculator" 10/05/1968.

D: Bruce Bilson W: Phil Sharp

Guest Cast: Leon Askin (Gen. Burkhalter), Noam Pitlik (Major Lutz), Victoria Carroll (Lila Fenster), Dave Morick (Capt. Dingel).

Storyline: In a German pub, Luftwaffe Major Lutz discusses his plan to defect by delivering a homing device lifted from a new rocket prototype into the hands of his Underground lover, Lila Fenster. Lila whispers that she is ready to sneak the device through their secret network to London, but Lutz is overtly cautious as his presence is being watched by the Gestapo. Back at camp, Lila meets with Hogan to discuss how they can move the homing device from Lutz to London. Meanwhile, Carter has perfected a rabbit trap which he gamely demonstrates to the other men. The sudden appearance of Schultz inspires Hogan to quickly feign that the men are attempting to construct a "gonculator." His brainstorm is to pretend the POWs are secretly building this device to undermine the German war effort, and that Major Lutz, an electronics expert, is currently experimenting with similar devices at Stalag 19. The men continue to adorn the rabbit trap with spare radio parts and wiring while Schultz keeps a close surveillance on their activity. Burkhalter is summoned and he and Klink snoop in the barracks and examine the gonculator while the POWs have been dispatched to the Motor Pool. A befuddled Major Lutz is brought to Stalag 13 and ordered to examine the gonculator and compare it to the German prototype. Hogan is able to tip off that he is Lila's partner in the Underground. Once the gonculator is plugged into the wall, a fireworks show of sparkle and smoke showers the barracks, and during the confusion, Lutz is smuggled out of camp along with Lila and the homing device.

The irony is in their ignorance. Bob Crane poses with the fictitious "gonculator," another headache for Klink and Burkhalter. Author's collection/CBS TV Inc.

Program Notes: This is the first of six, unrelated, guest appearances for Victoria Carroll who kept busy during the 1960s and 1970s working with such show biz legends as Jack Benny, Jerry Lewis, Sid Caesar, Larry Storch, and the "King" himself, Elvis Presley. Many of her avid fans also remember her appearance with George Lazenby in "That's Armageddon," one of the *calmer* segments of *The Kentucky Fried Movie* (1976).

Assessment: The irony is in the ignorance as Klink, General Burkhalter, and their entire company eagerly accept that old Hogan and his men are up to no good in their construction of a make believe device that could be more effective than the German prototype, which, naturally, does not exist. The opener in the bier hall is a rarity in that it features two characters viewers have never previously encountered: gorgeous Lila Fenster and her soon to be defecting lover, Major Lutz. Guest stars Victoria Carroll (in her HH debut) and frequent visitor Noam Pitlik work marvelously well together (including his admission of not even knowing her name!) and launch the ship in the right direction. The thrust of the dramatic action is to find a way to get Lutz to Stalag 13 and to eventual escape and the fictitious "gonculator" is the chosen method of transportation. Series regular Dave Morick, as the caught-off-guard supply Captain, unknowingly and humorously aids and abets Hogan's cause by blatantly lying to Klink and Burkhalter about the classified nature of the make believe device. Leon Askin, in his customary excellence, has a brilliant, blink-and-you'll-miss-it-moment, when he blankly responds to Klink's newfound technical knowledge in the barracks. The fiery demo of the device is a sparkling good show, but whether or not this is a sufficient cover for Lutz to slip out unseen through those sneaky bunk beds is questionable. Driving the final ironic nail into the coffin is General Burkhalter, who in order to not admit his own ignorance, fails to question at any time with his inimitable squeal, "What in the name of the war effort is a gonculator and what brilliant German device are we supposed to be comparing it to, Klink?"

Season 4, Episode 3: "How to Catch a Papa Bear" 10/12/1968.

D: Bruce Bilson W: Laurence Marks

Guest Cast: Sigrid Valdis (Hilda), Alan Oppenheimer (Wilhelm), Jay Sheffield (Gestapo Officer), Horst Ebersberg (SS Sgt.), and Fay Spain as (Myra).

Storyline: A plate of apple strudel gets Schultz to divulge to LeBeau that Klink will be making a surprise bed check around midnight, right when Hogan is scheduled to meet a new unit of Underground allies. Hogan decides to send Newkirk in his place (as "Papa Bear") and the men dummy up a replacement in Hogan's bed, along with a phonograph playing loud snoring, in order to fool Klink and Schultz into believing the English man is sleeping off a bad cold. Newkirk meets in a barn with Myra, Wilhelm, Franz and Gunther, but their plans are quickly spoiled by the arrival of a Gestapo unit and their arrests. Newkirk and Myra are held in a cell while Hogan continues to stall Klink concerning Newkirk's "illness." In reality, Myra and Wilhelm are Gestapo spies who are trying to ferret out the Underground and their leader, "Papa Bear." Myra makes successful radio contact with Hogan's crew and they agree to have her brought in through their tunnel. Myra explains that she and Wilhelm were able to escape, but that Newkirk and the other two men are imprisoned. Hogan decides it's too risky to attempt the rescue of Newkirk, and to the disappointment of his men, he plans to sabotage a munitions dump instead. Hogan requests Myra make additional radio contact with Wilhelm, and this tips her hand when she fails to use the proper security words. Hogan and Carter, dressed as Gestapo, force Myra to lead them into Gestapo HQ to spring Newkirk, while Kinchloe and LeBeau successfully blow up the munitions site.

Program Notes: Fay Spain drops in for her first of two guest appearances. Truly an actress with a well-earned cult following, she may best be remembered for her performances in the Mamie Van Doren-headlined, Albert Zugsmith-produced novelties: *The Beat Generation* (1959) and the condemned by the Catholic Church sex fantasy, *The Private Lives of Adam and Eve* (1960). Once again the stock shot of Gestapo HQ is lifted from "A Tiger Hunt in Paris," helping save production costs. Guest star Alan Oppenheimer happily recalled playing "Agent 498" for director Bruce Bilson in "The Man From YENTA," a second season *Get Smart* caper:

At the beginning of the second act, three of us come out robed as Arabs. And one says, "My name is Abu Ben Bubi." And the other guy says, "My name is Abu Ben Bubi." And I said as an ad lib, "Will the real Abu Ben Bubi please stand up?" Which was the line from a quiz show, *What's My Line?* And the star, (Don) Adams, says, "Hold it! Wait a minute! Let's go upstairs." They went and rewrote the entire second act based on my ad lib. And Bruce went with them, he directed it . . . Bruce was great to work with, because he was fun and loose as a goose. We all had a lot of fun. You can't do that today, you understand, because now they want it done yesterday.*

Assessment: A pretty good tale of espionage and deceit gets a little muddled with a few details that hinder the smoothness of the operation, despite the presence of the luminous Fay Spain. The best sequence involves the Underground meeting with Myra in the men's secret sanctuary, deep underground. Hogan's insistence not to attempt the rescue of Newkirk is actually the shrewd Colonel's strategy to find out if Myra is on the level or not. Ivan Dixon, in particular, is given the opportunity to show his contempt for the insensitivity of his ranking officer, and responds to Hogan's plan to destroy the ammo dump with the disappointed observation: "It's your war, colonel." Thankfully, Hogan quickly recovers the faith of his crew after exposing Myra and his true plans – to greedily rescue Newkirk and blow up the ammo dump simultaneously. This leads to the all too easy wrap up where Hogan, Carter, and Myra breeze their way through Gestapo HQ and the rescue of Newkirk. At one point Carter appears to just grab the firearm from an approaching and all too cooperative cell guard. Adding to the doubtfulness of this endeavor is the immediate round up of all the principals – just in time to watch the munitions dump go sky high. As Fay Spain does not appear in this gang reunion finale one can only ponder her existence at this point. Meanwhile, Klink and Schultz are entrenched in buffoon mode, all too easily complying with the illness of the lifeless Newkirk, and the record playing snores produced from underneath Hogan's bunk. Even the snoring which inexplicably switches to the swing sounds of Tommy Dorsey doesn't perk the curiosity of our confused Krauts.

*Telephone interview with the author, November 27, 2020.

Season 4, Episode 4: "Hogan's Trucking Service... We Deliver the Factory to You" 10/19/1968.

P/D: Edward H. Feldman W: Bill Davenport

Guest Cast: Sigrid Valdis (Hilda), Bernard Fox (Col. Crittendon), Peter Bourne (Leader Four), Bob Garrett (Cpl. Kohler), and Howard Caine as (Major Hochstetter).

Storyline: The men stall the service of Klink's staff car at the motor pool while explosives are being secretly loaded into a supply truck. The plan is to have Newkirk drive the truck and park it at a ball bearing plant while Carter follows in the staff car. The plan also involves the Underground moving in to attack fuel tanks and possibly a rail depot once the SS guards are distracted by the initial truck explosion. All plans get halted due to the arrival of a "Colonel X," an escaped POW officer who is staging an attack on Stalag 16 to free ten of his men. Newkirk and Carter become detained by "Colonel X," and when Hogan shows up for answers he discovers his old British counterpart, Colonel Crittendon. Hogan pulls Crittendon into the scheme, who fails to understand the particulars and ends up driving the truck with explosives back to Stalag 13. He is apprehended by Klink, who together with Major Hochstetter, interrogate the ignorant Colonel. Newkirk posts a fake call as a Gestapo soldier requesting Hochstetter back at the ball bearing plant to question suspects. Discovering a flat tire, courtesy of Carter, Hochstetter takes Crittendon with him to the plant in the only available vehicle, the truck loaded with TNT. Later, Crittendon is captured trying to flee the plant and brought back to Stalag 13 just as a loud explosion is heard coming from the former ball bearing plant.

Assessment: Despite the humorous interference of Bernard Fox, the Heroes accomplish their mission although the plot mechanics become easier with age. More than ever, the POWs appear to come and go from Stalag 13 with complete ease, even to the point of driving German vehicles in and out of the front gates with unchallenged freedom. Still, most of the humor prevails including Crittendon's attempt to subdue a beefy German soldier with his judo technique and his subsequent interrogation by the exceedingly pleasant Klink and the perpetually sneering Major Hochstetter. Again the action is driven by the inclusion of fake phone calls and flat tires. Klink, on the other hand, gets saddled with his sidecar as once again the gang prove their inefficiency as motor pool mechanics, even costing the Kommodant a dinner date with Hilda. We even get treated to the timeworn gag of the stranded sidecar as the motorcycle speeds away, a chestnut dating back to Groucho and Harpo and *Duck Soup* (1933). The final gag, with LeBeau having removed the brake cable from Klink's car, is more cruel than funny. And what of Major Hochstetter? We have to assume that somehow the diminutive Gestapo man survived the ball bearing plant explosion much the way Hogan has survived yet another unwelcome collaboration with the notorious "Colonel X."

Season 4, Episode 5: "To the Gestapo with Love" 10/26/1968.

D: Bruce Bilson W: Arthur Julian

Guest Cast: Sabrina Scharf (Inge Wagner), Christiane Schmidtmer (Heidi Baum), Inge Jaklin (Anna Manheim), and Howard Caine as (Major Hochstetter).

Storyline: The men are busy wiring two bridges to explode to stall an incoming Panzer division. The first blows up and the men flee back to camp, except Carter loses a button off his uniform. When the second bridge fails to explode, Carter and Newkirk argue over who was supposed to set the timer. While Hogan contemplates a solution, Hochstetter grills Klink over the found button with the inscription "US." Suspicious of the prisoners, Hochstetter brings in a triple threat: beautiful frauleins Inge, Heidi, and Anna, who have shown much success getting suspects to divulge information. LeBeau is ordered to meet the women first, and he lets some Underground info slip regarding a radio man that works from Strasbourg without realizing it. Hogan arranges to leave camp with Inge for his interrogation, and he drives them to the second bridge where he manages to finally set the timer while kissing Inge. Upon his request, Hogan is filled in by London Intelligence about several intimate details regarding the three women. That night Hogan manipulates the conversation by divulging several of these details and pitting the women against one other. The women quickly accuse each other of having loose lips which starts a big fracas until Hochstetter dismisses them. He suggests to Klink that the Gestapo will go back to "the old methods" and that at least no sabotage has taken place with Hogan under their watch. His confidence is short lived as a huge blast is heard.

Program Notes: Sabrina Scharf packed in a lot of acting work in a relatively short career, including a performance in the landmark counter culture classic, *Easy Rider* (1969). She was married for nearly fifty years to Bob Schiller, who was legendary for his long writing association with Lucille Ball. Scharf would return for the season six episode, "The Experts." Christiane Schmidtmer graced the March 1966 issue of *Playboy* magazine just after playing the German flight attendant/lover to swinger Tony Curtis in *Boeing Boeing* (1965). This was the second and final visit from Viennese beauty Inge Jaklin.

Assessment: Producer Feldman fills the frame with a trio of pleasing visuals meant to demonstrate new techniques in Gestapo interrogation methods in this diverting program. The major weakness stems from the Germans' supposedly allowing Hogan to drive off campus with Inge for his private interrogation, which conveniently allows him to set the timer on the bridge explosive. Since there is no scene building up to this action, it's just too incredible to believe that Hochstetter would allow the excursion, particularly without an armed escort. It also belies the Major's later assertion that Hogan has been kept under complete observation. The fun filled fact sheet from London about the girls' private lives is also far too convenient. London Intelligence has sure done their homework if they are on to the "schnapps problem" of Heidi's mother! Still the story moves at a lightly humorous clip punctuated by such silly sights as Carter dancing with a broomstick and Kinchloe's observation that Carter and Newkirk are fast "becoming the Laurel and Hardy of demolition teams." Finally, there's also those three heavenly visions – too bad they're working for the Gestapo.

Season 4, Episode 6: "Man's Best Friend Is Not His Dog" 11/02/1968.

D: Bruce Bilson W: Phil Sharp

Guest Cast: Katherine Henryk (Hanna Vogel), Chet Stratton (Bonner), Dick Wilson (Kraft), and Leon Askin as (Gen. Burkhalter).

Storyline: While the men perform calisthenics in the compound, a procession of new model tanks roll into camp. Carter feigns a fainting spell as an excuse to lay on the ground and take snapshots of the tanks to deliver to London. Hogan learns that they will be in touch with "Rumplestiltskin," an Underground operative who will take possession of the tank photos. Klink announces that the Swiss Prison Commission will make a detailed inspection of the POW camp. Schultz discovers the camera that Carter had used earlier, and Klink tries to set a trap for Hogan and his men by putting it back where it was found and then ordering the men to police the area. Although the trick does not work, Hogan is concerned about Klink's interest and decides to keep the film on him until the contact arrives. The Commission arrives, escorted by a Nazi officer, Hanna Vogel, and they begin a barracks inspection. Hogan hides the film in a bone belonging to a stray dog that the men have adopted, and the dog runs off with it. While the men try to recover the bone with the film in it, Hogan tries to figure out which of the visitors is "Rumplestiltskin." He is surprised to learn that it is Vogel and she agrees to adopt the stray dog and to make sure and take along the pooch's favorite bone.

Program Notes: Chet Stratton, who recently played the jubilant desk clerk "Bruno" during Klink's ski lodge vacation, continues with his six episode series connection.

Assessment: Taking a cue from last season's "Monkey Business," this installment again embraces the charm meter. This leads to the most enjoyable and well-staged sequence of the gang chasing after the adorable little dog as he merrily leads his adoptive family from one buried bone to the next. The idea of having an Underground agent show up as a Nazi officer and escort to the Swiss Commission isn't particularly a strong one. In so many other cases, one of the Heroes would simply sneak out at night and hand off the film to their contact as if conducting business as usual. Still, the writers are looking to change it up a bit and some applause should be awarded for an original effort. Less applause rendered for the stunt of Carter fainting during exercises and then laying on the ground and taking photos in plain sight of anyone caring to watch – the viewing audience included.

Season 4, Episode 7: "Never Play Cards with Strangers" 11/09/1968.

D: Marc Daniels W: Laurence Marks

Guest Cast: Arlene Martel (Olga), Sigrid Valdis (Hilda), Dan Tobin (Gen. Von Treger), Jay Sheffield (Capt. Moss), David Morick (Lt. Vogel), Walter Kightly (Sentry).

Storyline: The Heroes, accompanied by their Underground ally, Olga, watch over a rocket fuel depot that is surrounded by tight security. The topography of the hillside area makes it difficult to access so Hogan suggests an air strike from London. They also observe General Von Treger's staff car access the front gate with ease, which Hogan keeps in the back of his mind. London radios Kinchloe and tells them they cannot get an air strike to that sector, leaving the fuel depot up to Hogan. Von Treger arrives, and Klink forces LeBeau to prepare a gourmet dinner after which the general suggests they play a round of bridge. Hogan's plan is to have Carter and Newkirk drive a German truck in uniforms and fall in with a convoy of trucks scheduled to enter the fuel depot. While playing cards, Hogan hears Von Treger order the security numbers of the trucks be changed at the last minute, which would clearly expose the unwelcome truck. The men figure the mission is a total scrub, but Hogan insists they carry on. The following night brings another fine dinner and another round of bridge, except LeBeau drugs the glasses of port and Klink, Von Treger, and his aide, Capt. Moss, all konk out. Hogan and Newkirk steal the hats and top coats of the German officers and bluff their way into Von Treger's staff car. The men successfully penetrate the front gates of the fuel depot and Hogan, dressed as a Captain, delivers cases of explosive wine as a "gift" from General Von Treger. To further the deception, Newkirk is seen in the backseat of the staff car making out with Olga, with his face hidden. Hogan assures the sentry that the general is "busy in conference," and they make a hasty return just as Klink and company arouse and learn of the destruction of the fuel depot.

Program Notes: Generally cast in the role of "Tiger," this is one of two occasions for Arlene Martel to appear as a different Underground character. This is the only stopover from Dan Tobin, who spent the 1950s quite busy lending support to comedians Joan Davis and Burns and Allen, and later essaying the recurring role of Terrance Clay in sixteen episodes of *Perry Mason*.

Assessment: *How* the Heroes pull off the demolition of another rocket fuel depot is at the forefront of this passably executed mission. The most intriguing aspect of the night takes place once the lights go out for our bridge playing Nazis. In a quick and nifty sequence, Hogan and Newkirk abscond with Von Treger's vehicle (yet utilize his driver), pick up the gussied up Olga along the route, and breeze into the fuel depot with the delivery of two very deadly cases of wine. Somehow, Newkirk gets the choice assignment of lounging in the backseat of the staff car with the lovely Olga, while Hogan smooth talks the guards into his confidence. Perhaps Crane and Dawson had to draw lots behind the scenes for these casting assignments. The drawback occurs when the three Germans all awaken from their sudden one hour nap, acknowledge that it occurred, and never bother to question why they all dozed off in unison. Not extremely curious these German officers are, are they now? The wrap up feels pretty tired too, with the sleepy eyed Klink and Von Treger numbly accepting the bad consequences of the night with mild indifference.

Season 4, Episode 8: "Color the Luftwaffe Red" 11/16/1968.

D: Marc Daniels W: Laurence Marks

Guest Cast: Leon Askin (Gen. Burkhalter), John Crawford (Gestapo Man), Arthur Hanson (German Colonel), James Vickery (Major Hogel).

Storyline: The Luftwaffe is opening a new HQ building in Hammelburg, and Hogan wants Kinchloe to plant a bugging device inside. Carter and Newkirk, dressed as a German civilian couple, attempt to bluff their way past the building guards in order to take photos but are run off the property. Hogan listens to Burkhalter bristle over a paint contract bid for the new HQ in Klink's office. The general demands that Klink pay the 450 marks out of his own budget. Hogan counters to have his own men paint the interior for 350 marks, and toss in a paint job for Klink's office as a bonus. Klink accepts the paint deal, and the men are taken to the Luftwaffe HQ with Schultz supervising. While the men shuffle about, Hogan steals a top secret war map off Major Hogel's desk while Newkirk distracts him concerning paint colors. Before they can leave, Hogel orders Schultz to search all the men as a precaution. Hogan casually tosses the war plans up into a ceiling light fixture and the men hastily exit. Determined to reclaim the war map, they head back to HQ in order to inspect the paint job from the previous day. Hogan references General Burkhalter's name in order to get past Hogel's initial protests. Hogan then manages to retract the map from the light fixture after pretending the light bulb is loose. All appears in order until Schultz insists that he buy the men a round of beers at the local beer parlor. A Gestapo Man shows up and reprimands Schultz for allowing the POWs to leave the HQ building without having been searched. The men again escape detection of the theft of the map thanks to the smooth, sleight of hand maneuvers of Peter Newkirk.

Assessment: A simple, yet highly effective, Laurence Marks script keeps the action moving by centering on a basic prop and its pesky travel movements. The details of the story succeed as the frequent, implausible elements of the series are removed, and the dramatic action continues forward with simple, yet concise logistics. There's plenty to enjoy in this episode, from the amusing opening with Carter and Newkirk as a German married couple, to the paint contract negotiations between Hogan and Klink. Great touches of suspense dot the landscape, including Hogel's sudden order to search the men and, later, Hogan's bluff concerning the faulty light bulb. There's even a brief moment within the latter plot point where Hogel and Hogan exchange some awkward movement, adding to the suspense. The quick-witted colonel stays on his toes throughout this episode, including the brilliant bit where he rapidly drops Burkhalter's name to convince Hogel to reenter the office. The final scene in the beer hall with John Crawford, back as another Gestapo Agent, is also terrific with the deftly deceptive Newkirk saving the day. Big laughs also come from Schultz, who in a stand out oddball moment, aims his rifle at the men and orders that they accompany him to the bar or else they "will be shot for trying to escape!" Also tops in the funny department is the final argument with Klink, who presents Hogan with a counter bill for *his* services. "A hundred-and-ninety marks for Schultz? You gotta be kidding!" This leads to the highly inspired conclusion where Hogan orders his men to abort the messy paint job in Klink's office on account of "losing the contract."

Classic Contract Negotiation:

Klink: (with utter seriousness) "Schultz will guard you, and if there's any attempt at an escape, his orders will be shoot to kill."

Hogan: "Not exactly union conditions, but we'll take the job."

Season 4, Episode 9: "Guess Who Came to Dinner?" 11/23/1968.

D: Marc Daniels W: Arthur Julian

Guest Cast: Milton Selzer (Otto Von Krubner), Marj Dusay (Heidi Eberhardt), Ned Glass (Max, the "Grocer"), Walter Morgan (Curt).

Storyline: Max is running a grocery store as a front for Allied communications, and here we find Colonel Hogan doing a little shopping. He meets with Heidi Eberhardt, and she confides her fear of detection by the Gestapo, and asks Hogan to slip her out of Germany. Without giving her too many details about his operation, he agrees. Back at camp, Kinchloe relays a message from London warning of the possibility of Eberhardt functioning as a double agent. Hogan regrets his earlier conversation. Klink welcomes to Stalag 13 the wealthy industrialist, Otto Von Krubner, who has munitions factories all over Europe. He is planning to expand into the United States once the war is over, and the country becomes "a new colony of Germany." Hogan meets Von Krubner and is shocked to discover that Heidi is the man's fiancée. As Klink begins a camp tour with Otto, Hogan speaks in private with Heidi. In order to gain Hogan's trust, she whispers that Otto has a secret factory in Rindelsgard. London confirms the location of the factory and plans an air raid to destroy it. At dinner that night, Hogan blows Heidi's cover by telling Otto he should tighten security around his factory in Rindelsgard. Otto calls the factory office and explosions are heard ending the phone conversation. Otto accuses Heidi of treason and makes a call to Gestapo HQ, which is intercepted by Newkirk, who says that a car in the vicinity will arrest her. The Gestapo Agent turns out to be Max, the grocer, and Heidi is relieved to know the past is now behind her. She trades a warm smile with Hogan as Max leads her out. Otto threatens Hogan that the Gestapo will conduct a thorough investigation of the bombing, so LeBeau provides an explosive dessert for Otto as a definitive take out order.

Klink taking a phone call in his office with Hogan present generally signals bad news for the Third Reich. Author's collection/CBS Television Inc.

Program Notes: This is the first of three visits from Marj Dusay, who memorably played "Kara" in the *Star Trek* fan favorite, "Spock's Brain" (1968). Milton Selzer was previously seen as the stern Sgt. Franks in "Colonel Klink's Secret Weapon." Ned Glass enjoyed a long, fertile acting career, including a number of appearances in Three Stooges comedies featuring "Curly" and later "Shemp" Howard.

Assessment: A serious tone pervades this war time tale of potential trust versus potential treason, and guest stars Marj Dusay, Milton Selzer, and Ned Glass all respond to the demands of the material. The series now takes a regular, new approach to launching the half hour with an "off campus" introduction, typically one where Hogan makes contact with an Underground agent in a public place. Here it's the grocery store setting with Glass as the congenial proprietor. Klink adds a lovely degree of pleasantry to the proceedings as he confides to Hogan his desire to relocate to the United States after the war, with his one sharp eyeball paying close watch on Palm Springs and the stories he's heard about the lovely girls there sporting even lovelier swimsuits. Hogan's choice to first rat out Heidi in order to actually save her is a well-written plan of strategy. Refreshing too is the sincerity established between the two characters and the poignancy of their farewell (or in other words, Hogan doesn't make a sexual play for her). This approach would take a complete, about-face turn, when Dusay would return later in the season as the sexy Baroness in "My Favorite Prisoner." Less justifiable is LeBeau's elimination of Otto Von Krubner, who, although he threatens Hogan with an investigation, is certainly not the typical, Nazi monster. The decision to have him blown to bits seems to be more reactionary to some unflattering comments he earlier made about France. The lesson learned, apparently, is that if you are going to enjoy French cuisine in a POW camp, don't insult France.

Season 4, Episode 10: "No Names Please" 11/30/1968.

D: Marc Daniels W: Laurence Marks

Guest Cast: Richard Erdman (Walter Hobson), James Sikking (Pvt. Berger), Howard Caine (Major Hochstetter), Roy Goldman ("Olsen"/Uncredited).

Storyline: During an Allied raid, the Heroes rescue an American paratrooper from a tree, war correspondent, Walter Hobson. The men hide the journalist in the tunnel and Hobson marvels at what a great story their operation would make. Hogan shuts down the idea and urges that their operation remain in secrecy. Newkirk retrieves a "music box" (i.e. radio) that London drops down for later delivery to the Underground. The men manage to sneak Hobson out of camp in the laundry truck while Schultz is distracted. About a month later, Hogan is anxious that they still have yet to deliver the radio. He is called into Klink's office where Hochstetter informs him that a news story has circulated around Europe concerning a sabotage and escape network operating within a prisoner of war camp in Germany. Hochstetter sends "Private Berger" into Stalag 13 as a spy to investigate Hogan. Hogan convinces Klink that the only way to appease Hochstetter and his goon is to "give him something." He explains that some time ago the men started building a tunnel out of Barracks Four, and that they could cue Hochstetter to halt a staged escape attempt. The two agree for Wednesday night, and Klink notifies Hochstetter. Not entirely trusting Hogan, Klink confides to Schultz they will strike on Tuesday night and without informing Hochstetter. In Barracks Four, Klink catches Hogan and Newkirk in the act, and they are all surprised by the sudden appearance of Hochstetter and Berger. While Klink and Hochstetter argue, Kinchloe and Carter sneak out with the "music box."

Program Notes: This is the first of three appearances for long time TV favorite, James Sikking, best remembered as the overzealous, Lt. Howard Hunter in 144 episodes of *Hill Street Blues* (1981-1987). Roy Goldman, who typically plays a silent but frequently visible POW, appears here as "Olsen," and enjoys a few lines of dialogue. Other sources have incorrectly cited Stewart Moss appearing as "Olsen," but he is not seen in this episode. The radio being called "the music box" is most likely a friendly nod to Laurel and Hardy's Oscar-winning short subject (1932), a tip of the derby hat, perhaps, to a great comedy team the series frequently references.

Assessment: This time it's an American ally that creates complications for Hogan and company, an original concept which generates plenty of laughs as Klink and Hochstetter get pulled into the scheme machine. There's a fun opening which combines stock footage of an air raid attack followed by a clever high angle shot, looking straight down at a parachutist stuck in a tree. The banter in Klink's office is highly spirited including Hogan's suggestion to "keep the war sensible" when accused of being our favorite saboteur. Klemperer continues to find audience sympathy, this time with his genuine, innocent concern of Hogan's possible spy activity. The Heroes appear to be growing into the Bowery Boys, with the addition of Olsen bringing the gang count to five. There's also plenty of comical spark in the finale when Klink uncharacteristically stands up to Hochstetter and the little Major's ballistic response. Some nicely timed suspense is also generated when Hochstetter and company almost walk in on Kinchloe and Carter and those flexible bunk beds, but once again Colonel Hogan is there to save the moment with the hurried and precisely timed announcement: "Major Hochstetter! The escape's happening in Barracks Four!"

Season 4, Episode 11: "Bad Day in Berlin" 12/07/1968.

D: Richard Kinon W: Laurence Marks

Guest Cast: Harold J. Stone (Major Teppel), John Stephenson (Decker), John Hoyt (Colonel Braun), Edward Knight (Major Metzger), David Wiley (Agent One).

Storyline: Hard-nosed Major Teppel of Abwehr Intelligence makes an inspection of the men's barracks and immediately starts an argument with Newkirk. Requesting a private conference with Hogan, Teppel proves he's an Underground agent as both men share halves of a playing card, the eight of spades. The two agree to arrange a meeting later. Klink is called away from dinner thanks to a fake phone call from a fictitious general. Hogan then learns that Teppel is actually Robert Morrison, of German/American descent, and was forced to turn traitor and join the German Army. Yet he has successfully continued to aid Allied Underground activity, and now his big concern is "Robin Hood," an agent who knows all about Teppel and Hogan's extracurricular activities. "Robin Hood" is actually "Decker," a German spy, and he's ready to bring down the house of cards by singing to the Gestapo in Berlin. Morrison wants to take Hogan and some of his men to Berlin for "questioning" where they can find a way to penetrate the Berlin Hotel and remove Decker. Morrison and Hogan, with Carter and Newkirk dressed as paramedics, arrive at the hotel in an ambulance. Morrison subdues Decker with a drug, and Carter and Newkirk remove the body on a stretcher. Morrison reveals the contents of Decker's briefcase bearing incriminating maps and papers. He also points out his "insurance policy," two killers across the street who will shoot if a man exits with the briefcase. Major Metzger arrives stating that Colonel Braun is in the lobby waiting, which forces Hogan to impersonate Decker. Hogan nervously stalls Metzger and tells Morrison to order his men not to shoot. Down in the lobby, Metzger detains Morrison from leaving the building as "Decker" joins the group. After awkwardly lighting up a cigarette, "Decker" bolts from the lobby leaving his briefcase behind. Colonel Braun helpfully chases after "Decker" with the briefcase and meets a hail of bullets, an opportunity for Hogan and Morrison to disappear in the ambulance.

Program Notes: This is the first of twelve directing assignments for Richard Kinon, already established as a very productive director of several episodes of *Perry Mason*, *Burke's Law*, and *Bewitched*. Harold J. Stone makes his debut with the series and would return for two more assignments. Another prolific actor with an expansive resume, Stone frequents the films of Jerry Lewis: *The Big Mouth* (1967), *Which Way to the Front?* (1970), and *Hardly Working* (1981/US release). On the more serious side of the street, Stone also played a key role in *The Harder They Fall* (1956), Humphrey Bogart's final feature.

Assessment: "It's a crazy war," smiles Harold J. Stone at the onset of a smart adventure that features a tricky assignment in Berlin filled with several moments of intrigue and suspense, and only a few wisecracks. Ironically, Hogan is baffled at first to meet an American hiding behind a German officer's uniform – a masquerade Hogan assumes on a near weekly basis. Laurence Marks' densely plotted script finds Hogan following the game plan of another schemer, and for a nice change of pace it's Hogan who has to sweat and dodge bullets this time around. Crane is well matched with the serious approach of guest star Stone, and the duo make an excellent team. The multiple plot points and their well-paced development move with precision. There's much to credit debuting director Kinon, who offers a *Dirty Dozen* style approach to the action. The finale, with Hogan making a bolt for the exit leaving John Hoyt holding the bag and on the receiving end of a barrage of bullets is a tough-minded conclusion that belies the gripes of the critics who all too frequently dismiss *Hogan's Heroes* as "hokum's heroes".

Season 4, Episode 12: "Will the Blue Baron Strike Again?" 12/14/1968.

D: Marc Daniels W: Arthur Julian

Guest Cast: Sigrid Valdis (Hilda), Leon Askin (Gen. Burkhalter), Jon Cedar (Cpl. Langenscheidt), Celeste Yarnall (Nanny), Laurie Mitchell (Honey Hornburg), Cynthia Lynn (pretty girl with Baron/Uncredited), and Henry Corden as (Gen. Von Richter, "the Blue Baron").

Storyline: Just before roll call, Corporal Langenscheidt helpfully fills in Hogan about General Von Richter, who will be opening a secret airfield near Hammelburg. Von Richter is renowned for having shot down seventy-five enemy planes during World War I, earning him the nickname "the Blue Baron." The corporal further explains that Klink knew him during air academy training where his cowardice permanently injured Von Richter's knee. Hogan is determined to learn the location of the air base and convinces Klink to throw a party for the Blue Baron and big brass. The men intercept Klink's mail delivery and find that all the invited guests have returned regrets. While Burkhalter reprimands Klink for wasteful party planning, Hogan gets Hilda to call back the party guests, who will miss out on "Honey Hornburg and the Stuttgart Steppers," an exotic dance troupe attending. The regrets quickly turn into RSVPs and even Burkhalter changes his tune. Hogan tells Klink the revised VIP guest list will easily persuade Honey Hornburg and her girls to attend. Hogan hopes the party will end by ten, follow Von Richter back to his airfield, and then signal Allied bombers to destroy it. The party gets rolling and while Burkhalter has a ball with Honey Hornburg, Von Richter sets his sights on a pretty blonde. No one wants to leave. Hogan and his men steal the hats and topcoats of the German brass and trick Von Richter's driver into taking them to the airfield. Hogan manages to ignite some oil drums which create a pretty, fiery show for the Allied bombers to zero in on. Later, the Blue Baron informs Klink that he is a "jinx," and orders him to never make contact again.

Program Notes: Colonel Klink's first-season secretary, Helga (Cynthia Lynn), makes her return as an unidentified, and uncredited, party guest. This is the third of five guest shots for Henry Corden. John Banner does not appear in this episode, which encourages Jon Cedar to return as Corporal Langenscheidt.

Assessment: The returns of Cynthia Lynn, Jon Cedar, and Henry Corden, along with a raucous performance from Leon Askin, bring plenty of good cheer. With the absence of Schultz, Langenscheidt returns and more than willingly conveys information regarding the Blue Baron to Hogan. Here's a corporal who appears to "know something" and is happy to share it. Much of the episode is devoted to Hogan and Klink's effort in arranging the party and guest list which includes a snappy, double talk scene in the office followed by Hilda's enthusiastic cooperation to playfully recruit the guests. Sigrid Valdis appears to fight a laughter fit on the telephone while explaining that Honey Hornburg and the Stuttgart Steppers is an "exotic dance troupe!" The party scene is loads of fun with Burkhalter dominating the action, inseparable from Honey Hornburg, and the droll Corden, in a woefully underwritten role, telling Klink he hasn't been able to dance since 1917 – when their test flight went down and his knee went out. The only complaint one can make about Corden's performance is that there just isn't *enough* of it. Arthur Julian borrows from the earlier "Never Play Cards with Strangers" plot point of having the men make use of a staff car and uniforms to further their sabotage efforts. Interestingly enough, while both of Klink's secretaries appear in this episode, they do not share screen time.

Greatest Revelation:

Honey Hornburg: "General! Are you always this friendly with the prisoners?"

Burkhalter: "When one feels this good, everyone's German!"

Season 4, Episode 13: "Will the Real Colonel Klink Please Stand Up Against the Wall?" 12/21/1968.

D: Richard Kinon W: Bill Davenport

Guest Cast: Leon Askin (Gen. Burkhalter), Noam Pitlik (Capt. Herber), and Howard Caine as (Major Hochstetter).

Storyline: In Berlin, Burkhalter reviews a map of unexplained sabotage attacks for Hochstetter and Herber. The discussion includes a doomed munitions train that was disguised as a hospital train, and a forthcoming train that will be transporting airplane parts for the Luftwaffe. Burkhalter explains that the transport activities are known to the three Kommodants in the vicinity, which leads Hochstetter to suspect Klink, although the General isn't as certain. Herber is to be planted as a new aide in Klink's camp where he can report any suspicious behavior back to Gestapo HQ. Hogan learns the Berlin Express will be used as a cover to transport the airplane parts and plans to derail it. Hogan denies Klink the use of his staff car claiming several parts have turned up missing. He sends Carter, dressed as Klink, out in the staff car to the station master, to deliver a special package that must travel with the train. After Klink retires, Herber witnesses the fake Klink leave camp and reports the odd behavior to Hochstetter. Herber is ordered to search Klink's office, and then notify the station master to "switch to the alternate plan." While Hogan stalls Herber in the office, LeBeau runs a phone line from the office to the barracks. Newkirk intercepts and receives Herber's phone call to the station master. To help establish an alibi for Klink, Hogan barges into his quarters causing Schultz to tumble through the bedroom door. Hochstetter accuses Klink of treason, backed by Herber's testimony, but Burkhalter is still uncertain. The German officers question Hogan and Schultz, but a phone call received by Hochstetter verifies the phone lines have been down all day, which belies Herber's claim that he contacted the station master earlier. Klink is released from suspicion, Burkhalter and Hochstetter gang up on Herber, and the Berlin Express blows up on cue.

Program Notes: This is the first episode to feature frequent guest stars Leon Askin and Howard Caine appearing together in the same program. Noam Pitlik chocks up his fourth of seven guest appearances.

Assessment: A well-conceived, character driven Bill Davenport script featuring Noam Pitlik's liveliest role yet, some cleverly timed trickery, and the monumental, long awaited, team up of General Burkhalter *and* Major Hochstetter, all contribute to one of the series' most enjoyable offerings. The story launches with a crackling opener where we first encounter both Burkhalter and Hochstetter sharing screen time and some choice dialogue with the Gestapo Major condemning Klink's "stupidity" and the Luftwaffe General defending it! Another choice encounter occurs late in the game with Hogan walking in on the very suspicious Capt. Herber in Klink's office, and the barrage of insults and offbeat comments fired with deft ease by our favorite, wisecracking POW. Pitlik proves to be a terrific foil to Crane's free flowing insolence. A delightful bit by Dawson as the jovial train station master, and the droll interjections of Askin, who continues to defend Klink based on his stupidity (!), keep this episode traveling with plenty of spark, right to the exciting conclusion where a large airplane part crashes through the window of Klink's quarters. The ruse of keeping Klink's car in the shop gets worked over yet again, and the absence of *any* stalag guards while Carter (dressed as Klink), LeBeau, and one of the guard dogs all clown around before mission time may raise the eyebrows of some fans, but for pure comedy derived from terrific characterizations, this episode is tough to beat. Truly, this is a fan favorite outing.

Season 4, Episode 14: "Man in a Box" 12/28/1968.

D: Richard Kinon W: Laurence Marks

Guest Cast: Sigrid Valdis (Hilda), Jill Donohue (Luise), Diana Chesney (Nazi clerk), Walter Janowitz (Schnitzer), Buck Young (Guard), and John Crawford (Gestapo Officer).

Storyline: In order to sneak LeBeau out of camp in a garbage truck, Hogan uses Hilda as an attractive decoy to distract Schultz from inspecting the outgoing cans. LeBeau is to rendezvous with the Underground agent "Luise," and together they will go to a German building where a magnetic mine is being developed, under the pretense of seeking employment. Using a gimmick cigarette pack, LeBeau will take photos of the building interior. Klink begins a fruitless search for LeBeau's recapture and finally allows Hogan to head into town to do so. Hogan meets with Luise in a pub and receives the trick camera, only to discover that he is being tailed by Schultz in civilian attire. While Luise flirts with Schultz, and then Klink, Hogan slips out the back exit. LeBeau sneaks back to camp, and Hogan explains his plan to destroy the research building. LeBeau will be crated in a box, Hogan's men will stop a supply truck en route to the research lab, and the box will be slipped into the rear. Hogan, pretending to be upset over Klink and Schultz's meddling, gives up on the search, but Klink persists that he try again. That night, the crate with LeBeau is successfully moved onto the supply truck and delivered to the lab. After planting explosives and igniting smoke bombs, LeBeau escapes and moves to his next appointed stop, an old barn just down the road. Hogan alerts Klink and his men to the location, and while Klink rambles outside, LeBeau sneaks into the back of the barn, then gives himself up.

Assessment: The most pleasing of diversions, Sigrid Valdis, walking across the compound, is certainly an eye catching way to launch this diverting, yet unsatisfying, caper off on the right note.

The ensuing proceedings, unfortunately, don't add up too well as we get stuck with routine, sitcom shtick, like the marginally funny sequence with Schultz and Klink proving their ineptness at tailing Hogan in a Hammelburg pub (a scene frequently snipped out of syndication re-runs). The mechanics of the plot all flow freely from any suspense or threat of opposition, such as the stopping of the Nazi supply truck and the deceptive addition of the title character. Ditto with the ease that LeBeau is able to detonate the research facility and make his escape with nary a witness. The final sequence, too, with the absent LeBeau supposedly holed up in the barn, and Klink and Schultz all too eager to accept and hear his presence until he finally does show up, feels more phony than funny. Klemperer, always the pro, makes the most of his hammy speech while we all wait for LeBeau to actually appear. However, we might be better off waiting for heavenly Hilda to sashay by one more time.

Season 4, Episode 15: "The Missing Klink" 01/04/1969.

D: Marc Daniels W: Bill Davenport

Guest Cast: Leon Askin (Gen. Burkhalter), Sigrid Valdis (Hilda), Dick Wilson (Capt. Gruber), Ann Prentiss (Ilse), Chris Robinson (Karl Wagner), and Howard Caine as (Major Hochstetter).

Storyline: Hogan and Carter scout out a Nazi building at nightfall where Hans Wagner, head of the Underground, is being imprisoned. His brother, Karl, pressures Hogan to think of an escape plan, but the colonel is uncertain since the building is a fortress. Knowing that Klink will be headed to the train station to pick up Burkhalter, Hogan suggests that Karl and his followers stop the vehicle and kidnap the general and arrange a prisoner swap. Klink and Schultz wait at the train station, but Burkhalter never arrives. Heading back, Klink's vehicle is stopped, and he is removed at gunpoint. Schultz hurries back to camp to report the kidnapping of Klink to his aide, Capt. Gruber. Hogan realizes that the Underground has mistaken Klink for Burkhalter. The General arrives at Stalag 13 after having waited at the *airport* for Klink for two hours. Burkhalter and Major Hochstetter seem complacent with the missing Klink, and Hogan realizes he must scheme to get him back. With Newkirk posing as British Intelligence, a phone call is placed to Klink's private line for "Nimrod," a British agent that has long confounded the Nazis. Hochstetter receives the call along with a secret code, which he spends two hours unsuccessfully decoding, much to the fatigue and doubts of Burkhalter. Newkirk is sent in under the pretense of cleaning the office, and claims he recognizes the code from his schooling days. Newkirk decodes the message as: "Secret plans hidden Hilda's desk." The men arrange for Hans Wagner to be traded for Wilhelm Klink, who Hochstetter is convinced is "Nimrod," and when Klink finally returns home he is delighted to find Burkhalter and Hochstetter waiting. Placed under arrest, Klink's delight is short lived.

Hogan enters to claim the model planes sent by the Red Cross, and he also grabs the model plane instructions – which happen to be the "secret plans from Hilda's desk." A final phone call from Newkirk sets Hochstetter straight by thanking him for returning Karl Wagner and confirming the return of Colonel Klink.

Assessment: Executive producer Edward Feldman must have realized midway through this fourth season that he had a goldmine with actors Leon Askin and Howard Caine at his disposal, and so Bill Davenport again pens a script that pairs Burkhalter and Hochstetter, and along with the always reliable Peter Newkirk pulling the strings, the duo carry the bulk of the run time with a high quota of laughs. Howard Caine is in focus and again the viewer is exposed to some humane details not seen since "War Takes a Holiday." Here the humor focuses on the little Major's frenzied attempt to crack the code planted by Newkirk's fake British agent, and Caine makes every moment decidedly deliberate, genuine, and very funny. Whether earnestly following directions to memorize the coded message and then swallow the evidence, to staging how he and the general should pose in a nonchalant manner while anticipating the return of Klink, Caine seizes each and every nuance with gusto. Aiding and abetting his efforts are the deadpan comments and expressions countered by Leon Askin, who effortlessly displays the attributes of the perfect straight man. Klink is allowed room to actually display some uncommon heroics during his kidnap and incarceration, and his genuine pleasure at discovering the general and the major awaiting his return is its own delight. Rounding out the character driven antics is Richard Dawson's crafty approach, both as a thoughtful Intelligence Agent and, later, as a one time student of cryptography. Just observe the way he deciphers the code and you will appreciate the relaxed smoothness of this expert character actor.

Season 4, Episode 16: "Who Stole My Copy of Mein Kampf?" 01/11/1969.

D: Bruce Bilson W: Phil Sharp

Guest Cast: Ruta Lee (Leslie Smythe-Beddoes), Alan Oppenheimer (Col. Sitzer), and Leon Askin as (Gen. Burkhalter).

Storyline: In the middle of the night, Kinchloe wakes up Hogan with an urgent coded message. While Hogan consults his code book, masked as a personal hygiene manual, Klink and Schultz barge in demanding why the men are still up. Hogan demurely admits they were plotting an escape involving the men dressed as dogs looking for bones! Klink orders the men to their bunks and leaves with Hogan's "hygiene book." Hogan plots to recover the book before Klink realizes its importance. He stages a rehearsed apology in Klink's office, actually a trick with LeBeau manipulating the book off Klink's desk. Later, General Burkhalter arrives with Colonel Sitzer from the Ministry of Propaganda. The men state that Klink will receive an award for his perfect record and his acceptance speech will be broadcast on live radio for Hitler. Hogan finally decodes the message revealing orders to silence Leslie Smythe-Beddoes of the Ministry of Propaganda. Hogan visits the Propaganda office dressed as a German captain assigned to deliver a (lethal) package to Beddoes, but he demures when he sees it's a woman. Klink continually hounds Hogan for advice about his acceptance speech while Hogan realizes an alternate plan to remove Beddoes. In a fake conversation with Carter, Hogan pretends to sympathize with Hitler's philosophies in his book "Mein Kampf." Beddoes recruits Hogan to appear along with Klink on the upcoming radio broadcast thinking it will please Col. Sitzer who has tired of their usual programming. During the broadcast, Klink's speech is cut short by Beddoes. Next Hogan goes on a rant that includes his mention of several stretches of prison time and the novelty of Hitler being a man who can do "the thinking of all men." He also opines his thoughts on Hitler's less than successful campaign with Russia. Sitzer cuts the broadcast short and fires Beddoes on the spot. Later, a phone call from Hitler renders a mandate; Beddoes will be turned over to the Gestapo, and the suggestion that if Hogan ever attempts escape, Klink should let him!

Program Notes: The series continues to make direct references to recent outings. In the first barracks scene, Hogan explains to Klink about their escape attempt involving the POWs dressed as "dogs burying bones" ("Man's Best Friend is Not his Dog"). Later, Hogan makes a clumsy exit after his botched delivery attempt by aping the limping walk of Henry Corden's Blue Baron. Alan Oppenheimer has worked with just about everybody in Hollywood, including Dan Rowan and Dick Martin in their 1969 horror spoof *The Maltese Bippy*. This is the second of three guest shots for Ruta Lee, who shared her general fondness for the cast: *

Bob (Crane) was adorable too! All the guys on that series were terribly funny. I mean terribly in the nice way. It was just one big laugh all the time. I was peeing my pants the whole time I was on the shoot . . . that's how much we laughed!

Assessment: A somewhat familiar theme already explored in "Axis Annie" gets a successful makeover aided by a gamy guest cast and Bruce Bilson's spry direction. Once again Klink confounds Hogan's plans with an unsanctioned action – here removing Hogan's book on "hygiene" - and without realizing the significance of that action. This leads to the most clever bit of the night, the men serenading Klink with an apology recital while LeBeau retrieves the book from Klink's desktop with the use of his third arm! Director Bilson pulls some inspired performances from his guest stars, including the hilarious sequence where Ruta Lee asks Klink a series of questions about his aptitudes and talents, only to receive a series of doubtfully silent and perplexed responses from the less-than-gifted Kommodant. Alan Oppenheimer injects a heavy dose of enthusiasm to his inspired, yet somewhat bored of it all, purveyor of radio propaganda.

He almost appears to have taken inspiration from the "Gavin MacLeod school of Nazi acting." Or perhaps it's the other way around. Lastly, Bob Crane gets to revisit his unique brand of rambling, political satire first launched in "Is General Hammerschlag Burning?" with his quirky, on-air opinions vocalized at the expense of Hitler and the Third Reich.

Hilter has just listened to Colonel Hogan's less than favorable radio commentary of the Third Reich's war campaigns and this means bad news for guest stars Ruta Lee and Alan Oppenheimer in "Who Stole My Copy of Mein Kampf?" Photo courtesy of Alan Oppenheimer/CBS Television Inc.

*Telephone interview with the author, December 4, 2020.

Season 4, Episode 17: "Operation Hannibal" 01/18/1969.

D: Bruce Bilson W: Laurence Marks

Guest Cast: Sigrid Valdis (Hilda), Louise Troy (Hedy Von Behler), John Hoyt (Gen. Von Behler), Jack Riley (Capt.), Dick Wilson (Capt. Gruber/Uncredited), John Creswell (German Private/Unc.).

Storyline: General Von Behler and his aide discuss "Operation Hannibal," a combat strategy involving guerrilla warfare that could prolong the war. His daughter, Hedy, visits the POWs while working near a railroad and offers them cheese sandwiches. Schultz confiscates the sandwich given to LeBeau and this leads to a mock trial in Klink's office which results in five days in the cooler for the Frenchman. Hogan removes the wrapper of the sandwich which contains a coded message from Hedy requesting a private meeting. Hogan slips out of camp dressed as a Luftwaffe officer and pretends to be Klink's aide, Capt. Gruber. In the palatial Von Behler residence, "Gruber" makes small talk with the General followed by private talk with his daughter. Hedy wants Hogan and his men to access the General's safe during a party and photograph the Operation Hannibal documents. If anything fails, she will back her father and Hogan's men will suffer the consequences. At the party, "Gruber" runs afoul of Klink, and also sets in place climbing rope outside the balcony to Von Behler's study. Hedy keeps the guard posted in the terrace busy with a plate of food while Carter and LeBeau scale the outside wall, enter the study, and open the safe using the combination Hedy provided. "Gruber" keeps the guard distracted while Carter and LeBeau make their escape from the study. Hedy says farewell to the Heroes in the parking lot and warmly embraces "Gruber" to again dodge Klink. Later, Klink chides the real, and confused, Capt. Gruber about his romantic charms and ponders to Hogan why his adjutant won't include his Kommodant in his social circle.

Program Notes: This is the third and final visit from Louise Troy. Jack Riley makes his debut with the series. A king of droll, often self depreciating humor, Riley had established himself as a busy, working actor when he landed his most familiar role, Elliot Carlin, one of the frequently seen patients on *The Bob Newhart Show*. Mel Brooks' vast devotees will probably remember Riley as one of the Roman soldiers inhaling the "Roman Red" and contemplating the fall of the Empire in *History of the World: Part I* (1981). Carter repeats the gag of attempting to swallow an important piece of paper, a task recently demonstrated by Major Hochstetter in "The Missing Klink." Director Bruce Bilson recalled some filming incidents:

They had to get into the castle; they were driving a jeep and we shot it on a stage with a big fountain in the center of the square and behind it was the wall with the exterior of the castle and it was rigged so they could climb up it . . . The jeep is supposed to drive in, whoever was driving hit the brakes, and it skidded and hit the fountain which was on wheels, and it just rolled away. Which was a great outtake shot. Someone has that . . . maybe Jerry (London) because he was in editing. So they go to climb the wall . . . Larry Hovis and probably Robert, certainly Larry. And it's really hard. It took forever and the whole crew was just holding their mouths trying not to laugh out loud. I remember it that way.*

Assessment: This caper works on several levels by focusing on a more humane objective, photographing the war plans to help end, not prolong the war. It's a lot of fun to watch the Heroes confound the Nazis by blowing up buildings and bridges, but in order for the series to succeed in the marathon, it's wise to get a break from such violent activity on occasion. Here the core relationship of a devoted Nazi officer and his even more devoted daughter succeeds thanks to some thoughtful Laurence Marks dialogue advocating the end of Hitler's war by a larger majority of the German population. Key factors that furnish the funny business include Carter's hilarious impersonation of Klink on the telephone to Von Behler, Hogan's "Gruber" reprimanding the guard in order to keep his eyes away from cat burglar activity, and Klink's prodding of the understandably puzzled Gruber about his social circle (the inimitable Dick Wilson). Less intuitive is the mock trial in Klink's office over the coveted cheese sandwich, an exercise in appropriately cheesy silliness which oddly ushers in one of the more realistic implementations of Klink justice – five actual days in the cooler for LeBeau!

*Telephone interview with the author, September 14, 2020. The 2016 CBS Home Entertainment DVD collection of the entire series contains a "gag reel," special feature which includes a brief snippet of Larry Hovis attempting to scale the wall as Bilson described.

Season 4, Episode 18: "My Favorite Prisoner" 01/25/1969.

D: Bruce Bilson W: Laurence Marks

Guest Cast: Marj Dusay (Baroness Von Krimm), John Orchard (Capt. Sears), James Sikking (Gestapo Officer), and Howard Caine as (Major Hochstetter).

Storyline: During a cocktail party in Klink's quarters, Hogan cozies up with a sexy German Baroness. Schultz implies to Hogan that he might be able to allow him out of camp to further the prospective romance. Hogan quickly realizes that both Klink and Schultz are in cahoots with the Baroness, and they hope the wily female will extract war secrets out of Hogan. The next night, Schultz allows Hogan to exit the front gates, and he enjoys a date with the Baroness in her home. They make idle chatter while Klink and Schultz eavesdrop with the help of a planted microphone. Back in the barracks, the men smuggle in British Captain Sears who possesses a phony invasion plan that London wants the Nazis to obtain. Hogan thinks the Baroness can be an unknowing instrument to their plans. Hogan again freely returns to the Baroness' home except this time he brings along Sears, who needs a hideout for a few days. When alone, the two men discuss the fake war plans and the Underground contact scheduled to meet Sears. Hochstetter, who has joined the snooping party, sets up Schultz as the contact and once the war plans are handed off, Hochstetter and his men burst in and arrest Sears. While Hogan enjoys yet another date with the Baroness, Carter, Newkirk, and LeBeau, trigger the escape of Sears from Gestapo HQ. When Hochstetter and Klink learn of the breakout, they find Hogan still cozy on the couch with the Baroness, releasing him from suspicious activity.

Program Notes: The epilogue sequence ends on a freeze frame of Klink along with a title credit for "executive producer, Edward

H. Feldman." The remaining programs would all utilize this freeze frame finish.

Assessment: A less than smooth plot line is mostly ironed out thanks to the game contributions of returnees Orchard, Dusay, and Sikking, and the always reliable Howard Caine. There's plenty of delights to go around, particularly the unusual novelty of Klink and Schultz deliberately scheming against Hogan, and the eventual addition of Major Hochstetter latching on to Klink's brainstorm. This is a rare instance where Schultz is a regular cooperative of the German side and less a buddy to the prisoners. There's also some ironic humor to seize in the regular intervals where the nonchalant Schultz calls down his guards as he freely allows Hogan to exit the gates at nightfall. One can only assume the stroll to the Baroness' abode is a short one. In a program that features the star player frequently in the arms of European babes, real chemistry is vividly apparent between the pairing of Bob Crane and Marj Dusay. They spend much of the half hour on the couch in an all too natural and pleasing lip lock. The plot gets confusing, however, regarding Hogan's attitude towards the phony invasion plans and *how* they should let the Germans discover it. Back at camp, Hogan worries about the Gestapo coming down on his operation if he is directly involved, yet apparently later he isn't too concerned with Capt. Sears being tossed under the Gestapo bus. Hogan casually delivers marching orders for the rescue of Sears, more concerned with his followup date with the Baroness. This attitude sets up another routine, easy as pie, rescue from Gestapo HQ, bolstered by the stoic presence of James Sikking and a very funny exchange with Carter regarding cell number *nein*.

Season 4, Episode 19: "Watch the Trains Go By" 01/18/1969.

D: Bruce Bilson W: Laurence Marks

Guest Cast: Leon Askin (Gen. Burkhalter), Alice Ghostley (Gertrude Linkmeyer).

Storyline: The Heroes are busy wiring railroad tracks for a late night blast party when LeBeau warns of an approaching German patrol. Hogan aborts the mission and the team flee back to camp. At Stalag 13, the boys observe tightened security with soldiers in and out of the fence line. Hogan elects Newkirk and Carter to slip down to the fence, cut the wire, and enter camp. The duo are immediately apprehended and hauled off to the cooler while the other access the tunnel. Hogan learns that the beefed up security is tied in to a pending inspection with General Burkhalter, and he plots to keep Klink distracted by persuading the general's sister, Gertrude, to accompany her brother to Stalag 13. Hogan secretly visits Newkirk in the cooler and has him forge a love letter to Gertrude. Burkhalter and Gertrude arrive together and Klink is uncertain about her presence. He seeks Hogan's advice to deter her romantic interest, and Hogan cooperates, provided Klink will release his men from the cooler. Their first conceived plan, having Klink continually act too busy to interact with Gertrude, backfires when Gertrude respects Klink's commitment to his work and heightened security. Meanwhile, London wants to have the Underground take over the railroad bombing job, but Hogan stubbornly wants to have his team finish it. Finally, Hogan convinces Klink to take Gertrude on a moonlight drive near the railroad tracks and tell her the truth of his disinterest. Hogan hides in the trunk of the car and later slips out and finishes laying the explosive wiring. He slips back into the trunk just as Klink orders Schultz to drive them back to camp following his disastrous break up date with Gertrude. Later, Burkhalter is furious, but Hogan appeases the general explaining how embarrassing it would be to introduce Klink as his brother-in-law to the Fuhrer!

Program Notes: Familiar comic actress Alice Ghostley takes over the role of Gertrude Linkmeyer, previously played twice by comic actress Kathleen Freeman. 1969 was an exceptionally busy year for the always working Freeman, who probably was tied to another commitment when this episode was produced. Freeman would return to the role, however, on two more occasions. Ghostley, a vastly gifted comic herself, is best remembered in sixteen episodes of *Bewitched*, as Samantha's cousin, the bumbling witch, Esmerelda. Ghostley would return to Stalag 13 in an unrelated role in the final season.

Assessment: Quite a few, strong, unusual elements surface above the story line and help submerge the weaker elements, and make this more than just another lopsided, Cupid comedy between Klink and Gertrude. In her only crack at the role, Alice Ghostley brings a sensitivity to the part not seen with the Kathleen Freeman interpretation. There's a bit of a melancholic aura that Ghostley's Gertrude favors and it's rather effective, especially considering that her presence at Stalag 13 is one of complete, insensitive manipulation on Hogan's part. The routine exercise of escaping in and out of camp is nicely addressed with the early scene of the whole gang plotting their way back into camp. Director Bilson includes a terrific, sloped angle of Newkirk and Carter sneaking their way down to the fence line. Contrived, to say the least, is Hogan's persuasion to get Klink to take Gertrude out on a moonlight drive *and* conveniently park the car right next to the railroad tracks that Hogan needs to revisit. If Klink is ready to dump poor Gertrude, why would he stage it around a drive and park to Lovers' Lane? Still, it ensues with the smoothest action of the night - Hogan's return to camp where he slips out of the trunk and then quickly assumes an awkwardly casual, upright gait as the car pulls away and Klink approaches. Smooth, Colonel Hogan, quite smooth.

Season 4, Episode 20: "Klink's Old Flame" 02/08/1969.

D: Bruce Bilson W: Arthur Julian

Guest Cast: Ben Wright (Count Von Heffernick), Norma Eberhardt (Marlena Schneider), Leon Askin (Gen. Burkhalter), Sigrid Valdis (Hilda), Norbert Schiller (Hans, the farmer), Arthur Hanson (Willy).

Storyline: An unusual meeting inside a haystack takes place between Hogan and "Willy," an Underground contact. Willy has five shortwave radios that must be delivered to their allies in France. Hogan takes on the assignment not certain how the delivery will occur. Count Von Heffernick is preparing to visit Stalag 13, calling for increased rolls calls and bed checks. Hogan wants to find a way to get LeBeau and the radios to France so he has LeBeau attempt a phony escape. This includes having one of the guard dogs wake up Schultz in order to arrest LeBeau! Klink sends LeBeau to the cooler, but Hogan suggests that a transfer to the POW camp near France would make for an even more bittersweet punishment. Klink approves the transfer but changes his mind when Count Von Heffernick arrives and objects to the idea. It seems that the Count's fiancee, Marlena Schneider, was an old girlfriend of Klink's, and the Count wants to make certain that the old flame no longer burns for either party before their marriage and honeymoon in France. He threatens Klink who turns to Hogan for his usual sage advice. Hogan helps Klink transform into a completely disheveled, womanizing alcoholic which repulses Marlena and satisfies the Count. He endorses a promotion for Klink, and he and his fiancee leave Stalag 13 for France not realizing that Kinchloe has hidden the five radios inside the dashboard of their auto. Later, a staff car enters the camp and Klink, assuming that the Count has returned, reverts to his drunken alter ego by seizing Hilda in a warm embrace. General Burkhalter enters, observes the behavior, and tears up the promotion recommendation.

Assessment: Two different plot elements are at work in this episode, but they seem to almost work against one another. The essential story concerning the delivery of five shortwave radios to France gets encumbered with details that don't resonate. Generally Hogan is protective of his team, but here he is ready to have LeBeau transferred to another POW camp, supposedly near France, in order to move the radios. As a result, we presume that LeBeau is permanently leaving and that his new stalag will be equally accomodating. Hogan implies that LeBeau's transport truck will be stopped by the French Underground (with the radios hidden inside by Carter) but what happens next with the Frenchman is unexplained. It's only for sheer luck that Hogan cuts a deal with Klink and manages to rescind LeBeau's transfer, now to Stalag 14, which is nowhere near France. This bridges the other plot element which is essentially a one-set comedy piece. Fortunately, it's a strong one thanks to Klemperer's wildly funny interpretation of the alcoholic Kommodant, who alternates between jovial and somber instances. Julian's one liners during this sequence are especially spirited topped by Klink's passionate kiss with Hilda - "in duplication." Not surprisingly, Klink goes back to Hilda for seconds climaxing in one of the briefest, and funniest, visits yet from General Burkhalter. Other choice bits include the bizarre opener, cleverly staged inside a haystack, and LeBeau's phony escape attempt, which includes having the guard dog lick Schultz's face and kicking Schultz in the shin to wake his sleeping ass!

Classic Revelation:

Marlena: "I've never heard of a prisoner of war camp like this!"

Hogan: "Yeah, neither have we. Around here, punishment is like not getting white wine with the fish!"

Season 4, Episode 21: "Up in Klink's Room" 02/15/1969.

D: Bruce Bilson W: Harvey Bullock, R. S. Allen

Guest Cast: Forrest Compton (Major Zimmer), Sigrid Valdis (Hilda), Victoria Carroll (Pretty Nurse Gerda), Muriel Landers (chubby nurse), and Henry Corden as (Dr. Klaus).

Storyline: During a chess game in Klink's office, Hogan manages to swipe the train schedule from Klink's desk and most of his chicken dinner. Carter tells Hogan that one of their American operatives posing as a German officer has been injured and taken to the local hospital. "Major Zimmer" is in possession of top secret info and Hogan plots to pay a hospital visit. Hogan and his men rig Klink's sidecar to fall off the motorcycle with Klink in it. Then Hogan insists that Klink be rushed to the hospital. He accompanies Schultz, and they pay the Kommodant a visit. Hogan learns that Zimmer will be admitted later that evening, but Dr. Klaus has approved Klink's immediate release. Hogan tries to get Klink to remain longer by encouraging a possible romance with Gerda, Klink's attractive nurse. When Klink finds out that Gerda has been replaced with a less desirable one, he hastens his plans for departure. Hogan studies the medical book that Dr. Klaus has written concerning diseases of the Arctic. Hogan pretends to have contracted a rare Alaskan disease, "polaris extremis," and begins to exhibit the symptoms including pain in the fingertips and desire to eat greens. When Hogan starts eating a house plant (!), Dr. Klaus quarantines him. Later, with Newkirk's help, Hogan retrieves the war plans from Zimmer. Before Newkirk can depart and notify London, Dr. Klaus returns and quarantines him along with Hogan. Using Hilda as an ally on the telephone, Hogan tricks Klink into believing they will lam it. Klink and Schultz return to the hospital, and with some prompting from Hogan and Newkirk, bring the boys, and their hot message, back to the ranch.

Program Notes: This is the second of six guest appearances for the beautiful Victoria Carroll, who was a semi-regular on *Alice* (nine appearances) and has enjoyed a very successful career as a voice actress for decades. Muriel Landers was a talented singer/comedienne who, in a truly diverse career, held key roles in *Bela Lugosi Meets a Brooklyn Gorilla* (a 1952 low budget quickie featuring Lugosi, a gorilla, and a Martin and Lewis imitation act!). She also earned a rare, co-starring title with the Three Stooges in *Sweet and Hot*, a 1958 Columbia short subject released during the Joe Besser era of Stooging. She would return in the following season's "Gowns by Yvette" (also directed by Bruce Bilson) playing the role of General Burkhalter's niece, Frieda. Frequent guest star Victoria Carroll commented on her early, professional experience with *Hogan's Heroes*:

They were so kind to me, bless their hearts! I was so very young, so very green and naive, and I thought . . . why did they hire me? In those days we always went into read, certainly at that point in my career . . . I think after the first one ("Klink vs. the Gonculator") Edward Feldman just called me in. It was wonderful! I was very shy, almost introverted on the set. These were my first jobs. I had to pour all my energy into concentrating and doing the best that I could."*

Assessment: Hogan gets separated from much of the crew in a spirited adventure that moves him off campus and into a hospital setting for most of the half hour. The chess game opener is an interesting irregularity in that it shows the two colonels behaving like two friends. The real sparkle here comes from the game guest cast, and the nice performances retracted from director Bilson, including the always delightful Henry Corden as Dr. Klaus, Victoria Carroll as a fetching nurse, and Muriel Landers as an exceedingly pleasant and plump one. The flirtations between chubby Landers and the chubbier John Banner are particularly charming. The ruse of Hogan coming down with a rare case of "polaris extremis" is a stretch but works well enough to keep the story moving. The best sequence involves the late night hospital escape by Hogan and Newkirk, and their prompting of cues for capture by the clueless Klink and Schultz – although this still feels like a humorous road we've already traveled. Bob Crane continues to amuse with his curiously goofy, although deceptive, line reads. Here his simple take on being "restricted to the motor pool" prompts giggles from this writer.

*Telephone interview with the author, November 24, 2020.

Season 4, Episode 22: "The Purchasing Plan" 02/22/1969.

D: Marc Daniels W: Laurence Marks

Guest Cast: Sigrid Valdis (Hilda), Leon Askin (Gen. Burkhalter), Inger Wegge (Heidi), Walter Janowitz (Schnitzer), and Howard Caine as (Major Hochstetter).

Storyline: Kinchloe brings word from London that several crates of ammunition will be dropped down, and that the Heroes are to retrieve and store it for the Underground. Schnitzer, the kennel trainer, arrives with his niece and while they keep Schultz occupied, the POWs move the ammo crates from his truck into the tunnel. London further instructs that the ammo crates must be delivered to four different locations. While the boys ponder this request, Burkhalter reprimands Klink about cost control measures. Having listened to their conversation, Carter suggests a plan that would save the Germans money by moving all their supplies to one central location prior to distribution. Hogan runs with the idea, and he and Carter stage a fake argument concerning the cost saving plan. Klink overhears the debate and takes Carter under his wing and also steals the idea as his own. Klink confers with Burkhalter in Berlin and the general approves his concept, although Major Hochstetter has his usual doubts. Supply crates for several stalags are brought to Stalag 13, and Klink has Carter act as supervisor for redistribution. The men are able to mix all the ammo crates (marked as W, X, Y, and Z) into the transport trucks for the other stalags. Hochstetter drops by just as Klink is preparing to launch the cargo fleet. The Major grouses about cases of wine being loaded until he learns they are for Hitler's birthday party. Later, Kinchloe reports that the Underground were able to stop each of the four trucks and remove the marked cases of ammo. In a gesture of goodwill, Klink invites Hogan and Carter into his quarters to toast the success of their plan.

Klink has retained one case of wine, but it is the crate marked Z which contains nitroglycerin. Hogan stalls Klink while Carter detonates the crate in the middle of the compound. Hogan blames it on Hochstetter saying the Major was furious to see a Klink plan actually succeed with Berlin.

Program Notes: Swedish actress Inger Wegge had a brief acting career with two appearances on *Hogan's Heroes* and two on *The Girl from U. N. C. L. E.* making up nearly the entirety of her professional career. Walter Janowitz appeared in a total of seventeen episodes with the series, nearly always as the POWs outside ally, Oscar Schnitzer, the guard dog keeper.

Assessment: This is a pretty mild caper since the key plot revolves around trying to reroute crates of ammo to the Underground, which might not be the most exciting thing to write home about. Still, it's always a blessing to savor a Klink/Burkhalter/Hochstetter scene, particularly one where Klink comes off pretty well, and the episode does harness a few other small delights. The silliest, and most likely funniest, scene involves the men moving the ammo crates directly through the bedroom of the sleeping Schultz and Hogan's encouragement that's it's all only a "dream, dream, dream." There's also a nice surprise payoff with the return of the dreaded crate "Z" and its quickly resolved departure although Hogan's implication that Major Hochstetter deliberately tried to plant the explosive case of "wine" out of envy is a tough grape to swallow.

Season 4, Episode 23: "The Witness" 03/01/1969.

D: Marc Daniels W: Richard M. Powell

Guest Cast: Nita Talbot (Marya), Howard Caine (Maj. Hochstetter), Larry D. Mann (Prof. Zagoskin), and Gavin MacLeod as (Gen. Von Rauscher).

Storyline: Visitors to Stalag 13 include Von Rauscher, his companion and Russian interpreter, Marya, and Prof. Zagoskin, a Russian who has invented a new guidance system for rockets. Marya has tipped off Von Rauscher that Hogan's behavior as a prisoner of war is not entirely "passive." The general tells Hogan that "the war is over" because of how lethal their rockets will become, and he plans to make Hogan a stateside witness to the fact, telling the Allies to surrender. At the rocket site, Von Rauscher brags about the efficiency of the project while Hogan calls Zagoskin a "traitor and a fool" for believing Germany will spare Russia. Major Hochstetter and his squadron storm the party announcing they are head of security and he argues with everyone in sight. Marya visits Hogan later in his cell and explains her real objective is to safely help the inventor back to Russia. They visit Zagoskin, now drunk, who sadly explains that after launch the rocket will return eighteen minutes later and destroy whoever is there. Hogan meets with his men in the woods, all outfitted as Gestapo soldiers. Carter starts a fake attack and diverts the main guards as Hogan's Gestapo unit blends in to continue watch over the rocket. Hochstetter dives into the fray, Klink runs away, and Schultz recognizes Newkirk and the rest of the Heroes dressed as Gestapo. Kinchloe goes to work sabotaging the rocket while the fake attack continues. Later, Hochstetter grouses about the unexplained diversion while Von Rauscher begins a countdown. The rocket falls over and explodes. Later, Hogan claims Hochstetter will cover their heads by sending the inventor back to Russia to similarly sabotage their own rocket effort in a plan "worthy of Himmler." The Germans buy it.

Program Notes: If you look quickly you can spot Nita Talbot in one of her earliest roles as a woman seated at the bar in the Ida Lupino/Robert Ryan film noir classic, *On Dangerous Ground* (1951). Another terrific, early role for Talbot was Rowena, "the veil dancer," in the "Murder on the Midway" episode of *Peter Gunn* (1959). You may remember Larry Mann as the train conductor who sets up the memorable poker game between Paul Newman and Robert Shaw in *The Sting* (1973).

Assessment: Some deliciously well calculated instances of "monkey business," the return of the White Russian, an uncorked Major Hochstetter, and Gavin MacLeod's final hurrah culminate in an exuberantly enjoyable installment. It's unfortunate that some of the plot details badly conspire against one another. The biggest question mark concerns the proposed target of the rocket test. Initially Von Rauscher states that the British battleship, "The Duke of York," is the intended target, but later the drunken, Russian inventor claims that the rocket will turn back and detonate in eighteen minutes. We are to guess that he and the others will perish but the actual, intended target of the special honing device is now contradicted – in fact it's just plain unclear. Generally the program would benefit if this scene was deleted altogether, especially since the segue from Hogan's prison cell to this new, undisclosed, house location is also clumsy and confusing. The logistics of Richard Powell's story fall apart here. Too bad, since the episode is crammed with so many delightfully loopful moments. Nita Talbot is her usual blast of fun energy; her glide into the frame and atop Klink's desk is just one of her many delicious bits. Gavin MacLeod closes out his four installment contract with the series with a wildly enthusiastic performance. When he questions Schultz about any "monkey business" taking place in a rather improvisational manner, John Banner appears to stifle the giggles in his response. Shot out of a cannon,

Howard Caine roars into the scene and delivers his trademark, triple timed inquiry "What is this man doing here?" with such gusto that MacLeod's General Von Rauscher appears to wilt with his meek response: "He's a vitness." Besides being hilarious, Hochstetter's accusation of Hogan as "the most dangerous man in Germany" is wholly accurate. The fake attack scene with Schultz slowly recognizing all the POWs in Gestapo garb is yet another funny exercise in an episode full of high energy fun.

★ ★ ★

Howard Caine's dynamic Major Hochstetter is on full display in "The Witness," an episode that manages to cram together terrifically loopy and humorous details in a dizzying amount of short time. Illustration courtesy of Larry Weber.

Season 4, Episode 24: "The Big Dish" 03/08/1969.

P/D: Edward H. Feldman W: Ben Gershman

Guest Cast: Howard Caine (Major Hochstetter), Laurie Main (Air Marshall Woodhouse), George Cisar (Gen. Boland), Chet Stratton (Prof. Burrows), David Wiley (Radio Operator), Walter Kightley (Technician), Paul Lambert (Gen. Reicher), and Karen Steele as (Lady Valerie Stanford).

Storyline: Hogan is brought to London to confer with high intelligence from Great Britain and the U. S. They project some 35mm slides of Lady Stanford, a brilliant, British scientist who defected to Germany. They believe she is developing a mobile radar system for the Nazis in the Hammelburg area, and they want Hogan to knock it out and convince her to come back to the Allies. Back at Stalag 13, a radar truck unit arrives along with Luftwaffe General Reicher and Major Hochstetter. Their plan is to conduct the radar test in the safety of a POW camp, but Hochstetter has his doubts. Hogan learns from Schultz that he has to play guard to Stanford at the Hammelburg Hotel. While Carter distracts Schultz, Hogan, dressed as a Luftwaffe officer, slips into Lady Stanford's room. Hogan enters her bathroom and delivers her robe and slippers while Lady Stanford finishes her bubble bath. She confesses that she was forced to comply with the Nazis, but once the radar test is conducted she will prove her British loyalty. They seal their agreement with several kisses. Hogan radios London asking them to halt any bomber missions but is too late. Using the new radar technology, the German artillery cripples an Allied air attack. Hogan realizes that Lady Stanford has played him for a sap. Later, Hochstetter takes Hogan to Klink's office stating that Hogan was spotted in Hammelburg dressed as a German officer. But first, Reicher and Stanford are ready to conduct another radar test. Carter, dressed as a German captain, orders the guard at the radar truck to follow a cable line leak. Kinchloe sneaks into the truck and receives instructions by radio from Professor Burrows to alter the components of the radar system. The test is a failure and later Reicher reports huge losses in Munich, Hamburg, and Dusseldorf. Hogan plays up his romance with "Valerie" and that's enough for Reicher and Hochstetter to have her taken into Gestapo custody as a traitor.

Program Notes: This is the only contribution from TV writer Ben Gershman, who penned multiple teleplays for such popular programs as *The Adventures of Ozzie and Harriet* (sixty-two episodes), *The Andy Griffith Show* (eight), and *My Favorite Martian* (eleven). This was the only guest appearance for Karen Steele who Trekkies will remember as one of "Mudd's Women" (1966).

Assessment: Ben Gershman's singular writing contribution is a strong one and similar, somewhat, in structure to the previous episode, "The Witness." The strength of the episode comes from Karen Steele's vivacious performance as Valerie, and, both in and out of the bubble bath, she is a delight. Producer and director Edward Feldman fills the program with an unusually large cast and kicks off the show with a slick opener in London featuring Hogan and the Allied big brass. There's also a rather personal moment here injected by Bob Crane as he admires the image of Valerie Stanford on a 35mm slide, a poignant moment considering the man's personal affinity for pretty girls and photography. Other choice instances include Carter's disguise as a German officer with a nose for "electricity leaks" and Hochstetter's condescendingly correct comments about Klink being a "natural hazard" and "a magnet for misfortune." In a particularly raw moment, Hochstetter offers Klink his gun and suggests that if he had any brains he would blow them out!

Season 4, Episode 25: "The Return of Major Bonacelli" 03/15/1969.

D: Jerry London W: Arthur Julian

Guest Cast: Sigrid Valdis (Hilda), Howard Caine (Major Hochstetter), Marion Brash (Gretchen), Diana Chesney (London Radio Op.), and Vito Scotti as (Maj. Bonacelli).

Storyline: British Intelligence is after the Heroes to take photographs of the latest German, anti-aircraft guns near Hammelburg. Hogan wants to contact their old ally, Major Bonacelli, who is the commander of a POW camp in Capizzio, but who actually works as an agent for the Allies. LeBeau and Carter return with a surprise guest, Bonacelli, who deserted his post after the Gestapo discovered his secret radio and now wants to flee to Switzerland. Hogan talks him into staying just long enough to get the photos they need of the anti-aircraft guns. Bonacelli drops in on Klink, whom he studied under, and with Hogan's prodding, Klink agrees to take Bonacelli on a tour of the anti-aircraft installation followed by a German lunch at the Hofbrau. At the anti-aircraft site, Bonacelli says he wants to snap a picture of Klink for sentimental reasons, and Klink happily obliges. Later, the men visit the Hofbrau and are seated by the lovely Gretchen, who Klink flirts with. Meanwhile, Hochstetter arrives at Stalag 13 on the trail of the traitor Bonacelli and learns from Schultz his location. Carter punctures the rear tire of the Gestapo staff vehicle to slow down the Major. Hogan, Newkirk, and LeBeau race to the Hofbrau to warn Bonacelli and overpower the chef. Hogan and Newkirk pretend to be Gestapo agents while LeBeau acts as chef. They sneak a note to Bonacelli in his weiner schnitzel entree warning him of danger, and he excuses himself to the kitchen. When Hochstetter arrives, the men hide in the freezer while LeBeau, hunched over the stove as the German chef, waves Hochstetter and Klink out the rear exit. The Heroes head out front and manage to leave in Klink's staff car while Hochstetter and Klink attempt to follow in the Gestapo vehicle with one flat tire.

Jerry London memorably launches his career as a television director, here sandwiched between guest star Vito Scotti (left) and Werner Klemperer during production of "The Return of Major Bonacelli." Photo courtesy of Jerry London/CBS Television Inc.

Program Notes: This marks the directing debut of Jerry London, who was already established as the associate producer and editorial supervisor. He would direct a total of ten episodes while continuing his production duties. Later, London directed several episodes of *The Six Million Dollar Man* (1974-75), *The Rockford Files* (1974-77), and the five-part mini-series, *Shogun* (1980). Vito Scotti takes over the role of Bonacelli, previously portrayed by Hans Conried. Scotti was one of the most familiar faces in the history of television, but many fans always connect him with his four appearances on *Gilligan's Island*. His evil scientist, Boris Balinkoff, visited the island twice, including the only occasion in the history of that show where the castaways actually left the island for an extended period of time. In that episode, "The Friendly Physician," Scotti was pared with film noir icon, Mike Mazurki.

Assessment: The history of Hollywood contains its own sub-history of replacement actors. Which means if you're a *M*A*S*H* fan, some nights you get Trapper John and other nights you get B.J. Hunnicutt. Tonight you get Vito Scotti's interpretation of Major Bonacelli, and, for the most part, a pretty fast-paced, fun little adventure to go with it. Jerry London's directorial debut contains any number of pleasant bits of business buoyed by Klink's exuberant energy to play the perfect German host. He enjoys a deliciously special moment at the Hofbrau when after obnoxiously flirting with Gretchen, the hostess, confides to Bonacelli in his most Jerry Lewis-ish swagger, "She's um – crazy about me." Top that Buddy Love. Much of the other dialogue, however, about pizza, garlic, and sauerbraten, becomes repetitious and unimaginative. Major Hochstetter, sadly, becomes a stooge here, with one flat tire, and most of his dialogue consists of snapping "BAH!" then exiting. Similar to the Bob Crane approach, Scotti breezes through his role of Bonacelli by coasting along on the strength of his sheer personality. It's a decent, workmanlike performance, but the heart and soul of the warmly befuddled Hans Conried interpretation is sorely missing.

Season 4, Episode 26: "Happy Birthday, Dear Hogan" 03/22/1969.

D: Marc Daniels W: Arthur Julian

Guest Cast: Sigrid Valdis (Hilda), Howard Caine (Major Hochstetter), Barbara Babcock (Mama Bear).

Storyline: In a Hammelburg movie theatre, Hogan makes contact with "Mama Bear," who warns him that the area around Stalag 13 is under scrutiny due to the sabotage taking place. She claims the Gestapo are planning to set a trap to determine where information is leaking. Each time a Gestapo agent appears, the couple pretend to be lovers. Back at camp, the men are contemplating a birthday gift and surprise party for Hogan. Hochstetter arrives and openly discusses to Klink that his men will be needed to secure an ammunition dump. LeBeau overhears the conversation and shares the news, which inspires Newkirk to suggest destroying the ammo dump as a surprise birthday gift. Kinchloe radios London to prepare the air attack, but Hogan returns and orders all sabotage activity to halt. He also points out the presence of a Nazi radar detection truck in the compound. The men race back to the tunnel to stop Kinch who is just about to radio London again to call off the air attack. The men ponder how they should abort the attack. LeBeau heads into town to meet "Mama Bear" at the movie house hoping the Underground can contact London. "Mama Bear" says their radio communications have ceased due to German scrutiny which sends LeBeau back to camp without a plan. The men finally explain the problem to Hogan who suggests they continue with his party and load the cake with treated Roman candles aimed at the radar truck. That night, the POWs stage an outdoor party complete with popping corn and party hats while Klink and Hilda observe. The cake rolls out and Schultz lights the candles which spark and shoot flames into the radar truck dismantling it. Kinchloe is able to immediately radio

London to abort the air attack on the ammo dump. Later, while Hochstetter badgers Klink about the radar truck, Hogan appears with two slices of birthday cake that cues the Major to storm out in disgust.

Program Notes: This is the second of three guest appearances for Barbara Babcock who has enjoyed a bountiful career spanning four decades including the regular role of Dorothy Jennings on *Dr. Quinn, Medicine Woman*. She was also frequently seen on *Dallas* (as Liz Craig) and enjoyed seventeen appearances on *Hill Street Blues*. Schultz makes a reference to his nephew Wolfie's birthday party in a nod to "What Time Does the Balloon Go Up?"

Assessment: The curtain comes down on the fourth season in an appropriately celebratory manner. The program opener recycles the "let's make out to avoid detection by the Gestapo" routine that keeps reappearing, here in two different scenarios. The general plot line, however, is completely unique and the wheels are set in motion with the unusually pleasant Major Hochstetter setting the trap in Klink's office. (Just the fact that he is so extraordinarily pleasant with Klink should tip off viewers that the game's afoot!) The chain of events triggered by the trap keep the story moving and allow the gang more screen time and dialogue than usual. Although typically silly moments threaten to undermine the party (Schultz playing "pin the tail on the donkey" so the men can remove his gunpowder certainly comes to mind), it's hard to complain when, in Hilda's words, "It looks like fun." Perhaps the nicest gift of all *is* the presence of Hilda, or more accurately, Sigrid Valdis. In a series consistently showcasing beautiful women, Valdis reasserts her position, whether gorgeously framed in the window of the office or sitting on her desk, leg crossed, and eating cake, she is one heavenly birthday wish. It's a contagious happiness, with the two opposing colonels eating their cake in amiable fashion and concluding the season with a memorable, freeze frame finish.

Primer for Season Five

Primary Cast

Colonel Robert Hogan:	Bob Crane
Kommodant Wilhelm Klink:	Werner Klemperer
Sgt. of Guard, Hans Schultz:	John Banner
Corporal Louis LeBeau:	Robert Clary
Corporal Peter Newkirk:	Richard Dawson
Sergeant James Kinchloe:	Ivan Dixon
Sergeant Andrew Carter:	Larry Hovis
Hilda (recurring character):	Sigrid Valdis
General Albert Burkhalter (recurring):	Leon Askin
Marya, "the White Russian" (recurring):	Nita Talbot
Colonel Rodney Crittendon, RAF: (recurring)	Bernard Fox
Cpl. Langenscheidt (recurring):	Jon Cedar
Oscar Schnitzer (recurring):	Walter Janovitz
"Tiger" (recurring):	Arlene Martel

and

Major Wolfgang Hochstetter, Gestapo: (recurring)   Howard Caine

Ivan Dixon in character as Sgt. James Kinchloe, Colonel Hogan's communications expert and default second-in-command. Dixon would be the only regularly featured actor to voluntarily walk from the series, tired of spending most of his footage as a radio messenger boy. Author's collection/ CBS Television Inc.

With the start of its fifth season, *Hogan's Heroes* moved back to its original time slot of Friday evening, 8: 30pm. For its previous two seasons, the program had aired on Saturday nights at 9: 00pm, and although still commanding a strong share of viewing audiences, it had slipped out of the top thirty programs as rated by the Nielsen system. A move back to its original time slot was a CBS strategy to reclaim its audience base.

Ivan Dixon, tired of being regulated to a largely background role, decided not to pursue contract negotiations and opted out at the end of the year. Due to the nature of several of the prisoners' missions involving the impersonation of German soldiers, Dixon missed out on a lion's share of the footage due to the color of his skin. Hitler's army did not include the African American race, which left Sgt. Kinchloe out of many of the more inspired adventures that took place away from Stalag 13. Post *Hogan's*, Dixon enjoyed a prolific career as a television director with multiple credits on such popular network programs as *The Waltons, Magnum, P. I.,* and *The Rockford Files,* before moving to Maui and owning and operating radio station, KONI – FM.

For the debut of its fifth season, producer Edward Feldman commissioned a one time writer, Tony Thomas, to draft a story, "Hogan Goes Hollywood," as a special call back to one of his favorite returning actors, Alan Oppenheimer, who fondly remembered the flattering experience:

"The year before, Feldman said to me, "I'm going to write a show for you next year." I said, "That's great." I had no idea it would be the opening show for the season. He sure did write it for me."*

The program continued its exterior production at Forty Acres with the interiors still shot at Desilu, which had now been renamed as Cinema General Studios. Jerry London, his association with the program dating back to the pilot episode as film editor, was now promoted to associate producer, and began to also direct episodes. The series continued to recruit top guest stars, faces very familiar to television audiences, including: Alan Oppenheimer, Victoria Carroll, Frank Marth, Bruce Kirby, Kathleen Freeman, Sandy Kenyon, Noam Pitlik, Harold J. Stone, Antoinette Bower, Fay Spain, Jack Riley, Muriel Landers, Forrest Compton, Marj Dusay, and Marlyn Mason.

During the off season, tragedy struck the family as the Director of Photography, Gordon Avil, passed from a heart attack on April 25, 1970, while vacationing in Barbados. Bruce Bilson:

"You probably know the story of his dying during one hiatus period. It was a shock to all of us. He was a wonderful, talented man."**

*Telephone interview with the author, November 27, 2020.

**E mail correspondence with the author, November 30, 2020.

Season 5, Episode 1: "Hogan Goes Hollywood" 09/26/1969.

P/D: Edward H. Feldman

Story: Tony Thomas   Teleplay: Richard M. Powell

Guest Cast: Alan Oppenheimer (Major Byron Buckles), Victoria Carroll (Nurse in film), Sigrid Valdis (Hilda) and Leon Askin as (Gen. Burkhalter).

Storyline: It's movie night as Klink presents an American service film starring Hollywood star, Byron Buckles. As a surprise, Klink announces his dream of producing a German propaganda film at Stalag 13 and then ushers in his newest prisoner, Byron Buckles. At first, Hogan is appalled that an American actor would consent to act in a German film, but then he realizes the filming could get him close to a bridge that London wants destroyed. Hogan convinces Buckles that he should direct the film and they both agree that Klink is not quite right for the role of the Kommodant. Schultz is chosen for the part leaving Klink to have to portray the sergeant of guard instead. Filming begins in the barracks and when Burkhalter shows up at Hogan's request, he too becomes involved with the production. Hogan convinces the crew that the film needs a big finish involving the destruction of a bridge by the POWs. The Germans agree after Hogan explains they will use fake explosives and insert a model. On location, Hogan entices Burkhalter, Klink, and Schultz to hit the plunger, and the bridge blows sky high. Realizing they've been tricked, the Germans consider Hogan's explanation that the bridge was destroyed by high flying, American bombers.

Program Notes: The opening scene with the black and white film-within-the-show was shot on the neighboring "Gomer Pyle USMC" set. This is the fourth and final guest appearance for actor Alan Oppenheimer in his only non-Germanic role. This is the only writing contribution to the series from Tony Thomas, who enjoyed great success as the executive producer of such popular series as *Soap, It's A Living,* and *Beauty and the Beast.* Victoria Carroll fondly recalled shooting the opening sequence with Alan Oppenheimer, who is still her dear friend today:

He's the most delightful human being and we just had a ball. We laughed so hard as we were very phony Hollywood actors in the 1940s supposedly. We just had a great time. He's a very close friend with my husband (actor Michael Bell) and they do the comic cons together. That scene was one of the most fun times, and that was primarily working with Alan. Ed Feldman almost had a stock company of actors.*

Guest star Alan Oppenheimer, as movie star Byron Buckles, shares screen time with Klemperer and Crane in "Hogan Goes Hollywood," a teleplay producer Ed Feldman had drafted specifically for him. Photo courtesy of Alan Oppenheimer/CBS Television Inc.

Assessment: This parody of Tinsel Town film making kicks off with one of the most unique prologues in the program's history, the black and white movie screening of the Byron Buckles war flick. Guest star Alan Oppenheimer, paired with Victoria Carroll (who may be wearing her same costume from "Up in Klink's Room"), make a memorably charming duo. Despite the clever and unusual opening, the story that unfolds is quite preposterous, and the parody of movie making feels underexposed. Fortunately, Oppenheimer sinks his pearly whites into his tailor made role of Buckles and squeezes much humor from what could have been a stock satire of a spoiled movie star. Sigrid Valdis lends more support than usual, whether stroking Klink's ego as a producer/star/director in his private quarters, or on the set in her fetching, Oktoberfest garb. We also enjoy a longer than usual look at how the men wire a bridge for explosion, prompting the hilariously accurate conclusion from Buckles that "Hogan is insane." Unfortunately, this leads up to one of the biggest absurdities in the show's history, that Burkhalter and Klink allow the POWs to wire the bridge without inspecting the explosives first. *Fortunately,* the writers do insert a longer than usual dialogue sequence with Hogan explaining away the problem of the destroyed bridge to Burkhalter and company with his usual deftness. *Unfortunately,* many syndicated broadcasts trim down or even remove this same dialogue sequence weakening the resolution.

*Telephone interview with the author, November 24, 2020.

Season 5, Episode 2: "The Well" 10/03/1969.

D: Bruce Bilson W: Laurence Marks

Guest Cast: Sigrid Valdis (Hilda), Michael Fox (Capt. Ritter), and Leon Askin as (Gen. Burkhalter).

Storyline: Burkhalter and Captain Ritter, of German Intelligence, arrive and convene in Klink's office. Hogan sends Carter and LeBeau in under the pretext of cleaning the office, and LeBeau slips into the closet where he lowers a false panel allowing him to spy through the cutout eyeballs in a portrait. He reports that Ritter is carrying a Luftwaffe code book, and he observed Klink lock it in the office safe. Hogan and Newkirk head into the office arguing about the windows that Newkirk poorly cleaned. Kinchloe stages a fake call which removes Klink from his office so Newkirk can crack the safe open and remove the code book. Klink confers with Schultz about improving his efficiency rating with the general, and Schultz suggests they try to recover five silver spoons stolen from the officers' mess. Schultz stops Newkirk as he is leaving the office and orders him to fall in for a surprise formation, forcing Newkirk to ditch the code book by dropping it into a dry well. The men stage a late night raid on the Hammelburg waterworks cutting off the supply of water to Stalag 13 which ruins Burkhalter's shower the next morning. Hogan suggests they dig for water and Burkhalter approves. The code book is recovered but Schultz demands a prisoner search first for the silver spoons, and now LeBeau has to dump the code book back into the well, which is filling with water. In a final effort, the men stage an escape involving LeBeau dressed as a German guard which pulls Klink and company out of camp. Carter makes a descent into the well and retrieves the book from the icy water.

Assessment: "The Well" revisits the theme established in the previous season's "Paint the Luftwaffe Red," in which the men must retrieve an inanimate object of great value. The premise is a decidedly workable one, but too many elements surrounding it don't add up in Laurence Marks' borderline incomprehensible script. First, we get the ridiculous maneuver of LeBeau spying on the office through the panel in the closet. Why don't they just listen in with their normal surveillance equipment? Typically we get some explanation of the bugs being removed from Klink's office to necessitate a new surveillance method. This episode doesn't offer up that explanation. Then we witness a most unconvincing sabotage of the Hammelburg water company with the boys gingerly tossing hand grenades over a fence and buildings blowing up a hundred yards away. This segues into Burkhalter's shower water cut off and Klink's men forming a bucket brigade supplying an endless mysterious source of water. (The staging of the sequence is well handled and very humorous; the logic is absent.) The details concerning the dry well and the ability to dig around it to discover a water supply are difficult to comprehend. Finally, Kinchloe states that Carter has a "half mile" descent down into the well, yet the boys pull off the maneuver in seconds. Meanwhile, Klink and his men fire their rifles into the woods at the escapee LeBeau who is framed a few feet away from the unobservant company. Perhaps this is intended as the ironic humor of the action, but it's missed on this writer. The best moments of the show, surprisingly, come from a more focused and threatening Sgt. Schultz, who hassles Newkirk into formation at gunpoint and later demands a spot search of the prisoners, furthering the hindrance of repeatedly losing the code book into the dry, then wet well. Meanwhile, thousands of Hammelburg civilians have lost their water supply thanks to an unsolicited mission on Hogan's part.

Season 5, Episode 3: "The Klink Commandos" 10/10/1969.

P/D: Edward H. Feldman W: Richard M. Powell

Guest Cast: Nita Talbot (Marya), Frank Marth (Count Von Waffenschmidt).

Storyline: Surprise guests to Stalag 13 include Count Von Waffenschmitdt, of the Gestapo, and our old friend, Marya, "the white Russian," who unabashedly flirts with Klink. The duo are en route to the Russian Front along with an attache case handcuffed to the Count's wrist. Klink sets up the Count in his quarters while Hogan plots to lift the attache case with the help of Newkirk. The men sneak into the Count's bedroom, but he instantly awakens with a German luger poised for target practice. The Count willingly explains that he knows Marya has several Underground contacts, and he has been tagging along with her to discover and bust up her ring of conspirators along the road to Russia. Moved to a cell, Hogan decides to set up Carter masquerading as a German general recruiting "volunteers" for a suicide mission to the Russian Front. He elects Hogan and his four men for volunteers and names Klink as the commander of the deadly mission. Now dressed in German uniforms, the POWs and Klink board the same train that is carrying Marya and the Count to Russia. Marya meets with Hogan and explains she needs Hogan's help to force the Count out of commission. She has put him to sleep with a mild sedative giving Hogan and Newkirk just enough time to tamper with the seal on his briefcase. When the Count awakens he finds Hogan pointing his gun at him and a new mission – his immediate defection to England. Meanwhile, the boys have taken charge of the engine car and planned an unscheduled train stop – Stalag 13 reached by reverse motion!

Assessment: The train setting provides a nice distraction from the usual capers in and around Stalag 13, but most of the proceedings here suffer from a tired, run-of-the-mill approach. Frank Marth – sporting the longest cigarette holder in Nazi Germany – brings his usual professional approach to his part of Von Waffenschmidt (!) but, he too, seems to suffer from battle fatigue by the time he receives the wake up call that his spying days are over. Even Larry Hovis's venerable Nazi General routine feels overtly pat and all too familiar, and Klink being shanghaied into the suicide mission by a general whom he's never met and without any signed orders is questionable. Not even Nita Talbot is given much material at her disposal, which is appalling, considering the sparkling talent in her possession. Richard Powell's script does not seem to know what to do with her. By the time the boys have effortlessly seized the engine car, long time fans might feel like they're sitting through an end of the line 1950s Bowery Boys programmer with Huntz Hall and Stanley "Stash" Clements still attempting to throw some coal into the fire.

Season 5, Episode 4: "The Gasoline War" 10/17/1969.

D: Richard Kinon W: Laurence Marks

Guest Cast: Marianna Hill (Louisa), Bruce Kirby (Franz), Richard Alden (Bartender), Eric Morris (Capt. Streicker).

Storyline: A large delivery of fuel barrels arrives at the camp, and the POWs quickly figure out that a gasoline station is being established in order to fuel up German convoys en route to France. The Underground set up a meeting with Hogan at the Hofbrau, but first he must throw Klink off the track by encouraging the Kommodant to stage a surprise bed check. After Klink's departure, Hogan heads to the bar and meets with Franz and Louisa, who request that Hogan's men destroy the gas station and stop the convoy. Hogan realizes that their living quarters, Barracks Twelve, is right next to the gas pumps and that it would be much safer to destroy the actual convoy instead. The men plan their attack using a small scale model of the gas station, barracks, and guard tower. Hogan sends Newkirk, disguised as an elderly fraulein, back to the Hofbrau to retrieve some extra explosives from Louisa. As the German trucks roll in to the gas pumps one at a time, the men slip under and attach dynamite to each truck. Newkirk poses as a soldier to help deflect interference from Klink and his aide, Capt. Streicker. Later, the trucks blow up under the observation of Hogan and Louisa. The next day, Klink states that the Gestapo are investigating the sabotage of the trucks, and he will shut down the gas station permanently.

Program Notes: During Klink's surprise bed check, all prisoners are reported present, yet Newkirk is inexplicably missing. This is the first of three, unrelated, appearances by prolific character actor Bruce Kirby, the father of late actor Bruno Kirby. With a career dating back to 1955, Bruce enjoyed the recurring role of Officer Kissel on *Car 54, Where Are You?* Two decades later, he would be seen in another unusual cop show, the short lived *Holmes and Yo Yo*, playing the police captain. Producer/director Jerry London recalled hiring Kirby frequently after both men had moved on from Stalag 13: "I liked Bruce. Nice guy and real, solid actor. I used him in a lot of shows. I had a group of actors that were like my stable . . . I liked to have them around me so I would use them, again and again."*

Assessment: A straightforward plot line, free from the lesser unsubtle qualities of the series, gets a nice presentation thanks to some well manufactured plot details. One of the choice bits involves the psychological double cross Hogan hatches to get Klink to drop in for a surprise bed check, freeing up Hogan to later head into town and meet his contacts at the Hofbrau. Hogan's request for a miniature model set lends realism to their mission as they review the specifics of sabotaging the convoy trucks without being spotted. Once again, Dawson turns up smiles as he inhabits the "Old Mother Riley" approach to a meeting by masquerade. The final fireworks show leads to yet another lip lock for Colonel Hogan, which now appears to be not only a series staple but perhaps a contract stipulation for Colonel Crane.

*Telephone interview with the author, February 14, 2020.

Season 5, Episode 5: "Unfair Exchange" 10/24/1969.

D: Richard Kinon W: Laurence Marks

Guest Cast: Leon Askin (Gen. Burkhalter), Kathleen Freeman (Gertrude Linkmeyer), Wendy Wilson (Maria Hoffman), and Howard Caine as (Major Hochstetter).

Storyline: While Hogan and Kinchloe take down information regarding Germany's war plans with France from Maria Hoffmann, Carter rushes in. The Gestapo approaches by car which means the boys need to evacuate from Weber's Farm, their meeting place with Maria. The girl insists on staying to keep the Gestapo occupied while the men flee. Later, Kinchloe reports the Gestapo have imprisoned Maria in Hamberg. While Hogan contemplates how to spring Maria, Burkhalter and his sister, Gertrude Linkmeyer, arrive. The general suggests to Klink that marrying in to his family would advance his career. Klink seeks advice from Hogan, who has decided to have Linkmeyer kidnapped, and then traded for Maria. Linkmeyer leaves camp under the false pretense of meeting Klink at a restaurant, but she is stopped and seized by Hogan's men. Burkhalter calls in Major Hochstetter for advice and the men consider their next move. Carter phones Klink's office posing as the kidnapper and demands the release of Maria as a trade for Linkmeyer. Hochstetter balks at releasing the prisoner, but Burkhalter's threat to call his old friend Himmler changes the Major's mind. After Maria is released, Carter calls again stating they can find Linkmeyer at Weber's Farm at 2200 hours. Newkirk forges a love letter to Schultz and he arrives at Weber's to discover Linkmeyer. Burkhalter, Hochstetter, and Klink all surround the barn and manage to rescue the general's sister and find Schultz, who has narrowly missed a spray of gunfire, while Hogan's Heroes all observe the shenanigans from a safe distance.

Program Notes: Kathleen Freeman returns as Gertrude Linkmeyer, previously played by Alice Ghostley. Freeman would revive the role in the final season's "Kommodant Gertrude."

Assessment: A family affair of Burkhalters, along with the appearance of our go-to Gestapo Agent, add up to the best of the Gertrude Linkmeyer episodes. This is one of those premises that could sink in silliness, but wisely Laurence Marks' script keeps the plot moving with mostly convincing situations. There's also some excellent contributions from the gang, including Carter's deviously evil kidnapper calls, and Newkirk's incarceration of the hostage down in the tunnel, which includes a clever, fake phone call. The signature scene in Klink's office with Burkhalter, Hochstetter, and Schultz is full of snappy one liners and a surprisingly high amount of blatantly disrespectful humor at the expense of Gertrude, which, somehow, Burkhalter takes in stride. The only weak link is Hogan's insistence on making Schultz the fall guy in stumbling upon and releasing the prisoner at the farm. It seems the boys could've easily tipped off the Krauts to Gertrude's whereabouts without bringing Schultz into the picture. As a result, the sad sack Schultz is unwittingly used as target practice to the supposed amusement of Hogan and company. More amusing is Schultz's earlier reactions regarding his mystery date, his growling reassurance to Hogan that "he knows what to do," and the risque comment regarding his duty restrictions: "I'll get off." Meanwhile, Klink parrots every one of Burkhalter's commands, much to the slow burn of Hochstetter, and humorous reaction of anyone watching the spectacle.

Classic Conference:

Hochstetter: "Klink, do you know any reason why Frau Linkmeyer would want to destroy herself?"

Klink: "We're just casual friends. How would I know?"

Burkhalter: "Klink and my sister were practically engaged."

Hochstetter: "Ohhh. That would be reasonable motivation for suicide."

Season 5, Episode 6: "The Kommodant Dies at Dawn" 10/24/1969.

D: Richard Kinon W: Arthur Julian

Guest Cast: Ben Wright (Major Feldkamp/Gestapo), Ned Wertimer (Field Marshall Kesselring), Inger Stratton (Fraulein Ziegler), Walter Janowitz (Vegetable Merchant).

Storyline: A vegetable merchant stops at the front gates, and the men persuade Schultz to allow him access to the camp. While Schultz loads up on fresh produce, a message for the Underground is slipped to Hogan concealed in a cucumber! Major Feldkamp arrives and orders the men back to the barracks and ejects the merchant. Hogan contemplates how they will deliver the message. Schultz informs the men they will be recruited as waiters for a cocktail party to honor the arrival of Field Marshall Kesselring. Major Feldkamp instructs Klink to invite Hogan to the cocktail party as an opportunity to pick his brain about the war effort. Waiting for the guests to arrive, Hogan informs Klink about the inadequacies of Kesselring's air fighters. During the party, Klink tries to impress the lovely Fraulein Ziegler with the info Hogan fed him earlier. She informs Feldkamp who arrests Klink for leaking out information regarding German military secrets. In a holding cell, Schultz informs Klink that a firing squad is being formed with volunteers from Klink's own company. Hogan has Schultz sneak Klink out of his cell and into Kesselring's staff car, which won't start. The men help Klink push the vehicle which takes off with no driver and promptly explodes. When the Field Marshall and Feldkamp arrive on the scene, Hogan explains that Klink managed to escape and prevent an assassination attempt. The Field Marshall drops all charges and, later, Klink happily heads into town to the Hauserhauf unaware the Underground message has been hidden inside his belt for delivery.

Program Notes: Frequent guest star Ben Wright would return as the Major Feldkamp character later in the season in "The Big Gamble."

Assessment: Some strong character profiling between Hogan and Klink elevate this episode although the plot, much like Klink's unlikely getaway car, sputters out of gas towards the finish line. Hogan again demonstrates his brilliant knowledge of aeronautical combat to Klink, who unfortunately sets up a date with the firing squad when he attempts to woo a pretty fraulein by showboating his newly acquired military "genius." The dialogue between Hogan and Klink in his cell is first rate with the German admitting his weakness for pretty ladies, and the American berating his big mouth. Schultz also delivers some classic good news/bad news one liners regarding the recruitment of volunteers for the Kommodant's firing squad, including deserters who have now returned for the assignment. Their clumsy escape sequence is well matched by the prisoners' comparisons to the great comedy team of Laurel and Hardy. The resolution suffers from the hastily concocted wrap up that threatens many an episode. Since there is no support scene or dialogue, we must assume the men have not only wired the Field Marshall's auto for demolition, but they also have somehow tampered under the hood. Feldkamp, much like his colleague Major Hochstetter, accepts Hogan's helpful explanation of the assassination attempt without even suggesting an investigation into the apprehension of the culprits responsible for the mysterious car bombing.

Season 5, Episode 7: "Bombsight"   11/07/1969.

D: Richard Kinon W: R. S. Allen, Harvey Bullock

Guest Cast: Leon Askin (Gen. Burkhalter).

Storyline: Schultz hustles all the men back into the barracks and away from the windows while the Nazis unload some mysterious supplies into a warehouse. Newkirk slips out and notices a German word written on the crates that Kinchloe translates as "chicken hawk." Hogan figures it as a code name for some secret project and wants to get hold of the blueprint plans that Burkhalter has secured in Klink's safe. On their surveillance unit, Hogan and company learn that the "chicken hawks" are a new type of bomb that zeroes in on radio targets and the first demonstration will take place at Stalag 13 in front of German brass. Hogan brings his watch to Klink for safe keeping claiming a thief is loose in the barracks and as Klink puts it in the safe Newkirk spies the new combination numbers with binoculars. Hogan pulls Klink outside his office, but the Kommodant quickly returns and the two colonels find Newkirk in the office alone. Hogan pretends he is the thief and removes him for disciplinary action. Still after the blueprints, Hogan spots Klink bustling about with the rolled-up plans and the POWs perform a switch. Newkirk photographs the blueprints and the men switch the real ones back for the fakes. While Newkirk uses a closet as a development room, Klink decides to forgive Newkirk and pulls open the closet door unknowingly spoiling the photo negatives. Finally, Hogan decides to give up on the blueprints and rig the demonstration for failure by having the men stash walkie-talkie radios in vehicles around the camp. The German bombers identify the wrong targets and the demo is an explosive failure as is the unexpected destruction of Burkhalter's staff car.

Program Notes: Although several non-speaking actors appear as staff officers during the bomb demonstration, Leon Askin is the only billed guest star.

Assessment: This time writers Allen and Bullock dust off the premise of season two's "Tanks for the Memory," involving the demonstration of the latest in Axis war technology, doomed to failure, of course, thanks to the meddling of Hogan and friends. Much of the deceptions revolve around Hogan's manufacturing of a thief in the barracks, an attempt to get crafty Newkirk's fingers on the newly adjusted combination to Klink's safe. Dawson performs with terrific enthusiasm alternating between self-loathsome regret (his mother always promised him a watch speech) and frantic pleading for mercy from Klink as Hogan calmly removes him from the office. Other strong developments include Hogan trying to get Klink's signature approving Newkirk's disciplinary measures, his initial order is to have Newkirk shot, and Klink unknowingly ruining the photo development process by extending a gesture of compassion. Only the wrap up feels a tad too quick and easy with the unchallenged and convenient placement of walkie-talkies, but by this point the preceding factors should retain most viewers without disappointment.

Season 5, Episode 8: "The Big Picture" 11/14/1969.

D: Bruce Bilson W: Laurence Marks

Guest Cast: Sigrid Valdis (Hilda), Sandy Kenyon (Capt. Bohrmann), Diana Chesney (Hotel Clerk).

Storyline: While Hogan and Klink debate the wages for a proposed clean up project, Hilda announces the arrival of Gestapo Captain Bohrmann. After Hogan's dismissal, Bohrmann reveals a photograph of Klink and an old comrade who has been arrested for treason. Bohrmann threatens Klink with a conspiracy plot and extorts one thousand marks as a down payment on his silence. The men hear the conversation, and Hogan decides that it would favor their secret operation to remove the evidence from Bohrmann and protect Klink. Their first attempt involves Hogan and Newkirk checking into Bohrmann's hotel and securing the room next to the Captain's. Newkirk stages a hallway fire with an effective smoke bomb and clears out the frightened hotel guests. The plan fails since Bohrmann vacated the room with the photo. Later, Hogan and his men volunteer for the work detail that would take them outside the fence line, an opportunity to ditch Schultz and head back to the hotel. Klink unexpectedly scrubs the project due to lack of funds. Hogan, Newkirk, and LeBeau return to the hotel, and this time a drunken diversion in the hallway lures the crafty Capt. Bohrmann away long enough for Hogan to finally seize the blackmail negative. Later, Klink receives the same photo negative from an anonymous friend ("It's a negative, I'm positive," offers Hogan), and the Kommodant routinely dismisses the senior POW and burns the evidence, unaware of the painstaking efforts made on Hogan's part.

Left to right, Dixon, Crane, Hovis, a partially obscured Dawson, and Clary rehearse their reactions to Klink's cancellation of the work detail that would've saved his bacon in "The Big Picture." Note unidentified crew member far right. CBS Television Inc.

Program Notes: Early in his career, frequent guest star Sandy Kenyon was once paired with Forrest Tucker in the sit com *Crunch and Des*, a syndicated series that ran thirty-nine episodes. Kenyon would return for the final season's courtroom spoof, "Klink for the Defense."

Assessment: The series revisits the familiar theme of "Hogan intervening in order to save Klink's hide" with most favorable results. Much of the activity moves the characters into the hotel setting in Hammelburg and promotes some well-timed bits of development (Newkirk oiling the hinges of the door so Hogan can safely eavesdrop into Bohrmann's room, Hogan sneaking in and then quickly sneaking out just as Bohrmann returns from the washroom, etc.). Another successful, revisited theme centers on Klink's disciplinary decisions that unknowingly defeat the unsanctioned help offered by the POWs. Here Klink scrubs the work detail since he's run out of camp funds to pay the labor costs not realizing Hogan meant to use the job as an opportunity to try and retrieve the incriminating photo. The final ruse to finally secure the photo is also quite effective with Newkirk and LeBeau staging a drunken, hallway party. This boisterous behavior will resonate with any world-weary traveler who has lost a night's sleep thanks to some belligerent night owls stumbling back from the hotel lounge.

Season 5, Episode 9: "The Big Gamble" 11/21/1969.

D: Marc Daniels W: Laurence Marks

Guest Cast: Sigrid Valdis (Hilda), Ben Wright (Major Feldkamp), Chet Stratton (Dr. Wolfgang Becker), Noam Pitlik (Capt. John Mitchell).

Storyline: While Klink attempts to solicit donations from Hogan for the German winter relief fund, an air attack ensues above Stalag 13. An American pilot, Capt. Mitchell, is captured and brought to Klink who moves him to the cooler. The wreckage of his plane is hauled into camp. Hogan secretly pays Mitchell a visit and learns that the airplane houses a top secret direction finding device in the front fuselage. The direction finder must be removed before the Germans discover it. Hogan sends in Newkirk and Carter, dressed in German uniforms, to attempt a recovery but Major Feldkamp and a squad of Gestapo soldiers foil the plan. Hogan learns that the Germans are sending in Dr. Becker to examine the plane wreckage, and that Klink has obtained his dossier file. Becker arrives and quickly removes the direction finding box from the plane. Using a drawing provided by Mitchell, Carter manufactures a duplicate box. LeBeau sneaks into Klink's office and photographs the Becker files. Hogan's research yields the only weakness that Dr. Becker possesses is an interest in casino gambling. In order to drum up money for the winter relief fund, Hogan talks Klink into hosting a "Monte Carlo" night in one of the unoccupied barracks. The casino night takes off and Hogan tempts Becker to join the fun much to the protests of Major Feldkamp. Becker attends with a briefcase handcuffed to his wrist containing the direction finder box. With a packed house of gamblers, Hogan and his men start spreading smoke bombs around the room creating a fake fire that sends all the guests running. The men knock Becker unconscious, hustle him under the roulette table, and Newkirk and Carter make a switch with the contents of the briefcase.

Program Notes: This is the second and final appearance of series regular Ben Wright as Gestapo Major Feldkamp, which implies that Howard Caine was probably unavailable for these two episodes. Wright, Stratton, and Pitlik continue their contributions to the series.

Assessment: Laurence Marks' scripting appears to be running out of fresh ideas as his teleplay offers up a decent premise with few surprises or twists. Noam Pitlik's Capt. Mitchell sets up this premise but then his character vanishes, not to be mentioned further. Pitlik would enjoy a much meatier return later in the season with "Standing Room Only." Ben Wright's reprise of Major Feldkamp is adequate but will certainly suffer when compared to Howard Caine's incomparable Major Hochstetter. Although the story moves at a decent clip and the idea of running the casino night as a baiting device is a welcome one, this sadly plays out as a missed opportunity. Marks does not bother to use the intricacies of greed and casino gambling to further the story. Becker (the always delightful Chet Stratton) shows up, yet another phony fire is dully staged, and the briefcase is effortlessly unlocked with the switch being made. The tracking shot on Hogan moving through the smoke-filled chaos is more diverting than the "diversion" itself. The whole caper could have been played out during a bingo night and still achieved the same results. Meanwhile, none of the Germans bother to investigate the cause or damage assessed by the mysterious fire or discovery of the used smoke bombs. The POWs also continue to conquer any task without question, from Carter's perfect duplication of the direction finding box to the sudden appearance of the professional casino table games. For an occasional viewer of the program, none of the above may detract from one's enjoyment, but for all else, the lethargic placement of the smoke bombs seems to be a commentary by the actors on having "seen and done this all before."

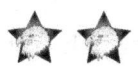

Season 5, Episode 10: "The Defector" 11/28/1969.

D: Jerry London W: Laurence Marks

Guest Cast: Harold J. Stone (Field Marshall Richter), Arlene Martel (Gretchen), and Howard Caine as (Major Hochstetter).

Storyline: After nightfall, Hogan, dressed as a civilian, meets up with Gretchen, his contact, by signaling her car on a country road. She tells him that help is needed to move a defecting Field Marshall safely to England. In order to bluff a passing German patrol, the couple become intimate until the soldiers move on. The next day, Hogan conveys the news to his crew as Klink receives unexpected guests: Field Marshall Richter, "the defector," and his personal secretary, "Gretchen." Hogan gets himself invited to dinner in Klink's quarters, waiting for his chance to brief Richter. Major Hochstetter arrives and is reprimanded by Richter for openly making insults about Klink's character. Hochstetter pulls Klink away to his office. He warns Klink about Richter being suspected of treason. Hogan directs Richter to take an after dinner stroll and head straight for Barracks Two, where his men will move him down to their tunnel. Hochstetter begins a thorough search after Richter goes missing. Fearing their tunnel system may be discovered, the men hide Richter in the cooler. The men then rig a dummy in Richter's uniform and a time bomb set for fifteen minutes, and plant both in Richter's staff car. After telling Schultz the car must be turned around, the dummy driver starts its leave from camp. Hochstetter and Klink tear out of the office, and wanting to take him alive, the Major fires at the wheels of the staff car – which promptly explodes. Klink announces he shot the gas tank instead and the Major panics until his superiors congratulate him on efficiently closing the file on Richter.

Program Notes: This is the second of three, unrelated, guest appearances for Harold J. Stone. Frequent guest star Arlene Martel appears as "Gretchen," who clearly looks and sounds like her typically featured Underground character, "Tiger." Producer/director, Jerry London, explained how casting typically worked:

The leads (guest stars) were cast by one of the Bing Crosby executives, and that was the only time that the Crosby company really got involved with the show. I can't remember the guy's name ... he would always suggest the lead actor as a guest star. After awhile, Eddie and I would cast the rest of the people.*

Assessment: Guest star Harold J. Stone, who made a strong impression in "Bad Day in Berlin," returns in another strong performance highlighted by one of the great sight gags of the entire series run. Most of the proceedings move at a pretty serious stride with few bits of outrageous business. In a nice change of pace, a Nazi superior (Richter) enjoys Klink's hospitality and admonishes Hochstetter for his openly contemptuous statements about Klink's character. Although the idea of a dummy somehow operating a moving vehicle is questionable, the resulting sight gag, along with Hochstetter's bewildered reaction, framed in a tightly jarring, extreme close up of the unexpectedly exploding vehicle, is more than memorable. The humor carries over into Klink's office, where the Major frets over his doubtful future in the Nazi party coupled with Klink's gleeful delight at his frequent adversary's misery. With the disappearance of Field Marshall Richter, we also must accept the disappearance of his secretary "Gretchen," certainly a character witness the Gestapo should've considered holding for questioning. This is a superior directorial accomplishment from Jerry London.

*Telephone interview with the author, February 14, 2021.

Season 5, Episode 11: "The Empty Parachute" 12/05/1969.

D: Marc Daniels W: Phil Sharp

Guest Cast: Parley Baer (Julius Schlager), Ronald Long (Major Blair), and Howard Caine as (Major Hochstetter).

Storyline: While Klink disciplines Hogan about the behavior of his men during a recent work detail in town, Hochstetter arrives with Julius Schlager, who has a briefcase handcuffed to his wrist. Hogan hurries back to the barracks so he can listen in on their conversation. Schlager possesses top secret information for Hitler, who will dispatch a Luftwaffe pilot for Schlager's retrieval. Hogan explains to his men that similar to safeguarding one's wallet by moving it to one's front pocket, they need to get Schlager to move the briefcase from his wrist to the safe in Klink's office. The men stash an empty parachute in the flower garden where they are working and allow Schultz to find and report it. Klink and Hochstetter believe an American has parachuted into camp in order to retrieve the briefcase, and so they lock it up in the safe. Hochstetter begins a dogged search of the entire camp for the whereabouts of the parachutist. Hogan has Kinchloe pipe in a radio address using a recorded Hitler speech, and while the Germans all stand at attention, Newkirk removes the briefcase. The men discover counterfeit US currency and metal engraving plates which they alter. Newkirk attempts to return the same but is pulled away for a work detail by Schultz. Running out of time, Hogan manages to remove a stick grenade from Schultz's belt. Klink unlocks his safe just as Hogan signals his men, and the stick grenade crashes through the office window creating a state of panic. LeBeau moves Schlager's briefcase to Hogan who returns it to the open safe before the Germans realize the stick grenade is a dud and that Schlager's briefcase is safe and ready to fly to Berlin.

Assessment: Despite the unusual and intriguing plot device of the discovered parachute and the search for the invisible intruder, and one key scene of suspense, nearly all of the other connecting developments implode. Since no explanation is provided, we must assume that the POWs are capable at will of piping in any recordings they please into Klink's office radio. This triggers the absurd sequence of Klink and company all in rapt attention of Hitler's radio address, as Newkirk opens the safe and lifts the briefcase within a *mere few feet* of his captors. Schultz's observation that Hitler's speech sounds exactly like the same one from the previous week is the only bright spot of this tepid scene. Although the build up scene of Hogan carefully opening the briefcase without it detonating is excellent, the counterfeiting angle is barely developed and just an excuse for the gang to prank Hitler by substituting his likeness on the American counterfeit plates. Guest star Parley Baer, in his fourth and final visit, makes zero impression as Julius Schlager, in a role that would've amounted to much more in the talented hands of, say, Noam Pitlik or Henry Corden. Finally, the return of the briefcase to the safe is also accomplished in less than satisfying fashion with Klink, and a woefully, underutilized Major Hochstetter (who spends much of the outing standing around Klink's office looking somewhat bored), pounding on an obviously unlocked door for all life's fears. Perhaps Helga, who was so unceremoniously dumped after the first season, returned to lock the bad boys in and enjoy one final romantic rendezvous with Colonel Hogan. Now that would have made for a truly unusual and intriguing plot device.

Season 5, Episode 12: "The Antique" 12/12/1969.

D: Bruce Bilson   W: Arthur Julian

Guest Cast: Sigrid Valdis (Hilda), Leon Askin (Gen. Burkhalter), Mari Oliver (Kristina Jerrold), Brenda Benet (French Girl).

Storyline: With heavy German troops patrolling outside the wire, the men anxiously await the return of LeBeau, who left to meet an Underground contact. Newkirk and Carter discover LeBeau entertaining the agent, Kristina, down in the tunnel. Kristina informs Hogan that their usual courier system has been disrupted and vital information regarding D-Day needs delivery. For the time being, Kristina must remain in the camp, which delights the other prisoners. Hogan finds Klink in his office with an armed guard. It seems two other prison Kommodants have been murdered, so Burkhalter has tightened security measures. Inspired by the cuckoo clock in the office, Hogan pretends it is a rare antique and forks over one hundred US dollars to buy it from Klink. Back in the barracks, the men wine and dine Kristina, now dressed like one of the prisoners. The men think their Colonel has gone cuckoo himself for paying Klink one hundred bucks for a cheap Hammelburg clock. Klink, knowing he can buy several clocks for dirt cheap, decides to go into the antique business. Hogan lays out a business strategy of sending one clock to each of five, different, European cities. These cities house the five agents that will receive the secret plans inside the clocks. Burkhalter arrives with the grim news that a third kommodant has been offed and plans to stay over in Klink's guest quarters, where Klink is storing several boxed clocks. Hogan plans to create a diversion with Burkhalter's unsanctioned help so they can finally sneak Kristina out of camp. When all the clocks hidden in the closet start ticking, Burkhalter fears a time bomb has been planted and screams for an emergency fire brigade which only succeeds in drenching Klink, ruining the clocks, and insuring Kristina's departure.

Program Notes: Director Bruce Bilson recalled working with Werner Klemperer and staging the sequence involving the fire hose:

I said to him, "Listen Werner, I'm not sure how this is going to be, I'd like to just let you try it and make sure you're okay with it." So we got out the fire hose and gave him a little shot. And he reacted very strongly, "Turn it off!" Now he knew and it was a very big mistake. Because when we got to shooting it, he knew what was coming and he braced for it, and fought it instead of trying to shrink away. It was funnier in the rehearsal than it was on film. If I hadn't given him a shot of it, it would've been a better performance, because now he knew what was coming!*

Assessment: Klink's weakness to greed gets exploited by the master of the double talk in a fitfully amusing story that dampens towards the finish. The strength of the half hour surfaces with Hogan's fanciful facts regarding rare, antique, cuckoo clocks garnered from his mother's supposed thirty years of experience in the business. The moment where the cuckoo clock birdie first makes its appearance triggering the idea in Hogan's brain is an inspired bit of timing. Crane's convincing rhetoric, along with Klink's scheming mind, help anchor the story and keep it moving in a fairly plausible manner. In a refreshing approach, the POWs take turns charming their house guest - the young, pretty, and impressionable, Kristina Jerrold – and successfully manage to jettison the occasional overtures of sexism and tackiness that accompany these situations between the horny prisoners and their female guests. The opening sequence, however, where LeBeau ignores orders by romancing the young agent down in the tunnels threatens to undermine the previous observation. Other details fizzle (with all the hype about the upped security it's never really explained how the clocks will be delivered) or just plain disappear (the intriguing subplot about a serial kommodant killer on the loose). The finale, despite the serious approach leveled by Leon Askin, goes soggy fast with Klink getting "hosed" again by the run amok prisoners, and the departing General Burkhalter not even curious as to what the hell just happened.

*Telephone interview with the author, Septmeber 14, 2020.

Season 5, Episode 13: "Is There a Traitor in the House?" 12/19/1969.

D: Marc Daniels W: Arthur Julian

Guest Cast: Sigrid Valdis (Hilda), Antoinette Bower (Berlin Betty), and Victoria Carroll (British Radio Officer).

Storyline: Before Hogan can report to London the location of a German ball bearing plant, an Allied air raid damages the tunnel and the men's radio transmitter. Klink pulls all the prisoners outside in the late evening cold air to listen to some radio entertainment, a propaganda speech from Berlin Betty. With her sexy voice and promises of physical comfort, Betty wants to coax the prisoners of Stalag 13 to willingly broadcast in favor of the Third Reich in an effort to demoralize the Allied war effort. Klink states that all of her broadcasts are heard in London which inspires Hogan to use her broadcast as a means of transmitting the factory location. Newkirk visits Klink under the pretense that he will cooperate with Berlin Betty's radio request. His radio speech will actually contain a coded message for London. Later, the men stage a convincing fight in the compound between LeBeau and Newkirk. Klink gets caught up in the physical mayhem before sending LeBeau to the cooler and inviting Newkirk to his office. Berlin Betty arrives and she suggests a private conference between her and Newkirk. Alone and over a bottle of champagne, Betty confides to Newkirk that her family is being held hostage and her radio addresses are strictly extorted cooperation. They become romantic. Newkirk, feeling guilty about the radio speech, slips out and seeks counsel from Hogan, who ultimately leaves the decision up to Newkirk. The radio address takes place and Newkirk tells a fable concerning the story of Papa Bear and Mama Bear, codes for London to pick up on. After the broadcast, Betty reveals her true colors explaining she used Newkirk romantically to assure his cooperation. Newkirk returns to his comrades confident he made the right decision. Later, an explosion is heard and the camp is pelted by the rainfall of ball bearings.

Program Notes: This is the third and final guest appearance from Antoinette Bower. Frequent guest star Victoria Carroll shared her warm feelings about actors Larry Hovis and, especially, Richard Dawson:

He (Dawson) was my favorite! He was one of the funniest human beings that I ever met in my life. And he made me laugh so hard. Very much a gentleman, never came on, never did anything inappropriate. Just so funny and entertaining. It was just a joy to work with him. He's a talented, talented man, very whimsical, and he enjoyed *being* funny, enjoyed what he was doing. I don't know if he was wasted on the show, but he sure did some wonderful things! And Larry Hovis! My husband (actor Michael Bell) worked with Larry Hovis a lot; I probably worked with Larry too because once you got into that comedy category in those days, we all worked a lot together . . . worked on the same shows, went out for the same things . . . and Larry's another funny, funny guy. A lot of talent on that show!*

Assessment: Richard Dawson takes center stage in this tale of wartime romance, propaganda, and, ultimately, one's duty. The broad comedy of the series is kept to the minimum with the episode favoring a more character driven approach. The opening sequence is well edited with Victoria Carroll's voiceover linked to the visuals of the radio antenna rising up from the rooftop of Klink's office. Here's one British Intelligence officer who is *so* obliging she even willingly offers up her physical measurements over the air! In a nice bit of irony, it's actually the Allies who become responsible for destroying the men's radio equipment during their air strike. The first scene during the night roll call as the men listen to Berlin Betty's sultry invitation is also well-produced. There's a good contrast presented among the men with all the POWs making their

When not making frequent visits to Stalag 13, Victoria Carroll kept very active in the 1960s appearing on all the hit shows, including The Jack Benny Program, a man Carroll called: "one of the nicest, kindest, most genuine of men. He treated everyone as if they were an old friend." Also pictured, singer Jack Jones. Photo courtesy of Victoria Carroll Bell/CBS Television Inc.

customary wisecracks while Newkirk remains silent and removed. Dawson is excellent throughout, whether playing shy and nervous around Klink, or creating genuine, romantic warmth with Antoinette Bower (also excellent as the manipulative, Berlin Betty). Betty gets a flashy intro as her lovely legs are revealed first upon entering camp, although Hilda quickly reasserts her role as *the loveliest* lady of Stalag 13 in a white sweater that would make any Allied prisoner defect. To remind everyone this is still a sitcom, we get the slapstick spectacle of Newkirk's cigar almost burning a hole through Klink. The scrap in the compound is also well-staged and quite raucous when Klink and his monocle get pulled into the fray. Although this episode rarely produces out loud laughter, it certainly succeeds as a wartime comedy drama and evidence to the critics that *Hogan's Heroes* is often more than just a ridiculous, screwball farce.

Memorable Radio Transmission:

Newkirk: (on radio microphone) "Mama Bear . . . this is Papa Bear. Uh, would you try and locate my girlfriend for me? Her name is Rita Nottingan. She's blonde . . . 34–24-36."

British Radio Operator: "Sorry, we cannot use the air for personal messages."

Newkirk: "Do me a favor. You're just jealous!"

British Radio Operator: "Why should I be? *I'm* 38-24-36."

Kinchloe: "Some Mama Bear!"

*Telephone interview with the author, November 24, 2020.

Season 5, Episode 14: "At Last – Schultz Knows Something" 12/26/1969.

D: Bruce Bilson   W: Laurence Marks

Guest Cast: Leon Askin (Gen. Burkhalter), John Myhers (Dr. Felzer), Jack Riley (Corrupt Guard), Dave Morick (Officer), and Fay Spain as (Carla).

Storyline: General Burkhalter and Dr. Felzer arrive and confer privately with Klink while the Heroes listen in. Felzer suggests they move the conversation to the privacy of Burkhalter's staff car. Before they drive off, LeBeau hides in the trunk of the car. Later, LeBeau reports to Hogan that Burkhalter wants Klink to head the security of a new secret laboratory developing atomic research for Hitler. No one, including Klink and Schultz, seems to know the location of the secret lab. The men team up with Carla, an Underground agent, in hopes to make a discovery. Carla suggests trying to use sodium pentothal - "the truth drug" - to get Schultz to talk. Newkirk poses as a Nazi physician and approaches Schultz late at night on the pretense that the sergeant must be inoculated. He moves Schultz into the barracks and injects him. LeBeau attempts to question Schultz, but the only information retrieved is that the lab is underground and that Flenzheim potatoes are served daily at meals. Carla checks with her contacts and learns that potatoes and produce are being delivered to an installation operating beneath a bombed out factory. She also learns the sentry guards regularly take the food items from the farmers. Hogan has Carter and the others plant several small time bombs in hollowed out potatoes and other food items. Dressed as farmers, Hogan, Carla, LeBeau, and Carter all ride a horse drawn wagon to the installation as if en route to Stalag 13. The corrupt guards seize all the food from the "farmers" and force LeBeau to help carry the baskets into the underground lab. Later, after making their escape, the "farmers" watch from a safe distance as the lab is blown sky high.

John Banner strikes a familiar pose incorporating concern and confusion in the aptly titled "At Last – Schultz Knows Something." Author's collection/ CBS Television Inc.

Program Notes: Although "Hilda" does appear briefly with Leon Askin in the opener of this episode, Sigrid Valdis does not receive billing during the final credits. This is the second and final stop from celebrated cult actress Fay Spain, who memorably taught Adam (Marty Milner) what a bed is used for in the sex comedy *The Private Lives of Adam and Eve* (1960), a joint directorial effort from producer Albert Zugsmith and mischief maker Mickey Rooney! Spain also played a Mafioso wife in *The Godfather: Part Two* (1974) before succumbing to cancer at the age of fifty.

Assessment: Several original ideas nicely surface in one of Laurence Marks' better fifth season offerings, and stronger collaborations, with director Bruce Bilson. What could've emerged as a long, drawn out scene regarding Schultz and the truth serum moves at a good clip and is more than buoyed by Richard Dawson's droll turn as the visiting doctor. Conjuring memories of mad doctor Phillip Van Zandt leveling a hypodermic towards the audience in 3-D in the 3 Stooges comedy *Spooks* (1953), Dawson's Nazi Doctor enjoys a similar, delicious close up handling the syringe in the barracks. The idea of hiding the timed explosives inside the food items is a novel approach, and the proceedings are consistently aided and abetted by the fetching Fay Spain, who somehow manages to avoid the typical, romantic entanglements usually rewarded to Colonel Hogan.

Memorable diagnosis:

Schultz: "Major, I cannot stand needles! Eh, whenever I see a needle, I faint and fall down."

Newkirk: (as fake Doctor) "You fall down? That would be a very interesting phenomenon to observe."

Season 5, Episode 15: "How's The Weather?" 01/02/1970.

D: Marc Daniels W: R. S. Allen Harvey Bullock

Guest Cast: Leon Askin (Gen. Burkhalter), Sigrid Valdis (Hilda), Dave Morick (Radio Operator).

Storyline: Radio London seeks weather information regarding air speed and direction as they are planning an air strike at a hydro-electric dam that Gen. Burkhalter is commanding. Using a volleyball filled with helium, the men inspire Klink to serve the ball up into the stratosphere as the POWs monitor its travel patterns. Later, using balloons that Newkirk is able to snag from the Non-Commissioned Officers' club, the men continue the pattern of releasing helium filled balloons and recording the wind movement. When Klink discovers the balloons in the barracks, Hogan says they were planning an anniversary party to honor Klink's installment as camp Kommodant. Klink approves the party although he has his suspicions. The night of the RAF air strike, the men present a cake to Klink. Suspicious of the absence of Sgt. Kinchloe, Klink and his armed guards move to the barracks where they open fire on the ice cream churner Kinchloe is operating, and where a radio is actually hidden. Seeing the ice cream leak out of the metal canister seems to calm Klink's suspicions, and the party moves back to the office. Needing to transmit a radio signal to tip off the bombers, Hogan persuades an intoxicated Klink to radio Burkhalter in thanks for the imaginary flowers he assumes the general sent. As Klink rambles and keeps the general tied up on the radio, the RAF bombers zero in on the dam target and strike. Later, an injured Burkhalter threatens Klink with removal. He reconsiders when Hogan convinces him that Klink was trying to divert the bombers and save the general's life.

Program Notes: Dave Morick amassed a total of seventeen guest appearances in the series, typically as a nameless, German soldier or officer.

Assessment: Stealing an idea from the third season's "What Time Does the Balloon Go Up?" (also directed by Marc Daniels), this Allen and Bullock variation establishes Klink as a suspicious, somewhat intimidating presence before an about-face sends him firmly back to the ranks of the goon squad. A few bizarre gags surface, notably the sight of Klink launching the volleyball into the heavens. There's also an unusually interesting one and only peek at Sgt. Schultz and his colleagues knocking down beers at the NCO club. The suspense just before the middle commercial break is well mounted with Klink, in a rare moment, threatening Hogan and his gang with armed guards. But once the ice cream churner, which apparently conceals a radio receiver, gets discovered, Klink's menace quickly melts like the pistachio ice cream riddled with machine gun bullets. The subsequent scene of a drunken Klink tying up Burkhalter on the radio waves is too much to ask for. Why wouldn't Burkhalter immediately cut off the radio signal knowing security is breached? Instead, he and the viewers listen to Klink drone on. The final double talk scene in Klink's office concludes the half hour in even less convincing fashion with Leon Askin's exit an indicator of script inefficiency. If there was ever an episode that starts out strong, shifts gears midway through, then crashes and burns, this is the one.

Season 5, Episode 16: "Get Fit or Go Fight" 01/09/1970.

D: Jerry London W: Bill Davenport

Guest Cast: Leon Askin (Gen. Burkhalter), Michael Fox (Maj. Kimmel), Corinne Conley (Gerda).

Storyline: Leaving his favorite restaurant in town, Klink enjoys the flirtations of Gerda, who is actually an Underground operative and who has a small child plant info in the hubcap of the car tire. The men retrieve the message at camp which details the German coastal defense plans. Burkhalter visits Klink and informs him that his Kommodants have gone too soft and must pass a physical exam, which gives Klink one week to get into shape or expect an extensive, exercise program at the Russian Front. To boost Klink's confidence, the men dummy up some barbells and encourage his new success in weight lifting – until Klink spots Carter moving the same barbells with ease in the barracks. The POWs put Klink on a strict regiment of exercise and muscle development. Gerda has more pending war info requiring Hogan to convince Klink he has made enough progress that he can reward himself with a trip back to Gerda's restaurant. Carter poses as a German doctor who has arrived one day early to administer Klink's physical so he can encourage Klink to head into town. To complicate matters, the real doctor, Major Kimmel, also arrives one day early requiring Hogan to pose as Klink and pass the physical. Eventually, Klink returns from town with lipstick on his face and more vital war plans stashed in the hubcap for Hogan.

Assessment: Colonel Klink, the unknowing carrier pigeon, is the crux of this story that ultimately becomes a gym comedy with mildly diverting results. The opener in town with Gerda is a welcome variation on the messenger system, particularly the novel idea of having a small child participating in the scheming machinations of the Underground network. The sight of Klink effortlessly lifting the dumbbells in the compound does provide a fun, cartoon-ish effect, although the subsequent efforts to get Klink into shape feel like a routine work out on the treadmill. The scene of Newkirk and LeBeau administering an extremely painful massage to their Kommodant is more mean-spirited than humorous. Larry Hovis offers a bemused, yet curiously mild, take on his visiting Nazi physician. His medical practice slightly suffers in comparison to Richard Dawson's recently whimsical turn as the doctor with the truth serum in "At Last - Schultz Knows Something."

Season 5, Episode 17: "Fat Hermann, Go Home" 01/16/1970.

P/D: Edward H. Feldman W: Richard M. Powell

Guest Cast: Nita Talbot (Marya), and Howard Caine as (Major Hochstetter).

Storyline: While Hogan reviews a map of a train route drawn on the door of a truck in the motor pool, Schultz busts out with the exciting news that Hermann Goering, Hitler's number two in command, plans to visit Stalag 13 and that Schultz has been summoned for a confidential meeting in town. In Hammelburg, Schultz finds Marya camped out in Goering's hotel room. She explains that Goering wants Schultz to pose as his double in uniform when he arrives at Stalag 13. Klink and Hogan witness the arrival of the fake Goering and Marya and their hasty entrance into Klink's private quarters, much to the confusion of both colonels. Hogan wants to hijack a train carrying stolen art for Goering and decides to kidnap Goering himself. Entering through the tunnel under the wood stove, Hogan and his men discover Marya, and Schultz, the "Goering" impersonator. Marya explains that a fake Goering will make it easier to lure the train and the art to Stalag 13. Then the artwork can be transported to either England or Russia. Klink's men receive the artwork at camp, and Hogan diverts the valuables into their tunnel network. Major Hochstetter bursts into Klink's office suspecting Klink of complicity in the recent robbery of Goering's train and cargo. Klink insists that he was acting under orders of Goering, and the two men find him with a face full of shaving cream, and Hogan and Marya in his company. Before Hochstetter can expose Goering as an impostor, gunfire breaks out near camp diverting the Major, Klink, and all their men into the fray. During the confusion the stolen artwork is flown out of Germany while, later, Hochstetter attempts to ponder what exactly has occurred. The Major finally decides to heed Hogan's advice and forget the whole debacle and report nothing to Berlin.

Assessment: Extreme silliness reigns at Stalag 13, along with a nonsensical storyline that ultimately compensates thanks to the game approach of its devoted cast members. Richard Powell's teleplay poses all sorts of question marks, particularly the unchallenged arrival of the artwork to Stalag 13. Yet later, Hochstetter informs Klink that the train was robbed and that Klink is the chief suspect, which doesn't seem to gel. The movement of the artwork is entirely confused as the men stash only the paintings and let the rest remain, while Hogan and Marya debate if the artwork will be moved to Russia or England. I think. A stock shot of an airplane taking off late in the episode is supposed to confirm mission accomplished, yet for all the viewers know, that plane could be headed to Edward Feldman's Beverly Hills residence! Fortunately, John Banner's delightful presence helps carry a lot of the muddled material, both in and out of his Goering disguise. Nita Talbot's enthusiasm also compensates for lulls in logic and her exclamation in Klink's office: "And rugs! Lots of rugs!" is deliriously fun. There's also a nice, thoughtful touch from Larry Hovis who confirms with his colonel if the evening's planned diversion should be from a battalion or a regiment. Thank goodness, also, for Howard Caine's Major Hochstetter. His opening dialogue in Klink's office, where he attempts to pleasantly engage Klink into an admission, is another example of the actor's rich command of diction and intention. His welcome presence notches this episode by one full eagle. By the time this caper comedy concludes, with Hochstetter exiting in frustrated confusion, he may very well be echoing the sentiments of the confused, yet entertained, viewer.

Season 5, Episode 18: "The Softer They Fall" 01/23/1970.

D: Marc Daniels W: R. S. Allen Harvey Bullock

Guest Cast: Leon Askin (Gen. Burkhalter), John Stephenson (Maj. Rudell), Ralph Medina (Capt. Stahl), James Savett (Corporal), Jon Cedar (2nd Corporal), and Chuck Hicks (Battling Bruno).

Storyline: In his office, Klink shows off "Battling Bruno," the reigning boxing champ of the Luftwaffe stalags. He orders Kinchloe to become Bruno's sparring partner. Klink clears Hogan and Kinchloe out of his office to make way for General Burkhalter and two guests, Major Rudell and Captain Stahl. Dressed as a Luftwaffe Captain, Carter enters the reception room and scares off the corporal posted at Klink's door allowing Carter to snoop on the meeting. Rudell and Stahl are developing a plan to eliminate the British radar network and Burkhalter plans to deliver it personally to Goering upon completion. Hogan wants to get the finished plans photographed for London and plots to use Bruno as a camp diversion. Klink and Burkhalter witness Kinchloe knock Bruno off his feet during a sparring exercise and this infuriates the General, enough to demand an actual match between Bruno and Kinchloe. The men all pretend to protest, but Kinchloe decides to agree for the good of his outfit. As an insurance policy, Klink instructs Bruno to line his gloves with iron. During the bout, loudspeakers have been installed around the camp for the posted guards to hear Carter's commentary. While Kinchloe tries to avoid Bruno's weighted gloves, LeBeau sneaks into the VIP quarters while the distracted guards listen to the fight. He photographs the Rudell/Stahl proposal. After LeBeau returns and signals Hogan, Kinchloe is able to finish the bout with a knockout punch. Hogan throws in the towel to stop the violence to one of his men and Klink declares Bruno the winner on a technicality. Later, Hogan and Kinchloe tell Klink that Bruno should be congratulated "once he wakes up."

Program Notes: The title pays respect to Humphrey Bogart's final film, *The Harder They Fall* (1956), a noirish crime drama set in the ring with a memorable role for former World Heavyweight, Max Baer Sr. This is the only appearance from former pro boxer Chuck Hicks, (born 1927) who was the Heavyweight Champ of the Navy's 6th Fleet. Hicks' pro acting resume spans seven decades, including playing "The Brow," a member of Chester Gould's rogues' gallery depicted in four color by director/star Warren Beatty's *Dick Tracy* (1990).

Assessment: The boxing drama serves as a terrific canvas for producing an original and very effective installment to the series. Ivan Dixon enjoys his last star assignment before exiting the series, in an episode with lots of great details. The early segment of Carter scaring off the posted guard, who may or may not be Cpl. Langenscheidt, effectively returns Larry Hovis to the masquerade of an irate Nazi officer, after some curiously low-key characterizations. He is matched by Jon Cedar's befuddled corporal, whose facial expressions in this encounter are hilarious. Cedar clearly appears to be a distant relative of Sgt. Schultz. Other choice components include Klink's diabolical scheming to fix the fight in his favor and spirited turn as the ring announcer, LeBeau hiding under the desk to avoid the prowling guards, and Schultz showing where his heartfelt allegiance belongs by deliberately ringing the bell early to save Kinchloe from a count out. Fitting the boxing landscape like a well-worn glove is Leon Askin's General Burkhalter. In a raw moment, Burkhalter comments on the devastating effects that would arise if word got out that a German fighting machine was knocked down by a black prisoner of war. Whether commenting on Hitler's racist reaction to Jesse Owens and his triumphs at the 1936 Olympic Games in Berlin, ordering Klink and Bruno to win the fight at any and all costs, or sitting ringside smoking his stogie, Burkhalter looms large.

☆ ☆ ☆ ¼

Season 5, Episode 19: "Gown by Yvette" 01/30/1970.

D: Bruce Bilson W: Arthur Julian

Guest Cast: Leon Askin (Gen. Burkhalter), Sigrid Valdis (Hilda), Muriel Landers (Frieda), Bruce Kirby (Gestapo Man), Dick Wilson (Count Von Hertzel), Bruno VeSota (2nd Gestapo Man/Uncredited), Leon Alton (Man in elevator/Unc.).

Storyline: An Underground contact possessing information regarding a mobile rocket factory will be in attendance at a wedding at the Hauserhof Hotel, and "Papa Bear" needs to retrieve it. While Hogan contemplates how he can crash the wedding party, he learns from Klink that it is Burkhalter's niece, Frieda, who will be married, and that Klink must make the necessary preparations. Hogan bluffs to both men that before capture LeBeau was known as "Yvette of Paris," a famous, bridal gown designer. After Frieda's measurements are taken, and Hogan learns his contact is being held in the hotel by the Gestapo, LeBeau uses Schultz as a model for the wedding gown fitting. This inspires Hogan to have Newkirk create a second, duplicate wedding gown. Following the wedding ceremony, LeBeau slips away and starts the air raid alarm panicking all of the hotel guests. In the confusion, the men trip up the two Gestapo agents, long enough for their contact to disguise himself with the duplicate gown. Newkirk helps with the deception and claims the valuable information for London. The groom, Count Von Hertzel, oblivious to the switch, claims his "bride" and exits the hotel to the pleasure of Hogan, Klink, Burkhalter and the other guests – until Frieda streaks by demanding her husband wait for her!

Program Notes: An unidentified actor portrays the Underground agent.

Assessment: This caper leans heavily on the sitcom format with another family affair revolving around the Burkhalter clan and Hogan manipulating the wedding party in his favor – *and* features the outrageous sight of Schultz in a wedding dress. Of course, one's enjoyment of this outing depends on the Germans (and the viewers) blindly accepting LeBeau as a famous French fashion designer. In his favor, the wedding gown designed by LeBeau and stitched by Newkirk, and the duplicate gown, actually look quite lovely. The hotel setting and its several rooms and halls provide a fun, romper room atmosphere for our heroes to dart in and out of. Muriel Landers, back for her second and final appearance, adds a nice kick to the proceedings, and proves she's no dummy when she catches LeBeau in the middle of a tacky insult. Return performer Bruce Kirby is given little material to elevate his Gestapo agent. He would have to wait for the final season's "The Gestapo Takeover" for a much better assignment. The finale involving the groom, Von Hertzel, exiting with the fake bride starts the confused climax, particularly when no one finds it odd that two brides are on the loose. Later, the General reports that the groom is suffering amnesia and cannot remember the wedding. This seems to imply that our Heroes knocked the groom unconscious in order to safely remove their contact. But why does Burkhalter also report that the man bears no marks on his head to indicate the amnesia. Perhaps the groom is having second thoughts?

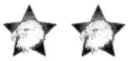

Season 5, Episode 20: "One Army at a Time" 02/13/1970.

P/D: Edward H. Feldman W: Laurence Marks

Guest Cast: Howard Caine (Major Hochstetter), Dave Willock (German Capt.), Dave Morick (German Sgt.), and Sigrid Valdis as (Hilda).

Storyline: On a night mission to destroy the Millheim Railroad Bridge, the Heroes, all dressed as German soldiers, decide to scrub the plan when an enemy patrol approaches. Hogan orders the men to split up and promptly return to camp, but Carter hesitates and finds himself surrounded by the patrol. Seeing the abandoned detonator box and dynamite, the patrol leader assumes Carter broke up a sabotage attempt and Carter is forced to "fall in." At the German base bar, Carter enjoys a round of beers with his new colleagues. A Captain arrives, inspects Carter's forged papers, and congratulates Carter for busting up the sabotage ring. Carter is made acting corporal in the Fourth Panzer Brigade. Major Hochstetter wakes up Klink and demands a night roll call due to the suspicious activity at the Millheim Bridge. Carter manages to slip back in to camp and make the roll call in time. Later, Hogan orders Carter to return to the Fourth Panzer Brigade in order to retrieve the dynamite and detonator box so they can complete their mission. Kinchloe fakes a phone call to Hochstetter which removes him from camp and Klink, in an effort to reassert his authority, cancels the night roll calls. The Heroes again suit up Luftwaffe style and rendezvous with Carter who arrives in the woods in a German tank! The boys wire the bridge with dynamite and use the tank's rotating cannon to spark the explosion in spectacular fashion.

Assessment: Larry Hovis finds himself in a highly ironic situation that is well-tailored around his easygoing charm and likability. The pacing of Laurence Marks' clever script is especially tight as Carter must continually hop back and forth between the Panzer Brigade base and Stalag 13 in order to accomodate Hochstetter's pesky roll call demands. The finale involving the stolen tank is fantastic in the least, but by this point in their fifth season of war time espionage antics it's quite enjoyable to see the boys ride the tank through the woods and destroy the Millheim Bridge with panace. This solid production from executive producer and director Feldman includes plenty of admirable moments including Carter's ill-fitted trousers slowing him up, Dave Morick as an encouraging and friendly German sergeant, Klink's hair net rejuvenator, Klink's line read: "Good riddance!", and Carter's urge to race back to the *other* camp to join the "guys" and watch a captured Betty Grable movie! Watching Carter and his new German buddies laugh over a round of beers is an encouraging reminder that despite being on opposite sides of a war, all men are skin and bone and must put their ill-fitted trousers on one leg at a time.

Best Dermatological Advice:

Hochstetter: "What is that thing on your head?"

Klink: "Oh, oh, that! Eh-heh-heh. It has a . . . a special ointment to uh – stimulate the growth of my hair. Yah-yah."

Hochstetter: "Any possibility it might stimulate some activity under the scalp?"

Season 5, Episode 21: "Standing Room Only" 02/20/1970.

D: Jerry London W: Laurence Marks

Guest Cast: Leon Askin (Gen. Burkhalter), Sigrid Valdis (Hilda), Forrest Compton (Capt.), Victoria Carroll (Sofia Lindemann), Eddie Firestone (Miller), and Noam Pitlik as (Major Strauss).

Storyline: While Klink successfully woos the beautiful Sofia Lindemann, Miller, a visiting prisoner unsuccessfully attempts an escape. Fortunately, Hogan retrieves Miller after bribing Schultz. Hogan's underground tunnel chambers are backing up with escaped POWs from Stalag 5 that are stuck due to heavy German patrolling. Meanwhile, Burkhalter is turning up the heat on Major Strauss because of these escapes. He orders Strauss to stay and observe Klink's methods while the General returns to take temporary command at Stalag 5. Both of the Colonels are deeply dissatisfied with the arrangement, particularly Strauss, who endures Klink's insulting comments. Studying Klink's ledger accounts, Strauss, along with the cheerful cooperation of Schultz, realizes that Klink has been borrowing camp funds to help finance his courting of Sofia. After Strauss threatens to expose him, Klink enters into a bargain with Hogan. Hogan insists he can get the escaped POWs from Stalag 5 to surrender in exchange for Strauss to drop his threats. Hogan also uses the rest of the escaped POWs to pose as German soldiers in order to remove the surrendering prisoners to safe and final freedom. When Strauss insists he accompany the transport vehicle back to Stalag 5, Hogan suggests to his costumed Nazi Captain that Strauss may want to hitch a ride "all the way."

After completing her successful six episode association with Hogan's Heroes, Victoria Carroll forged one of her favorite working collaborations with The Incredible Hulk and actor Bill Bixby: "who loved every aspect of his profession and was pure joy to work with." Photo courtesy of Victoria Carroll Bell/CBS Television Inc.

Program Notes: The series continues its homage to recently aired adventures (here, "Fat Hermann Go Home") when Strauss questions Schultz about the recent visit of Goering and whether or not Schultz was present at the time.

Assessment: Two plot developments, both excellent, are skillfully juxtaposed up and through the linking resolution, which resolves both Hogan and Klink's problems and concludes the best constructed episode yet of the fifth season. The opening scene of Miller attempting escape, while Klink romances Sofia Lindemann, is exceptionally well-mounted with a serious nature punctuated by machine gun fire, and Schultz's serious behavior. All of the action surrounding the subplot of the escaped POWs, their hiding out, and their exit operation is executed in a realistic fashion. The humor comes from Klink's frustration with having Major Strauss snooping around camp (thanks to a terrific set up scene from General

Burkhalter), and his eventual discovery of Klink's cooked books and cooperation received from Schultz. John Banner and guest star Noam Pitlik joyously work together. The round up of the surrendering POWs is also well-staged and features a juicy pan shot of Klink and Strauss inspecting the men along with the accompaniment of Jerry Fielding's taut music. The collusion of Hogan and Klink abandoning sides and working together continues to be a vibrant and successful theme. This episode also benefits from a terrific cast of *Hogan's Heroes* veterans: Noam Pitlik as the revenge driven Strauss, Forrest Compton as a German-acting American POW, Victoria Carroll as a beautiful woman *genuinely* attracted to Klink (her reminder to Klink that he had just been complimenting her eyes is a playful touch), and Hilda as just plain gorgeously cooperative Hilda. Jerry London and Laurence Marks effectively bookend this winner by reminding viewers who is really running this camp with Hogan's boys staging a diversion of gunplay, just so he can make time with Klink's girl – the ravishing Ms. Carroll and those sparkling eyes.

Season 5, Episode 22: "Six Lessons from Madame LaGrange" 02/27/1970.

D: Jerry London W: Laurence Marks

Guest Cast: Marlyn Mason (Lily Frankel), Leon Askin (Gen. Burkhalter), Howard Caine (Maj. Hochstetter), Edward Knight (Double Agent).

Storyline: At a quaint nightclub in Hammelburg, Hogan, dressed as a civilian, enjoys the singing of Lily Frankel. In reality, she is Hogan's contact, and after her number she informs Hogan that a double agent is meeting with Major Hochstetter in order to hand over an incriminating list of Underground agents, which includes Hogan and his Heroes. Hogan slips away to avoid the arriving Klink, who has been making nightly overtures to Lily. Back at camp, the men contemplate a mass escape attempt. Hochstetter arrives and stations his men around the stalag and prepares to move captured Underground agents into the barracks. Hogan informs Hochstetter about Klink's blossoming romance with Lily Frankel, and jealous, Hochstetter insists that he accompany Klink to the nightclub. The next day, Klink brags about his all night dancing with Lily while Hochstetter sat out, due to his lack of dance skills. When Hogan implies that LeBeau used to run dance schools in France, Hochstetter moves him to the cooler for "questioning." Hochstetter orders LeBeau to teach him the foxtrot until Klink and Burkhalter arrive and witness the spectacle. Burkhalter places Hochstetter under house arrest for "dancing with a prisoner," while Hogan slips into town, pretends to be the Major, and retrieves the incriminating list of names from the double agent.

Marlyn Mason's tribute to Marlene Dietrich in "Six Lessons from Madame LaGrange" is not only the highlight of this episode, but also a personal highlight of Mason's career. Photo courtesy of Marlyn Mason/CBS Television Inc.

Program Notes: Marlyn Mason debuts as lounge singer Lily Frankel, a role she would repeat in name only in the series' finale, "Rockets or Romance." In the opening scene, Mason performs Marlene Dietrich's signature song, "Falling in Love Again (Can't Help It)," made famous in the Dietrich/Emil Jannings film *The Blue Angel* (1930/directed by Josef Von Sternberg). The episode title references the 1941 Universal comedy/musical *Six Lessons from Madame LaZonga*, which paired the *Mexican Spitfire* team of Lupe Velez and Leon Errol.

Marlyn Mason gleefully recalled the filming of her tribute to Marlene:

They ran the old *Blue Angel* for me. When I saw it, her voice was very high. It wasn't the sultry voice she developed later. So I went with the sultry . . . I had this great top hat and tails. I said, "Jerry (London), you don't have a choreographer for this? This outfit really needs a choreographer." And out of the air comes this little French accent saying, "I am through working for the day. I will help choreograph something for you." It was Robert Clary. So he took me in hand and we went off to the side and in twenty minutes we worked out this little number and that's what you see on the screen. It was one of the most divine moments of my career, because that's how I started out, doing a number in top hat and tails, "Mister Tap Toe," when I was about twelve years old. They photographed it so well, the cameraman made me look like a million dollars!*

Assessment: The series pays tribute to *The Blue Angel,* with a beautiful opening scene in a small, but well decorated, nightclub set, and a spot on rendition of "Falling in Love Again," performed by Marlyn Mason. A most fascinating love triangle of sorts develops with both sappy suitors Klink and Hochstetter attempting to parlay the favor of the lovely Fraulein Frankel. This leads to the ridiculous notion of the Gestapo Major demanding lessons from Corporal LeBeau, in the cooler, nonetheless. Yet it's all worth it to catch the impeccable timing of Leon Askin who joins the dance party late in the game to witness the daffy display of Hochstetter and LeBeau "*not* dancing cheek to cheek." Mason performs exceptionally well with Crane in a sincere attempt at romance, particularly in her astute comment that Hogan "moves from one woman to another." But our unflappable Colonel Hogan ably wards off the jealous accusation resulting from the telltale, blonde hair on his face – actually a beauty mark acquired from his most recent Stalag 13 escape via the dog house!

*Telephone interview with the author, December 15, 2020.

Season 5, Episode 23: "The Sergeant's Analyst" 03/06/1970.

D: Bruce Bilson W: Bill Davenport

Guest Cast: Leon Askin (Gen. Burkhalter), Sigrid Valdis (Hilda), Norbert Schiller (Baker), Bard Stevens (Guard), and Richard Dawson as (Dr. Brunhilde Von Schramm).

Storyline: Supply Sgt. Schultz makes an unauthorized detour into Barracks Four to drop off food supplies for Chef LeBeau. Hogan and Newkirk secretly open a loaf of pumpernickel bread revealing another piece to a puzzle they are completing, a map of the German west wall. Exhausted, Schultz decides to take a nap in the barracks, especially since Klink is away from camp. General Burkhalter makes a surprise visit, and finding Schultz asleep on duty, orders his immediate transfer to the Russian Front. Hogan attempts to get Klink to reverse the orders as a fluke in the chain of command. It almost succeeds until Klink realizes that Burkhalter himself signed the orders. In another attempt to help Schultz stay, Hogan persuades Klink to contact Dr. Von Schramm (actually Newkirk) to administer hypnotherapy and convert Schultz into a tough, disciplined soldier. The ruse seems to work, aided by the men pretending to cower to the new, hardened Schultz. Burkhalter takes notice and is further impressed when Schultz delivers several confiscated goods from the prisoners and turns them over as gifts to the General. Burkhalter rescinds the transfer orders, and Hogan reverts Schultz to his former function of retrieving and delivering supply goods along with the final pieces of the puzzling west wall map.

Program Notes: Newkirk's masquerade as Dr. Von Schramm is a direct nod to the costuming and characterization of brilliant British comic Peter Sellers, and his performance as the quirky psychoanalyst in *What's New Pussycat?* (1965). Peter O' Toole took the role originally conceived by and intended for Warren Beatty while

Sellers enjoyed the part originally offered to Groucho Marx. The title Burt Bacharach song was performed by Welsh singer Tom Jones, who made it a recognizable part of his standard repertoire. Bruce Bilson recalled John Banner: "I loved him. He was such a good friend. I had this little teenie wife, about 5' 1" and one hundred pounds, and at the wrap party they danced together, and he was so light on his feet. It was something to behold."*

Assessment: A most curious series of events unfolds at Stalag 13 beginning with something we haven't witnessed yet, Schultz secretly delivering groceries to the prisoners' barracks. Of course, Colonel Hogan is only interested in the pumpernickel bread, the latest, ingenious, delivery system from the Underground. What should be the highlight of the episode, the psychoanalysis scene, is actually its downfall with the usually reliable Richard Dawson offering a curiously low key characterization. Although the sight of Dawson in his hermaphroditic skirt suit, and his mild flirtation with Klink, is amusing in its peculiarity, it never succeeds in big humor. It's all more bizarre than funny. Klink not being able to see through the obvious disguise further strains the thin logic. Perhaps Dawson himself wasn't that sold on performing a Sellers "rip off" sequence, explaining his absence of enthusiasm. It's also unclear whether or not Schultz is in on the caper. As is often the case, smaller nuances succeed, including Burkhalter's reprimand of Schultz with every sputtering word from the sergeant condemned as a lie, Klink again unwittingly foiling Hogan's plans by refusing the grocer's pumpernickel, and the rebirth of the toughened Schultz. But like Schultz's flattened, smuggled bread, this trip to therapy also falls flat.

*Telephone interview with the author, September 14, 2020.

Season 5, Episode 24: "The Merry Widow" 03/13/1970.

P/D: Edward H. Feldman W: Harvey Bullock, R. S. Allen

Guest Cast: Barry O' Hara (Sgt. Meadows), Bill Henry (Florist), and Marj Dusay as (the Countess Marlene).

Storyline: Kinchloe presents to Hogan film negatives revealing the Germans' new network of land mines that have stalled the Allied offensive. A tunnel cave-in has Hogan's men building a new tunnel out of Barracks Five. Schultz accidentally discovers the secret tunnel during a formation drill, along with a life-sized gopher, Corporal LeBeau. With LeBeau confined to the cooler and no way to secretly exit camp, Hogan plots to use Klink as his carrier pigeon. The Underground fly in a female agent to pose as the "Countess Marlene," a lovely vision who randomly chooses men for her affairs. Hogan and his men start a rumor in front of Schultz, who backs up the story when Klink receives flowers and an invitation from the Countess. Klink springs LeBeau from the cooler to make alterations to his uniform in time for his big date. LeBeau sews the film negatives into the lining of Klink's uniform and the Kommodant heads into town. While the Countess effectively removes Klink's coat and the negatives, Hogan receives word from Sgt. Meadows that the land mines have been significantly altered rendering the old negatives obsolete. A handheld model of the land mine design must now be delivered and the men hide it in the soil of a plant stolen from Klink's office. Schultz becomes the new, unknowing messenger carrying the plant to the Countess as a gift. But Klink's unexpected arrival spoils the affair. In a final effort before she flies out of Germany, the Countess arrives at Stalag 13 to woo Klink again and slip away with the plant and contents of its valuable soil.

Program Notes: This was the third and final appearance of Marj Dusay, who passed away shortly before contract for her involvement in this book could be made. Dusay and Leon Askin worked together in "Benvenuto . . . Who?," (1969), a sixth season episode of *Daniel Boone,* (1964-1970).

Assessment: Another "carrier pigeon" story that saddles Klink and Schultz as easily manipulated losers in love, this "Merry Widow" caper is never as merry as one would hope. Although Marj Dusay performs with relish, there's not much to like about the character since her only function is to woo Klink and split with the film. It's a good performance trapped in a one note, somewhat thankless role. Worse yet, the story lumbers to an unsatisfying conclusion. The actors compensate, somewhat, with their customary professionalism. Schultz is quite funny as he essentially repeats everything he has just heard in the barracks and sells Klink on the physical and intoxicating merits of the Countess Marlene. Also quite funny is the opening sight gag in the compound involving Schultz's unexpected discovery of the tunneling LeBeau. The best scene is the most subtle, involving a chess game between Hogan and Klink and their discussion about women, and eventually the notion of revenge for heartburn. Here again, the duo function as buddies and not adversaries of war. When one of the most inspired moments of the night is Klink's contemplation of his next chess move, it's another testament to the man's acting, particularly when so much of the surrounding trifles are less inspirational.

Season 5, Episode 25: "Crittendon's Commandos" 03/20/1970.

P/D: Edward H. Feldman W: Bill Davenport

Guest Cast: Bernard Fox (Col. Rodney Crittendon).

Storyline: Area A-11 will be receiving six drop in's, parachutists on a mission to kidnap Field Marshall Rommel from a Hammelburg Hospital where he is recovering from combat wounds. Hogan's men are to round up the commandos and house them until mission time. With SS troops combing the woods, Hogan and company dress as German soldiers and steal a truck from the motor pool. In the woods, they encounter Colonel Crittendon, who is leading the Rommel mission with a tired, ragged crew. Hogan instructs all to move back to camp, but Crittendon insists that he and his men travel the twelve miles back to Stalag 13 on foot to avoid the possibility of a mass capture. Much later, Crittendon arrives via the emergency tunnel only to inform Hogan that the rest of his men were captured by a patrol. He also explains that the kidnapping of Rommel is to trigger a hostage exchange for Admiral Toddley. Hogan's Heroes decide to aid Crittendon in the kidnapping and again manage to snag a truck from the motor pool. At the hospital, Crittendon insists he will sneak into the cellar and shut off the main light switch while Hogan and his men move in on room 101 and grab Rommel. It almost works until the air raid siren is triggered instead. As the hospital staff clears out, Rommel is moved out on a gurney. Later, Schultz informs the barracks that Rommel will be making a camp inspection. Unclear the result of their mission, Hogan is informed by Crittendon by a submarine radio that the men actually captured Admiral Toddley instead, negating the hostage exchange.

Assessment: What should have been a natural winner, an adventure mission to kidnap the "Desert Fox," is a mild disappointment thanks to a subpar Bill Davenport script that never seizes the potential drama of the piece. Like the preceding episode, this caper also staggers to a sleepy finish with the unremarkable removal of Rommel from his hospital room. A ridiculously fast, quick change maneuver that suddenly puts Hogan and LeBeau in doctors' scrubs further undermines the action. The final explanation from Crittendon that the boys nabbed the wrong body *almost* explains away the complete ease of the previous night's operation. The smaller pieces of the puzzle are more enjoyable, such as the wild sight gag of Crittendon attempting to communicate with the periscope outside of the wire (and the funny finish with LeBeau being pulled up to the roof of the cave), and Carter's nervous, knuckle-cracking that throws Hogan's boys a loop while trying to make contact with the commandos. Klink and Schultz spend most of the action in the background, with the Sergeant having to suffer through an unfunny motor pool incident. The one standout scene is probably the simplest, a Hogan/Klink office scene bolstered by Klink's admonishment of Hogan as a "scheming trouble maker" who continually depresses him! This is the one spot where Davenport's dialogue sings, Klemperer more than sells the goods, and Crane counters with his dumbfounded innocence. Unfortunately, it's sandwiched within a mediocre mission.

Season 5, Episode 26: "Klink's Escape" 03/27/1970.

D: Bruce Bilson W: Harvey Bullock, R. S. Allen

Guest Cast: Leon Askin (Gen. Burkhalter), Tom Hatten (Lt.), Dave Morick (Sentry), and Pamela Curran as (Heidi Freiderich).

Storyline: While Hogan and his men set up travel itineraries for several escapees from Stalag 12, Klink entertains his latest girlfriend, the charming Heidi Freiderich. General Burkhalter interrupts the romance with news of recent stalag escapes, orders Klink to double the guard, and conduct complete, building inspections – while the General remains and makes overtures to Fraulein Freiderich. Burkhalter believes that an Underground "escape center" is being operated, a notion that Klink mentions to Hogan. Hogan and his men plot to destroy a railway tunnel that has proven difficult for the Allies to take out. Hindering this objective are the extra posted guards blocking the typical escape route. Hogan leaks to Schultz a false story about German prisoners of war who also operated a clearing station, and how the Americans *allowed* the German POWs to escape, were followed, and the escape center terminated. Schultz reports this information to Klink, who becomes obsessed with *encouraging* his POWs to escape in order to shut down their escape center and win favor with Burkhalter. Klink goes so far as to have the men remove the wire from a section of fencing, ignore the broken searchlight, and provide German uniforms and a staff car for Hogan's men. They use Klink as a cooperative hostage to get past Burkhalter's road blocks, divert their course to wire the pesky tunnel for detonation, and return to Stalag 13 to insure Klink that his no escape record remains perfect.

Program Notes: In the opening scene, Hogan reports to his visitors from Stalag 12 that including "you four," they have aided in the relocation of "519 customers, thirteen in just the past week." This is the only appearance of Pamela Curran who retired from show business shortly after this episode aired. This was the final broadcast episode with Gordon Avil as the program's Director of Photography.

Assessment: The curtain closer for season five focuses on characterization with the most desirable of results. Using a plot device from "The Merry Widow," Hogan plants a seed in Schultz's brain knowing it will be shared with Klink. The ensuing events allow Werner Klemperer to assume the role of the most obliging of prison wardens while the heroes must play hard to get waiting for London to supply a dynamite delivery. Klink's psychological approach includes sharing American magazines with the prisoners (his advice to Hogan to "look at the pin- up girls" strikes a sensitive nerve), allowing the men to remove fence wiring for the possibility of installing a new gate, and fueling up his staff car and having it parked outside the fence line. When Newkirk cheerfully offers to repair the broken searchlight, Klink hilariously snaps: "Request denied!" Schultz joins in the fun by pretending to lose his rifle during a work detail, only to have the prisoners helpfully return the rifle and exit whistling Jerry Fielding's theme music. This is *Hogan's Heroes* at its charming best. Other superbly timed bits include Klink acidentally triggering though not quite discovering the secret of the breakaway bunk beds, and Hogan rattling the paper ballots during the prisoners' bugged, and rigged, election. Meanwhile, Burkhalter enjoys a meaty supporting role as he attempts to sleaze his way into the charms of Heidi Freiderich, even unknowingly repeating the same come-on lines used earlier by Klink, and experiencing his own set of disastrous results. The pitch perfect pace keeps moving with Hogan casually pulling the puppet strings and reminding the team their future actions are all part of "Klink's Escape" - not theirs. There is also a first ever, ingenious use of a split screen image, as Klink and Schultz use a listening bug to snoop in on the prisoners' escape plan. Adding to the charm is the inclusion of Pamela Curran in the left side image, bubbily along for the ride with her constant champagne glass as a companion. Ultimately, "Klink's Escape" is a showcase for Colonel Klink, and Werner Klemperer seizes every nuance with relish. Watch the way he pleasantly works the men's barracks late in the game, comments on how good the prisoners look in German uniforms, removes his own sidearm to brighten his appearance, and then casually strolls over to the window to make a whimsical comment about the still broken, searchlight. Here is simple mastery. This is my favorite episode directed by Bruce Bilson, and my favorite Werner Klemperer performance.

Craziest Come-on:

Burkhalter: (to Heidi Freiderich) "I have this little hideaway chalet not very far from here. It's very comfortable. Full of meat and butter. Think about it, my dear."

★ ★ ★ ★

Larry Weber's brilliant realization of Colonel Wilhelm Klink seemed a fitting homage to celebrate "Klink's Escape," my personal favorite Werner Klemperer performance. Illustration courtesy of Larry Weber.

Primer for Season Six

Primary Cast

Colonel Robert Hogan:	Bob Crane
Kommodant Wilhelm Klink:	Werner Klemperer
Sgt. of Guard, Hans Schultz:	John Banner
Corporal Louis LeBeau:	Robert Clary
Corporal Peter Newkirk:	Richard Dawson
Sergeant Andrew Carter:	Larry Hovis
Sergeant Richard Baker:	Kenneth Washington
Hilda (recurring character):	Sigrid Valdis
General Albert Burkhalter (recurring):	Leon Askin
Colonel Rodney Crittendon, RAF (recurring):	Bernard Fox
Marya, "the White Russian" (recurring):	Nita Talbot
Oscar Schnitzer (recurring):	Walter Janovitz
Corporal Langenscheidt (recurring):	Jon Cedar
"Tiger" (recurring):	Arlene Martel
and	
Major Wolfgang Hochstetter, Gestapo (recurring):	Howard Caine

The final season Heroes, with Kenneth Washington as Sgt. Richard Baker (center) replacing the role vacated by Ivan Dixon, await Colonel Hogan's next brainstorm in "The Experts." Author's collection/CBS Television Inc.

With the departure of Ivan Dixon and "James Kinchloe," the series employed another African American actor to fill his combat boots, Kenneth Washington, as Sgt. Richard Baker, who performed, generally, the same communication functions as his predecessor. Following the same blueprint established with the exit of Helga after season one, no explanation was offered for the replacement of Kinch. Prior to his recruitment, Washington was most familiar to television audiences in the recurring role of Officer Miller on *Adam-12*.

With the sudden passing of Gordon Avil during the off season, executive producer Ed Feldman promoted Avil's camera operator, William Jurgensen, to take over as his Director of Photography. This was an early career assignment for Jurgensen, who took his experience from Stalag 13 and followed it up with a similar pattern established by his *Hogan's* collegues, joining the 4077th Mobile Army Surgical Hospital. Jurgensen would run the camera and lighting crew at *M*A*S*H* for 110 episodes, and although his tenure as DP appeared to terminate with the departure of Gene Reynolds as executive producer, Jurgensen continued on as an occasional director for the Korean War, comedy/drama.

Meanwhile, the transparent romance between Colonel Hogan and Hilda blossomed with a first and only in television history, a marriage ceremony performed on the set of a TV series. Bob Crane and Sigrid Valdis wed on October 16, 1970 in front of about two hundred guests on the *Hogan's set*. About seven and a half minutes of the wedding footage is included on the CBS Home Entertainment DVD box set of the entire series, and Valdis admits in her included commentary that despite being a very happy day for both her and Crane, the wedding was largely a publicity stunt ignited by CBS and Bing Crosby Productions. Contrary to previously cited reports, Richard Dawson did not serve as best man (although his voice can be heard off camera immediately after the ceremony playfully kidding Crane about flubbing his exchange of vows). Edward

Feldman is clearly seen standing next to Crane and handing the groom the wedding ring.

The cancellation of *Hogan's Heroes* during the off season came as a big surprise to the cast and crew, who assumed that "monkey business" at Stalag 13 would resume with the production start of its seventh season. CBS moved the series, again, to a new time slot, now 7:30 pm on Sunday evenings. Frequent guest star, Howard Caine, claimed the move compromised the program's core viewers, largely a younger viewing audience, that were already tuned in to NBC Television's *Wonderful World of Disney* and unlikely to switch the dial midstream. Associate producer and director Jerry London recalled: "It was sure a sad occasion. We were all a family and we thought we would keep going. CBS was trying to go for a change in the age of their viewers, or something like that . . ."*

The Stalag 13 camp at Forty Acres experienced a resurrection of sorts when a Canadian film group shot the 1975 sexploitation film *Ilsa, She Wolf of the SS* around those still standing, exterior, compound buildings. Depicting the medical atrocities performed in Hitler's concentration camps, and as vile and disheartening as a motion picture experience gets, purist fanatics of *Hogan's Heroes* may find some perverse joy in seeing the final destruction of Colonel Klink's old stomping grounds in the film's welcome finish. Reportedly, the set was loaned out knowing its climactic demise would save the costs of having it torn down.

*Telephone interview with the author, February 14, 2021.

Season 6, Episode 1: "Cuisine A la Stalag 13" 09/20/1970.

D: Jerry London W: Laurence Marks

Guest Cast: John Hoyt (Gen. Wexler), Chet Stratton (Karl), Dave Morick (Gestapo Officer), Jay Sheffield (Capt. Richter), Brenda Benet (Marie Bizet).

Storyline: LeBeau helps Klink host a dinner party for General Wexler while Newkirk photographs the contents of the briefcase of his aide, Capt. Richter, in the bedroom. The developed photos reveal some minor Nazi operations, but Hogan knows through Richter that Wexler will be returning with much more valuable information. While the info is delivered to the French Underground, Marie Bizet informs LeBeau that an official call has been placed for all French citizens to return to France and secure the nation's liberation. LeBeau requests permission to escape permanently, but Hogan wants him to stay as chef for the return of Wexler and Richter. Hogan finally approves LeBeau's request, but the capture of Marie by the Gestapo changes things. Posing as a security officer, LeBeau attempts to spring Marie from Gestapo HQ. Hogan and Newkirk arrive as Gestapo officers and back LeBeau's story securing the freedom of Marie. Back in camp, LeBeau prepares one final gourmet dinner while the men secure the new information being transported by Richter. In a change of heart, LeBeau realizes his value to Hogan's operation and decides to remain.

Program Notes: With the departure of Ivan Dixon, Kenneth Washington debuts as Sgt. Richard Baker. William Jurgensen takes over as Director of Photography for this final season.

Assessment: Kenneth Washington gets an unceremonious welcome as Stalag 13's newest resident in a flat opener to the final season. Although LeBeau's passion in wanting to return to France for its liberation is a patriotic and noble notion, the story that unfolds is hardly gripping. The best sequence is the sincerity of the players (Richard Dawson in particular) as they all wish Louie a heartfelt goodbye. Noteworthy too is the visit to Gestapo HQ incorporating the first time scheme of two, separate, masquerading units acting in collusion in order to free Marie. Brenda Benet isn't given much of a chance to show her appreciation for the effort or register any other emotion in a barely sketched character. Likewise, the Capt. Richter character, who is actually explained as Hogan's "inside man" with Wexler, suffers from zero development and never shares a scene with Hogan to discuss their cooperative effort. The resolution with LeBeau suddenly deciding he must remain a Hero also underwhelms since nothing really happens of great consequence to instigate his decision. When the most exciting set piece involves John Hoyt looking for his cigars in the bedroom, and Newkirk hiding under the bed to avoid detection, we know we've witnessed a sub par adventure at Stalag 13.

Season 6, Episode 2: "The Experts" 09/27/1970.

D: Marc Daniels W: Laurence Marks

Guest Cast: Sigrid Valdis (Hilda), Noam Pitlik (Capt. Metzler), Edward Knight (Major Stern), Barbara Babcock (Maria), Sabrina Scharf (Luisa), Walter Janowitz (Schnitzer).

Storyline: While Hogan romances Hilda in the backseat of Klink's staff car, a Gestapo unit headed by Major Stern wakes Klink from his sleep demanding the whereabouts of two of Klink's men: Sgt. Holtz and Capt. Metzler. Hogan witnesses through the camp periscope the sudden assassination of Holtz by his own countrymen. With Metzler on leave, Hogan reasons that the Captain will be taken down next, and Hogan wants to know why. Under the pretense of having Klink's file cabinet painted, LeBeau and Carter secure the personnel files on the two men. With the help of London, Hogan learns that Metzler and company were all involved in a top secret radio transmissions program, were transferred to Stalag 13 upon the project completion, and now the Nazis are eliminating any loose ends permanently. With the help of his contact, Luisa, Hogan learns that Metzler is spending his leave in town at his girlfriend Maria's apartment, and he and Newkirk make contact hoping to save his life in exchange for detailed information about the radio communications center. In order to convince the doubting couple of his earnestness, Hogan reveals everything about his secret operation at Stalag 13. Using Schnitzer's dog truck, Metzler and Maria are snuck into the tunnels through the kennel. While Luisa plants a fake call to sidetrack Stern and his men, Metzler reveals all the details about the radio center to Hogan, and gets fitted with a new suit and travel papers to England. Mission accomplished, Hogan resumes his date with Hilda.

Program Notes: In the outer office scene, Hilda cheerfully mimics Schultz's trademark lines: "I know nothing, I see nothing!"

This third appearance concludes Barbara Babcock's three-part connection with the series.

Assessment: The early plot set up depicts the most raw image yet witnessed in the series, the on screen murder of Holtz by his fellow Germans. This propels Hogan into a self-appointed mission of his own discovery to find out why the German brass is tying up some mysterious, loose ends. Most of the action favors a dramatic development, particularly Hogan and Newkirk's encounter with Metzler and Maria. Dawson is especially convincing in this sequence. Another series first also develops with Hogan admittedly revealing the aspects of his covert operations – and to a German officer, nonetheless. The dialogue here is quite intriguing with Hogan explaining that they are actually "based" out of Stalag 13, as if they were never captured initially nor sent there as prisoners of war. Although Klink and Schultz are missing from most of the action, some light, romantic comedy is served in the bookends of the piece, with Hogan comfortably enjoying some backseat action with Hilda, who reassures the Colonel that although their date comes to a premature end, she will keep her "motor running."

Season 6, Episode 3: "Klink's Masterpiece" 10/04/1970.

D: Richard Kinon W: Phil Sharp

Guest Cast: Victoria Carroll (Rhona), Jon Cedar (Cpl. Langenscheidt), David M. Frank (1st Underground Agent), Bard Stevens (2nd Agent), Karl Bruck (3rd Agent).

Storyline: Hogan picnics with his latest contact, Rhona, who runs an art gallery in town as a front for Allied activity. The plan is to destroy some German supply convoys, but Hogan is waiting on the route maps from another contact. Since the Gestapo has been eyeing Rhona, she provides a carrier pigeon for their future message exchanges. Back at camp, Klink admonishes Hogan for not having the prisoners engage in leisure activities like the other stalag prisoners. Baker delivers the route maps but they arrive completely shredded as their contact has been posing as a janitor and this was the only safe way to deliver the maps. Hogan and his men begin to assemble the maps and convince Klink and Corporal Langesnscheidt that they have taken up jigsaw puzzles as their leisure activity. Hogan sends word to Rhona via carrier pigeon just as a random bomb is dropped from a flier creating a tunnel cave-in and shutting down the usual exit route. Hogan and company convince Klink that he is a talented painter and encourage his hobby. Hogan sets up a rendezvous with Rhona's art gallery so he and Klink can have his "paintings" appraised. This is Hogan's excuse to sneak the assembled maps to Rhona in the back of the picture frames. At the gallery, Rhona's art collectors (actually three Underground men) buy the three worthless paintings from Klink without hesitation and exit with the secretive maps. Realizing he forgot to sign his babies, Klink sends for Rhona and buys the three paintings back at decidedly marked up price tags. Hogan informs Klink that *after* he dies the paintings will probably become priceless, which was the case for Gaughin and Van Gogh.

Program Notes: Writer Phil Sharp won a 1958 Prime Time Emmy award for his work on *The Phil Silvers Show*. This was the sixth and final guest appearance of frequent visitor Victoria Carroll, who discussed how a program about Nazi Germany overcame negative public opinion:

I think you could almost label it black comedy. The war? The camp? The Nazis? I think everyone said, "You can never do this! It can never be done!" They really ragged on it . . . I think you could also almost label it high satire, because they're making fun of that time and what happened, and that takes the curse off of doing a show about Nazis. He (Werner Klemperer) made the arch villian look foolish and that took the sting out of it.*

Although Victoria Carroll spent the 1960s lending comic support to everyone in the business, she credits her work with the improvisational group "The Groundlings" as where she truly discovered her funny bones. Here Carroll is pictured with the late Phil Hartman, "a brilliant improviser; one always felt safe on stage with Phil." Photo courtesy of Victoria Carroll Bell/The Groundlings Theatre & School.

Assessment: Colonel Hogan's latest brainstorm is to convince Klink that he possesses a brilliant, untapped creativity as an oil painter – and Hogan sells the idea in the most convincing of manners. The office scene is particularly strong with Hogan analyzing Klink's doodle pad in order to set the ball in motion. Ditto with the followup action in which Hogan considers the ruse of Klink as a master artist, decides it will work, then happily remembers he still has Klink's doodle in the pocket of his ever present bomber's jacket. The compound scene is also lots of fun with the men encouraging Klink to take paint to canvas, moving the emotional LeBeau to tears in the process. Klemperer plays the scene with his typical, quiet brilliance, first completely hesitant with his own skills, then becoming more confident, assured, and flamboyant with each subsequent brush stroke. This carries over into the barracks scene which finds the welcome return of Jon Cedar, as he and Klink slowly take interest in the map being assembled by helping with the placement of the puzzle pieces. In her largest role to date, Victoria Carroll adds a lot of charm *and* bewilderment to the role of Rhona, particularly in trying to stomach the notion of Klink as artist. She also has one of the most subtle, and effective, moments in the program when Hogan asks her on the sly about the fate of the German convoys, to which she simply replies: "Boom."

*Telephone interview with the author, November 24, 2020.

Season 6, Episodes 4 & 5: "Lady Chitterly's Lover"
Part 1: 10/11/1970. Part 2: 10/18/1970.

P/D: Edward H. Feldman W: Richard M. Powell

Guest Cast: Anne Rogers (Lady Leslie Chitterly), Harold Gould (Gen. Von Schlomm), Howard Caine (Major Hochstetter), Sigrid Valdis (Hilda) and Bernard Fox as (Col. Crittendon and Sir Charles Chitterly).

Storyline: (Part 1:) Dropping from the night sky by parachute is the British traitor, Sir Charles Chitterly, who is working for Hitler on a secret mission and bears an uncanny resemblance to our old friend, Colonel Crittendon. Hogan and his men attempt contact but are deterred by the unwelcome arrival of Schultz and the other stalag guards. Chitterly informs Klink to contact Berlin of his arrival, prompting Klink to welcome Chitterly as a VIP until an envoy, General Von Schlomm, arrives. Since both Hogan and London are in the dark regarding Chitterly's mission, Carter sneaks into Klink's quarters through the wood stove impersonating Von Schlomm. After ordering Klink away, "Von Schlomm" and Hogan force Chitterly down into the tunnels as their hostage. Meanwhile, the boys have sprung Crittendon from Stalag 12 and Hogan plans to use him as a double. The real Von Schlomm arrives and is bewildered by Klink's confusion. The General informs the fake Chitterly that his wife, Lady Leslie, will be arriving within the next day and then their mission can proceed. Leslie confronts her "husband" as a traitor to England and threatens him with a knife until Hogan intercedes and makes her realize that this "Charles" is a plant. She agrees to cooperate with Hogan and Crittendon. Hogan, already uncertain about the unfolding events, is further hindered by Radio London's advice to "play along and see what turns up."

(Part 2:) Von Schlomm receives orders from Hitler to have the Chitterlys transported to Berlin immediately where Chitterly will persuade England to surrender to Germany. In order to stall for time, Leslie pretends that Hogan is an old lover and insists that she and her husband stay on, entirely frustrating and perplexing Von Schlomm. Holed up in Klink's private quarters, Hogan knows that Crittendon's masquerade as Chitterly will never fool the Fuhrer. Arguing with Leslie, Hogan insists that they must abort Chitterly's secret mission at Stalag 13. Newkirk pops out of the wood stove (!) to inform all of the escape of the real Chitterly, who turns up in the dog kennel and is greeted by Klink. Chitterly explains his true identity and how he was apprehended by the prisoners, much to Klink's doubts. When Chitterly attempts to show Klink the entrance to their tunnel system, the Englishman burns his hands on the wood stove. Klink and Schultz go to convene in his office with Von Schlomm and the recently arrived Major Hochstetter. Hogan and his gang recapture Chitterly and again replace him with Crittendon. Upon Klink's return, Hochstetter also burns his hands on the wood stove. On the phone, Leslie convinces the Fuhrer that the surrender plans of England should be delivered to Berlin by Von Schlomm. She also insists that an invasion force be launched to England to further their surrender. Baker informs the Allies of this development, and while Klink, Von Schlomm, and Hochstetter celebrate the pending surrender of England, the invasion force is wiped out. Hochstetter has Von Schlomm and the recently re-escaped Chitterly arrested for treason as Leslie and Colonel Crittendon are smuggled out of camp.

Program Notes: Guest star Harold Gould held a Ph.D in Theatre Arts and was an instructor at Cornell University before pursuing a full time career as an actor in the 1960s. In 1972, Gould portrayed Howard Cunningham in the segment "Love and the Happy Days" on *Love, American Style,* which also featured Ron Howard, Anson Williams, and Marion Ross in the roles they would continue on the long running *Happy Days* series. Gould was asked to continue by appearing in the proposed pilot but declined due to an overseas theatrical obligation. This two-part adventure concluded his association with the series, and he was billed as a "special guest star." This caper also concluded Bernard Fox's eight episode run. Although in his most recent sighting, "Crittendon's Commandos," Rodney made it safely back to England, here he finds himself once again incarcerated as a prisoner of war.

Assessment: The double duty casting ploy earlier employed with Ivan Dixon and John Banner returns, giving the double assignment this time around to Bernard Fox, with modest results of success. Richard Powell's script contains some hiccups that don't settle easily such as the instant and unspectacular escape of Crittendon from Stalag 12 and, as a result, Schultz's mild acceptance of Carter and Newkirk missing at roll call. The mysterious masquerade of the first General Von Schlomm goes unchallenged *and* quickly forgotten after his sudden disappearance, despite the confusion it causes for Klink and the real Von Schlomm. That's too bad since Larry Hovis's turn as the fake Von Schlomm provokes some of the biggest giggles in the first half hour. Hovis joyfully balances his two favorite approaches to the Third Reich school of acting: the irate, noisy Nazi along with the thoughtful, droll mannered disciplinarian. Things perk up with the addition of Anne Rogers as Chitterly's wife who enters into an uneasy alliance with Hogan. Her sudden brainstorm in Klink's office, posing as an old lover of Hogan's, is a spirited moment and continues to perplex the mostly affable Harold Gould. (Delightful is her first scene where she dismisses Gould's concerns about sudden noises from the bedroom as observations of "quaintness.") Lightning strikes, naturally, with the arrival of Howard Caine, who dominates the final scene in Klink's office, whether arguing with Gould and/or Klink or, ultimately, getting duped by one of Hogan's signature double talk routines. The only real thing missing is better, more cleverly constructed material for Bernard Fox. Although he scores with several of his ironic line reads ("It's going to be a dull few days," comes to mind), Powell's script never really seizes the comic material of having two doppelgangers appearing and reappearing, missing out on what could have been a truly inspired *Comedy of Errors*.

Memorable exchange:

Chitterly: "Call me a Messerschmitt, General. I'm going back to England!"

Carter: (as fake Von Schlomm) "You are a Messerschmitt, and you're staying here!"

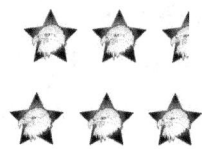

Season 6, Episode 6: "The Gestapo Takeover" 10/25/1970.

D: Irving J. Moore W: Laurence Marks

Guest Cast: Leon Askin (Gen. Burkhalter), Joseph Ruskin (Maj. Strauss), Bruce Kirby (Otto), Martin Kosleck (Gen. Mueller), Sigrid Valdis (Hilda), Forrest Compton (Capt. Geissler), Richard Alden (Bartender/Uncredited).

Storyline: Gestapo Major Strauss and a commando of soldiers arrive at Stalag 13 and quickly announce their takeover of command by orders of General Mueller. Klink attempts confirmation from Burkhalter, who quickly ends the phone conversation once the word "Gestapo" is mentioned. Although Hogan's men don't seem fazed by the sudden change in command, Hogan insists otherwise. His point is taken when a tunnel is discovered in the compound and Strauss has him hauled off to the cooler. LeBeau confers with Hogan in his cell, who instructs the corporal to have Baker make a recording of any phone conversations between Strauss and Mueller. He wants Newkirk to study, practice, and eventually imitate Mueller's voice. Klink and Schultz, fearing they will be transferred to Russia, seek Hogan's counsel who barters to be released. Using his contact, Otto, and a second Underground agent, Hogan plots an elaborate ruse to have Strauss sign a document for Mueller involving a plot to kill Hitler in exchange for ten million Swiss francs and safe passage to Argentina. Hogan moves the treasonous document to Klink who delivers it to Burkhalter in Berlin, who then confronts Mueller. Strauss is arrested and Mueller reluctantly returns the keys to Stalag 13 back to Burkhalter and Klink (and Hogan, for that matter).

Program Notes: This was the first of two directing assignments for Irving J. Moore, who began his long career as an assistant director for Jules White's short subjects department at Columbia Pictures. His early AD credits frequently placed him alongside The Three

Stooges (*Musty Musketeers* (1954), *Scotched in Scotland* (1954), etc.) In the 1980s, Moore dominated the prime time soap opera market, at the helm of fifty-two episodes of *Dallas* (spanning 1978-91), and fifty-nine episodes of *Dynasty* (1981-88). Long time character actor Joseph Ruskin will certainly be recognized by *Twilight Zone* trippers as the not-entirely-trustworthy Genie in "The Man in the Bottle" (1960). Richard Dawson is only visible in the radio room scenes indicating he wrapped his scenes in one day and in one location.

Assessment: Everything clicks like clockwork in one of Laurence Marks' brightest scripts allowing three guest stars to carry the key components of Hogan's scheme to fruition. Newkirk finalizes the brilliant ruse with his spot-on voice impersonation of General Mueller that is played for conviction and not for laughs. The supporting cast is uniformly excellent, with Joe Ruskin as a memorably oily Gestapo Major who looks and sounds as if born to play the role. His quiet approach is a welcome change from some of the more bombastic portrayals that have filtered through the stalag. Bruce Kirby enjoys his best role of his three visits bringing a highly believable demeanor to his impersonation of "Baum, the Swiss accountant." There's also a crisply directed document exchange as Baum and Geissler exit the office and encounter the unruly LeBeau and Carter. The terrific pace climaxes with a choice showdown between Burkhalter (who hung up on Klink at the top of the episode yet now gloriously saves the day) and the gravelly voiced Mueller, who sounds exactly like Peter Newkirk (with a pinch of Charles McGraw). Perfectly directed by first timer Irving J. Moore, here is an episode that showcases *Hogan's Heroes* at its finest by juxtaposing an entirely credible caper, functioning within the accepted staples of the series, along with doses of humor that never disrupt the dramatic flow.

Season 6, Episode 7: "Kommodant Schultz" 11/01/1970.

D: Marc Daniels W: Laurence Marks

Guest Cast: Leon Askin (Gen. Burkhalter), Eric Morris (Hercules), Jon Cedar (Cpl. Langenscheidt), Norbert Schiller (Farmer), Walter Janovitz (Oscar Schnitzer), Richard Alden (Bartender).

Storyline: Working outside the wire, the boys smuggle an Underground operative, "Hercules," and his package back into camp. The package contains uranium that the Nazis are mining, and London wants Hercules to deliver it. An oddball memorandum from Hitler, presented by General Burkhalter, states that all senior non-commissioned officers will receive commander training. During this period, Klink will be reduced to adviser status while Schultz assumes command. The timid Schultz seeks the counsel of Hogan, who uses the story of the "little train that could" as an inspiration for the sergeant to succeed. Storm warnings prevent Hercules from exiting camp so he remains in waiting. Schultz, now sporting a monocle, miraculously transforms into a complete tyrant by doubling the guard and enacting severe disciplinary measures. Klink, fearful that he will be displaced, also seeks Hogan's advice. The men try to sneak Hercules out of camp using Schnitzer's dog truck, but Schultz busts up the plan. Hogan orders Newkirk and LeBeau to escape and hide out in town which completely stymies Schultz. Burkhalter restores command to Klink dependent on his ability to reclaim the missing prisoners. Hogan leads Klink and company to the Hammelburg Hofbrau where the boys are enjoying the company of some lovely frauleins. After Klink manages to wildly shoot the place up with a machine gun, he orders Schultz to pay the damages as order is restored to Stalag 13.

Program Notes: Back to back appearances surface for Richard Alden as the Hofbrau bartender, who this time enjoys final credit billing. This is Jon Cedar's final turn as Corporal Langenscheidt, although he would reappear later in the season, reincarnated as Oscar Danzing.

The swiped cigar in Hogan's hand indicates he has once again taken control of the situation, as Klink anxiously awaits the brainstorm that will discredit "Kommodant Schultz." Author's collection/CBS Television Inc.

Assessment: After previously delivering a knockout script, Laurence Marks slips back into the comfort zone with a passable tale promoting Schultz to Kommodant. Although the concept was toyed with in season one's "The Great Impersonation," this time around Schultz actually takes the reigns of his new command with intense authority and determination, allowing John Banner to again show some range as a dramatic actor. The concept of Hitler actually ordering his NCOs to take temporary command of his stalags is pretty flimsy, but since this is *Hogan's Heroes'* take on WWII history, anything's possible. This episode could have benefited from a comparison scene involving Klink perhaps commiserating with a fellow Kommodant, and the results of the intrusive command change at a *different* stalag. Either way, the narrative moves with general successes in both the dramatic and comedic aspects expected from the show. Bright spots include the final appearance of Jon Cedar's Corporal Langenscheidt, who appears genuinely delighted to see his old Sergeant of Arms bumped up to Big Boss, and the hilarious sight of Colonel Klink demonstrating how to use a machine gun in a crowded beer parlor.

Season 6, Episode 8: "Eight O' Clock and All is Well" 11/08/1970.

D: Richard Kinon W: Laurence Marks

Guest Cast: Howard Caine (Major Hochstetter), Monte Markham (Capt. James Martin/Seifert), Roy Goldman (POW/Uncredited), Dick Wilson (Karl/Unc.).

Storyline: After Hogan and company successfully blow up a convoy of German trucks, Major Hochstetter visits Klink and shows him a map of several Allied sabotage attacks all surrounding Stalag 13. The guard is ordered to double up and radio detection trucks will begin sweeping the area. Hogan orders that all their extracurricular activities be temporarily curtailed. The POWs receive a new prisoner, Captain James Martin. Hogan has him screened to make sure he isn't an enemy plant before finally giving Martin a tour of their sabotage and escape center. The Heroes next mission is to destroy a German munitions train which will include Martin. During roll call, Martin starts a beef with Schultz, so Klink has him brought to his office. Knowing he is under surveillance, Martin writes Klink a note that explains his true identity, Captain Seifert of the Gestapo. Klink lets "Martin" off with a warning then summons Hochstetter. Hogan is suspicious of Klink's leniency and then observes a Gestapo soldier stand at attention when Martin passes. The men hold Martin as a hostage in the tunnels as they head out and efficiently destroy the train. Martin's jacket, which has been deliberately scorched, is left behind as evidence. Later, Klink and Hochstetter decide that Martin, learning about the train sabotage plot, went out on his own to take down the saboteurs and was blown up in the process.

Program Notes: The title of this episode bears no relation to the events that occur within the half hour creating an irregularity in the series.

Assessment: A decent recycling of events that dates back to the pilot episode, this undertaking begins with the most unconvincing spectacle of the demolition of a German convoy of supply trucks. Initially, LeBeau spots one truck moving along through his binoculars followed by an explosion where several trucks are already at a standstill. Fortunately, the final explosion of the munitions train effectively restores order. Monte Markham brings a consistently rugged and believable tone to his Capt. Martin facade, and the scene where he shoves Schultz surprises the viewers as much as the lovable sergeant himself. Roy Goldman's background POW gets a bump up in the action, including the task of keeping Martin "on ice." Typical benefits are also supplied by Howard Caine who brings one of his more relaxed visits to Stalag 13. Atypically, he lights up one of Klink's cigars during an office waiting game then ponders: "I'm trying to win the war, vot are you doing?" His final scene is a rare instance where one of Klink's suggestions is actually considered by Hochstetter important enough to take to Berlin. The climax with Martin's scorched pilot's jacket supposedly explaining away his disappearance is lifted from season three's "One in Every Crowd," again offering the unsolvable puzzle of what happened to the rest of his uniform and body. If he died a hero, with his boots on, those boots are nowhere to be found.

Season 6, Episode 9: "The Big Record" 11/15/1970.

D: Richard Kinon   W: R. S. Allen, Harvey Bullock

Guest Cast: Leon Askin (Gen. Burkhalter), Jack Riley (S. S. Man), John Myhers (Col. Schneider), Roy Goldman (POW/Uncredited).

Storyline: Klink presents to all the prisoners in the recreation hall the opportunity to record messages to be sent back home on phonograph records. He regulates that the only comments recorded must come from a strictly approved set of statements. S. S. soldiers arrive and Klink orders the rec room cleared while Hogan ponders what it's all about. Hogan tricks Schultz into admitting that the sudden enhanced security pertains to a pending visit from Colonel Schneider. Hogan and Newkirk pay Klink a visit pretending to seek his life story for the "camp newsletter." During the ensuing conversation, Klink leaks out that Colonel Schneider will be using the rec hall for a top secret meeting led by General Burkhalter discussing Luftwaffe, ground support, battle stations. Hogan wants to make a recording of the meeting for London, so the men rig a clothing line to the rec hall, but the S. S. men quickly kill the scheme. Hearing Schultz sing "Swanee" in the NCO shower, Hogan influences Schultz to sing for the recorder so they can send the record to Newkirk's uncle in England, an impresario always on the lookout for new, vocal talent. They move Schultz to the rec hall for "better acoustics," but Klink disrupts the plan insisting they should be recording his violin playing instead. While Hogan and Baker pretend to make the recording in the office, the real device records Burkhalter's meeting. Two weeks later, Burkhalter and Schneider return disgusted that their carefully planned ground forces were wiped out by the Army Air Corps. To make matters worse, Klink begins playing the "Air Corps" song with his violin under Hogan's guidance, adding salt to the General's wounds.

Assessment: A slim storyline nets so-so results with pacing being the key detriment. Schultz singing "Swanee" is good for a few chuckles but not when it gets worked over in the labored sequence in the barracks - although Schultz's exit and immediate return coupled with Hogan's unflinching movement is a sweet bit of business. Klink injects an inspired notion of suspicion regarding Newkirk's uncle, but this is merely buildup to Klink's real objective of having *his* egotistical talents promoted on record. The standout scene sticks to a fan favorite, the double talk scene in Klink's office, where both Hogan and Newkirk trigger information out of loose-lipped Klink. Off the record, most of the other material surrounding these few choice moments feels like only passable entertainment, perhaps like managing to sit through Klink's violin concerto.

Season 6, Episode 10: "It's Dynamite" 11/22/1970.

D: Bob Sweeney W: Laurence Marks

Guest Cast: Michael Fox (Berger), Lyn Peters (Elsa), Sigrid Valdis (Hilda), and Howard Caine as (Major Hochstetter).

Storyline: Through their periscope-in-a-rainwater-drum, Hogan observes several trucks roll into camp. Further surveillance with their coffee pot reveals Hochstetter's plan to use Stalag 13 as a storage center for crates of dynamite. The loaded crates will be driven to secret locations, and Klink and Hochstetter force Schultz to "volunteer" as their first driver. Hogan and his Underground contacts want to hijack the dynamite and begin studying road maps out of the stalag after Schultz indicates that Flenzhiem Road will be traveled. Their first night mission fails when Schultz and the truck disappear along the route, and the sergeant returns early the next morning with an empty truck. Hogan attempts to work Klink for information and spooks him with talk of explosive results, prompting Klink to approve himself for immediate furlough. Meanwhile, Major Hochstetter is using the prisoner's detention cells for storage and office facilities. Hogan figures the Major has maps and charts of their secret routes so Carter poses as the Hammelburg Fire Chief accompanied by Elsa, an Underground ally, posing as the Chief's personal secretary. As the beautiful Elsa flirts with Hochstetter commanding his attention, the "Fire Chief" spreads smoke bombs throughout the storage cells causing Hochstetter to yell: "Fire!" Hogan and the others slip in and pilfer the route maps while Hogan pretends to guide Hochstetter to safety, until Baker and the fire hose render him and his men all wet. Upon his return, Klink formally thanks Hogan and his Heroes for their bravery during the recent fire.

Program Notes: This is the seventeenth and final episode directed by Bob Sweeney. In addition to his directing assignments on over fifty network programs, Mr. Sweeney also amassed over one hundred professional acting credits, often in TV shows based on classic radio programs: *Burns and Allen*, *The Life of Riley* (the William Bendix version), and as Fibber McGee on *Fibber McGee and Molly*. Bruce Bilson expressed much admiration for Sweeney:

"My big break was working on *The Andy Griffith Show* and meeting Bob Sweeney, and he made me a director on *The Patty Duke Show*. Bob Sweeney and I were very close; he and Ed (Feldman) were good friends also."*

Assessment: Most of the plot action regarding truck routes and missing dynamite crates moves with precision and plausibility, until the resolution which threatens to send the whole enterprise up in smoke. Both of the scenes in Klink's office are strong ones: Klink and Hochstetter musing about electing the services of an "expendable" soldier and reputing Schultz's meek objections to the task, and the beautifully framed shot of Klink sharpening a pencil with a knife while Hogan attempts to "lean" on him. Bob Crane and Sigrid Valdis, married on the *Hogan's* set the previous month, certainly perform together like a couple of prospective newlyweds. The genuine mutual attraction between the couple is charmingly infectious. Despite the radiant features of Lyn Peters' "Fraulein Schmidt," who sexily lets her hair down to ease into the role of seductress, Larry Hovis's "Fire Chief" is given little material other than to casually strew smoke bombs about while sporting a ridiculously Milton-Berle-longish burning cigar. What about those charts and maps that Hochstetter attempts to frantically salvage and then immediately and conveniently forget moments later? By the time the viewer hits the finish line they may be feeling exactly like Hochstetter and his unit – all wet. (Although Klink's final promise of "wiener schnitzel on Saturday night" does instill some hope.)

*Telephone interview with the author, September 14, 2020.

Season 6, Episode 11: "Operation Tiger" 11/29/1970.

D: Jerry London W: Laurence Marks

Guest Cast: Arlene Martel (Tiger), Frank Marth (Capt. Steiger), Dick Wilson (Karl), Walter Janovitz (Oscar Schnitzer), Dave Morick (1st Guard/ Unc.), David M. Frank (2nd Guard/Unc.).

Storyline: Hogan's request to mount an operation and rescue "Tiger" from the Gestapo is denied by HQ. Angered by the response, Hogan is determined to save her, and his men hesitantly fall into agreement. They sneak into camp another agent, Karl, who possesses more information regarding her capture. Hogan pretends that one of the prisoners has been distilling liquor in the barracks, and when Klink confronts the prisoners a wild melee erupts. During the confusion, Schnitzer's kennel truck sneaks Karl in through the doghouse entrance, until Klink ends the party with machine gun fire. That night, Hogan and Karl alter the railway switchback bringing the train transporting Tiger to Berlin (along with a supply of munitions) to a halt. "Capt. Carterheim" discourages further use of the railway due to enemy land mines, diverting Capt. Steiger, his men, and their prisoner, Tiger, to Stalag 13. Klink reluctantly lodges Tiger in the cooler where Hogan manages a rendezvous and explains his "insane" escape plans. Newkirk phones Steiger pretending to be a Gestapo Major and informs him two more men will be added to his security team. "Carterheim" then takes the phone explaining the train can move out again the next evening. Hogan and Newkirk, dressed as Gestapo officers, board the train along with their phony travel papers. At a scheduled stop in Dusseldorf, Hogan and Newkirk take the guards hostage and have them bound and gagged and apply the same treatment to Steiger and his aide. The boys slip Tiger off the train through the compartment window after setting a time bomb, before the train begins moving again. The rescue party meets up with Karl and Schnitzer, and from a safe distance they observe the train explosion and the "elimination" of Tiger.

Program Notes: Several series regulars concluded their work with this episode, including Frank Marth (five appearances), Arlene Martel (seven), and Walter Janovitz (thirteen). In another throwback reference to a recent event, ("Kommodant Schultz"), Klink again fires a machine gun overhead, but this time with precision. "Tiger's" true name is revealed as Marie Louise Monet, "an Underground Leader." The final program credits now declare: "A Bing Crosby Production, in association with Bob Crane Enterprises, Inc., and The CBS Television Network." Jerry London cited this episode as his personal favorite of the ten he directed.

Assessment: A recycling of the general idea already witnessed in season two's "A Tiger Hunt in Paris," this time we get a more compact version of Tiger's latest and final rescue operation. Using "home brew" as an excuse to set up a special formation call, the men stage a wild free for all in the compound climaxed by a rare act of bravery on Klink's part, snatching a machine gun from one of his guard's and using it to restore order – an action that causes even the typically calm Colonel Hogan to flinch. Carter's take as the jovial "Carterheim," who warns Steiger that if they proceed along the rail tracks they could end up "flying to Berlin," is a decidedly daffy delight. His reappearance on the phone, along with Newkirk, further amuses the action and confounds Steiger. The actual rescue sequence aboard the munitions train is a somber affair with Hogan and Newkirk apprehending and binding the guards with complete ease. Worse yet, Steiger and his aide cooperatively watch Newkirk set a timer in an attache bag and place the same device directly in their presence. Even after Hogan and company depart, no effort of self preservation is exerted. After his lethargic experience in season five's "The Klink Commandos," you would think guest star Frank Marth would avoid train travel, especially anywhere near Stalag 13.

Season 6, Episode 12: "The Big Broadcast" 12/06/1970.

D: Jerry London   W: William Davenport

Guest Cast: Howard Caine (Major Hochstetter), Sigrid Valdis (Hilda), James Sikking (Hercules), Jay Sheffield (SS Man), Yvonne Dardenne (Bertha), John Crawford (2nd SS Man/Uncredited).

Storyline: Just as Baker finishes receiving the team's latest mission, he detects radio interference and terminates transmission. Radio detection trucks are in the vicinity which could interfere with their plan to meet their contact "Hercules," who possesses info that must be transmitted to Air Intelligence. Hogan wants to use Klink's staff car so the men warn Klink and Schultz that the brakes are overdue for replacement. While Newkirk argues with Schultz, LeBeau removes the brake line. To keep Klink's mind preoccupied, Hogan tells him about a new, rich young widow in Hammelburg that Klink should move in on. Hochstetter arrives demanding a garrison of volunteers to help search out and destroy the source of radio transmissions detected in the area. Klink summons for his staff car, and Schultz crashes the vehicle not able to stop. After completing car repairs, Hogan notes that the radio is missing, although Schultz insists that the car never had one. Hogan insists a two-way radio is standard issue and convinces him that one must be inserted. After completion, Klink takes over the wheel, ready for his date in town with the widow "Bertha," but changes his mind when realizing a radio and transmitter were installed. The men hijack the vehicle and give it a makeover, disguising it as a Gestapo staff car. Meeting with "Hercules," the Heroes, all dressed in Gestapo uniforms, are able to smooth talk a sentry into turning off his radar detection unit so "Hogan-Meier" can call in a report. Hogan slyly leaks out the coded information provided by Hercules on their specially equipped car radio as he pretends to make idle chatter with the sentry.

Program Notes: This is the third and final appearance from James Sikking, who gets to play one of the "good guys" this time. John Crawford completes his seventh and final appearance, sadly, in a non-credited role. Although Schultz drives off without the brake line, he strangely does not crash the vehicle until some time later.

Assessment: An entirely original scheme, some smooth double talking from Hogan, an off the rails Major Hochstetter, and a rare, happy ending for Klink, serve as the ingredients to a most satisfying dish. The scene where the boys must stall Klink and Schultz about the supposedly faulty car brakes is assisted by some extremely intense verbosity from Newkirk. (Dawson's protest that "he doesn't care what the Kommodant says!" rattles the rafters.) The atypical mood swings of the core characters make for highly engaged viewing, particularly Klink standing up to Major Hochstetter, then threatening to shoot Hogan if he doesn't have that darn car ready, and Schultz cutting right through the monkey business and demanding the same. The second Klink/Hochstetter scene ignites sparks when our two old adversaries debate in crisply framed profiles, and as the Major struts around the office loaded down with oversized stick grenades. A wild vision indeed. Bob Crane draws on his radio experience as the smooth voice of the airwaves, when he slyly incorporates the battle plans to his Allies in the air while maintaining a casual conversation with the sentry guard. The cherry atop the sundae arrives by motorcycle sidecar, when Klink's date, the widow "Bertha," turns out to be a delicious redhead. As a result, Klink's normally threatening clenched fist of frustration becomes a handshake offering of champagne in a case of rare gratitude.

Memorable Military debate:

Hochstetter: "Your men are cowards!"

Klink: "Now, just a moment."

Hochstetter: "Cowards! When I asked for volunteers for the assault force, every guard in this camp had night duty tonight."

Klink: (hopefully) "Ah, that proves they are not afraid of the dark, heh-heh-heh."

Director Jerry London poses with three of his Heroes while preparing to shoot a barracks scene: left to right, Larry Hovis, London, Robert Clary, and Richard Dawson. Photo courtesy of Jerry London/CBS Television Inc.

Season 6, Episode 13: "The Gypsy" 12/13/1970

D: Richard Kinon W: Harvey Bullock, R. S. Allen

Guest Cast: Sigrid Valdis (Hilda), Mat Reitz (Capt. Gruber), Roy Goldman (POW/Unc.).

Storyline: While Hogan complains to Klink about the leaky roof over the men's barracks, the Kommodant is more absorbed with his astrological chart. Hilda concurs that Klink's behavior is easily controlled by the stars and superstition. Capt. Gruber's unit arrives with an unusual, tank-like vehicle. It is kept under a large tarp and surrounded by several armed guards. The Heroes discover it is actually a new German anti radar unit, so they trick Schultz into posing for some photographs while they peel back the tarp and actually get several shots of its control panel for London to research. That night, LeBeau, angered by the rainwater leaking into their sleeping area, heads to the roof for a repair. A lightning bolt misses him but sends him toppling from the rooftop, ending the work detail but inspiring Hogan to convince LeBeau, and eventually Klink, that Louis has magically become a fortune teller. The boys raid Klink's office after hours and find some personal letters regarding Klink's mother and brother, information that LeBeau slips out during morning formation to indicate his powers of ESP. "The Gypsy" foresees a promotion to general if Klink moves all his soldiers to the front gate to head off an impending Allied attack. While Newkirk distracts Klink and his entire regiment with a fake battle using a barrage of fireworks, Baker and Carter enter the abandoned tank, steal its main instrument panel, and wire the vehicle to explode.

Program notes: Although Mat Reitz is credited as Capt. Gruber, he is only briefly seen when the tank unit/anti-radar device arrives and has only three words of dialogue.

Assessment: The fatigue seems to be showing in this final season outing with a typically absurd premise that gets little development.

Even for all their elaborate scheming, the idea of turning LeBeau into a struck-by-lightning fortune teller in order to convince Klink to move his guards away from the anti-radar vehicle seems woefully extreme. Klink is established as an astrological obsessive in order to sell the scam, but no great comic opportunities are seized to prey on his superstitions. Clary plays his "gypsy" role in a "white zombie" catatonic state, which is an okay acting choice but never really ignites sparks either. Some kind of a physical gag to reinforce his magical soothsaying ability is sorely missing. Likewise, Newkirk's fireworks show is a pretty tepid ploy here – a quick and easy ruse to lead Klink and company on a wild goose chase. As usual, Schultz is no help as a soldier and weighs down the war games with his typical cowardice-in-combat non-heroics. Even Hogan seems a little indifferent to the proceedings, as if waiting for a better caper to crock up. In the end, the only real glee is courtesy of, once again, Klemperer, who wildly leads his men into battle against an imaginary adversary and rejoices when discovering the "enemy" has retreated thanks to his brave leadership. Now there's some true spark.

Season 6, Episode 14: "The Dropouts" 12/27/1970

D: Marc Daniels W: Laurence Marks

Guest Cast: Howard Caine (Major Hochstetter), John Stephenson (Prof. Bauer), Ben Wright (Dr. Riemann), Gordon Pinsent (S.S. Capt. Steiner), Chris Anders (Guard/uncredited), Roy Goldman (POW/uncredited).

Storyline: On a night mission a few kilometers outside camp, Hogan and Carter, dressed in German uniforms, are mysteriously met by a German staff car carrying Capt. Steiner and two civilians. Carter loses his German accent when the crafty Nazi stomps on his foot. Hogan and Carter are forced to face away and kneel down at gunpoint, but Steiner and the two others oddly drive off. Hogan scrubs their mission and the men return to the barracks convinced their secret operations are now at peril. The following day, the three strangers arrive at Stalag 13, and Capt. Steiner requests accomodations from Klink as they are en route to Berlin for a secret briefing. In reality, they are three German rocket scientists and, appalled by the Third Reich's decision to harbor their research into atomic warfare, request Hogan's help to defect. Hot on their trail is Major Hochstetter, who arrives to find the three suspects have disappeared and vows he will return to the stalag daily until the traitors are captured. Actually Hogan has dressed them as POWs and engineered a simple, but brilliant, escape plan: each scientist will be smuggled out daily in the trunk of Hochstetter's staff car!

Program Notes: This was the fifth and final appearance of British born actor Ben Wright (1916-1989) who's film and television resume spanned six decades, appearing in the Burt Lancaster film noir *Kiss the Blood Off My Hands* (1948, filmed in England) and Billy Wilder's masterful adaptation of Agatha Christie's *Witness for the Prosecution* (1957). During the 1960s he was at work non-stop chocking up repeat appearances on everything from *Gunsmoke* (eleven appearances), *Have Gun Will Travel* (six), *Perry Mason* (three), and into *The Twilight Zone*, (three appearances, including the third season, concentration camp themed, "Deaths-Head Revisited").

Assessment: This is another "aid to defect" narrative and the escape plan of transporting each scientist out of the camp via the *unlocked* trunk of Hochstetter's staff car is a bit unimaginative. The opening sequence is a terrific one, with Hogan and Carter being held at gunpoint and for a brief moment contemplating the end. Strong components are comprised of Hogan's panic that their clandestine operations will be realized (summoned to Klink's office, Hogan instructs LeBeau to "burn everything" if he doesn't return), and Klink suddenly stopping Dr. Riemann, disguised as a prisoner on litter detail, only to point out he missed a scrap of paper on the ground! Nothing gets past Colonel Klink. Hogan shows rare trepidation on his part when, entering Klink's private quarters, he encounters the three Germans from the previous evening and, almost ready to surrender, woefully admits aloud: "Well, I suppose it had to happen." It's quietly acted moments like this that help make compensation for all the spectacular scheming and trickery of Robert Hogan, and remind the viewers (and Hogan) that they are not entirely infallible. Meanwhile, despite the Underground man that's to meet the escapees on the back end, the viewer must suspend disbelief and assume that Hochstetter's unknowing taxi service will deliver the defectors to safe haven and not Gestapo Headquarters.

Season 6, Episode 15: "Easy Come, Easy Go" 01/10/1971

P/D: Edward H. Feldman W: Laurence Marks

Guest Cast: Leon Askin (General Burkhalter), Stewart Moss (Lt. Mills), George Gaynes (General, U. S.), Tom Hatten (Air Force Captain), Judson Morgan (Schindler), Paul Lambert (Col. Forbes), Cynthia Lynn (Eva/Uncredited), Sheila Leighton (Greta/Uncredited).

Storyline: Klink invites Hogan to enjoy champagne and caviar at a private party hosted by General Burkhalter, who is accompanied by Eva and Greta, two beautiful, good-time frauleins. Burkhalter's true motive revolves around the American P 51 fighter plane, which is proving lethal to the Nazi war effort. He bargains with Hogan to fly to England and steal a P 51 and fly it back so the Nazis can study its components. In exchange, Hogan will receive one million in U.S. currency and safe transport to Switzerland. Burkhalter also renders Hogan an "insurance policy" by stating his men will be held as expendable hostages if the mission fails. Hogan, accompanied by Klink (posing as Major Davis), meet with U.S. Colonel Forbes with papers indicating they have made their escape from Stalag 13. After drugging Klink, Hogan confides to Forbes the true details of his mission and supposed cash deal with the Luftwaffe. Hogan claims he can use his role in the mission to help undermine the Germans' espionage unit in London. The US and British air command allow Hogan to steal a P 51, and he and Klink make their flight back to Germany. Hogan cuts off their fuel source forcing both men to parachute to safety and allowing the P 51 to crash. Hogan returns to Stalag 13, apparently having rejected the million in cash and one way ticket to Switzerland.

Program Notes: Character actor George Gaynes (1917-2016) appears briefly as an Air Force general. Audiences will remember him from his work in *Tootsie* (1982) and Mel Brooks' remake *To Be* *or Not To Be* (1984), which involved Polish Allies impersonating German officers. Gaynes put his stamp on the recurring role of Commodant Lassard in the long running *Police Academy* franchise (1984-1994). Cynthia Lynn ("Helga", season one) returns to the series in a non-credited, one shot appearance as Eva, one of Burkhalter's good-time girls.

General Burkhalter (Leon Askin) cheerfully lets down his guard between takes at Forty Acres. Behind him are assistant director Floyd Joyer (left) and producer/director Ed Feldman. Author's collection/CBS Television Inc.

Assessment: Mostly played as a light-hearted adventure, "Easy Come, Easy Go" is easily the most oddball entry in the entire canon. Apparently the only way the Luftwaffe can seize a P 51 fighter is by bribing a POW air flier to steal one back to Germany. That's the premise we are asked to accept in a narrative that's quite intriguing and mostly successful. Since the barracks boys are pushed into the background, the gang is offered one pleasant lights out scene where they ponder in bed whether or not their beloved Colonel will ditch them for the dough. Stewart Moss, who passed on a regular spot after the pilot aired, enjoys a larger than usual return role as the "drunken" Lt. Mills. At this late stage of the game, it's nice to see producer/director Feldman and longtime writer Marks explore completely original concepts. The final sequence as our two mismatched colleagues fly home, discuss the possibility of going into business together after the war, and must suddenly parachute to safety, makes for agreeable viewing. Still, ultimately, we may be left to wonder how and why General Burkhalter accepts the fate of his well calculated yet failed plan.

Season 6, Episode 16: "The Meister Spy" 01/17/1971

D: Bruce Bilson W: Harvey Bullock, R. S. Allen

Guest Cast: Alan Bergmann (Maj. Martin/Hans Strausser), Oscar Beregi Jr. (Herr Schneer), Dave Morick (Lt. J. B. Miller), Ray Hastings (Herr Mayerink), Eva Lynd (Fraulein Kissinger).

Storyline: When their fuel line malfunctions, two American fliers, Major Martin and Lt. Miller, parachute to safety outside Stalag 13 and are immediately captured. Miller confirms his identity, but Martin is revealed to be German spy Hans Strausser, as the Heroes eavesdrop on his conversation in Klink's office. "Martin" possesses top secret plans to thwart the Allied offensive but will not reveal the name of his secret contact in Berlin. Hogan discredits Strausser's story by manipulating Klink into believing Miller is the *actual* German spy and having "Major Martin," the impostor, deposited in the cooler. In an effort to get Martin/Strausser to reveal his Berlin contact, Hogan poses as a Gestapo agent, frees him from the cooler, and transports him blindfolded to, presumably, German Headquarters. After giving Klink's office a theatrical make-over, Carter poses as an irate Hitler and Newkirk as his long suffering aide, and fearing for his life, Strausser finally reveals his secret contact. Hogan then reveals he is actually an American prisoner as Schultz and company sequester "Major Martin" back to the cooler.

Program Notes: Alan Bergmann spent three decades balancing an acting and directing career, helming several episodes of *Night Court* and the service comedies *Private Benjamin* and *Operation Petticoat*, two TV series based on popular military films. Oscar Beregi Jr. completes his two episode mission, previously appearing in season two's "Operation Briefcase." Director Bruce Bilson discussed the initial, negative criticism launched at *Hogan's Heroes*:

A comedy? That was the point! It wasn't funny. The outcry was, don't make jokes about it! People died. The world changed. It's not a comedy. I had a friend, Harve Foster, who directed a whole lot of stuff. I was his assistant on a show called *Whirlybirds* (1957-1960). He had been a prisoner, and he wouldn't look at the show. "That's not funny to me." The reaction was about don't make funny . . . I think that's what it was. Don't make light of fucking World War II and the Nazis! And that was my first reaction. Until I got into it.*

Assessment: A fun, nutty, fast-moving adventure, punctuated by some dramatic moments of suspense, "The Meister Spy" is perfect evidence of the series still hitting a high batting average approaching the finish line. Oscar Beregi brings well-calculated anxiety during Hogan's masquerade as Strausser at the German intelligence meeting by inquiring which thumb Strausser lost in a previous combat mission. (Hogan is quick to credit "brilliant German surgery" for the restoration of his formerly missing thumb!) The real hilarity starts with the gang discrediting "Miller's" telephone reference by tapping in to Klink's phone call to the Tempelhof Hotel and supplanting it with Newkirk representing "Schimmel's Bakery." To take Strausser into his confidence, Hogan reroutes "The Meister Spy" to Berlin headquarters via a fake truck ride in ridiculously funny fashion (the vehicle is actually mounted off its wheels and the crew simulate motion by rocking and bumping it about!) Somehow, the gang have rapidly renovated Klink's office into Berlin Headquarters cuing Carter, in the episode's standout scene, to pose as a temper tantrum leaden Hitler and Newkirk as his exasperated, effeminate secretary. Dawson's line reads and facial tics are hilarious; proof positive of the actor's superb comic timing. Schultz mindlessly wandering into the foray and later spotting Carter's Hitler casually peeking out of his office are more contributors to a finely tuned, frenetically funny, half hour.

*Telephone interview with the author, September 14, 2020.

Season 6, Episode 17: "That's No Lady, That's My Spy" 01/24/1971

D: Jerry London W: Arthur Julian

Guest Cast: Alice Ghostley (Mrs. Mannheim), Diana Chesney (Berta Burkhalter), Wendy Wilson (Red Riding Hood), Jon Cedar (Oskar Danzing), Dave Morick (Patrol Leader), and Leon Askin (as Gen. Burkhalter).

Storyline: A rendezvous with Underground leader and "master of disguise" Oskar Danzing is broken up by the arrival of a German patrol and sudden gunfire. Although both parties escape, Danzing is wounded and requires penicillin to survive. London HQ schedules a penicillin drop by parachute, and Newkirk and Carter barely manage to recover the parcel and escape back to camp. With guards heavily on patrol outside the wire, Hogan figures a way to sneak the penicillin out to Danzing and his caretakers by having Newkirk masquerade as an old lady attending the tea party Klink and General Burkhalter are hosting for several wives of Luftwaffe officers. After Klink mistakes Mrs. Mannheim as Danzing in disguise by ripping off her wig, Newkirk offers to drive the horrified guest back to her hotel in town before his ruse is detected, and ultimately to deliver the badly needed penicillin.

Program Notes: Alice Ghostley, previously seen in the season four outing "Watch the Trains Go By," was a veteran of over one hundred network television appearances, permanently leaving a magical impression with viewers as the klutzy witch, Esmerelda, on the long running *Bewitched* series. A barely recognizable Jon Cedar makes his seventeenth and final guest appearance. This is the only occasion where we meet Mrs. Burkhalter. Associate producer and director of this episode, Jerry London, discussed the comedy mind of Richard Dawson:

The funniest guy was Richard Dawson. This guy was hilarious. We'd have a read thru of the script before we'd start shooting and this guy with his ad libs! He was always breaking people up. Dawson had an innate sense of humor, he was hysterical. Larry (Hovis), too, he was so subtle. Such a nice person, no ego.*

Assessment: A fun, pleasant excursion is uplifted by Dawson's character turns as the elderly German lady, and deaf civilian at the show's conclusion. This episode diverts from its usual executions of undermining the German war effort and supplants it with a basic need - the preservation of an ally's life. Although frequent guest star Jon Cedar is afforded the opportunity to step out of his "Corporal Langenscheidt" uniform, the actor is given little screen time to develop his "master of disguise" character. He spends most of his on-screen time lying on his back waiting for his drugs to arrive. It's more of a device to promote *Newkirk's* ability to successfully don disguises. Blustery Burkhalter falls in as one of the gang, as he banters jovially with Klink at the tea party, and even defends him after Klink's party foul of separating Mrs. Mannheim from her wig. A tasteless joke permeates the tea party, with LeBeau substituting dog food for pate, but comic experts Klemperer, Banner, and Askin roll with it by all admiring its unique taste! Burkhalter also makes the realization that the number of female guests is off-kilter and that one of the ladies must be an impostor. Unfortunately, Newkirk makes a hasty departure with Mrs. Mannheim before any connection is made, prompting Askin to exert more energy than usual as he runs between departing vehicles with aplomb. Naturally it's left up to Colonel Hogan to remind the German brass of the appropriately titled name of tonight's episode. Yet this brazen tip-off offers no inspiration for the Nazis to roadblock the departed vehicle.

Season Six episodes • 391

Richard Dawson in character as British Corporal Peter Newkirk, arguably the most talented member of Colonel Hogan's heroes. Author's collection/CBS Television Inc.

*Telephone interview with the author, February 14, 2021.

Season 6, Episode 18: "To Russia Without Love" 01/31/1971

D: Bruce Bilson W: Arthur Julian

Guest Cast: H. M. Wynant (Col. Becker), Ruta Lee (Olga), and Leon Askin (as Gen. Burkhalter).

Storyline: Colonel Becker, who has been stationed at the Russian Front, visits the camp with a unique proposal for Colonel Hogan. If Becker receives a permanent transfer to Stalag 13 as its new Kommodant, he will divulge his top secret papers in transport, and maintain the status quo of Hogan's secret operation. After a botched attempt to steal Becker's briefcase and secret papers, Hogan believes the colonel is in possession of material that could end the war, and, reluctantly, agrees to an alliance with Becker. Hogan enlists the aid of "Olga," a beautifully persuasive member of the Underground, to pose as a Russian girlfriend of Becker's and to convince Klink to put in for transfer to Russia. She sells the idea of wild parties at ski resorts and mineral springs, and that the German officers are especially enjoying the company of beautiful Russian women. Lots of them. When Olga announces its time to leave and purchase *another* swimsuit, this is enough for Klink to transform into a ruthless, unforgiving fighting machine, going so far as to plant land mines outside the fencing to dissuade potential escapes. Convinced by his changed behavior, Gen. Burkhalter approves Klink's transfer east and the reassignment of Becker to Stalag 13. When Becker attempts a double cross, Hogan and crew quickly dispatch the Nazi fink and hastily concoct a plan to reinstate Klink.

Program Notes: H. M. Wynant's career has spanned six decades (still active in 2018) including multiple guest shots on *Perry Mason*, *Mission Impossible*, and *The Wild, Wild West*, plus one unforgettable appearance in the second season *Twilight Zone* episode, "The Howling Man," which should merit four eagles in some other author's definitive, episode guide. This was Ruta Lee's third and final visit to Stalag 13, and she fondly described working with Werner Klemperer and Bob Crane:

I think he (Klemperer) was a rather amazing actor, and I think in most cases very underrated. There's a great talent in his family. He was very well read, I think I would call him a learned man but I don't know if he would . . . he was a damn good actor, he played the part seriously, the only way the comedy comes out is to play it seriously, and that's why it worked . . . I just loved (Bob) and I continue to do so. We used to play a lot of the same theaters when we were out on the road doing plays; either I would follow him into a theater or he would follow me, so we would see each other in Arizona or in Texas some place or other, because when one was following the other you went and saw the show and spent the evening with that person.*

Assessment: Colonel Klink burlesques Patton in a high spirited, at times intensely crafted, although slightly mean-spirited outing. In previous episodes, Hogan is completely content to retain the status quo and insure that Klink stays put as the Kommodant of Stalag 13. This time Hogan *knowingly sells out Klink* to a miserable future at the Russian Front in exchange for what he believes is a better deal – and that could leave a sour taste in the dedicated viewer's mouth. Guest H. M. Wynant's less comic, darkly dramatic turn, as Becker provides an excellent foil for Hogan and company and prompts a bittersweet admission from Hogan when Becker marvels at Hogan's successful manipulations. "I just happen to know the man's weaknesses," Hogan glumly acknowledges after years of manipulating Klink. It is an undeniably powerful moment at this late stage of the war games. As usual, General Burkhalter's presence further bolsters the proceedings. His disbelief that Klink willingly wants this terrible transfer and subsequent amazement at the new and improved "Patton-ized" Klink, provide exceptional moments. All too often the bombastic Burkhalter has threatened to transfer Klink to the

Russian Front; here is a case where he actually tries to talk Klink *out* of going. As if running out of time, the program rushes to its conclusion with Hogan actually revealing the location to their tunnel network via the breakaway bunk beds (a subterfuge to subdue Becker, who puts up the mildest form of resistance) and the immediate sabotage of the motorcycle and sidecar (which returns Klink to buffoon status in the eyes of Burkhalter). Ruta Lee injects a lot of energetic, sexy charm in her one – and it's a doozy - hilarious scene with Klink and Hogan. Her hand gesturing motions regarding her upcoming swimsuit purchase is enough to melt any man's monocle. She takes the scene by storm and is a dazzling firecracker on screen.

A jubilant couple indeed! Bob Crane and guest star Ruta Lee happily pose for the CBS still photographer during production of "To Russia Without Love," the one episode where Hogan sells out Klink and willingly conspires to transfer him to the dreaded Russian Front. Photo courtesy of Ruta Lee/ CBS Television Inc.

Memorable Curiosity:

Olga: "I am the farmer's daughter!"

Hogan: "Got any more where you came from?"

*Telephone interview with the author, December 4, 2020.

Season 6, Episode 19: "Klink for the Defense" 02/07/1971

D: Jerry London W: William Davenport

Guest Cast: Sandy Kenyon (Col. Hauptmann), Karl Brock (President of Court), Lynnette Mettey (Fraulein Hibbler), Leon Askin (as Gen. Burkhalter), and Howard Caine (as Major Hochstetter).

Storyline: German war hero Colonel Hugo Hauptmann has turned informant and possesses some Nazi submarine plans that he wishes to turn over to London, but the Gestapo apprehend him first (but not the plans). General Burkhalter and Major Hochstetter conspire to try him for treason in a court martial hearing they will stage at Stalag 13. The Nazis see an open and shut case – they possess wire recordings of Hauptmann phone conversations that his secretary, Fraulein Hibbler, secreted for the Gestapo. To further sew up their mock trial, Burkhalter will act as prosecutor and appoints Klink to the title position. In order to secure Hauptmann's innocence and retrieve the sub plans, Hogan's men steal the wire recordings from Klink's safe, modify them to implicate Hibbler as a British spy, and discredit her evidence thus acquitting Hauptmann and earning Klink a spectacular, courtroom victory.

Program Notes: It's a wrap for Sandy Kenyon after five guest gigs on *Hogan's Heroes*. *M*A*S*H* fans will probably remember Kenyon's wry turn as Master Sergeant Woodruff, who rigs a fake promotion to honor a poker debt in the fourth season episode "Lt. Radar O' Reilly" (1976). As Associate Producer and Editorial Supervisor, one of Jerry London's numerous tasks was to gather stock footage for the series, and he explained how that process worked:

Ed would call me and say, "I'm developing a script and I need a bridge blowing up. Find some stock for me." The military had a library of newsreel footage and they allowed me to go into the library whenever I needed it and pull out that footage. They would only write it if they knew that we had the footage, because we couldn't build bridges and blow them up! So that was one of my jobs to get that footage . . . it was on Cahuenga and Santa Monica Boulevard.*

Jerry London supervises Michael Kahn in the editing room at Desilu Studios, 1965. After London edited the pilot, Ed Feldman quickly promoted him to editorial supervisor, retaining Kahn as his chief editor. Photo courtesy of Jerry London/Desilu Productions.

Assessment: A terrific premise adequately carried out, "Klink for the Defense" promises slightly more than it delivers. The first half of the episode moves with assurance with Hogan's hilltop meeting with Hauptmann and a juicy Klink/Burkhalter/Hochstetter scene to savor, but the latter half misses laugh out loud opportunities by offering routine courtroom antics. What could've been a spirited spoof of *Perry Mason* doesn't quite surface as Klink never even gets to question his witness, which should've been the highlight of his titled tale. Although the trick of editing the wire recording by adding Newkirk's voice as a supposed British operative is a clever one, this is a rehash of the key scheme from "Hot Money." The late absence of Hogan and Hochstetter, who is relegated to the rear of the courtroom next to a nodding off Schultz, likewise detracts from the potential laugh meter. If you're going to have Howard Caine on your set, for goodness sake, give the little big man some material!

*Telephone interview with the author, February 14, 2021.

Season 6, Episode 20: "The Kamikazes are Coming" 02/21/1971

P/D: Edward H. Feldman W: Richard Powell

Guest Cast: Nita Talbot (Marya), Henry Corden (Dr. Otto Von Bornemann), Richard Alden (assistant), Chris Anders (Guard), and Howard Caine (as Maj. Hochstetter).

Storyline: An Underground ally ushers Hogan and his crew to the wreckage of a new German transport rocket. Unable to contend with it, they mask the rocket with foliage until a better idea presents itself. Klink welcomes Dr. Von Bornemann, who is searching for the whereabouts of his designed rocket and unexplained failed landing, and his female companion, Marya. She convinces Hogan to reveal the location of the rocket wreckage, and Klink's men haul it in to Stalag 13 so the scientist can render repair. Marya agrees to help Hogan relaunch the rocket to England (or maybe Russia) when repaired. She creates a diversion while the gang overpowers and ties up the stationed guards *and* Marya, to make her appear innocent. The Heroes continually move the rocket to different buidlings as Marya leaks out false clues to throw Klink and Von Bornemann off the track. When Major Hochstetter arrives, Hogan indicates the rocket thief escaped through the wire fence, and then proves his point by pushing over a huge wooden frame of barbed wire! With the Gestapo sidetracked, Hogan convinces Otto to defect and transports him to England – in his own rocket!

Program Notes: After thirty seven performances, this is Howard Caine's final appearance as the snide, surly, and, unforgettable, Major Wolfgang Hochstetter, a key component to the lasting success of *Hogan's Heroes*. It's also a wrap for the wonderful Nita Talbot (seven appearances as Marya) and the equally talented Henry Corden (five guest spots in five memorably diverse characterizations).

Assessment: A wildly spirited, deliriously daffy outing gets elevated by its excellent supporting cast, and reunites Hogan and the

"White Russian" for one final caper. Marya flits about like an intoxicated butterfly, Von Bornemann's eyes bug out in pursuit of his elusive rocket, and Hochstetter sneers his way with much sour disdain. Nita Talbot again sparkles in her final bow as Marya, especially when her and Crane rehearse her hostage scene. "Lie down," advises Hogan, and Marya purrs, "Oh, Darling!" Those two words and her obliging delivery were probably all the CBS sensors would allow with a set up like that, and that's right before she knocks herself unconscious with the butt of Hogan's gun! A potential sub plot that Marya and Otto are actually married oddly gets zero development. Henry Corden is his usual, terrific guest, and plays well with Klink each time they rush off to find that damn rocket. Klink's self-confirmed delight that the missing rocket isn't his fault, and droll indifference to the crisis are lovely, subtle amusements. Powell's writing in Hochstetter's first scene in Klink's office is tops, with our favorite, snarling Gestapo man verbally ping ponging with Klink, Otto, Marya, Schultz, and, eventually, Hogan. He even gets in his trademark gripe of disbelief: "What is this man doing here?" - among a blitzkrieg of one-liners and utter disgust with who the hell is actually running this camp. After the boys spend some ridiculous good fun moving the rocket from one camp location to the next, the episode completely settles into Bugs Bunny cartoon territory as Hogan all too conveniently convinces Corden to defect and become an unlikely rocket passenger. Never a curious bunch, the Nazis don't bother to investigate why Hogan knew the location of the rocket wreckage. But after such a fast moving, high energy half hour – who's to carp?

Favorite exchange:

Klink: (with great indifference, to Schultz) "Apparently his rocket is missing."

Von Bornemann: "Apparently?"

Season 6, Episode 21: "Kommodant Gertrude" 02/28/1971

D: Bruce Bilson W: Laurence Marks

Guest Cast: Kathleen Freeman (Gertrude Linkmeyer), Lee Bergere (Maj. Wolfgang Karp), Johnny Haymer (Gen. Sharp), Leslie Parrish (Karen Richter), and Leon Askin (as Gen. Burkhalter).

Storyline: An air attack outside camp delivers an unexpected visitor, General Harry Sharp, whom Hogan and company sequester into the barracks through their secret tunnel. Klink enjoys the company of Karen Richter, actually an Underground spy, who fills Hogan in on Klink's plans to move the camp's fence line back one hundred feet into the woods affecting the POWs future escape routes, and the opportunity to smuggle Sharp out in a timely manner. Burkhalter arrives with his sister, Gertrude, and her fiancee Major Karp. Klink, delighted not to be up for the part of groom, offers to host an engagement party for the couple. During the event, Gertrude makes her motives clear to Hogan. She will marry Karp and then get him promoted as the new stalag Kommodant, with her quietly pulling the puppet strings. To disrupt this plan, Hogan sets up a compromising position between Karp and Richter, who met and flirted during the engagement party, spoils the wedding plans, and returns all to status quo.

Program Notes: Johnny Haymer drops in for a one shot guest appearance, before moving his military service to another base, as the recurring character Sgt. Zelmo Zale on *M*A*S*H*. Lee Bergere completes his dual contract with the show, previously seen in the first season outing, "The Prince from the Phone Company" (season 1, episode 26). *Batman* fans should remember gorgeous Leslie Parrish as the crime moll/girlfriend to Eli Wallach's Mr. Freeze. Kathleen Freeman completes her visits as Gertrude Linkmeyer. Freeman's acting career spans half a century and fans with sharp ears may recognize her voice as Peggy Bundy's off-camera, obese mama on FOX Television's no-holds-barred comedy, *Married With Children*. Bruce Bilson discussed his long time friendship with Freeman:

Kathleen Freeman and I were in the very first class of graduates from the UCLA film school in 1950. Its original title was Theatre Arts Department. We became friends and I had my 1933 Ford convertible, and she often needed a ride home after rehearsals. We didn't work together professionally much, *Hogan's* may have been it. I believe I recommended her as a coach to some young actors ... I still think of her as a friend.*

Assessment: Gertrude's final stop over at Stalag 13 is a curiously mild, late series disappointment, with no memorable set pieces or true hilarious situations. Gertrude wants to take over Klink's command so Hogan screws up her plan. Laurence Marks' script underwrites the character of Major Karp, who wants to avoid service at the Russian Front by marrying a general's sister. Unfortunately, Hogan selfishly uses him as a pawn for his own gain. Even Hogan's bland observation to Richter about Karp – he dismisses the Major as "the slob she met at the party" – reeks petulance and crassness. Tacky too is the use of Richter as a Mata Hari who toys with the affections of two men to further a plot that may have benefited from spending more time tinkering with Klink's intriguing plan to reroute the fence line. The talented Kathleen Freeman deserved a much better send off.

*E-mail correspondence with the author, December 1, 2020.

Season 6, Episode 22: "Hogan's Double Life" 03/07/1971

D: Bruce Bilson W: Phil Sharp

Guest Cast: John Hoyt (Field Marshall Von Leiter), David Frank (Albert, Underground Member), Dick Wilson (Bruner, Underground), and Malachi Throne (as Major Pruhst, Gestapo).

Storyline: On a night mission, Hogan and his crew encounter two Undergound allies, and when each team's covert assignment details don't sync up, he scrubs the plan smelling a rat. The rat arrives at Klink's office the next day in the form of Gestapo agent, Major Pruhst, who is convinced that Col. Hogan is the man responsible for all the sabotage incidents taking place near Hammelburg. Pruhst has a female witness in Berlin who saw a man fitting Hogan's description at the recent destruction of the Milheim railroad bridge, and he secretly captures a photograph of Hogan to send to the witness for verification. In order to discredit his accusations, Hogan dons the disguise of Captain Shroffstein and crashes the party of Field Marshall Von Leiter, winning the senior officer's trust by posing as an old family friend and regaling the party guests with several researched anecdotes. Klink and Pruhst, suspecting "Shroffstein" is really Hogan in a flimsy disguise, hastily depart the party and race back to Stalag 13 to find the senior POW wrapping up a chess game with Carter. Now Klink and Pruhst are convinced that their witness mistook "Shroffstein" for Hogan.

Program Notes: Malachi Throne, in his only *Hogan's Heroes* appearance, amassed a fifty year career in show business and earned the bizarre credit: "Special Guest Villain ?" for his two-part portrayal of False Face on *Batman*. John Hoyt closes the file drawer on his seven episode association with the series. This is the twenty-fifth and final directing assignment from Bruce Bilson. Major Pruhst claims the witness spotted Hogan at the Milheim Bridge, which was destroyed by a tank in the finale of "One Army at a Time."

As Bruner, Dick Wilson refers to "Olga" in the opening scene, the character recently played by Ruta Lee in "To Russia Without Love."

Assessment: *Hogan's Heroes* episode or a tell-all expose of the secret life of Bob Crane? Actually, "Hogan's Double Life" is a sharply written, well-directed drama that shows the series still in superior form at the tail end of its run. From the secret camera in Pruhst's glove to the rigged chess game with Newkirk posing as a body double for Hogan (under the surveillance of Schultz), to the girl in the bikini tattoo on "Capt. Shroffstein's" left forearm, these unique details add up to a terrifically smart episode. It's a pity that this is the only contribution from prolific character actor Malachi Throne as he falls right in to the proceedings with the assurance of a regular player and works extremely well with Klemperer, even pleasantly *encouraging* Klink to attend the party as "his guest." (Major Hochstetter, in contrast, would probably balk at such a notion!) Throne's performance is quite fascinating, particularly in Klink's office where he ably conveys the frustrations of this agent who has attempted a one man investigation into Robert Hogan but has been continually blocked and mocked by Berlin. If the series had returned for a seventh season, I highly suspect that Mr. Throne would've undeniably been on Ed Feldman's return list. Self satisfying from start to finish, the only real objection a viewer can raise, is where *exactly* did the Field Marshall's chauffeur drop off Capt. Shroffstein? Next to the fake tree stump outside Stalag 13? Nevertheless, this is the last *great* episode of *Hogan's Heroes*.

Season 6, Episode 23: "Look at the Pretty Snowflakes" 03/21/1971

D: Irving J. Moore W: Arthur Julian

Guest Cast: Edward Knight (Cpl. Dietrich), Harold J. Stone (General Strommberger).

Storyline: General Strommberger's Panzer division is bogged down by heavy snowfall in Hammelburg, which also cancels out an Allied plan for an air attack further up the Hoffenstein Pass. Hogan and his men are willingly recruited to help clear the road so they can attempt an explosive attack of their own. This sabotage plan is foiled by the overzealous Corporal Dietrich, who orders the prisoners to vacate the transport truck before even leaving Stalag 13. Eventually the gang is transported to the Hofbrau pub in Hammelburg for their work detail to begin, and Hogan's mind to come up with a new battle plan. Klink changes the assignment strategy opting for snow plows instead, thus foiling Hogan's plan to deliberately stall the road clearing assignment and keep the Panzers dead in their tracks. Not trusting the POWs, Strommberger has the five men chained at the ankles and also leaks out warning of an avalanche advisory. Hoping to encourage the avalanche, the boys swing in to an impromptu jam session with the band equipment in the Hofbrau. Strommberger shuts down the band before they can succeed, but does not count on Klink's recently acquired cold. He releases a well-timed sneeze, triggers the avalanche, and effectively aborts Strommberger's Panzer advance.

Program Notes: This was the final episode to be filmed, although not the last to be aired, and marked Harold J. Stone's third and final contribution to the series. Edward Knight completed his tenth and final appearance, all as unrelated German characters. A wintry shot of the Stalag gates and guards replaces the typical one used at the tail end of the opening credits. Viewers get their only chance to catch gifted drummer Bob Crane tapping the skins. Frequent director Bruce Bilson recalled Crane and his beloved drum set always parked in his dressing room: "I remember particularly, it just came out, "Springtime for Hitler," and (Crane) would play that score and drum along to it. I remember that when that movie had just come out."

Assessment: A change of scenery and some fresh story ideas get slightly frozen out thanks to some less than fresh sight gags and dialogue routines. Carter, who typically shows little interest in the opposite sex, spends much of this outing fawning over a missed rendezvous with a female entertainer and mostly annoying his comrades with his repetitive dialogue. An extended verbal routine based on the word "gesundheit" also annoys more than amuses. In keeping with the comedy rule of "threes," we also get labored with three instances of a rooftop of snow dumping on Klink and Strommberger's heads. Harold J. Stone's underwritten General results in his least effective visit, marring an otherwise terrific track record. Although Edward Knight brings a strong sense of realism to his no-nonsense corporal, writer Arthur Julian unrealistically puts him out to pasture by having him and his transport truck blown sky high off camera. The supposed moral here becomes if you dare to push LeBeau around, and actually behave like a German captor, you will pay the severest of prices. The benefits of this escapade come from keeping the team together for the entire half hour, which grants Kenneth Washington his greatest amount of screen time of the season. Too bad it came at the very end of it. The standout sequence, and one that is nothing close to what we've yet witnessed, is the jam session that showcases Bob Crane's passion for the drums. It's rather poignant that it occurs in the last episode to be filmed, although the band members certainly did not realize at the time that this would be "the last waltz."

Klemperer, Crane, Dawson, and Clary during the last filmed episode of Hogan's Heroes - "Look at the Pretty Snowflakes." Author's collection/CBS Television Inc.

Season 6, Episode 24: "Rockets or Romance" 04/04/1971

D: Marc Daniels W: Arthur Julian

Guest Cast: Marlyn Mason (Lily Frankel), Kenneth Dumain (Guard), James Savett (Radio Operator), Norman Alden (Maj. Heintzen), and Leon Askin (as Gen. Burkhalter).

Storyline: During a work detail along a rural road, Major Heintzen pulls up with a flat tire and demands that Hogan's prisoners change it. Actually this is an excuse for an exchange of information from another one of Hogan's contacts. Three mobile rocket launchers are in the vicinity and preparing to attack England. Hogan needs to report two of their locations to London so they can order an air strike. The third launcher arrives and parks itself in the compound of Stalag 13 by order of General Burkhalter. Hogan's assignment is to meet "Frankel" at a hilltop lookout point, a shack that will also house wireless radio equipment. He instructs his Heroes to find a way to sabotage the resident rocket launcher during his absence. Hogan learns that "Frankel" is Lily Frankel, an attractive woman, and while the duo continue their surveillance of the main roadways, flirtations begin. Lily suggests that if Hogan's men were able to alter the gyroscopes of the third rocket, it would fly off course. An electromagnet is planted near the launcher by LeBeau and Carter under the pretense of cooking a dinner for Schultz. Meanwhile, Baker and Newkirk plant a radio in the woods to navigate a German radio detection truck away from Hogan's lookout shack and transmitter. Hogan and Lily spot the two rocket launchers and report the coordinates to the air team who quickly hit their targets. The next day, Burkhalter, fuming over the successful destruction of the first two rocket launchers, allows Klink to hit the button on the third and final rocket. Hogan's electromagnet does its job, and the misguided missile flies off course and heads straight for the closest neighborhood, and Burkhalter's house!

Program Notes: Marlyn Mason returns as Lily Frankel, but no connection is established with her previous appearance as Lily in "Six Lessons from Madame LaGrange." The shack on the hill set was recently seen in the opener for "Klink for the Defense" where Hogan meets up with guest star, Sandy Kenyon. This time around the film negative has been reversed offering a different look at the same location.

Assessment: A completely original teleplay, unfortunately, makes for a mostly humdrum mission, with most of the episode's running time spent in the shack as Hogan and Lily wait for the rocket launchers to make their entrances – and Hogan makes a play for Lily, again and again. Knowing this is the final adventure makes for a curious viewing experience as one might suspect that Hogan himself knows this is it – the last mission and the last opportunity to use his charm and wiles on the last of his beautiful co-conspirators. Sadly, it's almost like observing one of your fraternity brothers continue to hit on the same pretty co-ed all night long. Fortunately, it's the charming Marlyn Mason, who brings her usual, sympathetic sweetness to the role – a role that makes little demands of her exquisite talents. Even Mason herself confessed to me that she really didn't remember much about working on this one since all her scenes were played out in the tiny shack setting. The opening scene is a winner, another original idea to link up Hogan with a contact in a manner we have not witnessed before. There's also a strong bit of realism registered when the guard suddenly sprays machine gun bullets to scare the POWs away from the rocket launcher. Yet even though Burkhalter has demanded the complete security of the area, this doesn't stop Schultz from allowing LeBeau and Carter to set up their makeshift barbecue (i.e. electromagnetic field) several feet away from the rocket pad. The supposed destruction of Burkhalter's house may seem to offer some sort of satisfactory closure to the series, but if the production team had known the writing to be on the wall, perhaps a revisit to "War Takes a Holiday" would have been more appropriate. Then we would have been treated to the return of Major Hochstetter, who along with General Burkhalter and Kommodant Klink, could ponder what happens next now that the war is truly over.

Marlyn Mason returns as Lily Frankel, who appears to bear no relation to her earlier portrayal of the same named character, in "Rockets or Romance," the oddly downbeat finish to a one of a kind, upbeat series. Photo courtesy of Marlyn Mason/CBS Television Inc.

Special Guest Stars

My deepest amount of gratitude goes to the artists associated with *Hogan's Heroes* that so kindly offered their remembrances about working on the series and their observations about the business of show business. The next few pages celebrate the backgrounds of and contributions each has made to the world of film and television entertainment, and their invaluable contributions to the book you possess. The two observations that all my guest stars embraced were that Edward H. Feldman was a wonderfully terrific producer and human being, and that their associations with *Hogan's Heroes* was a delightfully happy time in all their careers.

Director Bruce Bilson and actor Richard Dawson pictured between takes on the Stalag 13 set at Forty Acres, Culver City, CA. Behind Dawson is Gordon Avil, the program's Director of Photography for its first five seasons. "Note the little horn on top of the magazine. The operator would blow it to announce the lighting was complete and ready for the first team - the cast and director." Photo courtesy of Bruce Bilson/CBS Television Inc.

Bruce Bilson

Mr. Bilson was in the first class of graduates from the UCLA film school in 1950, when it was called the Theatre Arts Department. He explained to me landing his first job in the business after leaving UCLA:

It took me about a year to get it. I was an assistant editor on something called "Snader Telescriptions." I got that job for sixty bucks a week because I knew how to use a hot splicer; it was a machine with a hot plate (35mm film cement splicer). Lou Snader was the boss and he asked: "Radio is dying, television is going to be it, so what are the disc jockeys going to do? I'm going to start making a library for them to broadcast on TV." He set up a little company, and two days a week, Monday and Thursday, a musical group would come in the morning, like Baby Rose Marie, and she would record five of her best hits. Duke Goldstone directed it with two cameras and a playback, and by lunchtime he would have five numbers filmed. After lunch, another group or singer, maybe Les Brown and His Band of Renown, would come in, and by the end of the day he had five more done. On Tuesday, Wednesday, and Friday, Duke would edit the week's filming and I would splice it . . . that was the first job. I used to take a walk when the guy from the union was coming by. Recently I read in Bob Crane's autobiography that when he was starting as a TV disc jockey, he was playing those same telescriptions that I was splicing.*

It was during this employment that Bilson made the fortunate acquaintance of another young man starting out in show business:

The publicist on that series was a young lady named Mary, and she had a boyfriend, or maybe a husband, who came around, and his name was Ed Feldman. That's where I met him, when we were both young and starting out, and we're talking about 1951.**

After his service in the Air Force in 1953, the editors' union recognized Bruce and he was hired to work as an assistant editor on "You Bet Your Life," the quiz show starring Groucho Marx, which was shot with eight cameras. ("I spliced it, I coded it, and synced it, that's what I did.") He finished his work early one day and went to visit his old boss, Duke Goldstone, who offered Bruce the opportunity to direct an exercise program in New York called *It's Fun to Reduce*, which "was my ticket to membership in the Screen Directors Guild! My head was spinning and I could hardly find my way home."** He spent the rest of the decade earning his stripes as an assistant director on such programs as *The Life and Legend of Wyatt Earp* (1957-1958), *Whirlybirds* (1957-58), and *U.S. Marshall* (1958-59). While working as Assistant Director on *The Andy Griffith Show*, Bruce made the friendship of director Bob Sweeney, who helped launch Bilson's network directing career on *The Patty Duke Show* (1965-1966).

Thanks to "Sween" and his own reputation of being a very talented, easy to work with director, Bilson's career flourished in the 1960s. He built two particularly strong associations during this prolific period: as director of twenty-two episodes of *Get Smart*, including a Prime Time Emmy win for the third season's "Maxwell Smart, Private Eye" (1967), and as the director of twenty-five missions for his old friend Ed Feldman and *Hogan's Heroes*. The rest of Bilson's directing career is like taking a trip through television history, which includes healthy stints with *The Odd Couple* (six episodes), *Love, American Style* (twenty-one), *The Doris Day Show* (eleven), *Hawaii Five-O,* (nine), *Barney Miller,* (ten), *The Fall Guy,* (nine), *The Love Boat,* (five), and *Dallas* (three).

Bruce is the patriarch of a true show biz family, with its talented tentacles reaching into nearly every aspect of professional entertainment. His father, George Bilson, ran the trailer department for Warner Brothers in the early 1930s. Later, he was the producer of dozens of two reel comedies starring Leon Errol, and the "master of the slow burn," Edgar Kennedy, at RKO Radio Pictures in the 1940s and early 1950s. Bruce's mother, Hattie, was a screenwriter in her husband's short subjects unit at RKO. Bruce's son, Danny, is an established writer, producer, and director of movies, television, and comic books, including *The Rocketeer*. Bruce's daughter, Julie Ahlberg, is a successful producer of TV documentaries. Bruce's wife, Renne Jarrett, is an accomplished actress guest starring on such network shows as *Archie Bunker's Place*, *Barnaby Jones*, and *The Misadventures of Sheriff Lobo*, in two episodes directed by Bruce. Renne's son, Drew Stauffer, is an accomplished television producer, editor, and graphic designs artist. Finally, Danny's daughter, Rachel Bilson, is an exceptionally busy actress, having played "Summer Roberts" on ninety-two episodes of *The O. C.* (2003-2007), and one spirited turn as Aubrey Plaza's promiscuous older sister, Amber, in *The To Do List* (2013).

*Telephone interview with the author, September 14, 2020.
**Telephone interview, March 9, 2021.

Victoria Carroll

Back when Hollywood still celebrated glamour. Case in point, Victoria Carroll and Anthony Franciosa, star of "Valentine's Day." "So wonderfully Italian, so wonderfully charming, so wonderfully handsome. Need I say more?" Photo courtesy of Victoria Carroll Bell/ABC Television Inc.

Born into a family of vaudevillians, Victoria found herself on stage at the age of seven in an act developed by her father, Oscar "OK" Ford, who along with his performing wife, "Buddy," toured their variety show, "Ford and His Little Lincolns." "As soon as I learned to speak, my brother and I learned this mind reading act, and I was billed as "the world's youngest mind reader," Carroll cheerfully recalled.* Years later, Carroll found herself touring as a dancer with one of her parents old colleagues:

I went on tour with Jimmy Durante. I danced professionally for about four years when I was a kid, about eighteen up to about twenty-one years old . . . when my folks were in vaudeville, they toured the Pantages and Orpheum circuit, with Jimmy Durante. When I worked with him, I said, "Do you remember OK Ford and Buddy Ford?", and he said, "Oh, my gosh! Say 'hello' to them!" He remembered them!*

Carroll's early Hollywood career was as a contract dancer for Warner Brothers, and she danced her way into *The Roaring 20s* (TV series, 1960-1962), *My Fair Lady* (1964), and *Robin and the 7 Hoods* (1964), an assignment she recalled as a day "being saved by Sammy Davis Jr., who was a complete and wonderful gentleman, and really understood the plight of the young actress in Hollywood."* Carroll flourished during the rest of the decade as she amassed an impressive acting resume, appearing in numerous hit television series, including *I Dream of Jeannie* (1965, "The Yacht Murder Case"), *Get Smart* (1966, "The Last One in is a Rotten Spy"), and *The Beverly Hillbillies* (1967, "His Royal Highness"), and her six appearances chronicled here on *Hogan's Heroes*. She also supported the premiere of *The Jerry Lewis Show* on ABC, playing a genuinely understanding, wholesome young woman, who suddenly reveals her rocking bikini body, sending Jerry into comic convulsions!

Although having played in numerous situation comedies, and having shared screen time with many of the greatest comedians in the business, Victoria believes her later work with "The Groundlings," a Los Angeles school and theater dedicated to improvisational comedy, was the definitive source of finding her funny bones. As an original, founding member, she considers this one of the greatest achievements of her successful career, and moved her firmly into the category of "comedy actress: "

I am an O. G. (Original Groundling). Being one of the founding members of The Groundlings was for me a life changing experience. Friendships were forged that have lasted over forty-five years. The basic principles of improvisation, "Yes, and . . . don't deny, add information" have been a road map for my path in life. The training taught me to enter into everything with the spirit of fun and adventure. The Groundlings' "Comedy Collage" literally launched my career. To this day it is my cherished family.**

The alumni of "The Groundlings" is a who's who of comedy, with many of its former members making the move to *Saturday Night Live,* including Laraine Newman, Phil Hartman, Jon Lovitz, Julia Sweeney, Will Ferrell, Kristen Wiig, Maya Rudolph, Mikey Day, and Heidi Gardner.

During and since her tenure with the "Groundlings," Victoria has kept busy with her appearances on *Charlie's Angels* (1977), *The Love Boat* (1978), *Alice* (1977-1983, nine episodes as "Marie,"), *Three's Company,* (1984), and enjoyed one of her favorite work relationships - Bill Bixby and *The Incredible Hulk* (1979-1981). Along with her husband, actor Michael Bell, Victoria has voiced well over one hundred animated characters for countless TV series, with "She Hulk" being a personal favorite. Victoria and Michael built and ran together The West End Playhouse, an Equity Waiver ninety seat theater (allows non-union stage actors to perform). She continues to celebrate "an era gone by" in her paintings of life in the 1920s, 1930s, and 1940s, in what she describes as "realism within the figurative tradition," and by only employing the color schemes of those distinctive periods in her art work. Victoria has exhibited and been awarded in the Andrew Carnegie Museum's classic competition, has been featured in *American Artist* magazine, and her paintings of tender realism are widely collected throughout the United States.

The actress who once avoided getting squashed with George Lazenby by a runaway ambulance in *The Kentucky Fried Movie* (1976), and her husband, the man who once played a shifty guru trying to scam Suzanne Somers out of her savings on *Three's Company,* have passed on those acting experiences to their daughter. Ashley Bell is an accomplished film and voice actress, and the writer, producer, director, and star of *Love and Bananas: An Elephant Story* (2018). In this extraordinary documentary, Ashley depicts the rescue of a seventy-year captive blind elephant, and her forty-eight hour trek across Thailand towards freedom, and into public awareness of how these poor animals are cruelly treated for human gain and consumption.

*Telephone interview with the author, November 24, 2020.
**E-mail correspondence February 24, 2021.

Ruta Lee

Ruta Lee helps her good friend Peter Marshall celebrate the taping of the 2000th episode of "The Hollywood Squares" in 1974. Pictured clockwise from left, Cliff Arquette as "Charley Weaver," Rose Marie, John Davidson, George Gobel, Kent McCord, host Peter Marshall, horror icon Vincent Price, Paul Lynde, Sandy Duncan, and Ms. Lee. Not surprisingly, Ruta has charmed Lynde out of the "center square" position for this family photo. Courtesy of Ruta Lee/NBC Television Inc.

The Lithuanian teenager who once was discharged as a cashier from Grauman's Chinese Theatre for a till shortage, now has a star on the sidewalk directly in front of the historic theater! Born in Montreal, Ruta Kilmonis graduated from Hollywood High School, an alma mater that "includes Carol Burnett, John Ritter, and Charlene Tilton."* An early break appearing on two episodes of *The George Burns and Gracie Allen Show* led to charming her way onto movie screens as Ruth, one of the *Seven Brides for Seven Brothers* (1954), and she's been charming her legions of fans ever since. Another key supporting role during this early career period was as Diana in the 1957 adaptation of Agatha Christie's *Witness for the Prosecution*, masterfully directed by Billy Wilder, "probably the funniest man I've ever known!"*

Lee's television acting career really exploded in the late 1950s and into the next decade, and she consistently brought her sparkling energy to scores of popular programs: *Highway Patrol* (1957, "Armored Car") with Broderick Crawford, *Maverick* (1957-1959, three episodes), *The Lineup* (1957-1959, eight), *Mickey Spillane's Mike Hammer* (1958, two), *77 Sunset Strip* (1958-1964, five), *Perry Mason* (1958-1965, five), and, of course, her three trips to Stalag 13.

During this prolific period, Lee co-starred with Werner Klemperer in the Allied Artists post- WWII drama *Operation Eichmann* (1961), a film that unexpectedly benefited her personal campaign to have her grandmother pardoned and safely moved out of the Soviet Union and into her home in California:

This was the first time that I worked with Werner, on that movie. A girlfriend of mine, who was then Erika Peters, was also up for my role and she was German, but I got it, and that goes to show you how Hollywood works . . . the interesting part about this is when I was going through that whole routine of getting my grandmother out of the Soviet Union . . . I found that there were two of my movies that ran constantly in the Soviet Union, even though they were not running American movies then; one was *Seven Brides* every twenty minutes and the same with *Operation Eichmann* . . . because it made the Russians look like the good guys . . . so when I needed the help and when a bit of notoriety and a bit of fame helped me with my grandmother, it was because of those two movies . . .*

For over six decades, Ms. Lee has been actively involved with The Thalians, a charitable organization that raises money and provides services for victims of mental health disorders. Along with her dear friend Debbie Reynolds, Lee has co-produced the organization's annual ball which is highlighted by the presentation of a "Mr. or Ms. Wonderful" trophy honoring that person's philanthropic generosity. The former recipients include a roster of the biggest names in the entertainment field, with Frank Sinatra, Shirley MacLaine, Gene Kelly, Lucille Ball, Bob Hope, Carol Burnett, Sammy Davis Jr., Mickey Rooney, Clint Eastwood, and Smokey Robinson comprising a small portion of that list of honorees. Lee continues to serve

The Thalians today as their Chairwoman of the Board Emeritus, and the organization's current focus on providing relief to our men and women in the military who suffer mental and spiritual stress.

I am exceptionally grateful for Ms. Lee's participation in this book, as she endured the loss of her husband of forty-six years, Webster Lowe, and longtime friend and co-host of the "High Rollers" game show, Alex Trebek, in 2020, but still made time to fondly share her memories of *Hogan's Heroes*: "For me, every visit to that camp was a joyous experience. I think that it just proved that laughter saves you no matter what condition or position you're in, and I believe that's why it was so popular for so many years."*

*Telephone interview with the author, December 4, 2020.

Jerry London

Down in the radio tunnel, Jerry London and Bob Crane get ready for the next set up during filming of the sixth season. Photo courtesy of Jerry London/CBS Television Inc.

With much affection and gratitude in his voice, Jerry London talks about being selected by Ed Feldman for his show about prisoners of war and their Nazi captors, as if it all happened two weeks ago. Generally in show business an artist's big break is typically a one-shot gig that puts that person's name into the public eye. London's early big break lasted six years:

I was a film editor and I was cutting commercials and I met Ed because he was with the agency in New York that handled Lucky Strike, etc. We'd do four or five commercials every six months and we got along really well. Then he called me one day and said, "Jerry, I've got a pilot, I want you to edit it for me." At that time I was over at 20th Century-Fox cutting the *Daniel Boone Show*. I said to him: "Ed, I got a steady job, I don't know if I want to leave for just a pilot."

And he said, "Jerry, I've got plans for you. I think you should come over here." The way he said it. He had such confidence in me early on, that it lured me away.*

The next step was getting that pilot edited, which proved to be a big challenge to deliver in a small amount of time:

We had to get the show ready very quickly. The pilot was ordered late for pilot season. By the time they finished shooting it, I had about four days to get the show ready and the show cut. I worked that weekend ninety hours . . . I guess I went home to change my clothes once . . . that was a heavy load. The guys came in Monday, we ran it, and they loved it. We got to get it over to CBS, so we sent the rough cut over there on Tuesday and on Wednesday we got the word that it was sold. It happened really quick!*

Over the next six television seasons, London worked on nearly every facet of the program, beginning as the editorial supervisor, quickly becoming an assistant producer, and finally being promoted as the associate producer and as a director of ten episodes, while still maintaining supervision of his first love, editing. London talked about juggling all his duties:

Ed's main thing was working with the writers, that was his bag. When he hired me, being the assistant to the producer, I was a sponge to learn everything about producing . . . including all the intricacies of the casting. (Ed) wanted to be relieved so he could spend all his time with the writers. I was doing just about everything. Checking the special props . . . if a new director would come in, I would go out there and I would indoctrinate him. He was a great guy to work with because he gave me so many responsibilities and that was great.*

After the unexpected cancellation during the off season of *Hogan's Heroes*, London quickly began directing scores of episodic programs in dozens of popular network series. Some of his more fertile associations include: *The Partridge Family* (1972-1973, six episodes), *The Bob Newhart Show* (1973, five), *Kojak* (1974-1975, four), *The Six Million Dollar Man* (1974-1975, six), and *The Rockford Files* (1974-1977, eight). He has also become one of the most successful directors of mini-series and made for television movies in the business. In 1980, London directed the five-part mini-series *Shogun,* based on James Clavell's novel, and NBC enjoyed its highest weekly Nielsen ratings in the network's history. London won The Directors Guild of America Award for "Outstanding Directorial Achievement" and was nominated for the Prime Time Emmy. He was later nominated for Emmys for directing *Chiefs* (1983, starring Charlton Heston and Wayne Rogers) and *Ellis Island* (1984, which featured Richard Burton, Faye Dunaway, and Peter Riegert in its all-star cast).

London continues to share his knowledge of the industry as an instructor of film production at UCLA and The Los Angeles Film School. He is very passionate about Hollywood history and quick to discuss the films of Stanley Kubrick, film noir, *The Untouchables* (series with Robert Stack), and one of his favorite actors, Montgomery Clift. He also still enjoys catching the re-runs of the series that launched his career, which, of course, continues his flow of memories:

Most of the negative criticism came out before the show, but once it came out and everyone saw the humor in it, it just sort of dissipated and then we never had a problem . . . the only tension between any of them was between Werner Klemperer and John Banner. John was a funny guy, hilarious, and Werner kept winning all the Emmys! I think (John) resisted that.*

*Telephone interview with the author, February 14, 2021.

Marlyn Mason

Eighty years young, Marlyn Mason continues to display the charm and sweet personality that have captured film and television audiences for over fifty years. Photo courtesy of Marlyn Mason.

Although Marlyn Mason has been displaying her buoyant singing and acting talents since childhood - "I started singing when I was five; my first television show was in 1949 (*The Doye O' Dell Show*),"* - it is her association with Elvis Presley in *The Trouble With Girls* (1969) that still leaves her fans all shook up. Marlyn proudly enjoys holding a spot as one of three women that actually sang an on screen duet with Elvis in their number "Signs of the Zodiac," "an awful song, and it goes on forever."* The other ladies holding that distinction are Ann-Margret in *Viva Las Vegas* (1964) and Nancy Sinatra in *Speedway* (1968), but Mason is quick to clarify: "Some people think Shelly Fabares (in *Girl Happy*, 1965), but that was done split screen, they were not together."* Talking in detail about Elvis makes Mason light up like a Christmas tree:

I was prepared not to like him, but he was just the best. I would have done anything for him. I wished I had worked with him earlier because we both got along so well. We both loved working together and acting together. We were almost the opposite, he was the male version of me and I was the female version of him, and we both just couldn't wait to work. He loved to rehearse. I got him when he was at the very best of his life . . . work wise . . . health wise . . . he was in great shape. He was stunning, and would almost take your breath away when he would walk on the set everyday. People asked me if you could describe him in one word, and I'd say, "There is no word." There was just something about him that still sticks today as if he were still alive. He wasn't so nice at the end, but luckily I didn't know that Elvis.*

In that wild decade of the 1960s, Mason was exceedingly good to show business, appearing in dozens of hit programs including: *Burke's Law* (1964), *Bonanza* (1964), *Valentine's Day* (1965), a six-part, character thread on *Ben Casey* (1965), *The Fugitive* (1967), and *The Invaders* (1967). She also earns the distinction of being the guest star on the final broadcasts of both *Perry Mason* ("The Case of the Final Fade-Out," 1966) and *Hogan's Heroes* ("Rockets or Romance"). During this exceptionally busy period of her professionalism, she also made the acquaintance of the two Eddies, as she enthusiastically explains:

The man I should've married was Eddie Rissien, who was the Vice President of Bing Crosby Productions. I had met him when I did the (six) part *Ben Casey* . . . it was through Eddie Rissien that I met Eddie Feldman. What a fine gentleman! These guys were the cream of the crop in producing. They were just great guys! Knowing him (Feldman) a bit socially, he was just fun, he was a cool guy. If I married anybody, it should have been Eddie Rissien! If you asked me who were the classiest guys in producing, those two names fly out of my mouth.*

Mason's TV career continued to percolate in the next two decades with constant work on such programs as *Longstreet* (twenty-three episodes as "Nikki Bell" with James Franciscus, and her longtime friend, Peter Mark Richman), *Vega$*, *Barnaby Jones*, *House Calls*, and *Dynasty*. She found herself sharing the TV screen with Ruta Lee in coincidental, back to back bookings on *Jake and the Fatman* (1989) and *Charles in Charge* (1990). Mason remembered during the *Charles* shoot Lee quipping: "You again? Jeez, you'd think we were joined at the hip!"**

Marlyn continues acting in various short film and feature projects while maintaining her rather non-celebrity surroundings at her home in Medford, Oregon. Two recent projects she is particularly proud of comprise the 2013 short film *The Right Regrets*, starring Mason and Maxwell Caulfield ("the director, Ralph Senensky, came out of a twenty-seven year retirement to direct that one"*), and the 2019 feature *Senior Love Triangle*. Kelly Blatz's beautifully made, independent film is based on the award winning photograph series by Isadora Kosofsky, which frames the longtime romance between three senior citizens in East Hollywood. In a bittersweet moment of art catching up with itself, stars Tom Bower and Anne Gee Byrd catch a screening of "Six Lessons From Madame LaGrange" in their senior assisted-living home, sentimentally celebrating Mason's Dietrich tribute, and poignantly capturing a loving close up of Bob Crane.

*Telephone interview with the author, December 15, 2020.
**Email correspondence with the author, December 20, 2020.

Alan Oppenheimer

Alan Oppenheimer in character as "just another misunderstood Nazi," Herman Freitag, in his Hogan's Heroes debut, "Two Nazis for the Price of One." Photo courtesy of Alan Oppenheimer/CBS Television Inc.

"It is hard to dig a tunnel when you're holding your sides laughing," observes General Burkhalter in "To Russia Without Love." A similar effect takes hold trying to maintain a phone interview with Alan Oppenheimer. At any given moment, you may find yourself talking to Don Adams in the middle of shooting a segment for *Get Smart*. Minutes later it might be the unmistakable voice of Sheldon Leonard taking over the conversation. Everything in between is a roller coaster ride of show biz memories and pointed observations on how the industry has changed since Alan made his four memorable stopovers to Stalag 13:

In today's so-called sitcoms, they're not filmed the way they used to be filmed. You don't have a long scene, you have close up, close up, close up, so you don't have to spend time lighting. It's all a cheat. I don't find it very funny, because you have a close up but you don't see the reaction of the other person. If you do it's another close up of a reaction . . . I watch the old stuff because the scenes are longer and there's writing . . . writing for God's sake!*

When Oppenheimer refers to the "old stuff," he should know as he has guest-starred on over one hundred classic television programs and movies. Audiences have enjoyed his work on *The Defenders* (1964), *Get Smart* (1967), *Ironside* (1969), *I Dream of Jeannie* (1971), *McCloud* (1971), *Bewitched* (1972), *Medical Center* (1975), and *Married with Children* (1991). He played the recurring role of the second Dr. Rudy Wells on *The Six Million Dollar Man*, (after Martin Balsam and before Martin E. Brooks), and has played unrelated roles in three different *Star Trek* series: *The Next Generation*, *Deep Space Nine*, and *Voyager*. His film appearances are plentiful, with roles in *In the Heat of the Night* (1967), *The Maltese Bippy* (1969, with Rowan & Martin and Leon Askin), *Westworld* (1973), *Helter Skelter* (1976), and *Private Benjamin* (1980).

Surprisingly, this is only a small fraction of Alan's professional resume, as he has been one of the busiest voice talents in the animated industry for over four decades in this or any galaxy.

"The unexpected highlight of my cartoon voice career is the success of Skeletor from *He-Man Masters of the Universe*, and Falkor, the voice of the Luck Dragon, in *The Never Ending Story* (1984)."** With a never ending voice resume that appears to rival Mel Blanc's and Henry Corden's combined, just some of Oppenheimer's choice voice work includes: *Inch High, Private Eye* (as Inch High, various/1973), *Tarzan, Lord of the Jungle* (various/1976-1979), *The Plastic Man Comedy/Adventure Show* (1979-1980), *Drak Pack* (as Count Dracula/1980), *Trollkins* (as Sheriff Pudge Trollsom/1981), *Flash Gordon* (as Ming the Merciless, various/1979-1982), and *He-Man and the Masters of the Universe* (as Skeletor, and just about anything else that moved and spoke/1983-1985). He continues to graciously meet his fans face to face as Alan has been a fixture at the Comic Cons in Los Angeles, Phoenix, and other cities for years.

Oppenheimer's recollections about his time with Hogan and his Heroes generate nothing but warmth and affection, whether discussing Ed Feldman, "thoroughly low key, respectful, and quiet humor,"* or guest-star Ruta Lee (in "Who Stole My Copy of Mein Kampf?"): "I have great respect and admiration for her, a brilliant woman."* When it comes to John Banner, a longer story surfaces:

I thought he was terrific on the show, so original and clever. Between takes one day, he said to me, "You know, Alan, I wasn't always this heavy. Let me show you." He opens his wallet and takes out a picture of this very, very handsome man, and he says, "You know I was a famous Austrian actor. This is what I look like when I was much younger." He showed me this picture and I said, "My God, John! Beautiful. You were so handsome!" What John did was he bought a picture in the drug store, took out the frame, took out the picture of the handsome model, put it in his wallet, and said, "That's what I looked like." Because the picture he showed me (laughing), the face, didn't look anything like a young John Banner. Not at all!"*

*Telephone interview with the author, November 27, 2020.
**Email correspondence with the author, February 21, 2021.

Larry Weber

Mr. Weber is a 1988 graduate of The Cleveland Institute of Art specializing in illustration. He has been a freelance artist in the Cleveland metro area ever since. With an impeccable talent comparable to the work of legendary *MAD* magazine artist Mort Drucker, Larry has always been a caricature artist. Recently he has taken his caricatures to a new level using a more detail- oriented, illustrative style. "I always enjoyed *Hogan's Heroes* when I was young and still enjoy the reruns to this day! I appreciate the chance to have my caricature illustrations be included in this celebration of that great show."* His illustrations of Howard Caine as Major Hochstetter and Richard Dawson as Peter Newkirk were commissioned specifically for this book.

Larry Weber captures Richard Dawson as Corporal Newkirk in a familiar task, impersonating a German dignitary on the telephone to further the Allied cause and one of Colonel Hogan's brainstorms. Illustration courtesy of Larry Weber.

*Email correspondence with the author, February 19, 2020.

About the Author

Brian R. Young is a freelance writer, actor, and casino dealer living in Portland, OR. He is one of three founding fathers of N.W. NOIR, a film noir appreciation society that screens triple features of actor-themed classic crime films in neighborhood bars on multiple screens. All donations from Brian's N.W. NOIR events are contributed to the National Film Noir Foundation in San Francisco, and its "Czar of Noir," Eddie Mueller. This is Brian's first published book.

Index of Episode Titles

A Klink, A Bomb, and a Short Fuse (season two/episode eight) 98-99

A Russian Is Coming (season three/episode twelve) 176-177

A Tiger Hunt in Paris: Parts one and two (season two/episodes ten and eleven) 102-106

Anchors Aweigh, Men of Stalag 13 (season one/episode fifteen) 42-43

An Evening of Generals (season three/episode thirteen) 178-180

Antique, The (season five/episode twelve) 313-315

Art For Hogan's Sake (season two/episode sixteen) 116-117

Assassin, The (season one/episode twenty eight) 71-73

At Last – Schultz Knows Something (season five/episode fourteen) 320-322

Axis Annie (season three/episode twenty three) 205-206

Bad Day in Berlin (season four/episode eleven) 246-247

Battle of Stalag 13, The (season two/episode five) 92-93

Big Broadcast, The (season six/episode twelve) 377-379

Big Dish, The (season four/episode twenty four) 277-278

Big Gamble, The (season five/episode nine) 307-308

Big Picture, The (season five/episode eight) 304-306

Big Record, The (season six/episode nine) 371-372

Bombsight (season five/episode seven) 302-303
Carter Turns Traitor (season three/episode sixteen) 185-186
Casanova Klink (season three/episode six) 162-164
Clearance Sale at the Black Market (season four/episode one) 223-224
Collector General, The (season three/episode twenty seven) 214-215
Colonel Klink's Secret Weapon (season two/episode twenty eight) 143-144
Color the Luftwaffe Red (season four/episode eight) 239-240
Crittendon Plan, The (season three/episode one) 151-152
Crittendon's Commandos (season five/episode twenty five) 345-346
Cuisine Ala Stalag 13 (season six/episode one) 354-355
Cupid Comes to Stalag 13 (season one/episode twenty nine) 74-75

D- Day at Stalag 13 (season three/episode three) 155-157
Defector, The (season five/episode ten) 309-310
Diamonds in the Rough (season two/episode three) 87-89
Don't Forget to Write (season two/episode thirteen) 110-111
Dropouts, The (season six/episode fourteen) 382-383
Drums Along the Dusseldorf (season three/episode thirty) 220-221

Duel of Honor (season three/episode twenty two) 202-204

Easy Come, Easy Go (season six/episode fifteen) 384-386
Eight O' Clock and All is Well (season six/episode eight) 369-370
Empty Parachute, The (season five/episode eleven) 311-312
Everybody Loves A Snowman (season three/episode fourteen) 181-182
Everyone Has A Brother-In-Law (season two/episode twenty three) 132-134
Experts, The (season six/episode two) 356-357

Fat Hermann, Go Home (season five/episode seventeen) 327-328
Flame Grows Higher, The (season one/episode thirty) 76-77
Flight of the Valkyrie, The (season one/episode four) 19-20
Funny Thing Happened on the Way to London (season three/episode five) 160-161

Gasoline War, The (season five/episode four) 295-296
General Swap, The (season two/episode seventeen) 118-119
German Bridge is Falling Down (season one/episode six) 23-24
Gestapo Takeover, The (season six/episode six) 365-366
Get Fit or Go Fight (season five/episode sixteen) 325-326

Index of Episode Titles • 435

Go Light on the Heavy Water (season one/episode eight) 28-29
Gold Rush, The (season one/episode seventeen) 47-48
Gowns By Yvette (season five/episode nineteen) 331-332
Great Brinksmeyer Robbery, The (season two/episode eighteen) 120-121
Great Impersonation, The (season one/episode twenty) 54-55
Guess Who Came to Dinner? (season four/episode nine) 241-243
Gypsy, The (season six/episode thirteen) 380-381

Happiness is a Warm Sergeant (season one/episode ten) 32-33
Happy Birthday, Adolf (season one/episode sixteen) 44-46
Happy Birthday, Dear Hogan (season four/episode twenty six) 282-283
Heil Klink (season two/episode twenty two) 130-131
Hello, Zolle (season one/episode eighteen) 49-50
Hogan and the Lady Doctor (season two/episode twenty) 125-127
Hogan Gives A Birthday Party (season two/episode one) 83-84
Hogan Goes Hollywood (season five/episode one) 288-290
Hogan Springs (season two/episode seven) 96-97
Hogan, Go Home (season three/episode nineteen) 192-194

Hogan's Double Life (season six/episode twenty two) 402-403
Hogan's Hofbrau (season one/episode twelve) 36-37
Hogan's Trucking Service . . . We Deliver the Factory to You (season four/episode four) 231-232
Hold That Tiger (season one/episode one) 12-14
Hostage, The (season three/episode fifteen) 183-184
Hot Money (season three/episode nine) 169-170
How To Catch a Papa Bear (season four/episode three) 228-230
How to Cook a German Goose with Radar (season one/episode twenty three) 60-62
How to Escape From a Prison Camp Without Really Trying (season three/episode twenty six) 21-213
How to Win Friends and Influence Nazis (season three/episode seven) 165-166
How's The Weather? (season five/episode fifteen) 323-324

I Look Better in Basic Black (season one/episode twenty seven) 69-70
Information Please (season two/episode fifteen) 114-115
Informer, The (season one/pilot episode) 10-11
Is General Hammerschlag Burning? (season three/episode eleven) 173-175

Is There A Doctor in the House? (season three/episode eighteen) 190-191

Is There A Traitor in the House? (season five/episode thirteen) 316-319

It Takes A Thief... Sometimes (season one/episode nineteen) 51-53

It's Dynamite (season six/episode ten) 373-374

Kamikazes are Coming, The (season six/episode twenty) 398-399

Killer Klink (season two/episode twenty four) 135-136

Klink Commandos, The (season five/episode three) 293-294

Klink for the Defense (season six/episode nineteen) 396-397

Klink Vs. the Gonculator (season four/episode two) 225-227

Klink's Escape (season five/episode twenty six) 347-349

Klink's Masterpiece (season six/episode three) 358-360

Klink's Old Flame (season four/episode twenty) 267-268

Klink's Rocket (season two/episode fourteen) 112-113

Kommodant Dies at Dawn, The (season five/episode six) 300-301

Kommodant Gertrude (season six/episode twenty one) 400-401

Kommodant of the Year (season one/episode two) 15-16

Kommodant Schultz (season six/episode seven) 367-368

Lady Chitterly's Love: Parts one and two (season six/episodes four and five) 361-364

Late Inspector General, The (season one/episode three) 17-18

LeBeau and the Little Old Lady (season three/episode twenty five) 209-211

Look at the Pretty Snowflakes (season six/episode twenty three) 404-406

Man in a Box (season four/episode fourteen) 253-254

Man's Best Friend is Not His Dog (season four/episode six) 235-236

Meister Spy, The (season six/episode sixteen) 387-388

Merry Widow, The (season five/episode twenty four) 343-344

Missing Klink, The (season four/episode fifteen) 255-256

Monkey Business (season three/episode twenty nine) 218-219

Most Escape-Proof Camp I've Ever Escaped From, The (season two/episode twenty six) 139-140

Movies Are Your Best Escape (season one/episode seven) 25-27

My Favorite Prisoner (season four/episode eighteen) 263-264

Never Play Cards with Strangers (season four/episode seven) 237-238

Nights in Shining Armor (season three/episode eight) 167-168

Index of Episode Titles • 437

No Names Please (season four/episode ten) 244-245

Oil For the Lamps of Hogan (season one/episode thirteen) 38-39
One Army at a Time (season five/episode twenty) 333-334
One in Every Crowd (season three/episode ten) 171-172
Operation Tiger (season six/episode eleven) 375-376
Operation Briefcase (season two/episode four) 90-91
Operation Hannibal (season four/episode seventeen) 260-262

Pizza Parlor, The (season one/episode twenty one) 56-57
Praise the Fuhrer and Pass the Ammunition (season two/episode nineteen) 122-124
Prince From the Phone Company, The (season one/episode twenty five) 65-66
Prisoner's Prisoner, The (season one/episode five) 21-22
Psychic Kommodant (season one/episode twenty four) 63-64
Purchasing Plan, The (season four/episode twenty two) 272-273

Reluctant Target, The (season two/episode thirty) 147-149
Request Permission to Escape (season one/episode thirty one) 78-79
Reservations are Required (season one/episode fourteen) 40-41

Return of Major Bonacelli, The (season four/episode twenty five) 279-281
Reverend Kommodant Klink (season two/episode twenty five) 137-138
Rise and Fall of Sergeant Schultz, The (season two/episode six) 94-95
Rockets or Romance (season six/episode twenty four) 407-409

Safecracker Suite, The (season one/episode twenty six) 67-68
Schultz Brigade, The (season two/episode two) 85-86
Scientist, The (season one/episode eleven) 34-35
Sergeant's Analyst, The (season five/episode twenty three) 341-341
Sergeant Schultz Meets Mata Hari (season three/episode four) 158-159
Six Lessons From Madame LaGrange (season five/episode twenty two) 338-340
Softer They Fall, The (season five/episode eighteen) 329-330
Some of Their Planes Are Missing (season three/episode two) 153-154
Standing Room Only (season five/episode twenty one) 335-337
Sticky Wicket Newkirk (season three/episode twenty) 195-198
Swing Shift, The (season two/episode twenty one) 128-129

Tanks for the Memory (season two/episode nine) 100-101

That's No Lady, That's My Spy (season six/episode seventeen) 389-391

The 43rd, A Moving Story (season one/episode twenty two) 58-59

To Russia Without Love (season six/episode eighteen) 392-395

To the Gestapo With Love (season four/episode five) 233-234

Top Hat, White Tie, and Bomb Sights (season one/episode nine) 30-31

Top Secret Top Coat, The (season two/episode twenty nine) 145-146

Tower, The (season two/episode twenty seven) 141-142

Two Nazis for the Price of One (season three/episode seventeen) 187-189

Ultimate Weapon, The (season three/episode twenty eight) 216-217

Unfair Exchange (season five/episode five) 297-299

Up In Klink's Room (season four/episode twenty one) 269-271

War Takes A Holiday (season three/episode twenty one) 199-201

Watch the Trains Go By (season four/episode nineteen) 265-266

Well, The (season five/episode two) 291-292

What Time Does the Balloon Go Up? (season three/episode twenty four) 207-208

Who Stole My Copy of Mein Kampf? (season four/episode sixteen) 257-259

Will the Blue Baron Strike Again? (season four/episode twelve) 248-250

Will the Real Adolf Please Stand Up? (season two/episode twelve) 107-109

Will the Real Colonel Klink Please Stand Up Against the Wall? (season four/episode thirteen) 251-252

Witness, The (season four/episode twenty three) 274-276

General Index

Excludes seven primary actors featured in opening credits of each episode. See Appendix for further references. **Bold** indicates photo illustration.

"A.K.A. the Fonz" (*Happy Days* episode) 188
"Amok Time" (*Star Trek* episode) 13
"Benvenuto . . . Who?" (*Daniel Boone* episode) 344
"Ceasefire" (*M*A*S*H* episode) 200
"Death in Slow Motion/The Riddler's False Notion" (Batman episodes) 148
"Deaths-Head Revisited" (*Twilight Zone* episode) 91, 383
"Falling in Love Again, Can't Help It" (song) 339, 340
"Howling Man, The" (*Twilight Zone* episode) 392
"Love and the Happy Days" (*Love, American Style* episode) 362
"Lt. Radar O' Reilly" (*M*A*S*H* episode) 396
"Lucy and Harpo Marx" (*I Love Lucy* episode) 166

"Mad's Snappy Answers to Stupid Questions" (*Mad Magazine* department) 189
"Man in the Bottle, The" (*Twilight Zone* episode) 366
"Mudd's Women" (*Star Trek* episode) 278
"Murder on the Midway" (*Peter Gunn* episode) 275
"Smilin' Jack" (*M*A*S*H* episode) 40
"Spock's Brain" (*Star Trek* episode) 242
"Springtime For Hitler" (song) 405
"Surf's Up! Joker's Under!" (*Batman* episode) 210
"That's Armageddon" (*Kentucky Fried Movie* segment) 226
"The Apple" (*Star Trek* episode) 209
"The Army Navy Game" (*M*A*S*H* episode) 98

"The Dentist Office" (*Abbott and Costello Show* episode) 79
"The Empath" (*Star Trek* episode) 213
"The Friendly Physician" (*Gilligan's Island* episode) 281
"The Man from YENTA" (*Get Smart* episode) 229
"The Menagerie" (*Star Trek* episode) 45
"The Rip Van Winkle Caper" (*Twilight Zone* episode) 90
"The Spanish Moss Murders" (*Kolchak: The Night Stalker* episode) 179
"To Serve Man" (*Twilight Zone* episode) 161
"Will the Real Martian Please Stand Up?" (*Twilight Zone* episode) 148
101 Dalmatians (1961) 60
20th Century Fox Film Studios 113

Abbott and Costello (comedy team) 79, 110
Abbott and Costello in the Foreign Legion (1950) 103
Abbott and Costello Meet Dr. Jekyll and Mr. Hyde (1953) 103
Abbott and Costello Show, The (television series) 79, 110
Abbott, Bud 210
Aberg, Sivi 209, 210, 211
Abwher, the (German Military Intelligence service) 203, 204
Adair, Tom 58, 59
Adams, Don 229
Adventures of Ozzie and Harriet, The (televisions series) 139, 278
Akins, Claude 9
Albert, Susan 137
Alden, Norman 32, 407
Alden, Richard 295, 365, 367, 398
Alice (television series) 207, 270
All in the Family (television series) 139, 196
Allardice, James 58, 59
Allen, R. S. 21, 118, 135, 269, 302, 303, 323, 329, 343, 347, 371, 380, 387
Allied Artists Pictures Corporation 126
Allyn, William 15
Alton, Leon 331
Alzmann, Walter 92
Anders, Chris 51, 90, 167, 199, 382, 398
Andy Griffith Show, The (television series) 6, 12, 34, 93, 112, 128, 278, 374
Argentina 202, 203, 204
Arkin, Alan 177
Arnold, Monroe 30, 31
Arsenic and Old Lace (stage play) 71
Askin, Leon 2, 5, 10, 11, 30, 38, 42, 58, 59, 63, 71, 74, 81, 82, 85, 86, 96, 97, 98, 100, **101**, 107, 110, 113, 114, 116, 117, 118, 125, 128, 132, 139, 141, **142,** 145, 153, 162, 163, 165, 167, 176, 178, **179,** 190, 191, 212, 216, 218, 225, 227, 235, 239, 248, 249, 251, 252, 255, 256, 257, 265, 267, 272, 285, 288, 291, 297, 302, 303, 313, 315, 320, 323, 324, 325, 329, 330, 331, 335, 338, 340, 341, 347, 351, 365, 367, 371, 384, **385,** 389, 390, 392, 396, 400, 407

Aubuchon, Jacques 92
Auto Focus (2005) 11, 108, 159
Avil, Gordon 8, 9, 287, 348, 352
Ayres, Jerry 76

Babcock, Barbara 171, 172, 282, 283, 356, 357
Bacharach, Burt 342
Baer Sr. Max 330
Baer, Art 112, 128, 137, 199, 200
Baer, Parley 34, 85, 135, 311, 312
Ball, Lucille 133, 234
Batman (television series) 7, 21, 45, 210, 400, 402
Beat Generation, The (1959) 229
Beatles, The (English rock and roll band) 8
Beatty, Warren 330, 341
Beaudine, William "One Shot" 77
Beauty and the Beast (television series) 289
Bela Lugosi Meets a Brooklyn Gorilla (1952) 270
Bell, Michael 289, 317
Ben Casey (television series) 6
Bendix, William 374
Benet, Brenda 113, 190, 191, 354, 355
Benny, Jack 133, 226, **318**
Beregi Jr., Oscar 90, 91, 126, 387, 388
Bergere, Lee 65, 400
Bergmann, Alan 387
Berle, Milton 374
Berlin Olympic Games (1936) 330
Besser, Joe 110, 270
Bewitched (television series) 19, 184, 247, 266, 389
Bieri, Ramon 49

Big Combo, The (1955) 148
Big Mouth, The (1967) 247
Billy the Kid Vs. Dracula (1965) 77
Bilson, Bruce 7, **81,** 187, 188, 189, 199, 200, 209, 210, 214, 215, 225, 228, 229, 233, 235, 257, 260, 261, 263, 265, 266, 267, 269, 270, 287, 291, 304, 313, 314, 320, 321, 331, 341, 342, 347, 349, 374, 387, 392, 400, 401, 402, 405, **411** (see Appendix)
Bing Crosby Productions 6, 310, 352, 376
Bishop, Joey 133
Bissell, Whit 94
Bixby, Bill **336**
Black Sleep, The (1956) 9
Blaine, Martin 78, 87
Blue Angel, The (1930) 339, 340
Bob Crane Enterprises, Inc. 376
Bob Newhart Show, The (television series) 261
Bochner, Lloyd 160, 161
Boeing Boeing (1965) 234
Bogart, Humphrey 123, 247, 330
Bold and the Beautiful, The (daytime soap opera series) 156
Bourne, Peter 231
Bower, Antoinette 185, 186, 202, **203,** 204, 287, 316, 317, 318
Bowery Boys, The (motion picture series) 245, 294
Box Brothers, The (television series) 6
Branded (television series) 141
Brandt, Thordis 30
Brash, Marian 279
Bridge on the River Kwai, The (1957) 172

Bronson, Charles 168
Brooks, Mel 28, 261, 384
Brooks, Peter 207
Brooks, Roland M. 9
Brosnan, Pierce 45
Bruck, Karl 125, 139, 140, 205, 358, 396
Buck Rogers in the 25th Century (television series) 113
Bugs Bunny 399
Bullock, Harvey 21, 118, 135, 269, 302, 303, 323, 329, 343, 347, 371, 380, 387
Bundy, Al 3
Bundy, Peggy 401
Burke, Walter 67
Burke's Law (television series) 247
Burns and Allen (comedy team) 238
Burns and Allen (television series) 374
Butler, Robert 10, 12, 15, 17, 44, 45
Buttler, Joseph **194**

Caesar, Sid 26, 60, 133, 226
Caine Mutiny, The (1954) 94
Caine, Howard 2, 44, **45,** 81, 82, 92, 93, 113, 130, 131, 137, 158, 159, 160, 181, 182, 187, 190, 191, 195, 197, 199, 201, 202, 204, 205, 207, 209, 210, 231, 233, 244, 251, 252, 255, 256, 263, 264, 272, 274, **276,** 277, 279, 282, 285, 297, 308, 309, 311, 327, 328, 333, 338, 351, 353, 361, 363, 369, 370, 373, 377, 382, 396, 397, 398
Car 54, Where Are You? (television series) 295
Carlsson, Carl 162

Carmel, Roger C. 21
Carradine, John 9
Carroll, Victoria 225, 226, 269, 270, 287, 288, 289, 316, 317, **318,** 335, **336,** 337, 358, **359,** 360, **415** (see Appendix)
Cattani, Henry Rico 12, 13
CBS Television Network 353, 376
Cedar, "John" 56, 57
Cedar, Jon 5, 12, 13, 17, 19, 23, 32, 38, 42, 81, 116, 117, 169, 170, 187, **189,** 248, 249, 285, 329, 351, 358, 360, 367, 368, 389, 390
Chandler, David 42, 49, 76, 77
Chaney Jr., Lon 9
Chaplin, Charles 47
Chesney, Diana 253, 279, 304, 389
Christopher, William 25, 26, 78, 107, 199, 200
Cinema General Studios 286
Cisar, George 277
Clements, Stanley "Stash" 294
Clue (board game) 186
Clute, Sidney 143, 158
Co-Ed Fever (television series) 207
Colman, Booth 67
Columbia Pictures Corporation 270, 365
Combat! (television series) 215
Comedy of Errors, The (Shakespeare comedy) 364
Comedy of Terrors, The (1963) 121
Compton, Forrest 23, 34, 107, 269, 287, 335, 337, 365
Conley, Corinne 325
Conried, Hans 56, 57, 280, 281
Constantine, Michael 51, 52
Cooley, Isabelle 65, 66

General Index • 443

Corden, Henry 25, 26, 102, 103, 105, 248, 249, 258, 269, 270, 312, 398, 399
Corman, Roger 69, 121
Cornell University 362
Cramer, Susanne 76
Crawford, John 25, 78, 116, 171, 239, 240, 253, 377, 378
Creswell, John 260
Criss Cross (1949) 154
Crunch and Des (television series) 305
Curran, Pamela 347
Curtis, Tony 234

D.O.A. (1949) 118
Dallas (prime time soap opera series) 283, 366
Daniel Boone (television series) 344
Daniels, Marc 207, 216, 237, 239, 241, 244, 248, 255, 272, 274, 282, 307, 311, 316, 323, 324, 329, 356, 367, 368, 382, 407
Dardenne, Yvonne 377
Dark City (1950) 67
Dassin, Jules 67
Davenport, William ("Bill") 139, 140, 145, 146, 162, 163, 192, 193, 212, 213, 231, 251, 252, 255, 325, 341, 345, 377, 396
Davis, Joan 60, 238
Day, Doris 122
Days of our Lives (daytime soap opera series) 156
Death Valley Days (television series) 141, 215
Defiant Ones, The (1958) 94
Dehner, John 17, 102, 103, 104
Demyan, Lincoln 207

DeNiro, Robert 54
DeRita, Joe 128
Desilu Productions 6, 286, **397**
Dick Tracy (1990) 330
Dick Van Dyke Show, The 58
Dietrich, Marlene 339
Dirty Dozen, The (1967) 247
Donohue, Jill 253
Dorian, Angela (Victoria Vetri) 151, 152
Dorsey, Tommy 230
Doucette, John 153
Dr. Quinn, Medicine Woman (television series) 283
Dr. Strangelove (1964) 84
Duck Soup (1933) 37, 232
Dumain, Kenneth 407
Dusay, Marj 241, 242, 243, 263, 264, 287, 343
Dynasty (prime time soap opera series) 65, 161, 366

Easy Rider (1969) 234
Eberhardt, Norma 267
Ebersberg, Horst 49, 228
Edge of Night, The (daytime soap opera series) 156
Edwards, Blake 210, 215
Elinson, Jack 122
Erdman, Richard 244
Errand Boy, The (1961) 74
Errol, Leon 339
Eustrel, Antony 67, 190, 191

Facts of Life, The (television series) 123
Falcon's Crest (prime time soap opera series) 65
Fantasy Island (television series) 93
Farrow, Mia 151

Fein, Bernard 6, 10, 40
Feldman, Edward H. 6, 8, 9, 10, 42, 71, 78, 93, 98, 101, 114, 128, 130, 131, 132, 139, 162, 173, 174, 183, 184, 188, 190, 192, 202, 210, 212, 215, 223, 231, 234, 256, 264, 277, 278, 286, 288, 289, 293, 327, 328, 333, 334, 343, 345, 352, 353, 361, 374, 384, **385**, 386, 397, 398, 403
Fibber McGee and Molly (television series) 374
Fielding, Jerry 9, 97, 337, 348
Firestone, Eddie 28, 90, 335
Flintstone, Fred 115
Ford, Barry 90
Fortune Cookie, The (1966) 7
Foster, Harve 388
Fox, Bernard 2, 19, **20,** 71, 81, 82, 151, 192, 193, **194,** 231, 285, 345, 351, 361, 363
Fox, Michael 291, 325, 373
Frank, David 96, 122, 128, 220, 358, 375, 402
Frankenheimer, John 83
Frawley, James 54
Freddie the Chimpanzee 218, **219**
Freed, Bert 54
Freeman, Kathleen 74, 162, **163,** 266, 287, 297, 298, 400, 401
French, Victor 15
Fugitive, The (television series) 186
Fuller, Kurt 108
Furley, Ralph 43

Garrett, Bob 231
Gaynes, George 384
General, The (1926) 117
Gerard, Gil 113

Gershman, Ben 277, 278
Gerstle, Frank 118
Get Smart (television series) 144, 188, 229
Ghostley, Alice 265, 266, 298, 389
Gibbons, Robert 100, **101**
Gilligan's Island (television series) 12, 56, 161, 280
Girl From U.N.C.L.E., The (television series) 273
Glass, Ned 241, 242
Gleason, Jackie ("the Great One") 36
Godfather: Part II, The (1974) 321
Goebbels, Joseph 206
Gold Rush, The (1925) 47
Goldman, Roy 23, **53,** 90, 110, 141, 162, 190, 244, 245, 369, 370, 371, 380, 382
Gomer Pyle, U.S.M.C. (television series) 6, 8, 12, 34, 112, 196, 288
Gone with the Wind (1939) 6
Good, Jack 56, 218
Gordon, Gale 6
Gorshin, Frank 148
Gosfield, Maurice 45
Gould, Harold 112, 155, 156, 361, 362, 363
Grable, Betty 334
Gray, Janine 92
Greene, Gilbert 49
Greenstreet, Sydney 123
Gregory, James 83, 84, 138
Groundlings, The (Los Angeles improvisational theatre) 359
Gunsmoke (television series) 85, 141, 179, 382

Hale, Jean 69, 70
Hall, Huntz 294

Hallelujah (1929) 8
Hamerman, Milt 7
Hanson, Arthur 120, 239, 267
Happy Days (television series) 188, 362
Hard Times (1975) 168
Harder They Fall, The (1956) 247, 330
Hardly Working (1981) 247
Hardy, Oliver 55, 113
Hartman, Phil **359**
Hastings, Bob 176, 177
Hastings, Ray 387
Hatten, Tom 47, 212, 347, 384
Have Gun - Will Travel (television series) 179, 383
Hawaii Five-O (television series) 93
Hayden, Sterling 86
Haymer, Johnny 400
Hayworth, Rita 195, 196
Hedstrom, Barbro 187, 189
Heldfond, Roger 36
Hellmann, Peter 90, 160
Henry, Bill 343
Henryk, Katherine 235
Herbert, Pitt 47
Here's Lucy (television series) 166
Hicks, Chuck 329, 330
High Anxiety (1977) 28
Hill Street Blues (television series) 245, 283
Hill, Marianna 295
History of the World: Part I (1981) 28, 261
Hogan, Robert 40
Hollander, Howard 9
Holmes and Yo-Yo (television series) 295
Horton Hears a Who! (animated special) 56

Howard, Curly 242
Howard, Shemp 242
Hoyt, John 147, 148, 155, 156, 178, 179, 246, 260, 354, 355, 402
Hunt, Heidy 214

I Dream of Jeannie (television series) 161
I Love Lucy (television series) 85, 166, 207
I Was a Teenage Frankenstein (1958) 95
I Was a Teenage Werewolf (1957) 95
Ilsa, She Wolf of the SS (1975) 353
Incredible Hulk, The (television series) 336
Information Please (radio quiz show) 115
Ingram, Elisa 56, 141, 142, 218
Inspector Clouseau (Peter Sellers characterization) 193, 210
Invasion of the Bee Girls (1973) 152
It's A Living (television series) 289

Jaffee, Al 189
Jaklin, Inge 21, 233, 234
Jameson, Joyce 120, 121, 158, 159
Jannings, Emil 339
Janowitz, Walter (also billed as "Janovitz") 5, 10, 81, 96, 135, 153, 253, 272, 273, 285, 300, 351, 356, 367, 375, 376
Jewison, Norman 177
Joelson, Ben 112, 128, 137, 199, 200
Johnson, Van 7
Jones, Bonnie 107
Jones, Jack **318**
Jones, Tom 342
Joseph, Jackie 69

Josie and the Pussycats (animated series) 69
Joyer, Floyd **385**
Julian, Arthur 28, 56, 69, 181, 190, 207, 209, 218, 220, 233, 241, 248, 249, 267, 268, 279, 282, 300, 313, 316, 331, 389, 392, 404, 405, 407
Jurgensen, William 352, 354

Kahn, Michael **397**
Karloff, Boris 121
Keaton, Buster 117
Keitel, Harvey 54
Kentucky Fried Movie, The (1976) 226
Kenyon, Sandy 58, 59, 110, 169, 170, 287, 304, 305, 396, 408
Kesselring, Joseph 71
Kightley, Walter 237, 277
Killing, The (1956) 86
Kinnear, Greg 108
Kinon, Richard 246, 247, 251, 253, 295, 297, 300, 302, 358, 369, 371, 380
Kinskey, Leonid 5, 8, 12
Kirby, Bruce 287, 295, 296, 331, 332, 365, 366
Kirby, Bruno 295
Kiss the Blood Off My Hands (1948) 382
Klute, Sidney 96
Knight, Don 114
Knight, Edward 30, 69, 94, 139, 165, 212, 213, 246, 338, 356, 404, 405
KNX-AM radio 7
Kobe, Gail 155, 156
Kolchak: The Night Stalker (supernatural series) 179

KONI – FM (Maui, Hawaii radio station) 286
Kosleck, Martin 365
Krugman, Lou 85, 223, 224
Kubrick, Stanley 86

Lambert, Paul 87, 88, 173, 174, 277, 384
Lancaster, Burt 206
Landers, Muriel 269, 270, 287, 331, 332
Landman, Hannie 76, 77
Laurel and Hardy (comedy team) 31, 131, 234, 245, 300
Lauter, Harry 56
Lazenby, George 226
Lee, Ruta 8, 125, **126**, 127, 257, 258, **259**, 392, 393, **394**, 403, **419** (see Appendix)
Leighton, Sheila 384
Lewis, Jerry 74, 226, 247, 281
Life of Riley, The (television series) 374
Life with Lucy (television series) 207
Little Shop of Horrors (1960) 69
Lock Up (television series) 154
London, Jerry (Foreword) 261, 279, **280**, 281, 286, 296, 309, 310, 325, 335, 337, 338, 353, 354, 375, 376, 377, **379**, 389, 396, **397**, **422** (see Appendix)
Long, Ronald 311
Longet, Claudine 51, 52
Lorne, Marion 184
Lorre, Peter 123
Losey, Joseph 67
Love Boat, The (television series) 49, 93, 112
Love, American Style (television series) 121, 362

Lowens, Curt 125
Lucy Show, The (television series) 6, 85, 166
Lugosi, Bela 9, 270
Lupino, Ida 275
Lynch, Hal 23, 58
Lynd, Eva 387
Lynn, Cynthia **5,** 10, 12, 17, 19, 23, 25, 28, 30, 32, 36, 38, 40, 42, 44, 47, 51, 58, 60, **61,** 63, 65, 71, 76, 78, 82, 248, 249, 384, 385

M (1951) 67
M*A*S*H (television series) 21, 23, 26, 40, 98, 108, 200, 352, 396, 400
MacLeod, Gavin 49, 50, 214, 215, 223, 224, 259, 274, 275, 276
Mad Magazine 189
Magnum, P.I. (television series) 286
Main, Laurie 94, 151, 218, 277
Maltese Bippy, The (1969) 258
Manchurian Candidate, The (1962) 83
Mann, Larry D. 71, 147, 274, 275
Manners, Mickey 139, 140
Mannix (television series) 186
Marcus Welby, M.D. (television series) 207
Marcuse, Theodore 120, 121, 126, 147, 148, 183, 184
Markham, Monte 369, 370
Marko, Peter 83, 199
Marks, Laurence 15, 17, 18, 23, 25, 30, 32, 34, 36, 38, 40, 44, 47, 54, 67, 76, 77, 78, 87, 88, 90, 94, 96, 100, 107, 110, 114, 115, 116, 125, 132, 133, 141, 153, 154, 158, 160, 167, 169, 171, 172, 178, 205, 206, 214, 223, 228, 237, 239, 240, 244, 246, 253, 260, 261, 263, 265, 272, 291, 292, 295, 297, 298, 304, 307, 308, 309, 320, 321, 333, 335, 337, 338, 354, 356, 365, 366, 367, 369, 373, 375, 382, 384, 386, 400, 401
Marriage on the Rocks (1965) 30, **31**
Married with Children (television series) 3, 401
Marsac, Maurice 34, 178, 179
Martel, Arlene 12, 13, 81, 82, 102, 103, **104,** 105, 130, 237, 238, 285, 309, 351, 375, 376
Marth, Frank 36, 122, 123, 124, 199, 200, 201, 287, 293, 294, 375, 376
Martin and Lewis (comedy team) 270
Martin, Dean 30, **31**
Martin, Todd 76
Marx Brothers, The (comedy team) 37
Marx, Groucho 232, 342
Marx, Harpo 232
Mary Hartman, Mary Hartman (soap opera series) 32
Mary Tyler Moore Show, The 49
Mason, Marlyn 287, 338, **339,** 340, 407, 408, **409, 425** (see Appendix)
Massey, Jayne 34, 69
Matthau, Walter 7
Maude (television series) 139
Mazurki, Mike 281
McGraw, Charles 366
McHale's Navy (television series) 49, 50, 176
McNair, Barbara 173, 174

Medina, Ralph 329
Mell, Joseph 63
Melville, Sam 114
Mettey, Lynnette 396
Mexican Spitfire (motion picture series) 339
Milner, Marty 321
Mims, William 38
Mission: Impossible (television series) 186
Mitchell, Laurie 248
Mitchell, Mary 78. 79, 132, 133
Montaigne, Lawrence 28
Moore, Irving J. 365, 366, 404
Morgan, Judson 384
Morgan, Walter 241
Morick, Dave 102, 173, 192, 214, 225, 227, 237, 320, 323, 333, 334, 347, 354, 375, 387, 389
Morris, Eric 295, 367
Morris, Howard 25, 26, 28, 34, 38, 42, 47, 51, 58, 59, 67, 69, 74, 76, 145, 146, 185
Morrison, Barbara 135
Moses, Marian 216
Moss, Stewart 5, 10, 11, 17, 65, 143, 153, 195, 245, 384, 386
Murphy, Mike 40
Music Box, The (1932) 245
Musty Musketeers (1954) 366
My Favorite Martian (television series) 278
Myhers, John 118, 185, 186, 320, 371

Nabors, Jim 6
Naked City, The (1950) 67
Naked Gun 2 ½: The Smell of Fear, The (1990) 161

Naked Gun 33 1/3: The Final Insult, The (1994) 163
Neise, George 102
Neon Rider (television series) 186
Newman, Paul 275
Night Court (television series) 387
Nightfall (1956) 83
Nillson, Britt 49
Noose Hangs High, The (1948) 79
Norton, Cliff 132, 133
Nutty Professor, The (1963) 74
Nye, Louis 31

O' Brien, Edmond 8, 118
O' Hara, Barry 343
O' Malley, J. Pat 60, 155, 156
O' Toole, Peter 341
Old Mother Riley (British film character) 296
Oliver, Mari 313
On Dangerous Ground (1951) 275
One Day at a Time (television series) 122
Operation Eichmann (1961) 125, **126**
Operation Petticoat (television series) 387
Oppenheimer, Alan 187, 188, **189,** 228, 229, 257, 258, **259,** 286, 287, 288, **289,** 290, **428** (see Appendix)
Orchard, John 21, 112, 263, 264
Orlandi, Felice 2, 137, 167, 168, 173, 176
Osmond, Cliff 151
Outer Limits, The (television series) 179
Owens, Jesse 330

Parfrey, Woodward 15, 162
Parrish, Leslie 400

Party, The (1968) 215
Patsy, The (1964) 74
Patty Duke Show, The (television series) 374
Perry Mason (television series) 238, 247, 383, 392, 397
Peter Gunn (television series) 275
Peters, Lyn 212, 213, 373, 374
Phil Silvers Show, The (television series) 45, 359
Picerni, Paul 171, 172
Pickering, Robert 181
Pinsent, Gordon 382
Pitlik, Noam 10, 11, 181, 182, 225, 251, 252, 287, 307, 308, 312, 335, 337, 356
Plan 9 From Outer Space (1959) 9
Playboy Magazine 151, 234
Polanski, Roman 151
Police Academy (movie series) 385
Powell, Richard M. 10, 12, 19, 51, 65, 71, 83, 85, 92, 102, 130, 131, 137, 151, 155, 173, 183, 184, 185,
Prentiss, Ann 255
Presley, Elvis 226
Private Benjamin (television series) 387
Private Lives of Adam and Eve, The (1960) 229, 321

Radilac, Charles 76
Rathbone, Basil 9
Reed, Alan 26
Reitz, Mat 380
Remington Steele (television series) 45
Reynolds, Gene 19, 21, 23, 30, 32, 36, 40, 49, 54, 56, 57, 60, 63, 65, 83, 85, 87, 88, 90, 94, 96, 98, 100, 107, 110, 116, 117, 118, 125, 137, 141, 143, 151, 153, 155, 156, 158, 160, 167, 352
Rich, John 195, 196, 197, 205
Ride the Pink Horse (1947) 154
Riley, Jack 260, 261, 287, 320, 371
RKO Forty Acres Lot 6, 91, 103, 286
Robertson, Dennis 40
Robinson, Chris 255
Robinson, Jack H. 42, 49, 76, 77
Rockford Files, The (television series) 280, 286
Rogers, Anne 361, 363
Romero, Cesar 210
Rommel, Erwin (the "Desert Fox") 345, 346
Room 222 (television series) 52
Room Service (1938) 37
Rooney, Mickey 321
Rosemary's Baby (1968) 151
Rowan and Martin (comedy team) 123, 258
Rowan and Martin's Laugh In (television series) 123
Ruddy, Albert S. 6, 10
Ruskin, Joseph 365, 366
Russians are Coming, The Russians are Coming, The (1966) 177
Ryan, Robert 275

Sage, Willard 36, 90, 141, 212, 213
Sarracino, Ernest 56
Savett, James 329, 407
Scharf, Sabrina 233, 234, 356
Schiller, Bob 234
Schiller, Norbert 32, 116, 126, 267, 341, 367
Schmidtmer, Christiane 233, 234

Schrader, Paul 11, 108, 159
Scorsese, Martin 54
Scotched In Scotland (1954) 366
Scotti, Vito 279, **280,** 281
Sellers, Peter 341, 342
Selzer, Milton 143, 144, 241, 242
Sennett, Mack 70
Sergeant Preston of the Yukon (television series) 8
Sharp, Phil 60, 63, 74, 98, 120, 121, 143, 147, 165, 176, 187, 225, 235, 257, 311, 358, 359, 402
Shaw, Robert 275
Sheffield, Jay 195, 212, 228, 237, 354, 377
Shield for Murder (1954) 8
Shogun (television mini-series) 280
Sikking, James 244, 263, 264, 377, 378
Silvers, Phil 60
Sinatra, Richard 10
Singleton, Doris 165, 166, 223, 224
Six Lessons From Madame LaZonga (1941) 339
Six Million Dollar Man, The (television series) 188, 280
Smith, Hal 128
Soap (television series) 289
Spain, Fay 228, 229, 230, 287, 320, 321, 322
Spooks (1953) 322
St. Clair, Michael 42
Stack, Robert 172
Stalag 17 (1951) 172
Stalmaster, Lynn 7
Star Trek (television series) 7, 21, 45, 207, 209, 213, 242
Steele, Karen 277, 278
Stephenson, John 28, 114, 143, 171, 172, 214, 246, 329, 382

Stevens, Bard 34, 56, 125, 139, 140, 153, 176, 205, 223, 341, 358
Stevens, Naomi 151
Stewart, Paula 36
Sting, The (1973) 112, 275
Stone, Harold J. 246, 247, 287, 309, 310, 404, 405
Storch, Larry 226
Stratton, Chet 205, 212, 213, 226, 235, 277, 307, 308, 354
Stratton, Inger 74, 300
Stromstedt, Ulla 87, 195, 196, 197
Sullivan, Margareta 100
Sutton, Frank 6
Sweeney, Robert ("Bob") 6, 92, 102, 112, 120, 122, 135, 147, 165, 169, 171, 176, 178, 181, 218, 220, 373, 374
Sweet and Hot (1958) 270
Swenson, Karl 165
Swimmer, The (1968) 206

Talbot, Nita 2, 82, 102, 103, **104,** 105, 183, 184, 274, 275, 285, 293, 294, 327, 328, 351, 398, 399
Tales of Terror (1962) 121
Tamiroff, Akim 9
Tarzana, California 172
Tata, Joey 56
Tedrow, Irene 76
Thomas, Danny 122
Thomas, Tony 286, 288, 289
Three Stooges Meet Hercules, The (1962) 128
Three Stooges, The (comedy team) 128, 242, 270, 322, 365
Three's Company (television series) 43
Throne, Malachi 402, 403

To Be Or Not To Be (1984) 385
Tobin, Dan 237, 238
Tonight Show, starring Johnny Carson, The 22
Tootsie (1982) 384
Traeger, Rick 47, 153
Triesault, Ivan 155
Troy, Louise 19, 205, 206, 260, 261
Tucker, Forrest 305
Twilight Zone, The (supernatural series) 58, 90, 148, 161, 179, 366, 383, 392
Tyne, George 74, 110

Universal International Pictures 103
Untouchables, The (television series) 85, 172

Valdis, Sigrid 30, **31, 81,** 82, 83, 85, 88, 92, 96, 98, 112, 122, 130, 137, 145, 155, 160, 167, 181, 182, 190, 191, 199, 209, 212, 214, 216, 218, **219,** 220, 223, 228, 231, 237, 248, 253, 255, 260, 267, 269, 272, 279, 282, 283, 285, 288, 290, 291, 304, 307, 313, 316, 321, 323, 331, 333, 335, 341, 351, 356, 361, 365, 373, 374, 377, 380,
Van Doren, Mamie 229
Van Lynn, Vincent 100, **101**
Van Zandt, Phillip 321
Velez, Lupe 339
VeSota, Bruno 331
Vickery, James 239
Victor, Ina 116
Vidor, King 8
Von Bismark, Otto 173, 174
Von Sternberg, Josef 339

Waldis, Otto 128
Wallach, Eli 400
Waltons, The (television series) 286
Ward, Fred 163
Wayne, Fredd 42
Weber, Larry **142, 276, 349, 431** (see Appendix)
Wegge, Inger 145, 272, 273
Wertimer, Ned 300
What's My Line? (television quiz show) 229
What's New Pussycat? (1965) 341
Which Way to the Front? (1970) 74, 139, 247
Whirlybirds (television series) 388
White, Jules 365
Wild, Wild West, The (television series) 12, 392
Wilder, Billy 7, 382
Wiley, David 128, 145, 246, 277
Willock, Dave 333
Wilson, Dick 110, 235, 255, 260, 262, 331, 369, 375, 402, 403
Wilson, Wendy 297, 389
Winston, Edgar 51
Witness For the Prosecution (1957) 382
Wonderful World of Disney (television series) 353
Wood Jr., Ed 9
Wright, Ben 178, 179, 267, 300, 301, 307, 308, 382
Wynant, H. M. 392, 393

Yarnall, Celeste 209, 210, 248
Yarnell, Bruce 32
Young, Buck 34, 128, 253
Young, L. E. 83, 205

Zugsmith, Albert 229, 321

www.ingramcontent.com/pod-product-compliance
Lightning Source LLC
Chambersburg PA
CBHW071939220426
43662CB00009B/917